International Papers in Political Economy

This series consists of an annual volume with a single theme. The objective of the IPPE is the publication of papers dealing with important topics within the broad framework of Political Economy.

The original series of *International Papers in Political Economy* started in 1993, until the new series began in 2005, and was published in the form of three issues a year with each issue containing a single extensive paper. Information on the old series and back copies can be obtained from the editors: Philip Arestis (pa267@cam.ac.uk) and Malcolm Sawyer (e-mail: mcs@lubs.leeds.ac.uk).

More information about this series at https://link.springer.com/bookseries/14844

Philip Arestis · Malcolm Sawyer
Editors

Economic Policies for Sustainability and Resilience

palgrave
macmillan

Editors
Philip Arestis
University of Cambridge
Cambridge, UK

University of Basque Country
UPV/EHU
Leioa, Spain

Malcolm Sawyer
University of Leeds
Leeds, UK

International Papers in Political Economy
ISBN 978-3-030-84287-1 ISBN 978-3-030-84288-8 (eBook)
https://doi.org/10.1007/978-3-030-84288-8

This Palgrave Macmillan imprint is published by the registered company Springer Nature Switzerland AG
The registered company address is: Gewerbestrasse 11, 6330 Cham, Switzerland

Preface

This is the eighteenth volume of the series of *International Papers in Political Economy* (*IPPE*). This series consists of an annual volume with eight papers on a single theme. The objective of the *IPPE* is the publication of papers dealing with important topics within the broad framework of Political Economy.

The original series of *International Papers in Political Economy* started in 1993 until the new series began in 2005 and was published in the form of three issues a year with each issue containing a single extensive paper. Information on the old series and back copies can be obtained from the editors: Philip Arestis and Malcolm Sawyer.

The theme of this seventeenth volume of eight papers is Economic Policies for Sustainability and Resilience. The papers in this volume were scheduled to be presented in late March 2021 at a one-day conference in Cambridge, UK (Downing College), organised by the Department of Land Economy, University of Cambridge, under the aegis of the Cambridge Trust for New Thinking in Economics. The papers were intended to be presented subsequently at the annual conference, entitled *Developments in Economic Theory and Policy*, held at the University of the Basque Country, Bilbao, Spain in June 2021. These conferences had to be cancelled as a consequence of restrictions on meetings and travel in response to the COVID-19 pandemic. We are grateful to the organisers of the Cambridge Trust for New Thinking in Economics, and to the organisers of the *Developments in Economic Theory and Policy* conference series, for funding and help in the organisation of annual conferences over a number of years, which have enabled presentation of the relevant papers; and subsequently published in the *International Papers in Political Economy* series.

Cambridge, UK — Philip Arestis
Leeds, UK — Malcolm Sawyer

Contents

Editors and Contributors

About the Editors

Philip Arestis is Professor and Director of Research, Cambridge Centre for Economics and Public Policy, Department of Land Economy, University of Cambridge, UK. Professor of Economics, Department of Applied Economics V, Universidad Del País Vasco, Spain. Distinguished Adjunct Professor of Economics, Department of Economics, University of Utah, US. Research Associate, Levy Economics Institute, New York, US. A Visiting Fellow, Centre for Globalization Research, Queen Mary College, University of London, UK. He was awarded the British Hispanic Foundation 'Queen Victoria Eugenia' award (2009–2010). Awarded the 'homage' prize for his contribution to the spread of Keynesian Economics in Brazil by the Brazilian Keynesian Association (AKB), 15 August 2013. Also, was honoured through the Thomas Divine Award of the Association for Social Economics (ASE). The award was given at the meeting of the ASSA, Philadelphia, USA, at the annual meeting of 4–6 January 2018. He served as Chief Academic Adviser to the UK Government Economic Service (GES) on Professional Developments in Economics

(2005–2013). He has published widely in academic journals, a number of books, and chapters in edited books. He is on the editorial board of a number of economic journals.

Malcolm Sawyer is Emeritus Professor of Economics, Leeds University Business School, University of Leeds, UK. He was the principal investigator for the European Union funded (8 million euros) five-year research project Financialisation, Economy, Society and Sustainable Development, involving 15 partner institutions across Europe and more widely. He was the managing editor of the International Review of Applied Economics for over three decades. He has published widely in books, co-edited books, chapters and research papers in heterodox and ecological macroeconomics, fiscal and monetary policy, financialisation, and industrial policy.

Contributors

Juan-Francisco Albert is a Ph.D. fellow in Economics and a teaching assistant at the University of Valencia (Spain). Juan-Francisco Albert holds an M.Sc. in Economics from the University of Alicante (Spain) and an M.Sc. in Philosophy from the UNED (Spain). Juan-Francisco Albert's research interest covers Monetary Policy and Theory, Economics of Inequality, Welfare Economics and Applied Macroeconomics. Juan-Francisco Albert has published several scientific articles in international peer-reviewed journals such as Structural Change and Economic Dynamics, Papers in Regional Science, Journal of Economic Policy Reform and Health Education Journal. During his Ph.D. period, Juan-Francisco Albert has been Visiting Researcher at the London School of Economics (UK) and De Nederlandsche Bank (Netherlands). Juan-Francisco Albert has been awarded as a young researcher to carry out different projects related to his doctoral thesis (the effects of monetary policy on income, wealth and racial inequality) by the Ministry of Science in Spain, Fundación Alternativas and Fundación Banco Sabadell.

Anna Coote is a Principal Fellow at the New Economics Foundation (NEF). A leading analyst, writer and advocate in the field of social policy, she has written widely on social justice, sustainable development, working time, public health policy, public involvement and democratic dialogue, gender and equality. Earlier posts include Director of Health Policy at the King's Fund, Deputy Director of the Institute for Public Policy Research, Editor of current affairs television at Diverse Productions and Deputy Editor of the New Statesman. She was Commissioner for Health with the UK Sustainable Development Commission from 2000 to 2009. Anna Coote's recent publications (with sole or co-authorship) include: The Case for a Four Day Week (Polity Press: 2020), The Case for Universal Basic Services (Polity Press: 2020); Universal Basic Income: A Union Perspective (PSI: 2019); Building a New Social Commons, (NEF: 2017); Local Early Action: How to Make it Happen (NEF: 2015); People, Planet Power: Towards a New Social Settlement (NEF: 2015;) and Time on our Side: Why we All Need a Shorter Working Week (NEF: 2013).

Diane Elson is an Emeritus Professor of Sociology at the University of Essex, UK. Diane Elson is Chair of the Commission on a Gender Equal Economy set up by the UK Women's Budget Group. Diane Elson is also a member of the UN Committee for Development Policy, adviser to UN Women and a former Vice President of the International Association for Feminist Economics. Diane Elson has published widely on gender equality, economic policy, and other related subjects. Diane Elson has been awarded the 2016 Leontief Prize for Advancing Frontiers of Economic Thought by the Global Development and Environment Institute at Tufts University, USA. In addition, Diane Elson was awarded the International Book Prize, Japan Society of Political Economy in 2018. Diane Elson's most recent publications are 'Push No One Behind' Journal of Globalization and Development (2019), available at: https://doi.org/10.1515/jgd-2018-0026, and 'Intersections of Gender and Class in the Distribution of Income', The Japanese Political Economy (2019), available at: https://doi.org/10.1080/2329194X.2019.160825.

Katie Kedward is an economist and Policy Fellow in Sustainable Finance at the Institute for Innovation and Public Purpose, University

College London. Katie Kedward's research interests span Post-Keynesian and Ecological Economics approaches, focusing especially on money, banking, and the intersection between finance and the environment. Katie Kedward started her career in capital markets at the Royal Bank of Canada, as a government bond and derivatives specialist. Prior to joining UCL, Katie Kedward worked in green banking at ShareAction, the responsible investment NGO, and as a researcher for George Monbiot, focusing on sustainable food systems. Katie Kedward holds an M.Sc. degree in ecological economics from the University of Leeds and a First Class degree from the University of Cambridge. Katie Kedward enjoys speaking about finance and economics at grassroots events, and has contributed to publications such as Open Democracy. Katie Katie Kedward sits on the advisory panel for Positive Money UK, an NGO campaigning for a fair, democratic, and sustainable financial system.

Natalia Martín-Fuentes is a Ph.D. student in Economics at the University of Malaga (Spain), where she has been a Research Assistant and a Substitute Professor. Natalia Martín-Fuentes holds an M.Sc.in Economic Analysis from the University of Malaga and is currently enrolled in a MicroMaster Program in Statistics and Data Science taught online by the Massachusetts Institute of Technology. During her Ph.D. period, Natalia has been a Visiting Researcher at the Cambridge Centre for Economic and Public Policy (University of Cambridge) under the supervision of Professor Philip Arestis. Natalia Martín-Fuentes's research interests cover Monetary Policy, Macro-finance, Trade and Inequality. Natalia Martín-Fuentes has been a Trainee at the European Central Bank (Directorate General International & European Relations) and she works as a Financial Stability Analyst for the same institution (Directorate General Macroprudential Policy and Financial Stability). Natalia Martín-Fuentes has developed research on the distributional effects of monetary policy for the Institute for Fiscal Studies of Spain (Ministry of Finance).

Jonathan Michie is Professor of Innovation and Knowledge Exchange at the University of Oxford, where he is Director of the Department for Continuing Education, and President of Kellogg College. Previously he was Director of the Business School at the University of Birmingham. Before that he held the Sainsbury Chair of Management at

Birkbeck College, University of London, where he was Head of the School of Management & Organisational Psychology. In addition, before that was at the Judge Business School, Cambridge, where he was also a Fellow & Director of Studies in Economics at Robinson College, and a Research Associate of the ESRC Centre for Business Research. He moved to academia from Brussels, where he was an Expert to the European Commission. Jonathan Michie became Chair of the UK's Universities Association for Lifelong Learning (UALL) in May 2020. He is Managing Editor of the International Review of Applied Economics, was joint secretary of the 2019 Centenary Commission on Adult Education, and is an 'interdisciplinary' Panel Member for Management & Business in the UK's Research Excellence Framework (REF) 2021 exercise.

Salvador Pérez-Moreno is Associate Professor of Economic Policy at the University of Malaga, Research Associate of the Cambridge Centre for Economic and Public Policy, University of Cambridge, and Affiliated Researcher of UNU-MERIT, United Nations University and Maastricht University. He is a founding researcher of the research group Public Economics, Equity, and member of different international research networks (EQUALITAS, ECINEQ, European Economic Association, etc.). From the perspective of economic policies, his research interests lie in the fields of economic inequality and poverty and socioeconomic development, with special interest in the wellbeing of children and other vulnerable groups. The results obtained have led to numerous publications, including some books and chapters in prestigious publishers and a number of articles in refereed journals such as Economic Modelling, Economics and Human Biology, European Planning Studies, Journal of Business Research, Journal of Contemporary European Studies, Journal of Economic Policy Reform, Journal of Social Policy, Review of Economics of the Household, Review of Income and Wealth, Social Indicators Research, etc. He has participated in numerous research projects and contracts and has been Visiting Researcher at various universities, among others, University of Cambridge, LSE, Free University of Berlin and University of Florence.

Ann Pettifor was one of few to predict the Great Financial Crisis in The Coming First World Debt Crisis (Palgrave 2006). In 2008 Ann Pettifor jointly co-authored the original The Green New Deal (New Economics Foundation). In 2017 Ann Pettifor published The Production of Money (Verso) on the nature of money, debt and banking. In 2019 Aher book, The Case for The Green New Deal (Verso) was published. In 2018 the Heinrich Boll Foundation awarded Ann Pettifor the Hannah Ahrendt Prize. Ann Pettifor is a fellow of the New Economics Foundation, and a trustee of the PREP Foundation for pluralist economics. In 2000 the University of Newcastle awarded Ann Pettifor an honorary doctorate for leading an international movement for cancellation of $150bn of debt owed by 35 poor countries, Jubilee 2000. In 2004–2005 Ann Pettifor worked with Nigerian Finance Minister, Ngozi Okonjo-Iweala to clear debts of $30 billion owed to official creditors.

Hector Pollitt is a director and the head of modelling at Cambridge Econometrics. He is also a research fellow at the Cambridge Centre for Environment, Energy and Natural Resource Governance (CEENRG) at the University of Cambridge. Hector is a post-Keynesian economist who is currently working to incorporate insights from complexity theory into a post-Keynesian modelling framework. The aim of his research is to develop a linked micro–macro model that can explain technology development and long-run growth from first principles, within a demand-driven economy that includes a realistic representation of the financial system.Hector has worked with Cambridge Econometrics' global macro-econometric model E3ME for more than 17 years. In that time he has contributed to several high-level European policy assessments of European climate and energy policy, including the targets that have been set for greenhouse gas emission reduction, renewables deployment and energy efficiency savings. He has previously co-edited two books on the policies needed to promote sustainable development in East Asia and is currently working on sustainability policy in China, India and Brazil.

Josh Ryan-Collins is Head of Finance and Macroeconomics at UCL's Institute for Innovation and Public Purpose. His research interests include money and banking, sustainable finance and the economics of land and housing. He is the author of three books, two co-authored: Where Does Money Come From? (2011, New Economics Foundation); Rethinking the Economics of Land and Housing (2017, Zed books) which was included in the Financial Times' top 12 economics books of 2017; and Why Can't you Afford a Home (2018, Polity). Josh Ryan-Collins was previously Senior Economist at the New Economics Foundation (NEF), one of the UK's leading progressive think tanks where he worked for 11 years. He has published on the topics of monetary policy, credit and asset-price cycles and financial stability, monetary-fiscal policy coordination, inflation and the role of central banks in advanced and emerging markets in dealing with climate-related and nature-related financial risks. His work has featured in journals including *Nature Climate Change*, *Environment and Planning A*: *Economy and Space*, *The British Journal of Sociology*and the *International Journal of Finance, Money, Institutions and Markets.*

List of Figures

List of Tables

1

Macro-Economic and Financial Policies for Sustainability and Resilience

Philip Arestis

1 Introduction

This chapter focuses on fiscal, monetary and financial stability policies; their aim is to achieve sustainability and resilience. Sustainability and resilience are defined as "the capacity of a process to be endured or to be maintained and improved" (Vercelli, 2017, p. 15). This contribution relies on our macroeconomic model (Arestis, 2019), which goes beyond the New Consensus Macroeconomic (NCM) model, which has been employed by central banks especially before the Global Financial Crisis (GFC). NCM contains serious problems as the GFC demonstrated (Arestis & González Martinez, 2015), and the recent era of stagflation. There are assumptions of the GFC, which imply that the NCM is lacking

P. Arestis (✉)
University of Cambridge, Cambridge, UK
e-mail: pa267@cam.ac.uk

University of Basque Country UPV/EHU, Leioa, Spain

P. Arestis and M. Sawyer (eds.), *Economic Policies for Sustainability and Resilience*, International Papers in Political Economy, https://doi.org/10.1007/978-3-030-84288-8_1

sustainability and resilience (see, also King, 2016a, who suggests that "The conceptual framework used by central banks was, and remains, flawed"; this framework relies heavily on the NCM paradigm). Our model's macroeconomic policies for a sustainable and resilient economy, do not account of the NCM assumptions. This enables our contribution to deal properly with fiscal, monetary and financial stability policies, which should be properly coordinated to achieve sustainable and resilient economies. Haldane (2020), correctly argues that, "the extra-ordinary degree of uncertainty about the economic outlook" implies "monitoring the economy closely, and setting policy to support it", are "more important than ever" (p. 1).

We proceed in Sect. 2 to highlight our theoretical model. Section 3 discusses the economic policies of our model. Section 4 deals with the coordination of these policies. Finally, Sect. 5 summarizes and concludes.

2 Our Theoretical Model

Our theoretical model (Arestis, 2019), is summarized in the Appendix, and discussed below, with its policy implications discussed in Sect. 3. The main objectives of our analysis are sustainability and resilience, as well as equitable economic growth at full employment. Achieving such objectives requires the maintenance of a high level of aggregate demand and sufficient productive capacity. Our model relates to a monetary production economy in which finance and credit play a significant role, along with relevant distributional aspects.

Our model comprises of five blocks. Block I (Eqs. 1–7) includes both the aggregate demand and supply of the economy. The demand variables are expenditure, income, employment and output. Aggregate demand determines the level of economic activity. Distributional effects are accounted since changes in economic activity affect the rate of change of prices and wages, thereby changes in the distribution of income emerge. These changes have effects on the level of aggregate demand through consumption. Aggregate demand is a volatile component, and it creates productive potential, thereby establishing interdependence between demand and supply. The supply of the economy contains the following characteristics: the interaction between production decisions of firms in the light of the (expected) level of aggregate demand; and the consequent decisions on employment. Investment, an important part of aggregate demand, influences the supply side of the economy since it is the main determinant of potential output and labour productivity.

Block II (Eqs. 8–13) focuses on the distributional aspects and the inflationary process. The most important variables of this block relate to the struggle over income shares, the level and rate of change of aggregate demand, cost-push factors emanating notably from the foreign sector (changes in import prices and the exchange rate). There are other factors as in the relevant equations of this block. In view of the distributional aspects of this block, it is important to emphasize the role of trade unions, which bargain with employers over conditions of employment and wages. Under such conditions, there is a conflict of interest, since the distribution between wages and profits is determined by the real wage demands of labour and the profit objective of firms. Unemployment restricts the extent trade unions are able to press for their claims, since it relates to the state of the labour market. The desired real wage is predetermined according to the expectations and aspirations of unions.

Block III (Eqs. 14–18) relates to money, credit and other financial aspects. Money is endogenously created within the private sector; it responds to changes in the behaviour of the private sector rather than only to policy actions of the monetary authorities. The behaviour especially of banks, but also of other credit institutions, is relevant; namely, the extent to which these financial institutions are willing to provide loans, and the terms upon which are provided, have an important impact on the level and structure of aggregate demand. The supply of credit depends essentially on demand. It is thereby the determinants of demand that influence the flow of credit and thus money. Central Banks are not able to have complete control of the quantity of money. They can of course control the supply price of credit via interest rate changes or through direct intervention in the financial markets. This is the way that enables Central Banks to provide the 'base' money to the banking and the rest of the financial system. Block III implies that the demand and supply of money are interdependent in view of the determinants of money demand that influence the flow of credit and thus money.

Central Banks cannot have a grip over the quantity of money; they can only control the supply price of money via the base rate, which is under their control. Financial stability policies are paramount in terms of the Central Banks being able to influence the financial sector. The main aim of financial stability should be to discourage financial institutions to provide credit for speculative rather than for productive activities, so that they support the productive aspects of the economy. When speculation causes liquidity to increase excessively, direct controls should be implemented to curb it. These aspects are highlighted in Eqs. (16) and (17), and discussed in Sect. 3 as part of 'financial stability' policies.

Block IV (Eqs. 19–23) portrays the government sector, with its expenditure and taxes along with the public sector borrowing requirement, and are endogenized. This blog includes the relevant fiscal policies.

Finally, Block V (Eqs. 24–27) deals with the open economy. An important dimension of the foreign sector is that exports and imports are included in the aggregate demand equation. They are endogenized as shown in this block. Another important dimension of this blog is the inclusion of the effects on aggregate demand (and hence employment) of variations in the exchange rate.

It is paramount for the implementation of relevant economic policies that our model is cyclical and could potentially account for periods of instability. Economic policies should then be employed to stabilize the economy and lead it to high levels of aggregate demand along with employment and output. Thereby the role of public institutions, especially in terms of Blocks III, IV and V, is essential. Governments and Central Banks should collaborate and pursue relevant policies in an attempt to reduce the amplitude of the cyclical behaviour of their economies. Central Banks in particular should support their banking and non-banking sectors to create credit, in view of their role as lenders of last resort. It is also important that national policy institutions should interact with the relevant international institutions, in terms of the 'open' economy aspect.

Our macroeconomic model clearly suggests that economic policies are paramount for sustainability and resilience of economic systems. The section that follows concentrates on the economic policies that emerge from our macroeconomic model.

3 Economic Policies

The objectives of economic policies should be to achieve and maintain a high level of aggregate demand and sufficient productive capacity, along with full employment of the labour force, so that full utilization of capacity is achieved, along with fair distribution of income. Policies employed in a co-ordinated manner (see, also, Arestis, 2012, 2015) help on this score. In addition to fiscal and monetary policies, financial stability policies, which had not been sufficiently considered prior to the GFC, are important (see, also, Arestis, 2016, 2018). Bank of England (2015) suggests, "The pre-crisis regulatory system was also ill-equipped to recognise and deal with threads to financial stability emanating from non-traditional banking activities or risk outside the regulatory perimeter" (p. 11). Financial stability policies enable financial development to produce healthy growth. We elaborate on these types of economic policies below.

Between August 2007 and 2011, the OECD countries experienced a banking crisis with their median loss of output around 5% of GDP, and to more than 10% in some small European countries, with unemployment increasing substantially and inflation dropping below central banks' targets (Bernanke, 2004; Ollivaud & Turner, 2015). The recovery from the GFC was slow, "with tepid economic growth, sluggish employment growth and subdued inflation" (CGFS, 2019, p. 6). More recently the economic situation has been weak due to the COVID-19 syndrome. We refer below to economic policies pursued recently, but most important to the required policies to achieve sustainability and resilience, accounting for recent developments due to the GFC and COVID-19. We refer mainly to the USA, the UK and the Euro Area.

3.1 Fiscal Policy

Fiscal policy should be employed in the short and long run to address demand issues. The ex-IMF Managing Director, suggests, "Under the old paradigm, fiscal policy was definitely the *neglected child* of the policy family. Its role was limited to automatic stabilizers letting budget deficits move up and down with the cycle and discretionary policy was regarded with deep suspicion. But fiscal policy had a *Sleeping Beauty* moment during the crisis with monetary policy running out of steam, and with the financial system on its knees, the forgotten tool arrived to prop up aggregate demand and save the world from an economic freefall. We need to rethink fiscal policy" (Strauss-Khan, 2011, p. 3). Frequent utilization of fiscal policies in view of macroeconomic developments is necessary. Such a conclusion relies heavily on the objectives of macroeconomic policy to be sustainable, along with equitable economic growth. Within these objectives, the main focus of macroeconomic policy should be the achievement of full employment of the available labour force. Achieving such an objective would require, inter alia, the maintenance of a high level of aggregate demand consistent with full employment of labour. Also, sufficient productive capacity to enable the achievement of full employment is required, where sufficient should be interpreted as quantity, quality and geographical distribution; thereby industrial and regional policies are clearly required to enhance supply. Public expenditure, particularly investment, should be structured to ease supply constraints; especially so public infrastructure plays a key role in this respect, and helps productivity to increase. Schwartz et al. (2020) suggest, "The economic recovery from COVID-19 presents a unique opportunity for countries to build a bridge to the future through well-designed and well-implemented public infrastructure. Public investment to stimulate weak aggregate demand can help boost more inclusive growth, reduce inequalities, and create economic opportunities for all"; this is important now in view of the COVID-19 pandemic. However, under the current COVID-19 pandemic, raising taxes too quickly would risk harming potential economic recovery. There is also the argument that due to possible 'secular stagnation' (Hansen, 1939; see, also, Summers, 2014),[1] long-term negligible or no growth and thereby lack of long-run demand, fiscal policy should be used extensively, especially so since unconventional policies cannot really help on this score. Monetary policy, in the form of QE and very low interest

[1] Secular Stagnation was suggested (December 1938) by Alvin Hansen in his Presidential Address to the American Economic Association, entitled "Economic Progress and Declining Population Growth".

rates, has not helped in view of its underperformance, in that "bank lending to the private sector and the broad money supply have stagnated and the recovery has been weak" (Goodhart, 2015, p. 20). The IMF Chief Economist, Gita Gopinath (*Financial Times*, 3 November, 2020), suggests that under the current global liquidity trap, with monetary policy having very limited effect, big fiscal stimulus is needed. Pérez-Moreno and Bárcena-Martín (2019) propose that inequality is another important cause of secular stagnation since higher inequality is a factor in reducing aggregate demand; low productivity is also relevant. Fiscal policy is thereby paramount.

Fiscal policy is not employed as required based on worries about increases in government deficit and debt. Such increases should not be a worry, especially currently with the record-low official interest rates. Over the 2000 years of recorded interest rates, they have never been as low as recently, which enables governments to borrow. The IMF (2020a), suggests for each dollar of government spending on infrastructure enhances output by nearly three dollars more, and higher tax receipts thereby emerge. Also, when the rate of economic growth is greater than the interest rate, governments that borrow to finance the initial spending as well as the subsequent interest bill would experience falling debt as a share of GDP (Arestis & Sawyer, 2003; Blanchard, 2019). Moreover, in a growing economy debt is reduced as tax revenues grow and outpace debt. Also, "the effect of public debt on GDP growth is small and is zero in recent data. ... many policy decisions to confront public debt via austerity have hinged on the presumption of a threshold. There is no evidence of a public debt threshold above which growth is substantially reduced in any of the data, using any method" (Ash et al., 2020, p. 25). Clearly, fiscal stimulus increases GDP by more than it would increase nominal debt, thereby stabilizing aggregate demand, increasing current and future taxes, and reducing government debt. In addition, not only does fiscal stimulus protect jobs but increases them and enables investment to enhance future growth. Auerbach and Gorodnichenko (2017) examine similar questions in the case of a sample of developed countries to conclude that government spending not only does it increase output, but it also reduces the debt-to-GDP ratio. This result is particularly relevant in periods of economic weakness.

Kelton (2020) deals with 'The Deficit Myth', whereby deficits are harmful, undermine growth, and thereby deficits produce fiscal crises; so return to fiscal surplus is the proper fiscal state of affairs; governments should rely on monetary policy, not on fiscal policy. Kelton (op. cit.) suggests that by "tearing down these myths" (p. 233), the Modern Monetary Theory (MMT) produces a relevant understanding of "a *description* of how a modern fiat currency works" (p. 233). And "Both the US Treasury and its fiscal agent, the Federal Reserve, have the authority to issue the US dollar" (p. 17). The USA, therefore, has monetary sovereignty, which means that the country makes the monetary system work for its people and does not have to worry about how to pay for it all. Government spending in countries that issue their own currency with a floating exchange rate and no debt denominated in foreign currency, can never run out of money. Since a 'sovereign' government cannot run out of money, an increase in government spending does not have to be 'paid for' by either an increase in taxes or a reduction in spending. However, inflation should be accounted for and thereby government spending should stop when the economy reaches the point of 'over-heating and inflationary pressures emerge'. Kelton (2020) suggests, government spending should be undertaken with respect to its impact on inflation and not on budget deficit. Government debt does not need to be fixed, and "The national debt poses no financial burden whatsoever" (p. 75). Clearly, Kelton (op. cit.) does not support unlimited government spending or monetary financing; the "MMT considers *fiscal policy* a more potent stabilizer and one that can be used to target even broader measures of well-being" (p. 243). An important part of government spending is job guarantee, whereby the government introduces a job guarantee scheme, thereby the government offers to hire the unemployed, along with providing them with new skills (Tcherneva, 2020); also, decent training and education programme. Kelton (2020) suggests that the job guarantee scheme is "not an emerging measure to be turned on during crisis and then shut down as private sector job growth recovers. Instead, the job guarantee is a way to equip our economy with a more powerful driverless stabilizer" (p. 253). Decent training and appropriate education programme are also relevant schemes.

Another relevant issue is the extent to which fiscal austerity affects economic activity. Fiscal austerity was implemented in many countries after the GFC. Jorda and Taylor (2016) provide empirical evidence using "local projections (LPs), rather than structural auto-regressions (SVARs)" (p. 221). The reason for such usage is that "LPs are a convenient pedestal on which all extensions of existing estimation methods can rest. The unified framework provides the reader a way to compare the results across a set of nested estimation strategies. LPs provide a flexible semi-parametric regression control strategy to estimate multipliers and include, as a special case, impulse responses calculated with the SVAR technique. LPs accommodate possibly non-linear, or state-dependent responses easily, and indeed we find that the effects of fiscal policy can be different in the boom and the slump, as emphasized by Keynes in the 1930s" (p. 221). Using LPs along with instrumental variables (IV), and inverse probability weighting (IPW) estimations, the results show that the effect of fiscal consolidation is negative. A 1% of GDP consolidation results in a 3.5% reduction in real GDP over five years. The IMF has also suggested (as reported in the *Financial Times*, 15 October 2020) that countries, which can borrow freely, do not need to pursue austerity, contrary to the IMF's suggestion a decade ago. These countries have a low cost of servicing their government debt, well below their growth rates. Both the IMF and the World Bank have changed their positions on austerity recently. Senior officials of both at their annual 2020 meeting encouraged countries to avoid 'fiscal orthodoxy' and replace it with 'fiscal activism' (*Financial Times*, 17 October 2020).

McCausland and Theodossiou (2016), deal with the impact of fiscal stimulus on public debt and economic activity, for 11 OECD countries (Belgium, Canada, Denmark, France, Germany, Italy, Netherlands, Norway, Sweden, UK and USA) for the period 1881–2011, using annual data. A standard fixed-effects regression model is utilized for their econometric approach and for the 11 OECD countries panel. Their empirical results show that fiscal contraction deteriorated public debt as a percentage of GDP. The implication of these results is that fiscal austerity deteriorates economic activity and increases unemployment. These empirical results are supported by Chick and Pettifor (2011), who compare and contrast the pre-World War II in the UK, when fiscal consolidation emerged and the public debt ratio to GDP increased and macroeconomic conditions worsened, with the post-World War II period, when fiscal expansion took place, the debt ratio to GDP fell and economic expansion materialized. These results demonstrate that in recessions government spending produces multiplier effects, increasing GDP and productivity, and thereby tax revenues, with the ratio of debt to GDP reduced.

Sawyer (2011), and for the UK experience after the GFC, examines the case of budget deficits to argue that there is a serious danger in trying to eliminate budget deficits; this is so because economic activity is influenced negatively and substantially. Sawyer (op. cit.) suggests that fiscal policy reduces budget deficits without influencing negatively economic activity. To achieve it requires high and sustainable level of aggregate demand and economic activity. Also, reducing inequality substantially would greatly help to increase aggregate demand. Sawyer (2012) discusses the UK post-2010 experience, when fiscal austerity was introduced, to conclude that his proposal as in Sawyer (2011), were very relevant and valid to account for the failure of the post-2010 experience with fiscal austerity. Governments around the world, but especially the ones considered in this contribution, have initiated substantive fiscal action in response to COVID-19. This should be maintained as long as it is needed to avoid long-lasting economic damage. A relevant example is the EU's fiscal rules of the Stability and Growth Pact, which the European Fiscal Board (EFB) suggested should be permanently suspended; this, according to EFB should promote 'growth-enhancing spending' (*Financial Times*, 21 October 2020).

3.2 Monetary Policy

Monetary policies, including unconventional monetary policies, pursued by countries since the GFC, are discussed. Quantitative Easing (QE) has been used internationally in view of the Central Banks' main interest rate reduced to the Effective Lower Bound (ELB). Thereby, QE has become one of the main tools of monetary policy for many Central Banks around the world (CGFS, 2019). Dario et al. (2020) review the impact of the

Fed's Forward Guidance (FG) and QE after the Fed's federal funds rate reached the ELB, to conclude that these tools should have been used more forcefully. They also examine the European Central Bank (ECB) and Bank of Japan, which employed similar tools, and suggest that more forceful use of these tools might still fail to achieve their inflation targets.

The Fed's 2% inflation target, and according to its Chair Jerome Powell, at the 27 August 2020 meeting of the annual Jackson Hole symposium, is abandoned in its current version; maximum employment on top of the Fed's objectives, is placed, because of consistently missing the 2% inflation target. A new monetary policy strategy emerges, which is more tolerant of inflation changes, along with more discretion. Instead of the 2% inflation target, an average of it over time will be the focus of monetary policy. Jerome Powell suggests that periods below the 2% inflation target, inflation should be offset by inflation above the target. However, the averaging period is missing. This change puts more emphasis on boosting growth and employment in the USA. This change is vital because of the dramatic reduction in economic activity and the risks of the COVID-19 syndrome. As a result of the Fed Chair's statement, USA Treasury yields rose, particularly the long-term ones. The difference between the 5-year bond yields and the 30-year bond yields widened by 119 basis points (*Financial Times*, 28/29 August 2020). A further point made by Jerome Powell is that FG in the USA relating to low interest rates will continue in the future. The current change is different from the Federal Reserve Reform Act of 1977, according to which the USA Congress gave the Fed three main objectives in the following order: maximum employment, stable prices, and moderate long-term interest rates. In the 1980s Paul Volcker, the then governor of the Fed, gave the greatest emphasis to stable prices. In January 2012 Ben Bernanke suggested 2% as the inflation target, and maximum employment consistent with stable inflation. Currently, maximum employment, the utilization of full capacity labour force, should be attained all the time, unless the average inflation target is severely threatened. These suggested changes to Fed's monetary policy could produce a case of global shift in Central Banks's monetary policies, along similar lines to Fed changes. Jerome Powell, though, has not explained how the Fed would undertake specific policy actions to affect growth and inflation.

A similar suggestion by the ECB's President, Christine Lagarde on 30 September 2020 (as reported in the *Financial Times*, 2 October 2020), is of the possibility of the ECB adopting average inflation targeting.

Andrew Bailey (2020), the Governor of the Bank of England, at the Jackson Hole meeting, stated that the enormous recent expansion of the Bank's size of its balance sheet, larger now than at any point in its history, was undertaken to support the objectives of both monetary and financial stability policies. In terms of the monetary policy objective, the aim is to achieve the inflation target, to provide sufficient liquidity to stabilize the money markets and support corporate financing. The QE approach of the Bank of England (2009) is to provide stimulus in the form of purchasing assets, mainly government debt, concerning the range of assets purchased. In terms of the financial stability, the increase of high-quality assets of the banks (including central bank reserves) has been the main objective of the Bank of England. This is so in view of prior to the GFC, banks had held insufficient high-quality liquid assets. Forward Guidance (FG) has also been introduced, "stating that the Committee does not intend to tighten monetary policy until there is clear evidence that significant progress is being made in eliminating spare capacity and achieving the 2% inflation target sustainably" (Bailey, 2020, p. 6). The Bank of England has also helped the government in its massive expansion of government expenditure over the COVID-19 crisis by providing finance directly on a temporary basis. An interesting comment made repeatedly at the Jackson Hole meeting was that monetary policy alone would not be sufficient to restore growth, and government intervention was needed to boost the economy.

An interesting question is how QE works. According to Bailey (2020), it works through a number of channels: "including signalling of future central bank intentions and thus interest rates; so called 'portfolio balance' effects (i.e. by changing the composition of assets held by the private sector); and improving impaired market liquidity" (p. 4). More recently (March 2020) the then QE (£200 billion) also included "a sustainable volume of inflation to target" (p. 4). Whether QE has been effective, Bailey (op. cit.) suggests that it "may be more important during a period of market dysfunction associated with a widespread shock to liquidity demand" (p. 4). Bailey (2020) also confirms that despite the very low interest rates, central banks do not lack ammunition to tackle recessions.

The ECB's monetary policy changes are also evident. Low-cost loans stimulus (known as 'Targeted Longer Term Refinancing Operations', TLTRO), which was introduced on 5 June 2014 until March 2020, was tied to the ECB's benchmark interest rate. The link changed in March 2020, and banks that meet the relevant lending criteria can access funds at a lower rate of interest of −1%. Dual interest rates were thereby introduced, since the TLTRO rate is different from the ECB's interest rate on bank reserves. Further changes in interest rates have not been undertaken since the ECB has relied mainly on QE. Relevant reductions in interest rates that aim to encourage firms and households to borrow, and thereby spend more and save less, might not work in that depositors might choose to hold cash, which reduces banks' ability to lend. An interesting development occurred in the EU. The EU proposal (18 May 2020), by Germany and France, the Next Generation EU (NGEU) fund of €750 billion, borrowed from the financial markets (€225 billion of which would be of green bonds), for pandemic recovery as part of the fiscal response to the COVID-19 for the worst-affected countries, has been under marathon talks as EU leaders battled over its details. On 21st of July, after five days of intensive discussions, there was an agreement to use €390 billion in the form of non-repayable grants to COVID-19 stricken EU countries (far less than the €500 billion originally suggested); the rest, €360 billion, will be in the form of loans and more than originally proposed. This is a recovery fund, alongside the EU's €1.074 billion seven-year budget (the Multiannual Financial Framework). Netherlands, Denmark, Austria, Sweden and Finland had misgivings about the collective debt, and cut the grant portion as above. The ECB proposes that the NGEU should become permanent (*Financial Times*, 24 September 2020). Still many of its details are to be worked out, and differences over it still exist. Hungary and Poland opposed it on 16 November 2020, in that NGEU violated the EU 'rule of law'. A compromise was reached, however, on the 10th of December at the European Council's meeting. This compromise, and the recovery fund, although temporary, could be the beginning of fiscal federalism, which is desperately needed in the EU (Arestis & Sawyer, 2019).

QE may be able to provide a transmission channel in terms of liquidity effects, especially so in terms of market stress, market dysfunction and illiquidity. Also, in times of market dysfunction QE may have positive effects on financial stability. The role of QE depends on where the liquidity stress originates in terms of illiquidity. The lessons from the GFC and the COVID-19 highlight the role played by the Central Bank balance sheet in terms of providing relevant policies, which can achieve monetary and financial stability. Whether these policies have been effective, especially in response to the COVID-19, is an interesting question.

CGFS (2019) discusses four unconventional monetary tools that have been implemented by Central Banks over the last decade or so. These are "negative interest rate policies, new central bank lending operations, asset purchase programmes, and forward guidance" (p. iii). It is also suggested that these policies had been implemented well before the GFC, but there is an important difference. "What set this period apart was the breadth of use and the scale of the tools' deployment, which marked an important innovation with respect to the conventional policy framework as understood prior to the GFC" (CGFS, op. cit., p. 11). It should be noted, though, that negative interest rates had not been pursued prior to the GFC; also, the FG policy has been different from the past, in that "It was directed at signalling central banks' willingness to pursue extraordinary policy actions for an extended period of time" (CGFS, 2019, p. 12). In terms of negative interest rates, a number of Central Banks introduced them since July 2009, among them the ECB, on the reserves of banks with them. CGFS (op. cit.) suggests that "negative rates may reduce the spread between lending rates and deposit rates, shrinking net interest margins and bank profitability, but intermediaries may temper this effect by shifting their portfolios towards riskier assets and/or by raising fees. Very low rates also push up asset prices, allowing banks to book profits on their security holdings and raise the value of collateral at their disposal. The improvement in overall economic conditions induced by lower rates may help borrowers to meet their debt obligations and banks to reduce loan loss provisions" (p. 18). There are a number of studies on the effect of negative interest rates, which produce different and opposing results (CGFS, 2019).

The FG policy was introduced after the GFC to reduce uncertainty about future monetary policies. The Fed introduced it in December 2008, with the ECB and the Bank of England in July and August 2013 respectively. The Fed, the ECB and the Bank of England introduced it to ease monetary policy because their inflation rates were below their targets; poor output and employment were also relevant concerns. Initially the relevant FG statements were vague, but over time they have become more concrete in view of low economic developments. The effectiveness of FG clearly depends on the Central Bank's credibility.

The conclusion of the CGFS (2019) is that these unconventional monetary tools "helped the central banks that used them address the circumstances presented by the crisis and the ensuing economic downturn" (p. iii). The overall conclusion of the CGFS (2019) is that the relevant Unconventional Monetary Policy Tools (UMPTs) have been effective but they also have their limits. According to the CGFS (op. cit.) "Their effectiveness is significantly enhanced when deployed in the context of a strategy that encompasses other types of public policy, in addition to monetary policy, in order to mitigate their side effects and boost their effectiveness" (p. 1). It is suggested that "Similarly, the action of other policy agencies, alongside the central bank, in addressing large systemic crises after they materialise would avoid an overreliance on UMPTs and help central banks to pursue their respective mandates" (p. 4). These are important conclusions and support the main conclusion of our contribution in terms of coordinating economic policies. It is further suggested that these unconventional tools were not really very different from the tools Central Banks had used in the past and well before the GFC. What differentiates them from their previous ones is "the broad use of these tools and the scale of their development" (CGFS, 2019, p. 1).

Supporting monetary policy with other policies enables it to be more effective. Prudential policies can create policy space in that they can ensure that financial institutions do not take excessive risks (see, for example, Altavilla et al., 2019). Bank regulation can ensure responsible lending when lending operations do not function properly. Macroprudential policy can add to the stimulus by releasing countercyclical capital buffers in stress situations. Fiscal authorities can support monetary policy by addressing negative demand shocks through the use of discretionary policy actions. Policymakers should avoid rules and employ judgement and thus discretion. A relevant contribution is Aikman et al. (2018a), who discuss the 'discretion versus rules' case to conclude that 'constrained discretion' has emerged since the GFC/GR (GR stands for Great Recession) in view of the fact that "Regulatory rules provide the constraint within which policymakers exercise discretion" (p. 24).

According to the IMF (2020a), Chapter 1, the 2020/2021 global economy is expected to experience the worst recession since the Great Depression, and also surpassing the GFC. The clear suggestion of the IMF (op. cit.) is that countries should maintain fiscal stimulus after the current COVID-19 crisis to ensure proper recovery. It should also be noted that environmental neglect was continuous despite heightened ecological awareness. A better balance is urgently needed.

After the GFC, Central Banks in advanced countries intervened and managed to save their banking sectors from collapse. Very low-interest rates along with QE, and as Bernanke (2020) defines it, "large-scale purchases of financial assets" (p. 944), and FG, "explicit communication of central bank's outlook and policy plans" (Bernanke, op. cit., p. 944), were pursued. Furthermore, fiscal policies introduced after the June 2009 G20-countries meeting, avoided another Great Depression. However, at the June 2010 G20-countries meeting, 'fiscal sustainability' was abandoned and 'fiscal consolidation' was suggested. Fiscal policies were abandoned, and austerity policies were introduced in 2010. Monetary policies did not work. The IMF (2018, footnote 17), reported that aggregate banking credit-growth to the private sector declined in a number of countries. In a sample of 47 countries, with relevant data, credit to the private sector declined from the pre-crisis period (2000–2007) to the post-crisis period (2010–2015) in 27 countries; and it did not increase in the rest. Goodhart (2015) suggests that although financial support did help initially after the GFC, subsequent monetary policy was not effective in terms of restoring robust recovery. Bank lending to the private sector did not increase as had been expected. Giansante et al. (2020) examine empirically the extent to which the UK QE enhances bank lending to the real economy, to conclude that there is no evidence that such relationship exists. Banks under such circumstances reallocate their assets towards lower-risk investments, such as government bonds, rather than provide more credit. Central banks should, though, be involved in climate change policies, and 'green finance/bonds'. Financial stability should be included as one of the objectives and instruments of the Central Banks.

3.3 Financial Stability

Financial stability comprises of microprudential (individual financial institutions), and macroprudential (whole financial system). We focus on macroprudential, which was mentioned for the first time at the meeting of the Cooke Committee (28–29 June 1979), the forerunner to the Basel Committee. Implemented after the GFC, unlike microprudential that has been around since 1979.

Financial stability focuses on controlling the financial sector to become useful to the economy as a whole, especially to the productive parts of the economy; and funds are channelled from surplus-sectors to shortage-sectors. Financial institutions, should serve the needs of their customers rather than targeting huge profits and excessive gains for shareholders. Assessment and monitoring of systemic risks, so that financial systems are robust, and "guard against the financial system disrupting the wider economy" (Brazier, 2018, p. 6), are important. Whether macroprudential regulation could prevent crises, Aikman et al. (2019) suggest, "a macroprudential regime with a suitably strong mandate, coupled with powers to adjust financial system leverage and maturity/liquidity transformation and to limit household sector indebtedness, could have significantly ameliorated the macroeconomic fall-out from the collapse of the real estate bubble" (p. 127). Forbes (2019) proposes, "Macroprudential policy should improve the economy's ability to withstand shocks and allow the financial system to function effectively under adverse conditions" (p. 471).

Aikman et al. (2018a), suggest "One of the greatest intellectual errors made in the run-up to the crisis was a classic 'fallacy of composition': it was assumed that the resilience of individual financial institutions was both a necessary and sufficient condition to ensure the resilience of the financial system as a whole" (p. 30). Aikman et al. (2018b) argue that prior to GFC "prudential regulations sought to ensure the safety of individual banks. This regime allowed major fault-lines in the financial system to develop unchecked, which materialised to devastating effect in 2007–08. Macroprudential frameworks were a 'missing ingredient' from the pre-crisis regime ..... and their development has been one of the major policy responses to the crisis" (p. 1). Financial deregulation, prior to the GFC, produced redistribution effects in favour of the financial sector thereby allowing it to undertake greater risk and achieve excessive profits. Redistribution emerged to the financial sector, enabling it to undertake greater risks, which led to a credit crunch, and the GFC (Arestis, 2016). Financial institutions should serve the needs of their customers rather than taking excessive risks. Therefore, financial stability should be the priority of Central Banks. An interesting relevant example is from the Bank of England's Financial Policy Committee (FPC) in terms of its financial stability implementation. The Bank of England (2016) states that "The primary responsibility of the Financial Policy Committee (FPC) .... is to contribute to the Bank of England's objective for maintaining financial stability. It does this primarily by identifying, monitoring and taking action to remove or reduce systemic risks, with a view to protecting and enhancing the resilience of the UK financial system". The Bank of England suggestion is that the aim of financial stability should be to provide essential services to the real economy. Clearly then, financial stability requires the development of alternative policy instruments along with the downgrading of the interest rate policy and its focus on inflation targeting, as the only instrument of monetary authorities; and abandoning the NCM assumption of price stability being the only objective of monetary authorities.

Aikman et al. (2018c) discuss the financial stability institutions in the case of US and UK (the Financial Stability Oversight Council in the US and the Financial Policy Committee in the UK). They conclude that in the US there are no 'macroprudential levers', because the US committee does not have appropriate macroprudential powers. By contrast, in the UK the Financial Policy Committee is in a position to avoid a similar crisis to the GFC; however, for such a success political backing is necessary. Edge and Liang (2017) show that many countries, fifty-eight in total, have established financial stability committees. Only eleven of the relevant committees have direct control of macroprudential policy tools. Most committees, though, are not properly organised to produce and account for countercyclical macroprudential policies. Consequently, these committees cannot meaningfully address financial stability concerns. Further proposals to account for financial stability have been proposed since the GFC; these proposals are extensively discussed in Arestis (2020). In this contribution we summarize them very briefly as follows.

The USA Dodd-Frank Act was signed in July 2010, with its main proposal being the Volcker Rule, namely to eliminate proprietary investments, which prohibits banks to use insured deposits to run trading operations. Banks are prohibited to own hedge funds.[2] This Act has not been implemented properly, in view of serious criticisms from the 18 USA top banks, and the USA President. There was also the UK Vickers Report of the Independent Commission on Banking, appointed by the government in the summer of 2010, and produced their report in September 2011. The UK's Prudential Regulation Authority, which is part of the Bank of England, would have the responsibility to regulate the ring-fenced banks. The ring-fencing aims to protect retail-banking activities from losses incurred in investment-banking operations. It thereby recommends 'ring-fencing' banks' retail operations from their riskier investment activities. Each part of the ring-fenced bank is a separate legal entity with its own board. The ring-fencing applies to the largest UK banks that have more than £25 billion deposits. There are disagreements on the Vickers report between the Bank of England and the Chair of the Vickers committee, and also serious complains from the banking sector. The UK Treasury started a review of the report early February 2021 (*Financial Times*, 8 February 2021) to be submitted within a year. The European Union-Commission committee, headed by the Finnish Central Bank Governor, made a ring-fence proposal in 2012. This proposal suggests ring-fencing banks' trading business

[2] An important aspect of the Volcker Rule is a reminder of the Glass-Steagall Act of 1933 in terms of the separation of investment and commercial banks to avoid their undertaking of excessive risks.

from their retail activities, opposite to the Vickers' report proposal. The report's objective is to contain "banking group's incentives and ability to take excessive risks with insured deposits"; and to "prevent the coverage of losses incurred in the trading entity by the funds of the deposit bank, and hence limit the liability of taxpayer and the deposit insurance system" (Liikanen Report, 2012). In October 2017 the European Commission withdrew its proposal. The main reason was the lack of progress. There was also the IMF proposal (Claessens et al., 2010), which includes high capital and liquid asset requirements; and taxing the financial sector, which is designed to ensure that financial institutions bear the direct costs of crises, not the taxpayers. Australia, Brazil, Canada and Japan, the least affected countries by the GFC, objected to this proposal. Their central banks argued that taxing banks would reduce their capital, thereby making them more, not less, vulnerable to financial crises. Countries resisted reform, on weak grounds, but with powerful lobbying. Another proposal was the Basel III, which was proposed by the 27-member countries of the International 'Basel Committee on Banking Supervision' (BCBS) of the Bank for International Settlements with the Group of Central Bank Governors and Heads of Supervision, at their meeting on 12 September 2010, and at the 2011 G20 meeting in Paris. The 'Basel III Package' (2010) proposes bank capital and liquidity standards for banks, which are required to hold equity requirements to 9.5% of their risk-weighted assets (RWA), calculated by risk-coefficients, based on credit ratings; and liquidity standards with banks required to meet a 3% leverage. The most serious problem of Basel III is that the group failed to achieve agreement on the RWAs. In December 2017, the BCBS published a package of reforms referred to as 'Basel IV', which proposes a nine-year implementation timetable, along with a five-year 'phase-in' period to commence on 1 January 2022, with full implementation from 1 January 2027. Whether Basel IV would be implemented properly and timely, is an interesting question.

Further policies are required to achieve and maintain financial stability (see Arestis, 2020). Especially so in terms of the IMF's (2020b) expected negative 2020 world economic growth of −4.9%, this is due to the increasing global economic uncertainty and the COVID-19. Keynes's (1936) theoretical contribution that the future is uncertain, along with

Minsky's (1986, 1992) financial instability hypothesis, which is also based on uncertain environment, help to explain the importance of financial stability policies (see, also, Crotty & Epstein, 2014).

Financial stability policies are important, and should be employed to increase the resilience of the financial system. The most important one is that the financial sector should have sufficient capital, with relevant quality, to absorb losses of future crises. This is the 'Counter-Cyclical Capital Buffer' (CCyB), which is an amount of capital, financial institutions should set aside to avoid breaching their minimum capital requirements. The GFC exposed banks in that their capita cushions and liquidity were inadequate and of insufficient quality to account for losses. Financial institutions should be required to hold more capital during upturns (in addition to institutions' capital requirements); and reduce it to absorb losses in bad times, so that to ensure that credit is available during a crisis. Financial stability policies should be coordinated with monetary policy to minimize the overall loss function of the central bank. Both policy objectives should be included in the loss function of a Central Bank.

Further suggestions include the Liquidity Coverage Ratio (LCR), a requirement that includes a portion of high-quality assets (cash and short-term government debt, and relevant foreign exchange assets). Targeted leveraged ratios (total debts/total assets, which restricts banks to exceed a minimum ratio), loan-to-value ratio, debt-service-to-income ratio and limits on foreign currency loans, when financial risks emerge, are further measures. There is also King's (2016b) proposal, what is called 'Pawnbroker for all Seasons'; banks should pay yearly a compulsory insurance premium so that in a crisis they can access funds from the Central Bank. Loan-to-value ratios and debt-to-income ratios are relevant and important financial stability policy suggestions. Another relative, new financial stability policy, is what the Fed Chairman suggested at the press conference following the Fed's monetary policy meeting on the 29th of January 2020. This proposal is a firm control of the yield curve, which depicts the difference between the yields on government short-term and long-term bonds.

CCyB's higher bank capital increases the resilience of the financial system, and also its loss-absorbing capacity. Properly introducing CCyB reduces the likelihood of a financial crisis (see, also, Forbes, 2019). The Bank of England Financial Policy Committee (FPC) proposed that appropriate setting of the CCyB should be "in the region of one percent in standard risk environment" (Kohn, 2019). It is also of paramount importance that the CCyB should be applied to the non-bank financial institutions, especially to the shadow banking, which has expanded enormously recently (Arestis, 2020).[3] Propose that CCyB should account for short-term and long-term bonds (see, also, Bernanke, 2020). This policy would require the central bank to intervene in the bond market to keep yields on target, in the same way as it intervenes to set its base rate.

A relevant statement was made by Broadbent (2019) on financial stability policies. In terms of the CCyB, Broadbent (op. cit.) suggests that "The aim is to ensure that, in the event of a downturn and losses on their books, banks don't make it worse by actively cutting back on lending" (p. 17). Furthermore, "Key priorities include completing implementation of the leverage ratio and of frameworks for the cross-border resolution of banks and for insurer solvency. Macroprudenial authorities must also have an adequate toolkit with which to contain systemic risks. Existing progress in challenging areas such as bank compensation practices and use of credit rating agencies must be built upon,[4] but new thinking may also be needed. Financial sector reform efforts must continue to be coordinated internationally" (p. 56). Miles et al. (2013) propose that banks should use equity capital to finance lending rather

[3] Vercelli (2017, pp. 155–177) discusses 'The Genesis of Shadow Banking' as well as its development since the early 1970s, and suggests that its emergence was "cause and consequence of deep structural changes in the financial system" (p. 155). Especially so, according to Vercelli (op. cit.), in view of "a continuous flow of flexibility-enhancing financial innovations and deep regulation change that aimed to liberalise banks and financial markets from any form of pressing regulations, control, and supervision" (p. 155). Arestis (2016) suggests that the shadow banking system and its operations were one of the main causes of the GFC in relation to their securitization, which became very crucial in the 1970s, especially so with their Collateralized Debt Obligations (CDOs) innovation. Arestis (2016) suggests that an example of successful banking regulation was the 1933 Glass-Steagall Act, which proposed separation of the activities of commercial banks from the risk-taking 'investment or merchant' banks, along with strict regulation of the financial services industry. It was successful until its abolition in 1999.

[4] An interesting, and important, recent development is China's suspension for three months of one of its top credit rating agencies in view of massive bribes to a former executive of the Golden Credit Rating (*Financial Times*, 16 December 2020).

than debt. Their analysis suggests that optimal bank capital of 20% of RWAs reduces significantly the probability of financial instability.

Stress tests, the focus of which is on identifying whether financial institutions, could manage large losses that might arise from financial crises (Bank of England, 2013) is another suggestion for financial stability. In addition, Central Bank Digital Currency CBDC), and actually Central Banks are increasingly interested in CBDC. Nuno (2018) discusses possible CBDC as a potential source of financial stability, which consists of credit cards, payments such as mobile ones and the technological innovations of what is called 'cryptocurrencies'; and its possible implications for financial stability (also, BIS, 2019). CBDC would be a deposit at the Central Bank by households and firms, and considered as legal tender by the government. The Central Bank could control it in terms of financial stability. However, financial stability could be negatively affected in the case of a financial crisis. Holders of CBDC might consider it safer than bank deposits, and thereby withdraw their funds from banks and deposit them in CBDC accounts. This would exasperate the financial crisis, and negatively affect financial stability.

Another relevant financial stability proposal is separation of retail banking from investment banking (Arestis, 2020). Such separation would deliver a more stable financial system, and avoid the high-risk taking of the combined financial institutions, commercial and investment banking. The success of the USA relevant Act, the 1933 Glass-Steagall Act, clearly implies that such change would be greatly beneficial for financial stability. Also, and as Russell (2014) suggests, the Glass-Steagall Act lessons "provide important insights for contemporary projects of progressive financial reform" (p. 101). In addition, control of the non-bank financial institutions, especially the shadow banking, is urgently required. Policymakers should develop and deploy new tools, and there are plenty of them as suggested above, with appropriate coordination between them to achieve financial stability. This is vital to contain another crisis. Also, and from this contribution's focus, to achieve sustainability and resilience of the economy.

When Bernanke (2020) discusses the relevant costs of QE and FG, he reaches a very relevant conclusion for financial stability, namely that their most serious cost is financial instability. Bernanke's (op. cit.) relevant conclusion is that monetary policy makers should account for it very seriously and introduce relevant financial stability policies. A relevant and additional suggestion to Bernanke's (2020) suggestion, from this contribution's point of view, is properly coordinated financial stability policies with monetary and fiscal policies. Such coordination would reinforce the achievement of the financial stability objectives and limit potential policy conflicts. Woodford (2016) discusses the possibility of QE and ELB causing financial instability; they might encourage 'risk-taking' of the kind that produced the GFC. Woodford's (op. cit.) conclusion is that such possibility is not expected, "if the increased supply of safe liabilities by the central bank is combined with a sufficient tightening of macroprudential measures" (p. 79).

Sustainable finance is an important aspect of financial stability. Sustainable finance accounts for environmental (climate change mitigation, green bonds[5]) and adaptation (like, for example, pollution prevention); it also accounts for social and governance considerations (like for example inequality, labour relations, human rights issues), and governance of public and private institutions, whereby social and environmental considerations are included in the decision-making process. Environmental, social and governance investments are more resilient than traditional investments (*Financial Times*, 15 September 2020), Environmental policies, however, have weakened since the late 1990s, especially as a consequence of the GFC and GR, and in many countries.[6] And as Vercelli (2017) suggests this is due to the NCM view that "the environmental policy measures disturb the self-regulation mechanisms of the market, which would otherwise solve spontaneously also the environmental problems in the more efficient and timely way" (p. 189). This NCM view is simply a myth. Environmental policy measures, especially on climate changes that pose serious risks to the financial systems,

[5] Green bonds are debt instruments, with their proceeds used to finance projects that support environmental- and climate-related projects. As reported in Ehlers et al. (2020), "the market for green bonds has been growing fast" (p. 31).

[6] China's unexpected recent commitment to make the country carbon neutral by 2060 is an important way forward (*Financial Times*, 28 September 2020). Also Cambridge University's £3.5 bn 'to divest from fossil fuels' by 2030 (*Financial Times*, 2 October 2020).

are very important to support sustainable finance and thereby financial stability (for further analysis on environmental problems, and relevant policies, see Dafermos & Nikolaidi, 2019).

4 Coordination of Policies

The Fed Chair proposes more fiscal stimulus that is necessary in the USA; and recovery is always stronger if monetary and fiscal policies *w*ork 'side by side' (*Financial Times*, 7 October 2020). Arestis (2012), suggests, "the time has come to assign a strong macroeconomic role to it, along with coordination with other relevant economic policies" (p. 93).[7] Fiscal policy should be coordinated with monetary and financial stability policies, along with discretion (Arestis, 2015). Woodford and Xie (2020) propose in 'finite planning horizons', fiscal policy in the form of countercyclical transfers, is relevant at the Zero Lower Bound; especially so because conventional monetary policy is constrained. Stabilization of both aggregate output and inflation is possible. This, however, requires monetary accommodation, a commitment to keep the nominal rate of interest at its lower bound, even if the inflation rate is not at its target; FG is also needed.

Eggertsson's (2006) empirical evidence shows that under fiscal and monetary policy coordination, fiscal multipliers are higher than when no policy coordination prevails; actually they are higher than those of the traditional Keynesian literature. The fiscal policy spending multiplier is 3.4, and 3.8 under the deficit spending multiplier. When no policy coordination is present, the real spending multiplier is unchanged, while the deficit spending multiplier is zero. Coordination of these economic policies is thereby paramount. Actually there is a great deal of empirical evidence that is very supportive of the coordination of the two policies (Arestis, 2012). We further argue of course that financial stability policy coordinated with fiscal and monetary policy is of paramount importance.

[7] Van der Ghote (2018), utilising a dynamic calibrated macroeconomic model that contains a financial intermediary sector with a leverage constraint, with common objective maximising social welfare, reaches the conclusion that coordination of monetary and macroprudential policies reduces substantially the risk of a financial crisis.

According to Coenen and Straub (2005), fiscal policy is most effective when monetary policy is accommodative, "With no monetary accommodation, the inflation pressures lead to an upward movement in real interest rates and thereby offset, in part, the effects of the fiscal stimulus on GDP. In contrast, with monetary accommodation and nominal interest rates held constant, the increases in inflation give rise to decreases in real interest rates. As a result accommodative monetary policy complements the fiscal policy stimulus and intensifies its effects on real GDP" (p. 51). Under such coordination central bank independence is not helpful. Actually, the experience of Central Bank independence around the world since its introduction has not been successful. This is investigated in Angeriz et al. (2008), with relevant analysis, and conclude that the experience with central bank independence was not a success, especially so when all relevant characteristics of Central Bank independence were accounted for in their investigation. Our analysis in this contribution clearly suggests that the main operation of any Central Bank should be directed towards financial stability. The events leading to the GFC and the GR testify to this important requirement. With the objective of financial stability, Central Banks would become more like Central Financial Agencies (CFA). They would be responsible for policies, which seek to influence the credit and lending policies of the full range of financial institutions.

In terms of coordination of monetary, fiscal and financial stability policies, the creation of fiscal councils to be independent bodies from the political ones, is of paramount importance. Such independent fiscal councils should be delegated the responsibility for the fiscal process. Barwell (2016) suggests that such coordination by an unelected fiscal council and Central Bank clearly avoids "failure of the political process to deliver good outcomes in a particular area" (p. 448). Barwell (op. cit.) also suggests such fiscal council is in place in the UK, and was established in interim form in May 2010. This is the Office of Budget Responsibility (OBR), and could become such a fiscal council. An interesting example is the statement of the Governor of the Bank of England, who proposes that in view of the COVID-19 the Bank of England finances the government response to the relevant crisis (*Financial Times*, 15 May 2020). The total UK's government fiscal response to the COVID-19 crisis is expected to total £123 billion, around 6% of national income (*Financial Times*, 15 May 2020). This is an interesting example of coordination, but more is required as suggested in this contribution.

Another important policy that should be part of coordination of policies, as suggested above, is a relevant policy to account for inequality. It is indeed the case that inequality is another factor, which carries the seeds of current and future disruptions unless growth can become more inclusive. As it is very clear from our theoretical model, inequality and thereby distributional effects should be a major objective of policy (see, also, Arestis & González Martinez, 2015). The recent sharp rise in inequality clearly suggests that there is considerable support of this proposition. Inequality had risen prior to the GFC, and has been rising since then. Dabla-Norris et al. (2015) provide clear evidence that rising income inequality has emerged in developed, developing and emerging countries. Especially so in the OECD countries (OECD, 2008, 2011), where inequality has become obvious and very worrying, with the top income groups increasing their shares substantially, especially the financial sector (see Arestis, 2016; Arestis & Karakitsos, 2011, 2013, where it is argued that inequality was one of the main causes of the GFC, especially in the Anglo-Saxon countries, and most prominently in the USA). In the case of the USA the share of the financial sector to GDP, almost doubled in size between 1981 and 2007, and subsequently accounted for 8% of the US GDP (Philippon, 2008). Vercelli (2017, p. 103) suggests the impact of financialization on income distribution has serious negative effects. This makes inequality of income distribution inconsistent with social sustainability (see, also, Keynes, 1936. pp. 150–151). Wealth and gender inequalities emerged as significant and relevant issues (see, for example, Arestis & Sawyer, 2018, chapters 6 and 7). Distributional effects, therefore, should be a major objective of economic policy. Not only should economic policies focus on achieving sustainability and resilience but should also focus on reducing inequality. Onaran and Galanis (2013), Lavoie and Stockhammer (2013) provide relevant empirical evidence that supports these propositions.[8] It is also very important to account

[8] There is a difference in the context of between wage-led vs profit-led economies, and the significance for policy as in the text. See the contributions of Onaran and Galanis (2013) and Lavoie and Stockhammer (2013).

of universal policies such as universal basic income. Reducing inequality should be taken seriously and account should be taken, of universal basic services.

Distributional economic policies should primarily include pro-labour policies with an important priority to promote wage policies, strengthening the status of trade unions and collective bargaining—and incomes policies should not be forgotten (see, for example, Arestis & Sawyer, 2011). In addition, raising the minimum wage and indexing it to inflation is another important tool to fight inequality. In terms of government spending, social spending, which includes investment in skills and education, is also important from the government spending point of view. Reforming taxes to make them progressive is another relative and significant aspect of fiscal policy (Atkinson, 2015; Piketty, 2014). The IMF (2014) notes that "fiscal policy is the primary tool for governments to affect income inequality" (p. 1). Government expenditure and taxes affect the distribution of income, both in the short and long run, and increase growth simultaneously. IMF (op. cit.) shows that findings from empirical studies support these propositions. Berg and Ostry (2011) suggest that a redistributive tax system is associated with higher and more sustainable economic growth and thereby less inequality. Such policies should be supported by monetary and financial stability policies, which should be concerned with reforms in an attempt to regulate and avoid the type of financial architecture that led to the GFC (Arestis, 2016). Such regulation had been neglected prior to the GFC. Neglect of proper regulation of the financial system does not work as the proponents argue; indeed, it leads to greater inequality (see, for example, Angeriz & Arestis, 2008; Angeriz et al., 2008; Arestis, 2017; Stiglitz, 2013, chapter 9). Relevant taxes include raising corporation tax, capital gains tax, land value taxes, environmental taxes, are all appropriate. Taxing globally financial transactions is also relevant, which requires international cooperation.

Such policies should be supported by fiscal, financial stabilty and monetary policies, along with proper coordination of them; the main focus should be the clear objective of achieving and maintaining full employment, and thereby reducing inequality. Reduced inequality matters for growth, and also for its sustainability and resilience.

5 Summary and Conclusions

The focus of this contribution is on the relevant macroeconomic policies required for sustainability and resilience of the economies. It begins with the theoretical model that underpins the proposed economic policies. It is clear from our approach that relevant policies are fiscal, monetary and financial stability. The latter had not been properly accounted and introduced prior to the GFC, but even since then not properly introduced. The relevant argument of this contribution is that financial stability should be the primary objective of the Central Banks's policies.

Fiscal, monetary and financial stability policies have been discussed in this contribution, but the most important discussion and proposal that follows, is that these policies need to be properly coordinated if sustainability and resilience are to be achieved. Also policies should include in their objectives inequality and sustainable finance. The latter accounts for environmental and adaptation objectives. Properly implemented, these policies, along with their proper coordination with the rest of the policies discussed above, should properly produce sustainability and resilience in the countries where they are implemented. International coordination of policies is also relevant, whereby central banks around the world undertake "policy actions formally agreed upon and taken by groups of policy makers to achieve beneficial outcomes for the international monetary system as a whole" (Bordo, 2020, p. 2).

Appendix

There are five blocks in terms of our model as follows.

The following relationships summarise Block I. We start with the standard income identity as in Eq. (1):

$$Y = C + I + G + (X - Q) \tag{1}$$

where Y is national income, C is consumption, I is investment, G is government expenditure, X is exports and Q is imports, and thus $(X - Q)$ is net exports (NE), including net income flows.

We proceed to endogenise C and I, with G discussed in block IV, and $(X - Q)$ endogenised in Block V. We begin with the consumption function:

$$C = C\left[\underset{+}{\mathrm{WE}(1-\mathrm{tw})},\ \underset{+}{\Pi\,(1-\mathrm{t}\pi)},\ \underset{-}{R},\ \underset{+}{\Delta\mathrm{BLP_h}}\right] \tag{2}$$

where W is wages, E total employment so WE is the wage bill, tw is the tax rate on wages, Π is total profits, $\mathrm{t}\pi$ is the tax rate on profits, R is the rate of interest, and $\Delta\mathrm{BLP_h}$ is changes in bank lending to households. The consumption function relates to net of tax wages and profits, the distribution of income variables, along with the rate of interest and bank lending to households.

The signs reported below the variables are the signs of the partial derivatives of the dependent variable in relation to the independent variables; this is also the case with all below equations.

Next, we endogenise the investment relationship.

$$I = I\left(\underset{+}{\Pi/K},\ \underset{+}{Y/\mathrm{Ya}},\ \underset{-}{R},\ \underset{+}{\Delta\mathrm{BLP_f}}\right) \tag{3}$$

where the symbols are as above with the exception of K, which is capital stock, Ya, which is a measure of capacity output and corresponds to the 'desired level' of operation, and $\Delta\mathrm{BLP_f}$ that stands for changes in bank lending to firms. Equation (3) relates to Kalecki's (1971) proposition that the most important variable is profits in relation to capital; we also include the rate of interest. In addition, our investment relationship is related to the ratio of output to capacity output, and bank lending to firms.

Capacity output is endogenised next:

$$\mathrm{Ya} = \mathrm{Ya}\left(\underset{+}{E},\ \underset{+}{K},\ \underset{+}{\mathrm{ST}}\right) \tag{4}$$

so that Ya would change over time in the same direction as changes in employment, capital stock and the state of technology (ST).

There is a level of employment (Ea) that corresponds to the capacity-output measure:

$$\mathrm{Ea} = \mathrm{Ea}\Big(\underset{+}{Y/\mathrm{Ya}},\ \underset{+}{K},\ \underset{+}{\mathrm{ST}}\Big) \tag{5}$$

where Ya is taken as a benchmark output for firms' investment decisions and employment.

The aggregate supply of output (Ys) is endogenised as follows:

$$\mathrm{Ys} = \mathrm{Ys}\Big(\underset{+}{E},\ \underset{+}{K},\ \underset{+}{\mathrm{ST}}\Big) \tag{6}$$

where the aggregate supply output is determined by employment, capital stock and state of technology, with all three affecting the aggregate supply of output positively. The symbols are defined as above.

There is a level of employment (Es) that corresponds to the aggregate supply of output (Ys):

$$\mathrm{Es} = \mathrm{Es}\Big(\underset{+}{Y},\ \underset{+}{K},\ \underset{-}{\mathrm{ST}}\Big) \tag{7}$$

and the variables are as above. Output influences the level of employment that corresponds to the aggregate supply of output positively, while capital and state of technology negatively.

We proceed with Block II (Eqs. 8–13), with the following relationships summarising this blog. We begin with the profit rate relationship:

$$\pi = \pi[\underset{+}{(P/\mathrm{ULC})},\ \underset{+}{Y/\mathrm{Ya}},\ \underset{-}{R},\ \underset{-}{\mathrm{dR_f}}] \tag{8}$$

where the variables, in addition to the ones already defined, are: π is the profit rate, P is the level of prices, ULC is unit labour cost, and $\mathrm{dR_f}$ is the debt ratio of firms, defined as total debt to total assets of firms. So the ratio of the level of prices in realtion to the unit labour cost, the ratio of output to capacity output, the rate of interest and the debt ratio of firms are the variables that affect profitability as shown in Eq. (8).

The unit labour cost is defined as in Eq. (9):

$$\mathrm{ULC} = W/\mathrm{PR} \tag{9}$$

where W is the level of wages, and PR is productivity, which is treated as exogenous..

The wage rate relationship, as in (10), is firmly based on conflict theory:

$$w = w\{\underset{+}{[(W/P)^{\mathrm{d}} - (W/P)]}, \underset{+}{(Y/\mathrm{Ya})}, \underset{+}{p}, \underset{-}{U}, \underset{+}{\pi}, \underset{+}{w^{\mathrm{e}}}\} \tag{10}$$

where the variables are as above with the exception of the wage rate (w), the bargaining position of workers, defined as the difference between their desired real wage $[(W/P)^{\mathrm{d}}]$ and the actual real wage (W/P); p is inflation, U is unemployment, which is taken in relation to labour force, and w^{e} stands for expectations of the wage rate. The difference between the workers' desired real wage $[(W/P)^{\mathrm{d}}]$ and their actual real wage (W/P) is the variable that portrays the struggle of workers over income shares.

Unemployment is negatively related to the ratio of output to capacity output and productivity as shown in Eq. (11):

$$U = U[\underset{-}{(Y/\mathrm{Ya})}, \underset{-}{\mathrm{PR}}] \tag{11}$$

where the variables are as defined above.

Inflation as in Eq. (12) is related to the wage rate, the ratio of output to capacity output and rate of change of productivity, inflation expectations, foreign factors, namely the rate of change of the nominal exchange rate, and also the rate of change of raw material prices.

$$p = p[w, (Y/\mathrm{Ya}), q, \ \mathrm{er}, p_{\mathrm{rm}}, p^{\mathrm{e}}] \tag{12}$$

where the variables are as defined above, with the exception of q, which is the rate of change of productivity, er is the rate of change of the nominal exchange rate, p_{rm} is the rate of change of the prices of raw materials, and p^{e} that stands for inflation expectations.

The last equation of Block II is the rate of change of the prices of raw materials as in Eq. (13), which relates to the rate of change of the exchange rate and world trade:

$$\mathrm{p_{rm}} = \mathrm{p_{rm}}\left(\underset{-}{\mathrm{er}}, \underset{+}{\mathrm{WT}}\right) \tag{13}$$

where the variables are as defined above with the exception of WT that stands for world trade.

Block III (Eqs. 14–18) relates to money, credit and other financial aspects. The following relationships summarise Block III:

$$\Delta M = \Delta \mathrm{BRBC} + \Delta \mathrm{BDP} \tag{14}$$

where ΔM is changes in the money supply, which is equal to the sum of changes in bank reserves with the Central Bank, including currency (ΔBRBC), and changes in total bank deposits held by the public (ΔBDP). In view of the small proportion of ΔBRBC of the total money supply, we treat it as the residual in the following identity:

$$\Delta \mathrm{BRBC} = \Delta \mathrm{BLP} + \Delta \mathrm{BLG} + \Delta \mathrm{BLES} + \Delta \mathrm{NBL} - \Delta \mathrm{BDP} \tag{15}$$

Identity (15) then defines ΔBRBC as the sum of changes in bank lending to the public (ΔBLP) and to the government (ΔBLG) as well as of changes in bank lending to the external sector (ΔBLES), and changes in non-bank lending (ΔNBL), which includes lending provided by the shadow banking and other relevant issues like securitisation, derivatives and collateralised debt obligations, minus ΔBDP. ΔBLES and ΔNBL which are treated as exogenous variables and with ΔBLG endogenised in Block IV (see Eq. 19), with the remaining variables in Eq. (15) are endogenised as follows.

We endogenise changes in bank lending to the public as in Eq. (16).

$$\Delta \mathrm{BLP} = \Delta \mathrm{BLP}\left(\underset{+}{\Delta Y}, \underset{-}{\Delta R}, \underset{-}{\mathrm{MP1}}\right) \tag{16}$$

where the variables are as defined as above, with the exception of the variable MP1, which stands for monetary policy variables such as credit-rationing by the authorities; this is of course in addition to changes in the rate of interest, which as Eq. (18) below shows, are influenced by changes in the bank rate. Changes in bank lending to the public depend, therefore, on changes in the level of income and interest rate as well as monetary policy variables.

Changes in bank deposits to the public are endogenised as in Eq. (17):

$$\Delta \mathrm{BDP} = \Delta \mathrm{BDP}\left(\underset{+}{\Delta Y}, \underset{-}{\Delta R}, \underset{-}{\mathrm{MP2}}\right) \tag{17}$$

with the variables defined as above, with the exception of MP2, which stands for monetary policy variables. Changes in bank deposits to the public depend, therefore, on changes in the level of income, reflecting the flow of funds into the banking sector as a result of changes in the level of economic activity; interest rate changes that account for possible portfolio effects, as well as monetary policy variables.

Both MP1 (Eq. 16) and MP2 (Eq. 17) can be thought of as financial-stability policy variables as discussed in the relevant Sect. 3.3.

Finally in terms of Block III, changes in the nominal rate of interest are explained in Eq. (18):

$$\Delta R = \Delta R\left(\underset{+}{\Delta \mathrm{BR}}, \underset{-}{\Delta \mathrm{EF}}, \underset{+}{\Delta \mathrm{PDC}}\right) \tag{18}$$

where in addition to the ΔR variable as defined above, ΔBR stands for changes in the bank rate, ΔEF stands for changes in external financing, defined as in Eq. (24), and ΔPDC that stands for sales of public debt to the non-bank public including currency. Changes in the nominal rate of interest are related to changes in the bank rate, thereby the Central Bank is able to exert considerable influence on the rate of interest. Changes in the external financing can also have an impact on changes in the interest rate, reflecting foreign demand for domestic government securities. Also, sales of public debt to the non-bank public have an impact on changes in the rate of interest.

Block IV (Eqs. 19–23) deals with the government sector. The relevant relationships are as follows.

$$\Delta \text{BLG} = \text{PSBR} + \Delta \text{EF} - \Delta \text{PDC} \quad (19)$$

where the variables are defined as above with the exception of PSBR that stands for the public sector borrowing requirement. The Bank of England (1982) is clear on this point, "Normally, that part of Government's borrowing requirement which is not financed by the sale of debt outside the banking system is met by the sale of debt – in particular Treasury bills – to the banking system, which thus acts as the residual source of borrowing for the Governent" (p. 87).

PSBR, as portrayed in Eq. (20), is simply defined as the difference between government expenditure (G) and tax revenues (T) along with other government revenues (OGR).

$$\text{PSBR} = G - T - \text{OGR} \quad (20)$$

We treat OGR as exogenous and hypothesise G and T to be determined as shown below in Eqs. (21) and (23) respectively.

$$G = P_G Q_Q + W E_G + U U_B + \text{ID} \quad (21)$$

where the symbols, with the exception of G, W and U, are defined as follows: Q_Q, the amount of goods and services bought by the government, with P_G being their prices; E_G, the number of employees in the government sector, U_B, unemployment benefits, and ID, interest payments on government debt. E_G is defined as in Eq. (22), with the rest of the variables treated exogenously, with the exception of U that is endogenised as in Eq. (11):

$$E_G = E - E_P - U \quad (22)$$

where E is is total working population, as defined above for the purpose of Eq. (2), and E_P is employment in the private sector. Clearly $E_G + E_P = E$ that is total employment.

Taxes are endogenised as in Eq. (23) in terms of wage earners' and profit earners' incomes:financial transaction

$$T = T(\underset{+}{WE}, \underset{+}{\Pi}) \tag{23}$$

Block V (Eqs. 24–27), the final blog, covers the open economy. We begin with the identity for changes in external financing:

$$\Delta EF = CB + \Delta KM - OEF \tag{24}$$

where ΔEF is equal to the current balance of international payments (CB) plus changes in capital movements (ΔKM) minus other external financing (OEF); the latter variable includes external lending to the public sector plus domestic bank lending to the public sector in foreign currencies. We treat OEF as exogenous and endogenise CB and ΔKM.

The current balance of international payments is the sum of net exports and other current balance as in Eq. (25):

$$\begin{aligned} CB = NE + OCB &= X\left(\underset{+}{WT}, \underset{-}{RER}\right) \\ &- Q\left[\underset{+}{WE(1-tw)}, \underset{+}{\Pi(1-t\pi)}, \underset{+}{RER}\right] + \underset{+}{OCB} \end{aligned} \tag{25}$$

where in addition to CB, NE and WT as above, OCB stands for other earnings on foreign investments minus payments made to foreign investors; RER is the real exchange rate (where the exchange rate is defined as foreign to domestic currency), with WE(1 – tw) and $\Pi(1 - t\pi)$ being the income distribution terms as they influence imports. All these variables are in real terms.

Equation (26) defines ΔKM:

$$\Delta KM = \Delta KM\left[\underset{+}{(R/R_W)}, \underset{-}{(er)^e}\right] \tag{26}$$

where the ratio of domestic interest rates (R) to world interest rates (R_W) is included, along with the expected rate of change of the nominal exchange rate variable $(\mathrm{er})^{\mathrm{e}}$. The variables that influence ΔKM depend on the assumption that capital flows are sensitive to returns available internationally and on expected exchange rate movements.

Equation (27) endogenises the real exchange rate:

$$\mathrm{RER} = \mathrm{RER}\left[\underset{+}{(R/R_{\mathrm{W}})}, \underset{-}{\mathrm{Y}}, \underset{+}{\mathrm{WT}}, \underset{+}{(\mathrm{er})^{\mathrm{e}}}\right] \tag{27}$$

where the variables are as defined above. The real exchange rate relates to the ratio of domestic to world interest rates, income, the world trade and expected rate of change of the nominal exchange rate variable.

References

Aikman, D., Haldane, G. A., Hinterschweiger, M., & Kapadia, S. (2018a). *Rethinking financial stability* (Bank of England Staff Working Paper No. 712). Available at: www.bankofengland.co.uk/working-paper/Working-papers.

Aikman, D., Giese, J., Kapadia, S., & McLeay, M. (2018b), *Targeting financial stability: Macroprudential or monetary policy?* (Bank of England Staff Working Paper No. 734). Available at: www.bankofengland.co.uk/working-paper/Working-papers.

Aikman, D., Bridges, J., Kashyap, A., & Siegert, C. (2018c), *Would macroprudential regulation have prevented the last crisis?* (Bank of England Staff Working Paper No. 747). Available at: www.bankofengland.co.uk/working-paper/Working-papers.

Aikman, D., Bridges, J., Kashyap, A., & Siegert, C. (2019). Would macroprudential regulation have prevented the last crisis? *Journal of Economic Perspectives, 33*(1), 107–130.

Altavilla, C., Bouchina, M., Peydró, J., & Smets, F. (2019). *Banking supervision, monetary policy and risk taking: Big-data evidence from 15 credit registers* (ECB Working Paper Series).

Angeriz, A., & Arestis, P. (2008). Assessing inflation targeting through intervention analysis. *Oxford Economic Papers, 60*(2), 293–317.

Angeriz, A., Arestis, P., & McCombie, J. (2008). *Does central bank independence affect inflation persistence and volatility?* (CCEPP Working Paper). Cambridge Centre for Economic and Public Policy, Department of Land Economy, University of Cambridge.

Arestis, P. (2012). Fiscal policy: A strong macroeconomic role. *Review of Keynesian Economics, 1*(1), 93–108.

Arestis, P. (2015). Coordination of fiscal with monetary and financial stability policies can better cure unemployment. *Review of Keynesian Economics, 3*(2), 233–247.

Arestis, P. (2016). Main and contributory causes of the recent financial crisis and economic policy implications. In P. Arestis & M. C. Sawyer (Eds.), *Emerging economies during and after the great recession*, Annual Edition of *International Papers in Political Economy*. Palgrave Macmillan.

Arestis, P. (2017). Financial liberalisation, the finance-growth nexus, financial crises and policy implications. In P. Arestis & M. C. Sawyer (Eds.), *Financial liberalisation: Past, present and future*, Annual Edition of *International Papers in Political Economy*. Palgrave Macmillan.

Arestis, P. (2018). Importance of tackling income inequality and relevant economic policies. In P. Arestis & M. Sawyer (Eds.), *Inequality: Trends, causes, consequences, relevant policies*, Annual edition of *International Papers in Political Economy*. Palgrave Macmillan.

Arestis, P. (2019). Critique of the new consensus macroeconomics and propose a more Keynesian macroeconomic model. In P. Arestis & M. C. Sawyer (Eds.), *Frontiers of heterodox macroeconomics*, Annual Edition of *International Papers in Political Economy*. Palgrave Macmillan.

Arestis, P. (2020). Financial stability: Still unsettled for the future. In P. Arestis & M. C. Sawyer (Eds.), *Economic policies for a post neo-liberal world*, Annual Edition of *International Papers in Political Economy*. Palgrave Macmillan.

Arestis, P., & González Martinez, A. R. (2015). The absence of environmental issues in the new consensus macroeconomics is only one of numerous criticisms. In P. Arestis & M. Sawyer (Eds.), *Finance and the macroeconomics of environmental policies*, Annual Edition of *International Papers in Political Economy*. Palgrave Macmillan.

Arestis, P., & Karakitsos, E. (2011). Current crisis in the US and economic policy implications. In P. Arestis, R. Sobreira, & J. L. Oreiro (Eds.), *An assessment of the global impact of the financial crisis*. Palgrave Macmillan.

Arestis, P., & Karakitsos, E. (2013). *Financial stability in the aftermath of the 'great recession.'* Palgrave Macmillan.

Arestis, P., & Sawyer, M. (2003). Reinventing fiscal policy. *Journal of Post Keynesian Economics, 25*(4), 3–25. Reprinted in B. Laperche & D. Uzinidis (Eds.), *John Kenneth Galbraith and the future of economics* (Palgrave Macmillan, 2005).

Arestis, P., & Sawyer, M. (2011). The economic policies of the political economy of the Australian patriot and Cambridge economist. *European Journal of Economics and Economic Policies: Intervention, 8*(1), 129–145.

Arestis, P., & Sawyer, M. (2018). *Inequality: Trends, causes, consequences, relevant policies,* Annual edition of *International Papers in Political Economy*. Palgrave Macmillan.

Arestis, P., & Sawyer, M. (2019). European integration and the 'Euro Project'. In J. Michie (Ed.), *The handbook of globalisation* (3rd ed.). Edward Elgar.

Ash, M., Basu, D., & Dube, A. (2020). *Public debt and growth: An assessment of key findings on o causality and thresholds* (Political Economy Research Institute, Working Paper Series, Number 4433).

Atkinson, A. B. (2015). *Inequality: What can be done?* Harvard University Press.

Auerbach, A. J., & Gorodnichenko, Y. (2017). *Fiscal stimulus and fiscal sustainability* (NBER Working Paper 23789). Available at: http://www.nber.org/papers/w23789.

Bailey, A. (2020). The central bank balance sheet as a policy tool: Past, present and future. *Speech Given at the Jackson Hole Economic Policy Symposium,* August 20.

Bank of England. (1982, March). The role of the Bank of England in the money market. *Bank of England Quarterly Bulletin,* 86–94.

Bank of England. (2009, November 19). *The role of macroprudential policy* (Bank of England Discussion Paper). Available at: www.bankofengland.co.uk/working-paper/Working-papers.

Bank of England. (2013). *A framework for stress testing the UK banking system* (Discussion Paper). Available at: https://www.bankofengland.co.uk/news/2013/october/framework-for-stress-testing-the-uk-banking-system.

Bank of England. (2015, February). *One bank research agenda* (Discussion Paper). Available at: http://cryptochainuni.com/wp-content/uploads/Bank-of-England-One-Bank-Research-Agenda-Discussion-Paper-Feb15.pdf.

Bank of England. (2016). Financial stability report. Presented to Parliament Pursuant to Section 9W(10) of the Bank of England Act 1998 as Amended by the Financial Services Act 2012, *Issue No. 40*. Available at: https://www.google.com/search?q=Bank+of+England+%282016%29%2C+Financial+Stability+Report%2C+November+2016%2C+Issue+No.+40.&ie=utf-8&oe=utf-8&client=firefox-b-ab

Bank of International Settlements (BIS). (2019). *Proceeding with caution—A survey on central bank digital currency* (BIS Papers, No. 101). Bank for International Settlements. Available at: https://www.bis.org/publ/bppdf/bispap101.pdf.

Barwell, R. (2016). *Macroeconomic policy after the crash: Issues in monetary and fiscal policy*. Palgrave Macmillan.

Basel III Package. (2010). *Basel III: International regulatory framework for banks.* Basel Committee on Banking Supervision. Available at: https://www.bis.org/bcbs/basel3.htm.

Berg, A. G., & Ostry, J. D. (2011). *Inequality and unsustainable growth: Two sides of the same coin?* (IMF Staff Discussion Note 11/08). International Monetary Fund. Available at: http://www.imf.org/external/pubs/ft/sdn/2011/sdn1108.pdf.

Bernanke, B. (2004, February 20). *The great moderation.* Remarks Given at the Meetings of the Eastern Economic Association. Available at: https://www.federalreserve.gov/boarddocs/speeches/2004/20040220/.

Bernanke, B. (2020). The new tools of monetary policy. *American Economic Review, 110*(4), 943–983.

Blanchard, O. (2019). Public debt and low interest rates. *American Economic Review, 109*(4), 1197–1229.

Bordo, M. D. (2020, October). *Monetary policy cooperation/coordination and global financial crises in historical perspective* (NBER Working Paper No. 27898).

Brazier, A. (2018, February 1). Market finance and financial stability: Will the stretch cause a strain? *Speech given at the Brevan Howard Centre for Financial Analysis*, Imperial College.

Broadbent, B. (2019, January 23). Debt dynamics. *Speech Given at the London Business School*. Available at: www.bankofengland.co.uk/speeches.

Chick, V., & Pettifor, A. (2011). *The economic consequences of Mr Osborne. Fiscal consolidation: Lessons from a century of UK macroeconomic statistics* (Report). Policy Research in Macroeconomics (PRIME).

Claessens, S., Keen, M., & Pazarbasioglu, C. (2010, September). *Financial sector taxation: The IMF's report to the G-20 and background material* (The IMF's Report to the G-20 and Background Material). International Monetary Fund. Available at: https://www.imf.org/external/np/seminars/eng/2010/paris/pdf/090110.pdf.

Coenen, G., & Straub, R. (2005). *Does government spending crowd in private consumption? Theory and empirical evidence for the Euro Area* (IMF Working Paper 05/159). International Monetary Fund.

Committee on the Global Financial System (CGFS). (2019, October). *Unconventional monetary policy tools: A cross-country analysis* (CGFS Papers, No 63). Bank for International Settlements. Available at: https://www.bis.org/publ/cgfs63.pldf.

Crotty, J., & Epstein, G. A. (2014). The last refuge of scoundrels: Keynes-Minsky perspectives on the uses and abuses of the 'liquidity defense'. chapter 16 in G. A. Epstein, T. Schlesinger & M. Bernengo (Eds.), *Banking, monetary policy and political economy of financial regulation: Essays in the tradition of Jane D'Arista*. Edward Elgar.

Dabla-Norris, E., Kochhar, K., Suphaphiphat, N., Ricka, F., & Tsounta, E. (2015). *Causes and consequences of income inequality: A global perspective. IMF Staff Discussion Note, 15*(13). Available at: https://www.imf.org/external/pubs/ft/sdn/2015/sdn1513.pdf.

Dafermos, Y., & Nikolaidi, M. (2019). Fiscal policy and ecological sustainability: A post-Keynesian perspective. In P. Arestis & M. Sawyer (Eds.), *Frontiers of heterodox macroeconomics*. Annual Edition of *International Papers in Political Economy*. Palgrave Macmillan.

Dario, C., Gagnon, E., Martinez-Garcia, E., & Neely, C. J. (2020). *Monetary policy and economic performance since the financial crisis* (Finance and Economics Discussion Series 2020-065). Board of Governors of the Federal Reserve System. Available at: https://doi.org/10.17016/FEDS.2020.065.

Edge, R. M., & Liang, N. (2017). *New financial stability governance structures and central banks*, Hutchins Center Working Paper #32. Available at: https://www.brookings.edu/research/.

Eggertsson, G. B. (2006). *Fiscal multipliers and policy coordination* (Federal Reserve Bank of New York Staff Reports, No. 241). Federal Reserve Bank of New York.

Ehlers, T., Mojon, B., & Packer, F. (2020, September). Green bonds and carbon emissions: Exploring the case for a rating system at the firm level. *Bank for International Settlements (BIS) Quarterly Review*.

Forbes, K. J. (2019). Macroprudential policy: What we've learned, don't know, and need to do. *AEA Papers and Proceedings, 109*, 470–475.

Giansante, S., Fatouh, M., & Ongena, S. (2020, August). *Does quantitative easing boost bank lending to the real economy or cause other bank asset reallocation? The case of the UK* (Bank of England Staff Working Paper No. 883). Available at: www.bankofengland.co.uk/working-paper/staff-working-papers.

Goodhart, C. (2015). Why monetary policy has been comparatively ineffective? *The Manchester School, 89*(4), 20–29.

Haldane, A. (2020, September 30). Avoiding economic anxiety. *Speech Given at the Cheshire and Warrington Local Enterprise Partnership (LEP) Economic Summit*. Available at: www.bankofengland.co.uk/news/speeches and @BoE_PressOffice.

Hansen, A. H. (1939). Economic progress and declining population growth. *American Economic Review, 29*(1), 1–15.

IMF. (2014, January). *Fiscal policy and income inequality* (IMF Policy Paper). Available at: http://www.imf.org/external/pp/ppindex.aspx.

IMF. (2018, October). *A decade after the global financial crisis: Are we safer?* (Global Financial Stability Report). International Monetary Fund.

IMF. (2020a, April). Chapter 1: The great lockdown. *World Economic Outlook*.

IMF. (2020b). World economic outlook update. *World Economic Outlook*. International Monetary Fund.

Jorda, O., & Taylor, A. M. (2016). The time for austerity: Estimating the average treatment effect of fiscal policy. *The Economic Journal, 126*(590), 219–255.

Kalecki, M. (1971). Class struggle and the distribution of national income. *Kyklos, 24*(1), 1–9.

Kelton, S. (2020). *The deficit myth: Modern monetary theory and how to build a better economy*. John Murray Publishers.

Keynes, J. M. (1936). *The general theory of employment, interest and money*. Macmillan.

King, M. (2016a, September 26). The future of central banks. *Financial News*.

King, M. (2016b). *The end of alchemy: Money, banking and the future of the global economy*. Little Brown.

Kohn, D. (2019). How can the objective of macroprudential policy be operationalized, given the high uncertainty about the state of the financial system? *Speech given at the Joint Bundesbank-ECB Spring Conference, 15 May*. Frankfurt. Available at: www.bankofengland.co.uk/publications/Pages/speeches/default.aspx.

Lavoie, M., & Stockhammer, E. (2013). Wage-led growth: Concept, theories and policies. In M. Lavoie & E. Stockhammer (Eds.), *Wage-Led growth: An equitable strategy for economic recovery*. Palgrave Macmillan.

Liikanen Report. (2012, October). *Report of the European Commission's high-level expert group on bank structural reform*. Available at: https://en.wikipedia.org/wiki/Liikanen_report.

McCausland, W. D., & Theodossiou, I. (2016). The consequences of fiscal stimulus on public debt: A historical perspective. *Cambridge Journal of Economics, 40*(4), 1103–2016.

Miles, D., Yang, J., & Marcheggiano, G. (2013). Optimal bank capital. *Economic Journal, 123*(567), 1–37.

Minsky, H. P. (1986). *Stabilising an unstable economy*. Yale University Press.

Minsky, H. P. (1992, May). *The financial instability hypothesis* (The Jerome Levy Economics Institute Working Paper No. 74).

Nuno, G. (2018). *Monetary policy implications of central-bank issued digital currency* (Economic Bulletin 3/2018), Banco de Espana, Spain.

OECD. (2008). *Growing unequal? Income distribution and poverty in OECD countries*. OECD Publishing.

OECD. (2011). *Divided we stand: Why inequality keeps rising*. OECD Publishing.

Ollivaud, P., & Turner, D. (2015). The effect of the global financial crisis on OECD potential output. *OECD Journal: Economic Studies, 1*, 41–60.

Onaran, O., & Galanis, G. (2013). Is aggregate demand wage-led or profit-led? A global model. Chapter 3 In M. Lavoie & E. Stockhammer (Eds.), *Wage-led growth: An equitable strategy for economic recovery* (pp. 71–99). Palgrave Macmillan.

Pérez-Moreno, S., & Bárcena-Martín, E. (2019). Secular stagnation and income class structure in Europe: Policy and institutional implications. In P. Arestis & M. Sawyer (Eds.), *Frontiers of heterodox macroeconomics*. Annual Edition of *International Papers in Political Economy*. Palgrave Macmillan.

Piketty, T. (2014). *Capital in the twenty-first century* (A. Goldhammer, Trans.). Harvard University Press.

Philippon, T. (2008, November). *The evolution of of the U.S. financial industry from 1860 to 2007* (Working Paper). New York University.

Russell, D. E. (2014). Lessons from the Glass-Steagall Act. Chapter 7 in G. A. Epstein, T. Schlesinger & M. Bernengo (Eds.), *Banking, monetary policy and political economy of financial regulation: Essays in the tradition of Jane D'Arista*. Edward Elgar.

Sawyer, M. (2011). UK fiscal policy after the global financial crisis. *Contributions to Political Economy, 30*(1), 13–29.

Sawyer, M. (2012). The tragedy of UK fiscal policy in the aftermath of the financial crisis. *Cambridge Journal of Economics, 36*(1), 205–221.

Schwartz, G., Fouad, M., Hansen, T., & Verdier, G. (2020, September 3). *How strong infrastructure governance can end waste in public investment* (IMF Blog).

Stiglitz, J. E. (2013). *The price of inequality: How today's divided society endangers our future*. Penguin Books.

Strauss-Khan, D. (2011, April 4). Global challenges, global solutions. *An Address at George Washington University*. International Monetary Fund. Available at: http://www.imf.org/external/np/speeches/2011/040411.htm.

Summers, L. (2014). U.S. economic prospects: Secular stagnation, hysteresis, and the zero lower bound. *Business Economics, 49*(2), National Association for Business Economics.

Tcherneva, P. R. (2020). *The case for a job guarantee*. Polity Press.

Van der Ghote, A. (2018). *Coordinating monetary and financial regulatory policies* (ECB Working Paper Series, No. 2155).

Vercelli, A. (2017). *Crisis and sustainability: The delusion of free markets*. Palgrave Macmillan.

Woodford, M. (2016, May). *Quantitative easing and financial stability* (NBER Working Paper No. 22285).

Woodford, M., & Xie, Y. (2020). *Fiscal and monetary stabilization policy at the zero lower bound: Consequences of limited foresight* (NBER Working Paper 27521). Available at: http://www.nber.org/papers/w27521.

2

Can Economic Growth Last Forever?

Hector Pollitt

1 Introduction

In *The Affluent Society*, J. K. Galbraith (1998) describes the 'paramount position of production' in modern society. He tells a story of a US diplomat describing the second-best year in history, despite there being little evidence of progress in the arts and sciences, health, education or violent crime, and no discussion of the prospects for human survival or religious spirituality. The second-best year in history simply meant the year in which the US had its second-highest level of GDP.

Galbraith (1998) builds a comparison of GDP with religion, suggesting that questioning the importance of GDP is akin to blasphemy.

H. Pollitt (✉)
Cambridge Econometrics, Cambridge, UK
e-mail: hp@camecon.com; hbp22@cam.ac.uk

Department of Land Economy, Cambridge Centre for Environment, Energy and Natural Resource Governance, University of Cambridge, Cambridge, UK

P. Arestis and M. Sawyer (eds.), *Economic Policies for Sustainability and Resilience*, International Papers in Political Economy,
https://doi.org/10.1007/978-3-030-84288-8_2

He says that "the importance of production transcends our boundaries" (p. 100). Finally, he asks the question that haunts efforts to move away from GDP as the core economic indicator, "What else is there?" (p. 101).

Some of the insights from Galbraith (1998) have been lost in the modern discourse. The question of why we focus on GDP is an important one, which reflects the way that evolution has shaped the human race. Throughout history, we have lived through scarcity and increased levels of production (i.e. GDP) have translated directly to increased chances of survival. The idea of economic scarcity can be traced back to the eighteenth century work of Malthus (1798). It has found its way into 'econ 101' as one of the axioms of textbook economics: human wants are unlimited but resources are scarce.

It is not, however, clear that human wants really are unlimited anymore. People can only eat so much food and the 24 hours in a day limit how many services can be consumed. Growing shares of the younger population now eschew 'stuff' and live minimalist lifestyles. Nevertheless, predictions, including by Keynes (1930), that we would eventually stop demanding more, have not come true.

Nowadays, GDP growth is linked to maintaining high levels of employment rather than survival. Domar (1946) noted that this line of thinking goes back to Marx, and it is widely accepted that scarcity of income is still a major issue for the unemployed. Galbraith (1998), similarly suggests that the means of production may be more important than the ends: "It still seems more satisfactory to say that we need the goods than to stress the real point, which is that social well-being and contentment require that we have enough production to provide income to the willing labour force" (p. 144).

Ecological literature increasingly identifies GDP growth as a cause of natural destruction. The idea of 'degrowth' is that GDP growth should end (while employment rates are maintained) so that we live within our natural constraints. Ekins (2012) summarises the main points:

1. We live on a finite planet.
2. There are limits to what may be extracted from the planet.
3. These limits are now exceeded in many places.
4. Economic growth is responsible for pushing against the limits.

5. There are strong correlations between economic growth and resource consumption.
6. Rich countries should therefore reduce or end economic growth.
7. Ending growth may not lead to loss of economic and social welfare.

Ekins (op. cit.) notes that only steps 1–3 are uncontested. Few would disagree that we are now seeing the effects of pushing against environmental constraints. The effects of a changing climate are profound (IPCC, 2018, chapter 3) and are already becoming apparent. We are already using roughly double the material impacts we can take sustainably each year (Bringezu, 2015). Up to 1 million of the planet's 8 million species face extinction, many within decades (IPBES, 2019).

The Club of Rome and The Limits to Growth (Meadows et al., 1972) predicted many of these effects almost 50 years ago. The modelling in *Limits to Growth* predicted a collapse in production and population levels soon after, likely leading to the breakdown of society: "the human race may have very little time to react to a crisis resulting from exponential growth in a finite space" (Meadows et al., 1972, p. 51).

Technology optimists counter that human ingenuity will find a way to deal with these issues, creating 'green growth'. Many of the technologies required to limit climate change not only exist already but also are now cheaper than the alternatives. Where this is not the case, proponents say it is better to invest in research and development (R&D) now, let the technologies develop and allow markets to identify low-cost solutions when we have more wealth to do so (e.g. Nordhaus, 2019).

Authors on both side of the debate seem certain that they are correct but there is no consensus about whether indefinite GDP growth is possible. A poll by the futurist Azeem Azhar on Twitter in 2020 showed a roughly even split (40% each) between people who thought indefinite growth was possible and people who said we are near finite limits already. The remaining 20% said that there are limits but we are not yet near them.

It is nearly 50 years since *Limits to Growth* raised the issue but we still do not have an accepted understanding over a question that is fundamental to our societies and economic systems.

1.1 Why Write This Chapter?

In 2020 there were some major publications on a world without economic growth (e.g. Hickel, 2020; Kallis et al., 2020). However, this is still a relatively new strand of literature. Moreover, the degrowth literature generally takes by assumption the idea that GDP cannot increase forever. For example, Jackson (2017, prologue), which provides one of the more nuanced discussions, takes as given that 'human activity' cannot expand indefinitely. Kallis et al. (2020) describe the "mad idea of an infinitely large economy" (p. 25). Hickel (2020) suggests that indefinite economic growth would "disavow the most obvious truths" (p. 17) about ecological limits.

In a review of the degrowth literature, Weiss and Cattaneo (2017) confirm that degrowth authors generally believe that endless economic growth is not possible. The authors also point to a troubling political bias within the literature, drawing from Paul Krugman (2014) to say that "Degrowth is a marginal left-wing European position" (p. 227). They find that the majority of articles lean towards a degrowth position normatively and suggest that the degrowth literature "lacks rigid hypotheses testing through modelling and empirical assessments" (p. 227). Van den Bergh (2011) similarly notes that much of the degrowth literature is 'normative and idealistic', and often vague.

Many of the same criticisms could be levelled at the mainstream neoclassical economic literature and textbook economics. Georgescu-Roegen (1971) references Marshall's *Principles of Economics* and notes wryly that "some careful writers have even emphasized the point that man can create neither matter nor energy" (p. 280). Many of the critiques of neoclassical economics describe assumption by omission (e.g. Beinhocker, 2007, chapter 3; Keen, 2011). It is easy to show that GDP can grow forever if you assume that there are no limits on the long-term availability of resources, or that resource productivity can grow indefinitely.

In this context, we can see how opinion on the topic of potential limits to growth can be so divided. Different views reflect both gaps in knowledge and differences in political opinions. This chapter avoids taking an ideological position and fills some of the gaps by combining three distinct strands of economic theory (see Sect. 2).

1.2 GDP as an Indicator

Proponents of both continued economic growth and degrowth note the limitations of GDP as an indicator of economic welfare. Degrowth advocates have proposed alternative indicators. For example, Kallis et al. (2020) suggest the goal is 'reorienting lives and societies toward well-being'. Hickel and Kallis (2020) discuss how economic value is determined, noting that there is no satisfactory theory (see the lengthy review and discussion in Mazzucato, 2019, chapter 1).

Degrowth authors frequently mention other shortcomings of GDP, such as ignoring domestic work and inequality (e.g. Ekins, 2012; Jackson, 2017, p. 6). More important for this chapter is the questionable link between GDP and happiness. Data show a lack of correlation between income levels (GDP) and happiness, which could be explained by 'adaptiveness', meaning that people are always chasing something they do not have already. Adaptiveness suggests that permanent increases in income have only temporary effects on happiness (beyond a subsistence level; Hickel, 2020, p. 178; Sterling, 2016). However, this analysis does not suggest that GDP is irrelevant to happiness; more that it could be the GDP growth rate, rather than level, that determines happiness.[1]

Van den Bergh (2011) notes that GDP is the interpretation of economic growth that it is likely to be understood best by economists, politicians and the general public. In this chapter, we therefore take GDP as the indicator of economic production for the analysis, while accepting the critiques. We use GDP in real terms.[2] We also frame the discussion in global terms to avoid issues of 'embodied' environmental damage in goods that are traded between countries (e.g. Ward et al., 2016). However, Sect. 5 acknowledges the difficulties of setting policy at a global level.

---

[1] Clinical psychology may soon be able to assess this issue (Burnham et al., 2016; Epstein & Chelen, 2016; Glimcher, 2016; Sterling, 2016).

[2] It is trivial to show that prices could increase indefinitely; however, this is not the relevant proposition most people are interested in.

1.3 Structure of This Chapter

The next section builds an assessment framework, drawing on three different schools of economic thought. Section 3 applies this framework to our core question and Sect. 4 discusses the key issues further. Section 5 concludes with a summary of the key insights from the analysis and suggested paths forward for society in general and economists specifically.

2 Building an Assessment Framework

2.1 Introduction

The general disagreement about limits to growth is reflected in the different schools of economic thought. Many of the schools ignore the possibility that there are limits to economic growth and therefore answer the question by assumption.

Mainstream neoclassical economics, and its extension to environmental economics, provides a prime example. Neoclassical economics treats the environment (at best) as an 'externality', meaning something that it is detached from economic production. Limits on physical resources are rarely acknowledged. Ironically, the core premise of neoclassical economics, of how to maximise production from a finite set of resources, would fit well with the question of how to make the best use of limited amounts of natural resources. It would not be a giant leap to introduce constrained supplies of resources into a neoclassical Computable General Equilibrium (CGE) model.

However, such an approach could do more harm than good. The models would only cover resource flows (and not stocks) in any meaningful way. The underlying assumptions of reversibility and easy substitution between natural and fabricated resources are often at odds with reality. The standard critiques of neoclassical economists' assumptions, including 'fictional self-regulating markets' (Kallis et al., 2020, p. 15), still apply.

We see these assumptions in the cost–benefit analyses used in forming environmental policy. There are numerous objections to the approach,[3] for example in the way values are put on human life and ecosystems (Kelman, 1981) and the use of discount rates that can greatly reduce the value of long-term environmental benefits (Stern, 2016). The approach cannot incorporate uncertainty, which is highly problematic if there is even a small chance of ecological or societal collapse (Sharpe et al., 2021; Weitzman, 2009). Distributional impacts are also typically ignored.

Neoclassical economics has also led to a focus on taxes (and subsidies) to 'fix' environmental problems by using prices to adjust behaviour (Pigou, 1920). Leaving aside the political practicalities of introducing such taxes, a failure to incorporate uncertainty again undermines the approach's validity. In the case of climate change, economists have long tried to estimate the 'social cost of carbon' (SCC), which is the cost of the emission of one tonne of carbon dioxide (or a gas with equivalent global warming effects). William Nordhaus was awarded the economics Nobel Memorial prize for his efforts to do this. However, the range of estimates of the SCC demonstrates the futility of the approach (Ricke et al., 2018).

Neoclassical economists claim that their analysis gets close enough to the 'right' answers and is better than alternative approaches (meaning to them no economics). However, to answer the question of whether indefinite growth is possible, an approach with stronger empirical foundations and more policy relevance is required. It is therefore necessary to consider alternative approaches.

2.2 Ecological Economics

Ecological economics was developed in the 1980s in response to the failure of both mainstream neoclassical and heterodox economics to account for real-world physical constraints (Spash & Asara, 2018). Ecological economists define the economy as a system that is placed within wider society, which itself must fit within natural constraints. The

[3] Ackerman (2017, chapter 2) describes the approach as 'steam engine' economics because it has not progressed from Walras' work in the nineteenth century (Walras, 1954).

logical conclusion is that there are limits to how much the economy can grow (in physical terms) and the original *Limits to Growth* (Meadows et al., 1972) could be seen as a starting point for ecological economics. More recent discussion of 'Planetary Boundaries' (Rockström et al., 2009) is consistent with ecological economics. Most degrowth literature is derived from ecological economics.

Nicholas Georgescu-Roegen is a key figure in ecological economics. His book *Entropy and the Economic Process* (Georgescu-Roegen, 1971) described a form of economics that moved from the first law of thermodynamics (exemplified by neoclassical economics) to the second law. The Law of Entropy states that the universe is gradually decaying to a chaotic state and that life itself is an attempt to prevent the spread of entropy within organisms. To achieve this outcome, however, living organisms must increase entropy elsewhere, by consuming dense energy sources and emitting waste products. Although a relatively short part of the book was devoted to what would now be recognised as ecological economics, Georgescu-Roegen (op. cit.) clearly suggested that the economic process accelerates the increase in entropy, leaving fewer useful resources behind for other organisms.

Georgescu-Roegen's (1971) analysis leads to two conclusions. The first conclusion is that economic processes cannot be fully reversible because this would violate the Law of Entropy. No technology can get around this basic law; as Georgescu-Roegen (op. cit.) describes, it is not possible that "a corpse may resuscitate to lead a second life in exactly the reversed order of the first" (p. 7).

The second conclusion links technology development to substitution. Georgescu-Roegen (1971, p. 303) describes the price of new technology as an increase in entropy creation. He also notes that technological advances often direct consumption away from renewable resources (e.g. human labour) towards finite resources (e.g. minerals). He concludes that every technological advance now allows fewer people to live in the future. The parallels to the conclusions from *The Limits to Growth* are notable.

Having only been around for 30–40 years, ecological economics is still not well defined. Spash and Asara (2018) list three separate branches, which differ in both theoretical and practical approaches, and even in philosophy. Some ecological economists prioritise adapting to the world we live in; others focus on trying to control it.

However, there are clear gaps in ecological economic theory, which mean that it alone cannot answer the question of whether GDP growth can continue indefinitely. For example, discussions about money and the financial system are often loose and ecological economics does not include a theory of economic growth, beyond stressing the importance of material and energy throughput in production. Innovation is often considered as a source of false hope for beating thermodynamic constraints, rather than as a core part of the economic process. Ecological economists regularly borrow insights from other branches of economics when addressing these issues (e.g. Jackson, 2017, chapter 2). We must do the same, starting with a basic description of the economic and financial system.

2.3 Post-Keynesian Economics

For a general description of the economy, we turn to post-Keynesian economics (King, 2015; Lavoie, 2014). Although only formally first defined in Kregel (1973) and Eichner and Kregel (1975), post-Keynesian thought has a much longer history, dating back to the work of Joan Robinson (1956), Kalecki (1954) and, of course, Keynes' *General Theory* (Keynes, 1936). Despite a lack of clarity in the *General Theory* (Carter, 2020, p. 257; Minsky, 1975, p. 12), the basic principles of post-Keynesian economics are now well established.

As Minsky (1975, p. 55) notes, we must go back even further to Keynes' *Treatise on Probability* (Keynes, 1921) to bring in the core post-Keynesian concept of fundamental uncertainty (see also Keynes, 1937). While such discussion may appear abstract, uncertainty is a theme that runs through the complete framework shown in Sect. 2.5. Fundamental uncertainty also puts post-Keynesian economics at odds with the neoclassical school and makes cost benefit analysis and the social cost of carbon logically incoherent.

Minsky (1975) and others have shown that uncertainty provides the foundation for the demand-driven economy; with 'unknown unknowns' it is not possible to optimise behaviour such that all available resources are used. The level of aggregate demand for goods and services, rather than the availability of resources, determines the level of production. Logically, economic growth can therefore only result from higher effective demand for products, supported by expectations of future growth that are reflected in investment.

Several authors suggest that post-Keynesian economics and ecological economics share common ground. Gowdy (1991), Kronenberg (2010) and King (2015, p. 122) reach similar conclusions, noting that both schools have incorporated Georgescu-Roegen's (1971) work and focus on production rather than transactions. Pollitt et al. (2016) suggest that post-Keynesian and ecological economics could link in the same way that neoclassical and environmental economics do.

Although post-Keynesian analysis rarely incorporates resource use,[4] it would not be difficult to do so. Limitations on the degree of substitutability between different types of capital find common ground with ecological economics. Kronenberg (2010) highlights irreversibility and path dependence as relevant common features. Galbraith (1998, p. 232) suggests that Keynes would have embraced such an approach, for example shifting focus from the aggregate level of production to distinguishing different types of production.

The linking of the two schools also creates some unresolved questions. Post-Keynesian theory stresses the importance of money for the financing of expenditure (Lavoie, 2020) and its representation of money has been shown to be both empirically accurate (Werner, 2014, 2016), and anthropologically consistent (Graeber, 2014). However, Kallis et al. (2020, pp. 25–26) cite money as a key source of environmental destruction and note the inconsistency between an unbounded money supply that drives production higher and fixed ecological constraints. Ever-increasing debt levels could be problematic in an economy that does not generate growth to repay debts with interest (Binswanger, 2009, 2015).

Keynes himself rarely considered issues of long-term economic growth. The main exception is *Economic possibilities for our grandchildren*

[4] Aside from the war effort, resource use was not an issue in Keynes' lifetime (Georgescu-Roegen, 1971, p. 2).

(Keynes, 1930) but its predictions that people would substantially cut working hours as wealth grew has not come to fruition. Keynes' (1930) error was putting too much weight on absolute needs and not enough on relative 'positional goods' that comprise much of our consumption today. Strong evolutionary pressures to display status and attract mating partners are not muted by a general increase in affluence (Veblen, 1899, pp. 15–20). Keynes (op. cit.) misinterpreted the reasons for continued economic growth, for which we must turn to a third school of economic thought.

2.4 Evolutionary and Complexity Economics

Veblen (1898) originally asked why economics is not an evolutionary science. Schumpeter (1934) designed an evolutionary framework for the economic system (although Schumpeter, op. cit., himself rejected the biological analogy) and Nelson and Winter (1982) built a model to show how economic sectors evolve when firms compete.

As the name suggests, evolutionary economics studies processes of change, in particular economic growth and development. It requires heterogeneity at micro level because if firms were identical, they would not compete and innovate, and no development would occur. Evolutionary Economics shows how this process of innovation creates *potential* macroeconomic growth. Although evolutionary economics focuses on the supply side, recent work has shown a high degree of compatibility with the post-Keynesian school (e.g. Dosi et al., 2010; Mercure et al., 2016) and recognising uncertainty is a common theme between the approaches.

The term 'complexity economics' was first used in Arthur (1999) and expands on the evolutionary school. Arthur (2010) outlines a theory of technological development that is close to Schumpeter's 'novel combinations'. Additional insights come from Anderson (1972) *More is Different*, which tells us that the nature of production changes with economic growth. Complexity theory adds that macro-level outcomes emerge from the combined interactions of the micro-level entities; adding to the macro analysis in ecological and post-Keynesian economics (see e.g. Di Guilmi, 2017; Metcalfe & Foster, 2010).

The main principles of complexity economics are familiar to both ecologists and ecological economists. As Hickel (2020) notes, "This is the thing about ecology: everything is connected… It is impossible to adequately understand our ecological crisis with the same reductive thinking that caused it in the first place" (pp. 9–10). Complexity economists often stress biophysical limits (e.g. Beinhocker, 2007, p. 449; Boulton et al., 2015, pp. 212–213; Nelson & Winter, 1982, p. 4).

We now bring these schools of thought together to build a framework for growth in an environmentally constrained world.

2.5 A Combined Analytical Framework to Assess Economic Growth

Economic growth is a reasonably recent phenomenon in human history (De Long, 1998), with productivity growth taking off after the industrial revolution. Most non-economists would be surprised to discover that we still do not fully understand what drives economic growth. Even more so that few economists study the topic. Kaldor (1932) noted, "Our knowledge of the subject remains, however, scattered in different sections of the standard works" (p. 180). If anything, the current 'standard works' have even less to say on economic growth. However, as Jackson (2017, chapter 2) points out, if we want to understand the limits to growth, we must first understand the process of growth.

In the ecological economics literature, Jackson (2017, chapter 2) and Binswanger (2009) give the best descriptions of economic growth, which are broadly consistent with Keynes (1936) and Schumpeter (1934). Georgescu-Roegen (1971, chapter 9) draws on Leontief and Marx to provide a long discussion that is often difficult to follow, but reaches the conclusion that economic growth is caused by the development of new 'processes'. He is consistent with Schumpeter (1934) and the evolutionary/complexity schools more generally; for example, Beinhocker (2007, p. 318) describes accumulated knowledge as the driver of economic growth and the incorporation of knowledge in the capital stock, which has long been acknowledged by (for example) Kaldor (1957). In the ecological literature, Ekins (2012) makes a similar point, noting that it was the knowledge of how to use fossil fuels, rather than the sudden appearance of the fuels, that drove growth after the industrial revolution. Based on complexity thinking, van der Leeuw (2016) suggests that a government-driven repurposing of knowledge and information using new ICT capabilities, including less concentration in the west, could provide the basis for future green growth.

Post-Keynesian economics has contributed relatively little to the discussion of long-run growth (Bellais, 2014; Domar, 1946; Eichner & Kregel, 1975) and has tended to focus more on capital accumulation and short-run development (notably Domar, 1946; Goodwin, 1967; Harrod, 1939; Kaldor, 1957). Although Setterfield (2010) includes more recent contributions, Dutt (2010) suggests that a new theory is needed and Keen (2013) suggests looking to the complexity school for this theory.

There is various work going on to build these linkages. Romero (2014) shows how a Schumpeterian approach can fit into a post-Keynesian framework, with the link between innovation and investment (via expectations) crucial for growth. Mercure et al. (2014) provide an operational example for the electricity sector and Dosi et al. (2010) builds a basic macro-modelling framework.

Figure 1 summarises the framework used in this chapter. Innovation arises when firms compete (Nelson & Winter, 1982; Schumpeter, 1934) to provide cheaper and better products to their customers. The innovation process may arise out of explicit R&D activities or through learning-by-doing. The aim of the innovation is to capture market share and to increase profits but, unless the innovation leads to a monopoly being established, the benefits are temporary because competing companies imitate and 'catch up' (Nelson & Winter, 1982).

As Fig. 1 shows, technological progress impacts the wider economy. We must make the distinction between process innovation (producing the same goods and services, but with fewer inputs, i.e. increasing productivity) and product innovation (producing different goods).

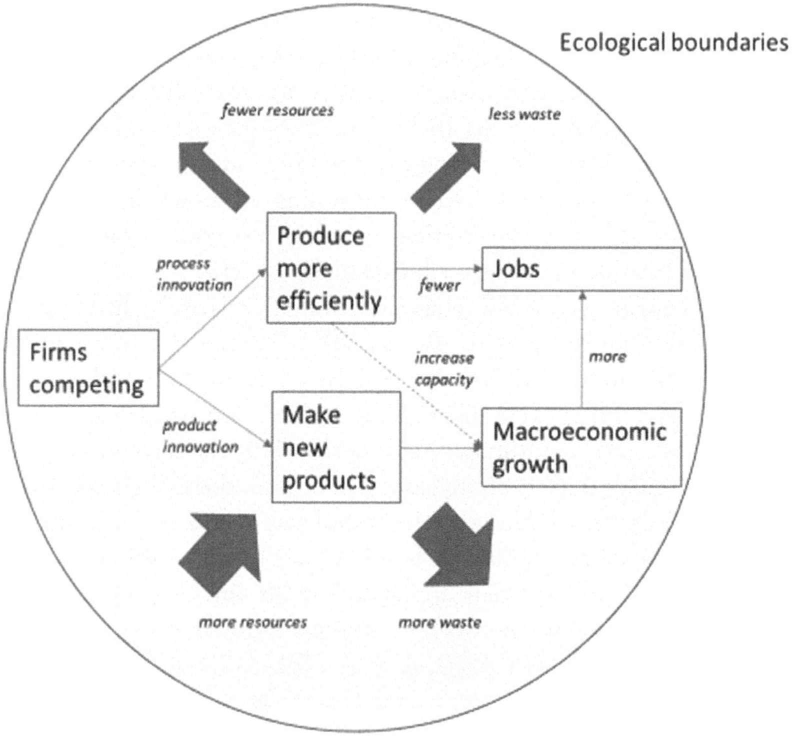

Fig. 1 The analytical framework (*Source* Author's construction)

Almost all the post-Keynesian literature focuses on process innovation.[5] For example, Kaldor (1957) states that: "The most important characteristic of capitalist business enterprise is the continuous change and improvement in the methods of production, as against the relatively unchanging techniques of peasant cultivation and artisan production" (p. 618).

Pollitt et al. (2021) describe the two different types of innovation. Process innovation increases economic capacity but induces a shift from labour income to profits unless cost reductions are fully passed on to

[5] The exceptions are Sasaki (2020) and Zagler (2004) but the model they use has an exogenous money supply that would be disputed by other post-Keynesian authors.

final consumers. In a wage-led economy (as most are, see e.g. Stockhammer et al., 2009), such an outcome leads to a reduction in aggregate demand and employment. Even if full cost savings are passed on to final consumers, some of the additional real income may be saved rather than spent on 'more of the same'. Process innovation may stimulate investment but only up to a certain point (otherwise, the resulting productivity improvements would not be worthwhile). In summary, higher rates of productivity may reduce aggregate demand, as Storm and Naastepad (2013) show happened for the Netherlands. As noted in Fig. 1, process innovation could, however, lead to lower resource use and amounts of waste.

The complexity school focuses on product innovation and 'more is different' (Anderson, 1972). Product innovation stimulates consumer spending by providing the 'novelty' that people desire (Galbraith, 1998, p. 120; Jackson, 2017, chapter 6; Sterling, 2016). The result is lower savings rates and a boost to aggregate demand and macroeconomic growth, although with more use of resources and more waste. For example, if no non-food products had ever been invented, economic growth and resource use would have been limited by high rates of 'forced saving' (Sasaki, 2020; Zagler, 2004) once everyone had bought and consumed as much food as they could physically manage. The introduction of non-food products, an early case of product innovation, thus allowed economic development to continue.

To summarise, the process of economic growth is driven by debt-financed investment for producing new goods and services and debt-financed consumption for using them, as Schumpeter (1934) first laid out, and Minsky (1986) built upon. Competition between firms to produce goods, as efficiently as possible, frees up labour and other resources to produce the new goods and services without hitting capacity constraints (including on natural resources). Product and process innovation thus co-exist and indeed drive one another, which has historically led to balanced growth without wild long-term swings in employment rates. Although the net effect on resource consumption is ambiguous, data have shown a strong tendency for resource use and waste to increase with economic growth, represented by the larger arrows linked to product innovation in Fig. 1.

3 Is Eternal Growth Possible?

3.1 Introduction

This section uses the economic framework outlined in the previous section to explore the question of limits to growth. We start with two basic questions:

- Can the human race continue to use increasing amounts of energy and material resources indefinitely?
- Can the economy grow indefinitely without using increased amounts of energy and material resources?

The first question is more physical in nature. The second question relates to the concept of 'decoupling', which is core to the idea of green growth. If 'absolute decoupling' is achieved, the economy can grow while using fewer physical resources and leading to less environmental degradation. Historical analyses have shown that absolute decoupling is possible in some countries at certain times (Hickel & Kallis, 2020). It is less clear, however, if it is possible at global level over a sustained period of time. Current data show no supporting evidence for global absolute decoupling, although this could reflect that the policies that would enable green growth have never seriously been attempted (van de Bergh, 2011).

We first discuss the immediate concerns around climate change and then broaden the discussion to consider a wider sustainability context.

3.2 Climate Change and the Immediate Threat

In 2015, the Paris Agreement on climate agreed to limit global average temperature increases to 'well below 2 °C' above pre-industrial levels, and to pursue efforts to limit the temperature increase to 1.5 °C. These targets in temperature change are arbitrary but reflect the precautionary principle based on Weitzman's (2009) dismal theorem, which was also expressed previously in Meadows et al. (1972, p. 81). The theorem states that beyond these boundaries, there is a non-zero risk of catastrophic change and we should do all that we reasonably can to avoid this risk. This formulation acknowledges uncertainty and replaces previous attempts by neoclassical economists to use crude cost–benefit analysis to estimate the optimal amount of global warming. The neoclassical economists' approach is now largely discredited (Ackerman, 2017, chapter 2; Keen, 2020; Pindyck, 2013; Stern, 2016).

The degree of temperature change is determined by the stock of greenhouse gases in the atmosphere. Given the long lifetime of the main greenhouse gas, CO_2, to limit climate change we must eventually either reduce new emissions of CO_2 to zero or find a way to remove an equivalent amount of emissions from the atmosphere (described as 'net-zero' emissions). The degree of climate change based on the stock of emissions is itself uncertain, but it is likely that the target of net-zero emissions will need to be attained shortly after 2050 at the latest (IPCC, 2018, chapter 2).

The majority of CO_2 emissions result from energy consumption and it is not feasible to reduce energy consumption to zero without reverting to a primitive society. Hence, we must rely on technological change and a decoupling of GDP and emissions to meet the targets. Fortunately, many of the technologies required for the decoupling already exist, and some (e.g. solar and wind power, or electric vehicles) are becoming cheaper than the alternatives that produce CO_2. The question to explore is thus whether these technologies can be rolled out fast enough, and whether continued economic growth is an impediment to doing so.

Underlying this discussion is the Kaya identity in Eq. 1 below (Kaya & Yokobori, 1998), which states that the total level of CO_2 emissions is the mathematical product of population (POP), per capita GDP (GDP/POP), the energy intensity of production (Energy/GDP) and the carbon intensity of energy (CO_2/Energy).

The Kaya identity

$$CO_2 = POP * \frac{GDP}{POP} * \frac{Energy}{GDP} * \frac{CO_2}{Energy} \quad (1)$$

A similar relationship may be obtained for non-energy and non-CO_2 greenhouse gas emissions.

In the western world, energy efficiency has improved (notably in lighting) in recent years, but most of the work of reducing emissions has fallen to the last term in the equation, the CO_2 intensity of energy. Initially this shift was driven by replacing coal-fired power plants with natural gas plants (which are less CO_2-intensive), but the gas plants themselves are now being replaced with renewable technologies.

The CO_2 intensity of renewables (in their use phase) is zero, which renders the rest of the Kaya identity irrelevant. However, there are some sectors such as aviation where there is currently no renewable option. There are also industrial processes where CO_2 is released regardless of the energy source (i.e. in chemical reactions). Most importantly, the pace of the roll-out of renewables must be balanced against the ever-reducing 'carbon budget', which is the remaining space before the stock of emissions reaches levels above those consistent with a 2 °C or 1.5 °C target.

The Kaya identity therefore remains important: a 1% increase in GDP offsets a 1% reduction in carbon intensity, effectively making the temperature targets harder to meet. To put it another way, the more economic production that takes place, the more wind and solar installations are needed to power it.

The modelling in the Intergovernmental Panel on Climate Change's (IPCC's) special report on the 1.5 °C target (IPCC, 2018, chapter 2) showed that it was possible to meet 1.5 °C, while still growing the global economy. However, although more advanced than the previous cost–benefit approaches, most of the models used in the report still make strong assumptions about perfect knowledge and rational behaviour. Such considerations are particularly important when considering the long lifetimes of infrastructure (e.g. buildings or roads) that result in CO_2 emissions.

There is a further issue with the IPCC model results. Many of the results rely on 'negative emissions' through a process of burning biomass and capturing the CO_2 emissions in the second half of the century. Even leaving aside the unproven nature of the technology and the potentially vast amounts of land required for growing the biomass (Anderson & Peters, 2016; Fuss, 2014), these results could be misleading because they confuse peak and final temperature change. This issue is important because climate processes are generally non-reversible, so the impacts of a 1.5 °C temperature change in 2100 are different if a higher temperature threshold was passed mid-century. For example, if high temperatures in 2050 drive a species to extinction, this species does not reappear when the earth subsequently cools 30 years later.

A more realistic modelling exercise has been carried out by Cambridge Econometrics, some of which was reported in Holden et al. (2018). The modelling incorporates endogenous rates of technological take-up (Mercure, 2012). These take-up rates can be exponential, cancelling out the exponential effects of economic growth (Grubb, 2018) that some authors suggest make meeting the climate targets impossible (e.g. Hickel, 2020, p. 21; Keen, 2020). The modelling finds that it is just possible to meet a 1.5 °C temperature target by 2050, without 'overshoot' that is corrected later by negative emissions. This scenario is highly investment-intensive, which leads to higher rates of economic growth than in the baseline case, suggesting that simultaneous decarbonisation and economic growth is possible (i.e. green growth).

How does this analysis relate to the framework developed in Sect. 2.5? The scenario shows rapid, targeted process innovation that is designed at reducing carbon intensity. The policies required to drive this innovation are extensive and require immediate introduction; if any policy or any major economy does not participate, the targets become unattainable. Product innovation continues, but is directed away from fossil fuel consumption through regulation. The process of decarbonisation itself generates economic growth but with carbon intensity reduced to zero, this does not matter.

Proponents of degrowth could use these results to suggest that ending or reversing economic growth (starting in the developed world) is required as a substitute for policy failure; it is politically infeasible that all policies will be universally implemented. However, if it is not possible to implement growth-inducing decarbonisation measures, changing the whole economic paradigm also seems impossible.

The conclusion is thus that economic growth may be a hindrance in meeting the climate challenge. Hickel (2020) is correct in saying that "Our insistence on perpetual growth is making our task much more difficult than it needs to be" (p. 138). However, there is no theoretical reason that enduring economic growth and a stable climate should be in long-term conflict, if innovation and the direction of growth are managed. The policy priority is to implement measures to reduce carbon and energy intensity. At least for now, this is more feasible than intentionally reducing rates of economic growth.

3.3 The Limits to Growth

Does the case for energy and CO_2 emissions generalise to other areas of sustainability? Alternatively, as Hickel (2020) puts it: "Once we have 100% clean energy, what are we going to do with it? … Clean energy might help deal with emissions, but it does nothing to reverse deforestation, overfishing, soil depletion and mass extinction" (p. 22).

The challenges that Hickel (op. cit.) cites are all the consequences, either directly or indirectly, of economic growth. Moreover, some of these challenges are being exacerbated by attempts to limit climate change. Solar panels, wind turbines and electric batteries require a range of different mineral inputs (ibid., pp. 139–140); none of these materials is properly included in the models described in the previous section. Economists also discuss the 'Energy-Water-Food' nexus, which describes how competing demands for food and energy supplies put pressure on available land and water resources (Brouwer et al., 2017; Paim et al., 2020).

The concept of limits on the size of the economy is not new. As noted previously, the original *Limits to Growth* was published in 1972 (Meadows et al., 1972), following discussions that began in 1968. Around the same time, Georgescu-Roegen (1971) wrote about how using limited stocks of mineral resources reduced possibilities for future generations.

More than two decades earlier, Domar (1944) pondered the same question: "In general it appears very unlikely that national income, or any economic series for that matter, can grow indefinitely at some constant percentage rate. The rate of growth achieved in the United States in the period 1879–1928 was due to technological improvements, growth of the labour force, and the discovery of new resources. Whether much reliance can be placed on resources still to be discovered is hard to say. It is true, however, that improved technological methods find new applications for known resources and thus may have the same effect as an actual discovery of new ones" (p. 819).

Economists have in general avoided the issue of limits to growth. For example, in his work on endogenous growth, Romer (1990) sidesteps the question, describing it as an empirical issue.

Chapter 2 of *The Limits to Growth* (Meadows et al., 1972) describes a situation in which the world faces shortages of food and mineral resources, with ever-increasing levels of pollution. Some of the predictions from the systems dynamics modelling in the book have proven to be accurate, but there are as yet few cases of resources running out. Although the authors suggest that shortages of energy are unlikely (although more due to nuclear rather than renewable power; p. 132), they suggest that the amount of environmental damage done by ever-increasing rates of mineral extraction will ultimately bound the level of human activity. Hickel (2020, pp. 120–121) makes a similar point that the danger is not running out of materials but of causing irreversible damage to ecosystems in extracting these materials.

At this point, we should note that many authors make the distinction between mineral and biomass resources. The difference is fundamentally one between stocks and flows. Biomass resources provide renewed capacity each year, whereas as mineral resources can only be used once. More importantly, the rate of renewal of biomass resources may be influenced by technology (see below), which is how Malthus's dire predictions were avoided, but Jevons' 'rebound' effects of increasing consumption of coal, even as productivity improved, have been proved correct (Georgescu-Roegen, 1971, p. 294; see next section). No such possibility of technologically-enhanced renewal mechanism exists for minerals.

While this situation naturally leads many to conclude that we should worry about the availability of minerals and not food and wood, Hickel's (2020) point about damage to ecosystems stands in both cases. Intensive farming causes just as much damage to ecosystems as mineral extraction does. Soil degradation is also a stock effect, making the distinction less clear-cut. Furthermore, improvements in agricultural productivity are often linked to the exploitation of mineral resources (going back to the plough). One can sense Georgescu-Roegen's (1971, p. 302) frustration in using the earth's limited 'natural deposits' to reduce dependence on labour and the unlimited energy provided by the sun.

Few people would therefore argue that, at least for the foreseeable future, the conclusion of Chapter 2 of *The Limits to Growth* that constraints exist because our planet's resources are finite is true. At present, the only way this constraint could be relaxed is if it would be possible to mine from asteroids that pass close to earth or other bodies in our solar system. Although there is the occasional story in the media on this topic, such activity is likely still to be decades away. Even further away is the theoretical possibility of transforming energy into matter, as demonstrated in *Star Trek's* fictional 'replicator' machines. Georgescu-Roegen (1971, p. 304) briefly considers the option but there is no prospect of such a technology arising any time soon.

The answer to the first question at the start of Sect. 3, about whether humans can continue consuming ever-increasing amounts of resources, is therefore a categorical no—we do not need an economic framework to tell us this. It also appears that we are already approaching the limits. As noted in the introduction to this chapter, Bringezu (2015) estimates that humanity is currently using double the amount of resources that is sustainable.

We now focus on the second question, which can also split into two parts; again, we can make the distinction between process and product innovation:

- Can we produce the same things using fewer inputs?
- Can we produce different things instead?

The first question relates to process innovation and is seen as the solution by technology optimists. It is addressed separately below. The second question asks whether it is feasible to transition our economies to focus on less resource-intensive products. Even *The Limits to Growth* (p. 175) suggests that some service sector activities could expand indefinitely. Ekins (2012) notes that "Economic (GDP) growth is growth in money flows/incomes/value added/expenditure. There is no theoretical limit on this kind of growth" (p. 63). Much of the degrowth literature also suggests that there should be a shift in production towards (non-financial and non-military) services, although Kallis et al. (2020, p. 6) describes an economy based on information and ideas as 'science fiction'.

It is undoubtedly true that a shift to an even more service-oriented economy would reduce material consumption (see Table 1). However, even if we accept the assumption that services use no mineral resources, the question remains of how we would grow the economy further once all non-essential production is in services. As we saw in Sect. 2.5, economic growth is driven by product innovation; if we reduce economic activity to service activities that people can do without tools, product innovation is reduced to the speed of human evolution and it is not possible for the economy to keep growing in any meaningful way.

Process innovation would also come to a halt. This is discussed further below but, for now, we can just note that productivity improvements in services are difficult without using mineral resources. For example, the barber needs his scissors and the taxi driver needs his car. As Georgescu-Roegen (1971) puts it, the role of capital "is not only to save labour, but also to amplify man's meagre physical power" (p. 266). Moreover, recent use of self-service supermarket checkouts and robots in warehouses has shown that the labour-saving aspect is still strong. Either way, it is difficult to escape the use of Georgescu-Roegen's (op. cit.) 'natural deposits' in production and the limits on the level of service-sector production seem impossible to overcome without using further material resources. A global economy based only on services will hit natural limits and cannot grow indefinitely.

Table 1 Direct purchases of resources, by sector (share of output, US in 2010)

Sector	Direct purchase (%)	Full supply chain (%)
Basic manufacturing	7.7	11.9
Advanced manufacturing	0.3	1.9
Construction	0.8	2.3
Services	0.1	0.7

Note Figure shows the proportion of output spent on biomass and non-energy mineral extraction. Includes intermediate purchases only and not investment goods
Source E3ME model database

3.4 Can Technology Solve the Problem?

We now come to the greatest point of contention between advocates of green growth and advocates of degrowth. Technology optimists suggest that innovation will allow our societies to keep on growing our economies while using fewer resources. Pessimists argue that technology is the cause of the problem and further advances will exacerbate environmental problems, as long as the current growth-driven economic system remains in place. Both views are only partially correct.

Much of the discussion in the literature appears to be ideologically driven. For example, in a much-read paper entitled *Is green growth possible?* (Hickel & Kallis, 2020), the authors use empirical analysis to show that green growth has not yet happened and attack theories of why green growth *might* be possible, but fail to address the question of whether it *can* be possible. Kallis (2011) asserts that 'throughput reduction is incompatible with further economic growth' and provides a list of supporting references but no further proof (before suggesting that a service-based economy cannot be ruled out). However, Sect. 2 of this chapter showed that Jackson (2017) is correct to note that "simplistic assumptions that capitalism's propensity for efficiency will allow us to stabilise the climate or protect against resource scarcity are nothing short of delusional" (p. 102). Van de Bergh (2011) gives a more balanced perspective, describing the strong correlations between economic and physical growth, but also noting the lack of corrective policy in the historical data.

Our economic framework from Sect. 2.5 describes how technology drives economic growth. For growth to take place in our current economy, it is necessary to have both product and process innovation. It is product innovation and the desire for novelty that have driven the increase in resource use over recent decades (Jackson, 2017, chapter 6), while process innovation has allowed the product innovation to take place by freeing up labour and other resources.

Is it possible that strong process innovation on its own could allow modern lifestyles to be maintained, without consuming ever-more resources? The story of 'green growth' usually follows this path. However, our framework suggests that such a path would lead to *degrowth* rather than *green growth* because, if no new products were invented, a steady state or declining economy would be a natural outcome (Pollitt et al., 2021). Our framework thus suggests that there is a major hole in the green growth story.

What if the economy was fixed so that process innovation could boost growth? This would require substantial intervention: either strict enforcement of cost reductions to be reflected in lower prices, or a full redistribution of additional profits for use in final consumption (with no additional saving).

This situation would lead to what economists describe as a 'rebound effect'. In the absence of product innovation, the product that consumers are most likely to spend additional (real) income on is the one for which prices have adjusted. This is called the direct rebound effect, as originally defined by Jevons in 1865 (Jackson, 2017, chapter 6). The indirect rebound effect is if expenditure is diverted to other products. For example, if food becomes cheaper, households might use any money they save on their purchases to buy luxury goods. Historically, product innovation has provided the goods that can be purchased.

This analysis already points towards problems; the direct rebound effect causes higher consumption of the resource-intensive goods that we are trying to make more efficient. The indirect rebound effect tends to divert consumption towards luxury goods that typically use more non-renewable resources. Hickel (2020, chapter 3) provides a broader description of how the rebound effect interacts with economic growth. Hickel and Kallis (2020) note: "… when technology improves labour productivity, we expect that this will lead to more growth and more jobs as the relative cost of labour declines – why some expect this to work differently in relation to resources is not clear" (p. 482).

The authors are describing the interaction of process and product innovation. For individual resources, cutting consumption may be possible but, taking material inputs as a single group, the degrowth authors are surely correct to raise this question. Hickel (2020) also makes the point succinctly: "the power of technology is that it enables capital and labour to be more productive – to produce more and faster. But it also speeds up the appropriation of nature" (p. 81).

If we consider the question temporarily from a supply-side perspective, we get to the same outcome: with a fixed number of people in the primary sector, improvements in productivity will increase the potential extraction of resources. The following extract from *The Limits to Growth* (p. 157), makes a similar point about how our economies respond to the 'negative feedback loops' caused by constraints on resource availability: "The growth-stopping pressures from negative feedback loops are already being felt in many parts of human society. The major societal responses to these pressures have been directed at the negative feedback loops themselves. Technological solutions, such as those discussed in chapter IV, have been devised to weaken the loops or to disguise the pressures they generate so that growth can continue. Such means may have some short-term effect in relieving pressures caused by growth, but in the long run they do nothing to prevent the overshoot and subsequent collapse of the system" (p. 157).

The passage describes a battle between mankind and nature, which has been recognised both inside and outside economics. As far back as 1899, Veblen (1899) recognised the line "drawn between mankind and brute creation" (p. 10), and the ambitions of people to rise above this battle.

The simplistic discussion of a mathematical race between resource efficiency and rates of economic growth (e.g. as in the Kaya Identity) ignores the interactions between efficiency rates, the two types of innovation and economic growth. The type of efficiency that reduces resource consumption is also likely to reduce economic growth. Even if we contrive to find a way in which it does not reduce growth, we get higher rates of resource consumption through rebound effects.

If we then factor in the way in which product and process innovation drive each other, things are complicated further. There is no obvious way to stop product innovation, which seems to be a deep-rooted human trait (Sterling, 2016). Trying to establish a world with only process innovation is a futile endeavour.

For authors that equate economic growth with the accumulation of knowledge (e.g. Beinhocker, 2007; Metcalfe & Foster, 2010), it is even more difficult to see how economic growth could be curtailed. It seems impossible (and surely undesirable) to stop the generation of new knowledge. Preventing actions based on this knowledge may be possible and there are some cases where restrictions are in place (e.g. in military technologies); but it would be difficult to regulate knowledge across the whole economy.

Finally, there are limits to how efficient a process can be. Ward et al. (2016) use a model to show that it is not possible to increase efficiency indefinitely because of physical (e.g. thermodynamic) constraints. It is not possible to take 100% of the material out of the product, for there would be no product left. Such arguments can also be applied to the 'circular economy', which effectively aims to turn the stock of mineral resources into an annual flow through reuse and recycling. However, Giampietro (2019) and Cullen (2017) note that full circularity is not possible because of product degradation, so some new extraction will always be needed to keep the circle going. It should also be noted that even a perfectly circular economy would still need new resources if it were to grow each year. Therefore, while a move to a circular economy would certainly help us to live within our ecological boundaries, it would not enable never-ending economic growth.

3.5 Economic Growth... It Had a Good Run

Returning to the questions at the start of this section, the analysis suggests that it is neither possible to keep on using more resources indefinitely, nor to continue growing the economy without using more resources. Logically, we must therefore conclude that economic growth will at some point come to an end. As noted in the introduction, with various environmental pressures already apparent, that end may be nearer than many people think.

The questions raised are profound and the subject of much of the degrowth literature. Is it possible to stop innovation and growth? How could we manage such a process? Does it spell the end for capitalism too? The following section briefly touches on some of these issues.

4 The Final Stages of Capitalism?

4.1 Introduction

Much of the degrowth literature starts by noting that economic growth will end one way or another; as the previous section showed, a combination of the laws of thermodynamics and an understanding of the processes that drive growth will ensure this outcome (Weiss & Cattaneo, 2017). To the degrowth authors, the question is whether the end of economic growth will be managed or chaotic. Again, these ideas are not new and were raised in the original *Limits to Growth* (pp. 170–182). However, it is debatable whether the call for more ideas about how to transition to a post-growth society in *The Limits to Growth* has been heeded and the general feeling from the literature is that there is still much to be resolved.

Kallis et al. (2020, p. 3) and Hickel (2020, p. 24) suggest that there is a lack of imagination in designing alternatives to the current growth paradigm. However, it could equally be argued that what is lacking is first a proof that the alternatives are viable and, second, a set of concrete measures to get there. The communal societies that the authors sketch out may appeal to particular groups in society but the reader is often left questioning why, if so good, we do not do much of this already.

Jackson (2017) summarises the situation well: "Even if it is true that economic growth is unsustainable, isn't it self-evidently true that its opposite or its absence is far from desirable too?" (prologue). Jackson (op. cit.) later describes an 'impossibility theorem' in that "the idea of a non-growing economy may be anathema to an economist. But the idea of a continually growing economy is anathema to an ecologist" (ibid., chapter 1).

One area where there is more consensus is the need for a better understanding of the macroeconomics. It is not realistic to expect society to move to a new economic system without fully understanding what this process entails. Jackson (2017) describes the development of new theory as a "precise and definable task" that is "entirely possible" (pp. 183–184). Our framework laid out in Sect. 2.5 may provide a good starting point. At a minimum, the new theory must include a proper understanding of technology development and the financial system, and most people would suggest a treatment of inequality too.

Having found a negative answer to our main question of whether GDP can keep growing forever, the remaining parts of this section discuss briefly how we might be able to extend the growth paradigm for longer and introduce some of the key issues with transitioning to a steady-state economy. The final sub-section considers this transition in the context of expected forthcoming developments in Artificial Intelligence (AI) and automation.

4.2 Prolonging the Growth Paradigm

While advocates of degrowth would suggest that immediate measures should be taken to curb natural resource consumption and GDP, there are two reasons to extend the current period of growth for now. First, extending growth for a few more years would give us time to understand properly what a transition to a steady-state economy would entail; and, second, the ultimate level of production at which the steady state occurs could be higher (although environmental damage would also be higher).

Seen against the following passage from *The Limits to Growth*, this process may appear to be continuing the fight against resource constraints, and such an interpretation would be correct to some extent. However, our final years of growth would also need to accept the finite nature of the earth's resources, and include a redirection of the fight towards eventually living within our environmental constraints. "Applying technology to the natural pressures that the environment exerts against any growth process has been so successful in the past that a whole culture has evolved around the principle of fighting against limits rather than learning to live with them. This culture has been reinforced by the apparent immensity of the earth and its resources and by the relative smallness of man and his activities" (p. 150).

Such an approach needs a much better understanding of the ecological space that we occupy and the limitations of that space. For climate change, the boundaries are uncertain but relatively well-researched

(IPCC, 2018); but for other areas of sustainability many people remain unaware that boundaries even exist.

The policies that can help us remain in this space are already relatively well known and are core to the green growth paradigm. They essentially involve:

- shifting the nature of production towards less resource-intensive activities (e.g. more services);
- directing process innovation towards reducing resource inputs rather than labour inputs;
- cleaning up pollution wherever possible.

As Grubb et al. (2014, chapter 2) explain, a combination of regulatory policy, market-based instruments and technology support is required to get the full benefits of each individual policy. The institutional context, particularly at international level, must be acknowledged in policy-making; there are limitations to what any one policy or institution can achieve.

Georgescu-Roegen (1971) wrote that 'bigger and better' washing machines, automobiles and superjets lead to 'bigger and better' pollution. If the focus shifts to 'better', and 'better' means a lower ecological footprint then, for a limited time, further sustainable economic growth may be possible.

4.3 Entering the Post-growth Era

We now turn to some of the key questions that the degrowth literature has sought to address, for which it is possible to provide only a brief summary here. Where relevant, we suggest ways in which insights from our framework may help address the issues.

A post-growth economy is likely to be more collectivist and less individualist than our current system. It is not yet clear to what extent capitalism could survive in a degrowth world. Fontana and Sawyer (unpublished) note that much reduced rates of investment and profits in a degrowth economy would make capitalism difficult to maintain.

Jackson (2017, pp. 222–223) leaves the question open. Kallis (2011) and Kallis et al. (2020) suggest that capitalism will not survive, describing degrowth as 'a radical political project' in which capitalism is undesirable.[6]

A more collectivist society leads naturally to discussions about inequality and the distribution of income. Weiss and Cattaneo (2017) note that a strong focus on inequality in the degrowth literature may reflect the roots of the degrowth movement in wider social movements. This discussion includes inequality both between and within countries. The same authors find that little of the published literature on degrowth has come from the developing world.

Kallis et al. (2020, chapter 4) suggest that most of the policies to promote degrowth are about inequality rather than absolute levels of production. The authors would likely agree with Galbraith (1998, pp. 79–80) that economic growth is often seen as a substitute for dealing with inequality. The past decade has shown the effects of increasing inequality compounded by slow economic growth. Galbraith (op. cit., pp. 97–98) goes on to discuss the broken window fallacy, as described by Keynes in the *General Theory*, as a last resort. Pointless production is exactly what degrowth aims to avoid, so the emphasis on reducing inequality would be even greater.

More generally, post-Keynesian thinking provides both support and obstacles to the degrowth agenda. For example, Jackson and Victor (2016) note that one potential conclusion of Piketty (2014) is that low economic growth rates will inevitably lead to higher inequality. However, the authors use a post-Keynesian framework to show that lower capital-labour substitution rates or modest policy intervention could reverse this trend.

More difficult for degrowth advocates, post-Keynesian economists would also question the conclusion in Hickel (2020, p. 183) that redistribution of income would automatically lead to lower levels of resource consumption (because luxury goods are more resource-intensive). This

[6] It should also be noted that the degrowth literature sometimes conflates capitalism with economic growth.

finding ignores the higher marginal propensity to consume among lower-income groups and the implication that a more equal share of income leads to higher rates of consumption and economic growth (e.g. Fisher et al., 2020; Keynes, 1936, pp. 114–115; Krueger, 2012; Skidelsky, 2010, p. 177). The suggestion in Ward et al. (2016) that rising inequality may lead to higher GDP with lower resource impacts (because wealthy people do not use their income to consume) is more questionable still.

Overall, a high-level discussion between prominent degrowth advocates and post-Keynesian scholars could yield important insights on issues relating to inequality. However, that discussion is likely to turn quickly to another matter of central concern to both groups: money and debt.

Many authors have rightly identified debt as problematic in an economy that is not growing (Fontana and Sawyer, unpublished). The contradiction between a money supply that can expand indefinitely and a real economy that cannot is often noted (e.g. Farley et al., 2013). Binswanger (2009, 2015) has shown that some growth is necessary for firms in aggregate to make profits, although Berg et al. (2015) demonstrate that it would still be possible to maintain interest and debt levels in a steady-state economy.

The consensus view is that monetary reform would be required in a post-growth economy, which could get around problems of debt (Jackson & Victor, 2016). Farley et al. (2013) suggest that the money supply could be brought under the control of central banks with a limited number of loans made. Kallis et al. (2020, p. 82) suggest limiting the use of 'general purpose money' and instead establishing more restricted (e.g. community-based or special purpose) forms of currency (Hornborg, 2017).

It is not always clear in these discussions how well the authors understand the nature of money and debt. As illustrated by Graeber (2014, chapters 1–3) and others, private debt existed well before anything like the modern economy and restrictions on the banking sector would not eliminate debt. There are many cases where restrictions on the use of official money have led to the development of parallel currencies (see e.g. Galbraith, 1975, chapter 5). Overall, much more research is needed in this area, which could be stimulated by recent proposals for central bank digital currencies.

Questions relating to innovation and technology development may prove to be even more difficult to address. Hickel (2020) tackles the question of whether we "need growth for innovation" (p. 197). Insights from complexity theory suggest that we do not but, as our framework shows, the real difficulty is in preventing innovation from leading to economic growth. As Jackson (2017, chapter 6) describes, the human desire for novelty and new products is natural. It would be impossible to ban all new products (especially in the military and medical sectors) but current experiences with illegal mining and deforestation suggest that policing the use of all natural resources also looks problematic. It is perhaps not surprising that a planned economy can appear attractive to degrowth authors, given these constraints.

As the next sub-section shows, the issue of limiting working hours may be closely related to technology. Reducing working hours is a core component of most degrowth visions because it can reduce production levels without increasing unemployment. Weiss and Cattaneo (2017) describe limiting working hours as "the single silver bullet through which degrowth can yield personal welfare gains, increase environmental sustainability, enhance democracy, and thus obtain the support of larger parts of the population" (p. 227). The authors provide several supporting references. As noted previously, in *Economic Possibilities for our Grandchildren*, Keynes (1930) also predicted a large reduction in working hours, albeit with the causality running in the opposite direction (i.e. higher productivity meaning people need to work less). In wider society, the idea of a four-day week has been put forward and was included in the UK Labour Party's manifesto for the 2019 general election.

There has been some research on how a shorter working week might work but many questions remain. Georgescu-Roegen (1971) questioned whether it would be possible to utilise capital fully if the volume of labour was restricted, which could be problematic if the volume of capital is itself restricted in a post-growth society. Van den Bergh (2011) suggests that shortening working hours is a blunt tool and we should remember that many people like working (in contrast to Keynes' time).

There are many practical issues and the idea of regulating working hours seems dated in a time when the gig economy forces many people to work irregular hours, sometimes at home where there is no way to monitor the time spent. Scaling down working time is unlikely to have uniform effects and the tasks that workers drop could be providing training to others or helping co-workers. Rules would be needed for how to treat on-call workers or the self-employed. Some jobs benefit from one person always being present, such as teachers to young children, soldiers in battle or the president of a country. Finally, the definition of work itself is not always clear-cut; would researchers be banned from reading outside their allotted hours?

While there may be answers to all these questions, the lack of a clear plan for the 'single silver bullet' shows just how far there is to go in proposing an alternative to economic growth until the planet can take it no more. With time running out, the need for further research is urgent.

Further research is also required to understand better the relationship between happiness and growth. As noted in Sect. 1.2, advocates of degrowth often point out the discrepancy between the levels of production and happiness within populations, but the link between the growth rate of production and happiness may be stronger. If so, in a degrowth scenario there could be a loss of happiness that must be replaced, particularly for people who are either individualistic in nature or object to the loss of liberty over their working hours. Some of this gap could be closed by a more equal distribution of income (e.g. Layard, 2005), although there may be limits to how far this can go. Competition between animals (including humans) for mates is a result of the evolutionary process and people will naturally compare themselves to their peers, even when beyond childbearing age.

Related to this issue, one area that may be relatively easy to address is reforming advertising. The effects of advertising are like those of product innovation in that they boost aggregate demand and rates of production, but the additional demand has been fabricated by the companies involved. Mercure et al. (2018) relate this process to business evolution and even mainstream neoclassical economists would criticise 'persuasive' advertising as inducing a misallocation of resources. Galbraith (1998) suggests that: "Consumer wants can have bizarre, frivolous or even immoral origins, and an admirable case can still be made for a society that seeks to satisfy them. But the case cannot stand if it is the process of satisfying wants that creates the wants" (p. 125).

It is, therefore, not surprising that many advocates of both degrowth and green growth would welcome restrictions on the self-perpetuating activities of the advertising industry. Advertising effectively drives GDP growth by taking away consumer satisfaction and then returning it in exchange for money.

To summarise, there are important contributions to the debate on happiness that must come from the evolutionary/complexity schools; and likely with inputs from psychologists and sociologists. A thorough analysis of degrowth more generally requires a joining of ecological, post-Keynesian and complexity economists. It must present a balanced view of the trade-offs involved in moving towards a degrowth position. To avoid politicising the issue (as has happened with climate change in the US), the political ideology that is currently present in the degrowth literature must be dropped.

4.4 An Automated Future Without Growth?

It may seem strange to end a chapter on the long-run sustainability of economic growth with a discussion about automation. However, it is possible that much of the work currently undertaken by humans will be automated within the next 50 years. If robots can do all the tasks that people can, we will not see workers moving into higher-value activities, as in the industrial revolution with. This time there may not be alternative jobs to move into.

As it stands, the 'fourth' industrial revolution represents a large positive shock to process innovation. Product innovation will likely follow, but probably in sectors that are already automated. Ford (2015, chapter 4) presents a picture of mass unemployment and Pollitt et al. (2021) confirm that this is a possible outcome, which could also reduce rates of economic growth. It is possible that Keynes' (1930) prediction of a 15-hours working week could come to fruition after all.

The non-linear nature of technology uptake means that the transition to an automated workforce could be fast once it gets underway (Mercure, 2012). Rapid economies of scale could easily push the costs of automated systems below those of current workers. Even if retraining is available, the expansion of automated systems into all economic sectors could limit opportunity.

The issue is important because maintaining full employment is one of the main challenges of both economic growth and degrowth. Jackson (2017, p. 144) describes work as the 'glue' of society. However, if the jobs are going to disappear anyway, does a degrowth strategy really need to consider how to maintain employment levels?

It is, therefore, worth thinking briefly about what a highly automated degrowth world would look like. There would effectively be unlimited amounts of both labour and capital. There may also be effectively unlimited amounts of renewable energy. We know that (with political will) the amount of money will be unlimited. The remaining supply-side constraints will be land and mineral inputs (and maybe biomass inputs).

The risk of rapidly using the available natural resources seems clear and some form of coordination would almost certainly be necessary (Ford, 2015, chapter 8). Under this scenario, the world may by necessity move towards a place where strict limits are put on resource use. The same artificial intelligence systems that manage the robots could assist with the coordination and we could end up moving towards a degrowth world by default.

5 Summary and Conclusions

The analysis in this chapter draws on three distinct strands of economic theory. Each one provides fundamental insights that tell an important part of the overall story: the physical world, the biological world and the socio-economic system in which we live.

The first strand is ecological economics, which tells us about the real physical limits on available natural resources. We can further divide natural resources into biomass stocks, which are replenished each year, and mineral stocks, which are not. However, there are also limits on biomass potential and the extraction of both types of resource may cause more damage to ecosystems than the use of the resources themselves.

The second strand is evolutionary and complexity economics. The combination of these two schools explains biological human behaviour and how humans interact with each other. Our natural desire for new products can be explained as an evolutionary process. Our natural inclination towards innovation and technological development can also be explained through these theories.

The third strand is post-Keynesian economics (with a nod to Schumpeter), which explains how a combination of innovation and debt drives the process of economic growth. If we are to understand degrowth we must lean heavily on this field.

The combination of these three lines of thinking suggests that economic growth will continue until it is unable to do so. What will happen then is less clear. As *The Limits to Growth* suggested 50 years ago, without intervention, the transition to the end of growth is unlikely to be smooth and could result in a collapse of society and population.

A strand of literature is thus developing about how the transition to 'degrowth' could be managed. Authors in this field are well versed in ecological economics and some of them also with complexity and post-Keynesian thinking. However, this literature remains at an early stage of development and needs to be advanced urgently.

So far, authors have identified two potential paths towards an economic system that consumes fewer resources. The first path involves abandoning capitalism and moving towards a managed economy in which governments determine levels of resource extraction. The second path puts an artificial constraint on the volume of resources that may be extracted each year; for example, through cap and trade systems. The choice of path would have important implications for the level of inequality in society and the two options fit neatly into the political divide of left and right. However, in both cases economic growth (as represented by GDP) would end.

There would be substantial difficulties to overcome in both cases. Even where there are already limits on extraction (e.g. in the Amazon rainforest), we have not been able to stop illegal activities. With enforced scarcity, prices would increase and the rewards for illegal extraction would be higher. However, managing resource extraction still looks easy compared to building a centrally planned economic system, as we saw in the twentieth century.

Furthermore, as long as the policy is set at the level of the nation state, there are strong disincentives to pursue degrowth. A higher GDP means more resources for the military and increased projection of national power. Economists who ignore this fact are doing little better than those who ignore the physical resource constraints that we must live within.

The current focus on climate change may prove to be instructive to long-term developments, although the direction of change is not clear. If the world can come together to keep climate change within agreed limits, this cooperation could provide the foundation to addressing other environmental concerns. However, it is also possible that success in averting dangerous climate change will be taken as evidence that environmental constraints can be overcome, while pursuing economic growth.

Eventually the limits on available resources will force change in our current economic systems and growth paradigm. There will likely be other pressures on the system too, because resource constraints are not the only fundamental issues that our economies will face in the coming decades. As well as automation and the potential end to our work-focused society, new technologies such as 3D printing could change how we produce goods. The challenges of an ageing and declining population have already impacted Japan's economy and will soon be felt across the developed world. The long-term impacts of covid-19 and any future pandemics on our societies remain unclear.

We conclude with the question about what economics can contribute to understanding this sea of change. With so much uncertainty, the services of economists should be more in demand than ever but the dynamic process of change does not fit well into equilibrium frameworks. As long as economists refer to the use of finite resources as 'externalities', their advice will be irrelevant or potentially even misleading.

As our economic system moves on, so must our understanding of economics. The combination of ecological, evolutionary/complexity (including the evolution of institutions) and post-Keynesian economics used in this chapter at least provides an appropriate toolkit that economists could use to carry out such analysis. These tools must be directed towards the barely addressed questions of how we move beyond the current growth paradigm.

Either way, there is a long road ahead—or at least we hope there is.

References

Ackerman, F. (2017). *Worst-case economics: Extreme events in climate and finance*. Anthem Press.

Anderson, K., & Peters, G. (2016). The trouble with negative emissions. *Science, 354*(6309), 182–183.

Arthur, W. B. (1999). Complexity and the economy. *Science, 244*(5411), 107–109.

Arthur, W. B. (2010). *The nature of technology*. Penguin Books.

Anderson, P. W. (1972). More is different. *Science, 177*(4047), 393–396.

Beinhocker, E. D. (2007). *The origin of wealth*. Random House.

Bellais, R. (2014). Post Keynesian theory, technology, policy and long-term growth. *Journal of Post Keynesian Economics, 26*(3), 419–440.

Berg, M., Hartley, B., & Richters, O. (2015, January). A stock-flow consistent input-output model with applications to energy price shocks, interest rates and heat emissions. *New Journal of Physics, 17*, Ref. 015011.

Binswanger, M. (2009). The growth imperative revisited: A Rejoinder to Gilányi and Johnson. *Journal of Post Keynesian Economics, 31*(4), 707–727.

Binswanger, M. (2015). Is there a growth imperative in capitalist economies? A circular flow perspective. *Journal of Post Keynesian Economics, 37*(4), 648–660.

Boulton, J., Allen, P. M., & Bowman, C. (2015). *Embracing complexity*. Oxford University Press.

Bringezu, S. (2015). Possible target corridor for sustainable use of global material resources. *Resources, 4*(1), 25–54.

Brouwer, F., Avgerinopoulos, D., Fazekas, D., Laspidou, C., Mercure, J.-F., Pollitt, H., Ramos, E. P., & Howells, M. (2017). Energy modelling and the Nexus concept. *Energy Strategy Reviews, 19*, 1–6.

Burnham, T. C., Lea, S. E. G., Bell, A. V., Gintis, H., Glimcher, P. W., Kurzban, R., Lades, L., McCabe, K., Panchanathan, K., Teschl, M., &

Witt, U. (2016). Evolutionary behavioural economics. In D. S. Wilson & A. Kirman (Eds.), *Complexity and evolution* (pp. 113–144). MIT Press.
Carter, Z. D. (2020). *The price of peace: Money, democracy and the life of John Maynard Keynes.* Random House.
Cullen, J. M. (2017). Circular economy: Theoretical benchmark or perpetual motion machine? *Journal of Industrial Ecology, 21*(3), 483–486.
De Long, J. B. (1998). *Estimates of World GDP, One Million B.C.—Present.* https://delong.typepad.com/print/20061012_LRWGDP.pdf
Di Guilmi, C. (2017). The agent-based approach to Post Keynesian macro-modelling. *Journal of Economic Surveys, 31*(5), 1183–1203.
Domar, E. D. (1944). The "burden of the debt" and the national income. *The American Economic Review, 34*(4), 798–827.
Domar, E. D. (1946). Capital expansion, rate of growth, and employment. *Econometrica, 14*(2), 137–147.
Dosi, G., Fagiolo, G., & Roventini, A. (2010). Schumpeter meeting Keynes: A policy-friendly model of endogenous growth and business cycles. *Journal of Economic Dynamics and Control, 34*(9), 1748–1767.
Dutt, A. K. (2010). Keynesian growth theory in the 21st century. In P. Arestis & M. Sawyer (Eds.), *21st Century Keynesian economics* (pp. 39–80). Springer.
Eichner, A. S., & Kregel, J. A. (1975). An essay on Post-Keynesian theory: A new paradigm in economics. *Journal of Economic Literature, 13*(4), 1293–1314.
Ekins, P. (2012). Sustainable growth revisited: Technology, economics and policy. *Mineral Economics, 24*(2012), 59–77.
Epstein, J. M., & Chelen, J. (2016). Advancing Agent_Zero. In D. S. Wilson & A. Kirman (Eds.), *Complexity and evolution* (pp. 299–317). MIT Press.
Farley, J., Burke, M., Flomenhoft, G., Kelly, B., Murray, D. F., Posner, S., Putnam, M., Scanlan, A., & Witham, A. (2013). Monetary and fiscal policies for a Finite Planet. *Sustainability, 5*(6), 2802–2826.
Fisher, J. D., Johnson, D. S., Smeeding, T. M., & Thompson, J. P. (2020). Estimating the marginal propensity to consume using the distributions of income, consumption and wealth. *Journal of Macroeconomics, 65*, article ID 103218.
Fontana, G., & Sawyer, M. (unpublished). *The macroeconomics of near zero growth of GDP.* Manuscript under review.
Ford, M. (2015). *The rise of the robots: Technology and the threat of mass unemployment.* Oneworld Publications.

Fuss, S. (2014). Betting on negative emissions. *Nature Climate Change, 4*(10), 850–853.

Galbraith, J. K. (1975). *Money: Whence it came, where it went, reprinted 2017*. Princeton University Press.

Galbraith, J. K. (1998). *The affluent society* (5th ed.). Penguin.

Georgescu-Roegen, N. (1971). *The entropy law and economic process*. Harvard University Press.

Giampietro, M. (2019, August). On the circular bioeconomy and decoupling: Implications for sustainable growth. *Ecological Economics, 162*, 143–156.

Glimcher, P. W. (2016). Proximate mechanisms of individual decision-making behavior. In D. S. Wilson & A. Kirman (Eds.), *Complexity and evolution* (pp. 85–96) MIT Press.

Gowdy, J. M. (1991). Bioeconomics and post Keynesian economics: A search for common ground. *Ecological Economics, 3*(1), 77–87.

Goodwin, R. M. (1967). A Growth Cycle. In C. H. Feinstein (Eds.), *Socialism, capitalism and economic growth*. Cambridge University Press.

Graeber, D. (2014). *Debt: The first 5,000 years* (3rd ed.). Melville House Publishing.

Grubb, M. (2018). Conditional optimism: Economic perspectives on deep decarbonization. INET *Is Green Growth Possible?* https://www.inetec onomics.org/perspectives/blog/growth-with-decarbonization-is-not-an-oxy moron

Grubb, M., Hourcade, J.-H., & Neuhoff, K. (2014). *Planetary economics: Energy, climate change and the three domains of sustainable development*. Routledge.

Harrod, R. F. (1939). An essay in dynamic theory. *The Economic Journal, 49*(193), 14–33.

Hickel, J. (2020). *Less is more*. Penguin.

Hickel, J., & Kallis, G. (2020). Is green growth possible? *New Political Economy, 25*(4), 469–486.

Holden, P. B., Edwards, N. R., Ridgwell, A., Wilkinson, R. D., Fraedrich, K., Lunkeit, F., Pollitt, H., Mercure, J.-F., Salas, P., Lam, A., Knobloch, F., Chewpreecha, U., & Viñuales, J. E. (2018). Climate–carbon cycle uncertainties and the Paris Agreement. *Nature Climate Change, 8*, 609–613.

Hornborg, A. (2017). How to turn an ocean liner: A proposal for voluntary degrowth by redesigning money for sustainability, justice, and resilience. *Journal of Political Ecology, 24*(1), 623–632.

IPBES. (2019). *The global assessment report on biodiversity and ecosystem services.* https://www.ipbes.net/sites/default/files/2020-02/ipbes_global_assessment_report_summary_for_policymakers_en.pdf
IPCC. (2018). *Global Warming of 1.5°C. An IPCC Special Report on the impacts of global warming of 1.5°C above pre-industrial levels and related global greenhouse gas emission pathways, in the context of strengthening the global response to the threat of climate change, sustainable development, and efforts to eradicate poverty*. IPCC. https://www.ipcc.ch/sr15/
Jackson, T. (2017). *Prosperity without growth: Foundations for the economy of tomorrow* (2nd ed.). Routledge.
Jackson, T., & Victor, P. A. (2016, January). Does slow growth lead to rising inequality? Some theoretical reflections and numerical simulations. *Ecological Economics, 121*, 206–219.
Kaldor, N. (1932, May). A case against technical progress? *Economica, 36*, 180–196.
Kaldor, N. (1957). A model of economic growth. *The Economic Journal, 67*(268), 591–624.
Kalecki, M. (1954). *Theory of economic dynamics: An essay on cyclical and long-run changes in capitalist economy*, reprinted 2009. Monthly Review Classics.
Kallis, G. (2011). In defence of degrowth. *Ecological Economics, 70*(5), 873–880.
Kallis, G., Paulson, S., D'Alisa, G., & Demaria, F. (2020). *The case for degrowth*. Polity.
Kaya, Y., & Yokobori, K. (1998). *Environment, energy, and economy strategies for sustainability*. United Nations University Press.
Keen, S. (2011). *Debunking economics: The naked emperor dethroned?* (2nd ed.). Zed Books.
Keen, S. (2013). Growth theory. In J. E. King (Eds.), *The Elgar Companion to Post Keynesian economics* (2nd ed., pp. 271–277). Edward Elgar.
Keen, S. (2020). The appallingly bad neoclassical economics of climate change. *Globalizations*. https://doi.org/10.1080/14747731.2020.1807856
Kelman, S. (1981). Cost-benefit analysis: An ethical critique. *AEI Journal on Government and Society Regulation, 18*(7), 33–40.
Keynes, J. M. (1921). *A treatise on probability*. Macmillan.
Keynes, J. M. (1930). Economic possibilities for our grandchildren. *Essays in Persuasion* (pp. 192–202). Classic House Books.
Keynes, J. M. (1936). *The general theory of employment interest and money*. Macmillan.

Keynes, J. M. (1937). The general theory of employment. *Quarterly Journal of Economics, 51*(2), 209–223.
King, J. E. (2015). *Advanced introduction to Post-Keynesian economics.* Edward Elgar.
Kregel, J. A. (1973). *Reconstruction of political economy: An introduction to Post-Keynesian economics.* Palgrave Macmillan.
Kreuger, A. B. (2012, January 12). *The rise and consequences of inequality in the United States. Address to the Council of Economic Advisers.* https://obamawhitehouse.archives.gov/sites/default/files/krueger_cap_speech_final_remarks.pdf
Kronenberg, T. (2010). Finding common ground between ecological economics and post-Keynesian economics. *Ecological Economics, 69*(7), 1488–1494.
Krugman, P. (2014, September 18). Errors and emissions. *The New York Times.*
Lavoie, M. (2014), *Post-Keynesian economics: New foundations.* Edward Elgar.
Lavoie, M. (2020). Was Hyman Minsky a post-Keynesian economist? *Review of Evolutionary Political Economy,* 1, 85–101.
Layard, R. (2005). *Happiness: Lessons from a new science.* Penguin Books.
Malthus, T. (1798). *An essay on the principle of population.* J Johnson.
Mazzucato, M. (2019). *The value of everything: Making and taking in the global economy.* Penguin Random House.
Meadows, D. H., Meadows, D. L., Randers, J., & Behrens, W. W. (1972). *The limits to growth.* Universal Books.
Mercure, J.-F. (2012). FTT: Power A global model of the power sector with induced technological change and natural resource depletion. *Energy Policy, 48*, 799–811.
Mercure, J.-F., Lam, A., Billington, S., & Pollitt, H. (2018). Integrated assessment modelling as a positive science: Private passenger road transport policies to meet a climate target well below 2°C. *Climatic Change, 151*, 109–129.
Mercure, J.-F., Pollitt, H., Bassi, A. M., Viñuales, J. E., & Edwards, N. R. (2016, March). Modelling complex systems of heterogeneous agents to better design sustainability transitions policy. *Global Environmental Change, 37*, 102–115.
Mercure, J.-F., Pollitt, H., Chewpreecha, U., Salas, P., Foley, A. M., Holden, P, B., & Edwards, N. R. (2014). The dynamics of technology diffusion and the impacts of climate policy instruments in the decarbonisation of the global electricity sector. *Energy Policy*, 73, 686–700.

Metcalfe, J. S., & Foster, J. (2010). Evolutionary growth theory. In M. Setterfield (Eds.), *Handbook of alternative theories of economic growth* (pp. 64–94). Edward Elgar.
Minsky, H. P. (1975). *John Maynard Keynes* (2nd ed.). McGraw Hill.
Minsky, H. P. (1986). *Stabilizing and unstable economy* (2nd ed.). McGraw Hill.
Nelson, R. R., & Winter, S. G. (1982). *An evolutionary theory of economic change*. Harvard University Press.
Nordhaus, W. (2019). Climate change: The ultimate challenge for economics. *American Economic Review, 109*(6), 1991–2014.
Paim, M.-A., Salas, P., Lindner, S., Pollitt, H., Mercure, J.-F., Edwards, N. R., & Viñuales, J. E. (2020). Mainstreaming the Water-Energy-Food Nexus through nationally determined contributions (NDCs): The case of Brazil. *Climate Policy, 20*(2), 163–178.
Pigou, A. C. (1920). *The economics of welfare*. Palgrave Macmillan.
Piketty, T. (2014). *Capital in the 21st century*. Harvard University Press.
Pindyck, R. S. (2013). *Climate change policy: What do the models tell us?* (NBER Working Paper 19244).
Pollitt, H., Lee, S., & Park, S.-J. (2016). Introduction to the modelling in this book. In S. Lee, H. Pollitt, & S.-J. Park (Eds.), *Low-carbon, sustainable future in East Asia* (pp. 29–41). Routledge.
Pollitt, H., Mercure, J.-F., Lin, X., & Alves, C. (2021). *The Link between innovation and growth in a demand-driven economy*. Cambridge Econometrics working paper.
Ricke, K., Drouet, L., Caldeira, K., & Tavoni, M. (2018). Country-level social cost of carbon. *Nature Climate Change, 8*, 895–900.
Robinson, J. (1956). *The accumulation of capital*. Macmillan.
Rockström, J., Steffen, W., Noone, K., & Foley, J. A. (2009). A safe operating space for humanity. *Nature, 461*, 472–475.
Romer, P. M. (1990). Endogenous technical change. *Journal of Political Economy, 98*(5), S71–S102.
Romero, J. P. (2014). Mr. Keynes and the neo-Schumpeterians: Contributions to the analysis of the determinants of innovation from a post-Keynesian perspective. *EconomiA, 15*(2), pp. 189–205.
Sasaki, H. (2020). Product and process innovation, keynesian unemployment, and economic growth. *Munich Personal RePEc Archive*. https://mpra.ub.uni-muenchen.de/101031/1/MPRA_paper_101031.pdf
Schumpeter, J. A. (1934), *The theory of economic development* (2nd ed.). Harvard.

Setterfield, M. (Eds.). (2010). *Handbook of alternative theories of economic growth*. Edward Elgar.
Sharpe, S., Mercure, J.-F., Vinuales, J. E., Ives, M., Grubb, M., Pollitt, H., Knobloch, F., & Nijsse, F. J. M. M. (2021). *Deciding how to decide: Risk-opportunity analysis as a generalisation of cost-benefit analysis. UCL Institute for Innovation and Public Purpose* (Working Paper Series [IIPP WP 2021/03]). https://www.ucl.ac.uk/bartlett/public-purpose/wp2021-03
Skidelsky, R. (2010). *Keynes: The return of the master*. Penguin Books.
Spash, C. L., & Asara, V. (2018). Ecological economics. In L. Fischer, J. Hasell, J. C. Proctor, D. Uwakwe, Z. Ward-Perkins, & C. Watson (Eds.), *Rethinking economics: An introduction to pluralist economics* (pp. 120–132). Routledge.
Sterling, P. (2016). Why we consume: Neural design and sustainability. *Great Transition Initiative viewpoint*. https://greattransition.org/publication/why-we-consume
Stern, N. (2016). Economics: Current climate models are grossly misleading. *Nature, 530*(7591), 407–409.
Stockhammer, E., Oznaran, O., & Ederer, S. (2009). Functional income distribution and aggregate demand in the Euro area. *Cambridge Journal of Economics, 33*(1), 139–159.
Storm, S., & Naastepad, C. W. M. (2013). Wage-led or profit-led supply: Wages, productivity and investment. In M. Lavoie & E. Stockhammer (Eds.), *Wage-led growth. Advances in labour studies*. Palgrave Macmillan.
van den Bergh, J. C. J. M. (2011). Environment versus growth—A criticism of "degrowth" and a plea for "a-growth." *Ecological Economics, 70*(5), 881–890.
van der Leeuw, S. E. (2016). Adaptation and maladaptation in the past: A case study and some implications. In D. S. Wilson & A. Kirman (Eds.), *Complexity and evolution: Towards a new synthesis for economics* (pp. 239–270). MIT Press.
Veblen, T. (1898). Why is economics not an evolutionary science? *The Quarterly Journal of Economics, 12*(4), 373–397.
Veblen, T. (1899). *The Theory of the Leisure Class*, reproduced in *Conspicuous Consumption* (2005). Penguin.
Walras, L. (1954). *Elements of Pure Economics*, translated by W Jaffé from original 19th century French version, reprinted 2003. Routledge.
Ward, J. D., Sutton, P. C., Werner, A. D., Costanza, R., Mohr, S. H., & Simmons, C. T. (2016). Is decoupling GDP growth from environmental impact possible? *PLoS ONE, 11*(10), e0164733.

Weiss, M., & Cattaneo, C. (2017, July). Degrowth—Taking stock and reviewing an emerging academic paradigm. *Ecological Economics, 137*, 220–230.
Weitzman, M. L. (2009). On modeling and interpreting the economics of catastrophic climate change. *The Review of Economics and Statistics, XC, I*(1), 1–19.
Werner, R. A. (2014). Can banks individually create money out of nothing?—The theories and the empirical evidence. *International Review of Financial Analysis, 36*, 1–19.
Werner, R. A. (2016). A lost century in economics: Three theories of banking and the conclusive evidence. *International Review of Financial Analysis, 46*, 361–379.
Zagler, M. (2004). A new look at old issues: Keynesian unemployment revisited. *International Review of Applied Economics, 18*(2), 209–224.

3

Forms of Ownership for Sustainability and Resilience: The Need for Biodiversity and Corporate Diversity

Jonathan Michie

1 Introduction

This paper makes four main arguments. First, that the 2007–2009 global financial crisis, and the resulting recession, which was the first on a global scale since the 1930s, was caused by globalisation—not by the 'fact' of globalisation, but rather by its 'form'. Globalisation is not a state in which the world either is or is not: there have been many degrees and forms of globalisation, most forcefully since the rise of capitalism as an economic system. So it is the nature and form of globalisation the main issue, not whether globalisation as a 'thing' is either present or absent, or good or bad. It was the particular free-market, 'capitalism

I am grateful for helpful comments on a previous version of this paper, and suggestions received, from Philip Arestis and Malcolm Sawyer.

J. Michie (✉)
Kellogg College, University of Oxford, Oxford, UK
e-mail: jonathan.michie@kellogg.ox.ac.uk

P. Arestis and M. Sawyer (eds.), *Economic Policies for Sustainability and Resilience*, International Papers in Political Economy,
https://doi.org/10.1007/978-3-030-84288-8_3

unleashed'[1] form of globalisation, which had been promoted since the 1980s that was the fundamental cause of the 2007–2009 global financial crisis—which along with a wasted decade of austerity left the economy and society across many parts of the globe badly resourced to face the 2020–21 Covid-19 pandemic.

Second, when the Covid-19 pandemic spread across the globe in the 2020 course, with subsequent variants in 2021, one might have expected the world to be better prepared than ever, given the 'early warnings' with other viruses in previous years posing clear global threats. However, despite these warnings, many countries were even less resilient than they might have been ten or twenty years earlier, due to the years of austerity and before that the 'anti-public sector' ethos behind the drive for privatisation and deregulation.

Third, none of this is inevitable. The 'capitalism unleashed' form of globalisation is not determined by technology, nor by any other single factor. It is the outcome of political and other choices made by a range of decision-makers. It was the collective effect of these decisions, and the forces behind them, which created the destructive form of globalisation, which has proven to be so costly to society. A different set of decisions, with different priorities, values and objectives should be pursued over the coming historical era. This would not abolish globalisation; rather, it would change its nature—for the better.

Fourth, amongst the priorities that should shape a new era of sustainable economic development is the need to protect the natural environment—to halt and if possible reverse climate change. In terms of the functioning of the economy, a key goal should be to promote a greater degree of corporate diversity, including in the financial services sector, replacing the current domination of 'too big to fail' shareholder-owned companies with a range of smaller, networked companies owned not by external shareholders but by their employees, customers and local communities. Such member-owned organisations tend to have different values and corporate purposes than do shareholder-owned companies, with concomitant differences in behaviours, policies and practices,

[1] 'Capitalism unleashed' was the term coined by Glyn (2006) to describe this phase of deregulated, destructive capitalism.

and different decision-making imperatives. Greater corporate diversity contributes towards increased economic sustainability and resilience; and replacing the 'greed is good' corporate culture as the dominant driving force in the economy makes less likely the sort of catastrophic consequences wreaked on the world's economic system by the 2007–2009 global financial crisis.

The chapter is structured as follows. In Sect. 2, the terms 'sustainability' and 'resilience' are clarified. In Sect. 3, the 2007–2009 global financial crisis is discussed, along with the resulting policy responses. In Sect. 4, attention is paid to the pledge that was made, most especially in the UK, to promote a greater degree of corporate diversity, both to reduce the likelihood of such financial crises being created, and to increase the economy's degree of resilience when faced with such crises. In Sect. 5, the relevance of corporate diversity for the financial services sector in particular is considered. Section 6 considers the corporate response to both the 2007–2009 global financial crisis and the 2020–21 Covid-19 pandemic. In Sect. 7, the need to shift the trajectory of the global economy to create a new historical epoch—a global green new deal—is argued. Finally, Sect. 8 summarises and concludes by considering how this agenda might best be promoted, including through changing the way people think about economics.

2 Sustainability and Resilience

"When I use **a word,**" Humpty Dumpty said, in a rather scornful tone, "it **means** just what I choose it to **mean**—neither more nor less".[2] Many have used the terms 'sustainability' and 'resilience' as Humpty Dumpty used words. We need, therefore, to make clear what the terms mean.

Sustainability is used to cover a range of concepts, including social, economic and environmental. This chapter takes all three concepts to be important, and indeed to be related—meaning it is important to consider all three together, rather than believing that one can be

[2] Humpty Dumpty, in Carroll (1872, p. 199).

adequately considered on its own. It is important, though, to be clear which aspect is referred to at any given time.

Whichever aspect of sustainability is considered, the term remains contested. Companies may claim to be behaving in a way that prioritises environmental sustainability, because they think the claim itself may have a positive impact on their brand image and reputation, quite separate from what their behaviours are. Such claims may be 'greenwashing', in the sense of presenting behaviours as being more driven by environmental considerations—and to be more environmentally friendly—than is in fact the case. Even where behaviours are honest and well-intentioned, there are clearly different degrees of ambition when it comes to actions taken in pursuit of sustainability—the date by which becoming 'carbon neutral' is targeted being an obvious example.

As for 'resilience', the term can be limited or even limiting if interpreted to mean that the aim should be that following 'shocks' to the system, society—or the economy—should be able to return to the *status quo ante*, rather than adapting and rejuvenating in ways that create a better outcome. The term is used here in the 'positive' sense, of being able to deal with shocks, rather than stagnating, so that society or the economy has the capacity and capabilities to 'bounce back' not necessarily to the 'good old days', but rather to a better future, having learned both from the 'shock' and from the process of change. So, notwithstanding the fact that 'resilience' can be interpreted to mean a rather limited response, the use here is in a more positive sense, as the alternative to not being resilient—the alternative to suffering long-term harm and damage from shocks, without the capabilities and capacity to recover, rejuvenate and 'build forward better'.

3 Globalisation and the 2007–2009 Global Financial Crisis

The 2007–2009 global financial crisis was caused fundamentally by the deregulatory, free-market values, policies and practices which constituted the era of 'capitalism unleashed'—the 'greed is good' phase of capitalism, which had been promoted by the Thatcher and Reagan administrations of the 1980s, and had gained momentum and ideological confidence following the collapse of the Soviet Union. The abolition of exchange controls promoted a vast market in international financial speculation. At the time it was argued that this would be a one-off movement, to make up for the inability of such funds to have moved previously—much like the removal of a dam creates a one-off flow of water. However, as so often with free-market economic arguments, the opposite proved to be the case. The financial flows led to the creation of new markets in speculation, which in turn drove further flows in a continuing cycle. The politics of the era enabled and sustained increased inequality within most countries. Those at the bottom of the income and wealth distribution turned to growing levels of credit to maintain living standards. The resulting US 'sub-prime' housing loans were diced and spliced to be added as ingredients for new 'financial products' traded in international markets. (On the role of inequality in creating credit growth amongst the poor, see for example van Treeck, 2015). Those at the top of the wealth distribution demanded ever greater returns on their money, leading in turn to more exotic 'financial products' to deliver historically—and what turned out to be unsustainably—high financial returns. The demands of the 'high net worth individuals' for greater returns fed this speculative frenzy, and played a significant role in the creation of the boom and its subsequent bust (as documented in detail by Lysandrou, 2019).

When the resulting global financial crisis of 2007–2009 was threatening to unleash a complete breakdown of the international financial system, a 1930s-style global depression was avoided only through the pursuit of an internationally coordinated Keynesian fiscal response, with governments boosting spending across the globe. This was accompanied by huge financial support provided to the banking sector, including in most countries nationalisation of many shareholder-owned companies. Ultra-low interest rates were accompanied by central banks pursuing 'quantitative easing'. Such measures played a role in stimulating economic activity, which by preventing too great a rise in unemployment, helped those at the bottom end of the income distribution. At the same time, though, these policies operated by boosting the price of assets, and hence most likely exacerbated the underlying economic inequality in society—by increasing the value of assets that were held by the already wealthy—that had contributed to the global financial crisis in the first place. Thus, the counterfactual need not be the absence of policy intervention, but rather the pursuit of a more egalitarian approach.

3.1 A Lost Decade Before Covid-19

There were pledges made for action on banking reform, rebalancing the economy away from finance towards manufacturing, promoting a greater degree of corporate diversity, pursuing industrial strategies, and ensuring regional balance. However, once the threat of a 1930s-style global depression had been averted—with only particular countries, such as Greece, suffering that fate, rather than the world economy as a whole—the forces that had led to the financial crisis in the first place, having not been removed or even seriously reformed, returned to pursue their previous agendas. Corporate leaders returned to promoting 'shareholder value', fuelling financial rewards for wealth-holders and those holding executive positions. In the face of such behaviour, the reaction of politicians and other policymakers also reverted to type, acceding to such behaviour through a failure to pursue any alternative of serious reform.

Thus, the initial Keynesianism—with coordinated fiscal stimuli—gave way to a return to orthodoxy, with governments pursuing 'austerity', involving public spending cuts at national, regional and local levels. This return to orthodoxy undermined—and in many cases actually prevented—the sort of economic recovery that would have usually followed from such a recession. The reform agenda, such as it was following the 2007–2009 global financial crisis, never really tackled the underlying causes of the crisis, namely the 'capitalism unleashed' form of globalisation that had been pursued since the 1980s in various forms across the world. This process—launched initially by the Thatcher and Reagan administrations—of deregulation, privatisation, demutualisation and financialisation, left nation states more fragile, regions less resilient and the international system more prone to contagion. These processes and the policy agenda that would be required to move to a more balanced, sustainable and resilient economy both within and across borders, have been analysed by various authors, including those brought together in Michie (2019).

This failure to pursue a sufficiently serious and appropriate reform agenda, left the global economy still prone to further such crises—and ill-prepared to deal with any such recurrence—by the time the Covid-19 pandemic struck in 2020–2021. Inequality within countries was as great as ever. Regional imbalances remained. Economies continued to be dominated by shareholder-owned companies, with share buy-back and other such policies still used to inflate share prices—and the concomitant executive bonuses. Global financial speculation remained largely unregulated. Tax evasion and avoidance continued on an industrial scale. The illegality of that tax evasion creates strong incentives for such funds to seek returns in markets operating 'below the radar'—through the 'dark web' and illegality generally, including the drugs trade, illegal arms trade and trade in people (on which, see Michie 2017b, chapter 9). Many of these problems have been exacerbated by the 2020–2021 pandemic, with both the health crisis and the economic crisis it sparked—via lock-downs and other measures—having hit the worst off the hardest, with the wealthiest having increased their share of wealth still further.

4 Alternative Corporate Forms: The Role of Mutuals

The term 'mutual' is used in a variety of different ways, varying across countries. It is sometimes used to refer quite narrowly to the mutual insurance sector, which in the UK is represented by the Association of Financial Mutuals. In this chapter the term is used in a much broader sense, to mean companies and other organisations that are owned by their members. These may be customers, as with financial mutuals. They may be employees, as with workers' co-operatives, or the John Lewis Partnership in the UK, where their 80,000 or so employees own the chain of John Lewis department stores and Waitrose food shops—or rather, the company is owned by a trust that is required to act in the interests of current and future employees.[3] Alternatively, the members may include both customers and employees, as with the National Health Service's Foundation Trust Hospitals, which are Industrial and Provident Societies—where 'members' may also include representatives of the local community or other such 'stakeholders'. Along with member (or stakeholder) ownership goes a corporate purpose of serving the interests of those members or stakeholders. This contrasts with having companies owned by private individuals, or by external shareholders, with the corporate purpose being to benefit those individuals financially.

4.1 Alternative Corporate Ownership Forms

A key component of any serious reform agenda needs to be tackling the dominance of the economy by 'too big to fail' shareholder-owned companies, driven to 'maximise shareholder value'. The operation of financial markets and institutions tends to exacerbate the short-term focus on the share price. Linking executive compensation packages to the share price was supposed to incentivise an interest in the performance of the company, but instead has incentivised behaviours that prioritise the short-term inflation of share prices—rather than promoting long-term investment in research and development, in education and skills and in the productive infrastructure more generally. A different approach is needed, to include the promotion of a range of alternative corporate forms, including public ownership at national, regional and local levels, and promoting 'member-owned' companies—employee-owned firms, worker and consumer cooperatives, financial mutuals and so forth (the need for this is argued in detail by Michie 2011a, and by the various authors brought together by Michie et al., 2017).

In the UK, the 2010–2015 coalition government (between the Conservative Party and the Liberal Democrats) pledged to create just such a degree of increased corporate diversity in the financial services sector, including by promoting mutuals (or member-owned financial institutions). Their lack of resolve might have been suspected from the

[3] For an excellent and detailed description and analysis of the John Lewis Partnership, see Cox (2010).

fact that they failed to introduce any *measure* of corporate diversity—so there was no way of telling whether they were succeeding in achieving this policy goal or not. Michie and Oughton (2014a and 2014b) developed a measure to track the results of this new government objective of creating a more resilient economy through fostering a greater degree of corporate diversity. The result of this tracking exercise was to find that the government's performance in boosting corporate diversity was disappointing. Rather than the degree of corporate diversity improving—which was so desperately needed, and was the clear commitment of government to bring about—it remained at the poor rate to which it had deteriorated in the run up to the crisis.

Full details regarding the conceptualisation and construction of this 'Diversity Index'—which factors are included, and with what weights—are reported and discussed in Michie and Oughton (2014a). But briefly, it focuses on diversity in corporate ownership (shareholder ownership versus member ownership), and also includes the degree of geographical diversity. Following the pledge to put things right, there was little progress—not even a return to the situation which pertained prior to the deterioration in the years leading up to the financial crisis. This is not surprising, as despite the government's pledge, they did little to promote the creation of new financial mutuals. There was no reversal of the disastrous policy of demutualisation, which had from the 1990s transferred the member-owned companies that provided most house-buying finance in the UK into shareholder-owned firms.

Perhaps the most blatant failure of government to honour its pledge was the case of Northern Rock, which had been for generations a successful member-owned building society, serving both to look after people's savings, and advancing them mortgages for their house purchases, but which had been turned into a private bank as part of the wave of demutualisation. It then gained international fame—or notoriety—by reinventing the bank run, which had been thought to be outdated, belonging to a bygone era before the financial services sector became regulated and hence trusted. As a—by then—private bank, it followed the above-described behaviour of chasing ever-higher returns through ever-riskier business practices. The point was thus reached when its customers began to doubt whether the bank had retained sufficient funds to repay savings should the customers seek to withdraw those funds. Thus, the customers queued up outside the bank to withdraw their funds. Sure enough, the funds proved inadequate. The bank was bankrupted. The bank run was reinvented. The government had to step in to take the bankrupt bank into public ownership.

One important aspect of corporate diversity—and hence of the diversity index—is that of regional diversity. The aim should be to have balanced economic development in a geographic sense, rather than having economic growth and prosperity concentrated in only one or a few regions within a country, with other areas stagnating and being left behind. In other words, to promote regional resilience. In addition, each individual region needs to be resilient in an economic sense, and this requires a productive economic infrastructure, appropriate levels of education, training and skills, and so forth. There is a large literature on this need for resilient regions—as brought together and discussed for example by Christopherson et al. (2010). The degree of regional inequality varies across countries, with Britain being the most unequal. Regional inequality deteriorated in most countries from 2000 to 2015, and the worst case of such a deterioration was in Britain.

At the time of the UK's Brexit referendum it was argued that the economy had recovered, and that living standards were by then already higher than they had been prior to the 2007–2009 global financial crisis. Yet the vote to leave the EU was widely seen as a protest vote against economic failure, austerity and a feeling of being 'left behind'. How can these two factors be reconciled, of economic recovery, yet voter disillusionment? The answer lies partly in regional imbalances. The recovery in GDP per head was concentrated in just two regions of the UK: London, and the South East. It was not the case in any other region, and support for Brexit was strongest in those regions left behind. Hence, perhaps, the vote.

4.2 Co-owned Business

In 2019, UK entrepreneur Julian Richer transformed his firm 'Richer Sounds' into an employee-owned partnership, like that used at John Lewis. A majority (60%) of the company's shares were placed in an employee ownership trust, with its 522 employees at 53 stores around the UK also receiving a share of a £3.5 m payout. Richer passed running the business to the management board, to be advised by a newly arranged advisory council made up of current staff. Work by Blasi and colleagues in the U.S. has consistently found that employee ownership delivers a range of benefits, including narrowing gender and racial wealth gaps (see Blasi & Kruse, 2017, and the various publications cited therein). Blasi's colleagues Janet Boguslaw and Lisa Schur, surveying 200 employees from 21 companies with employee ownership plans, found employees had significantly more wealth than the average US worker did. In addition, the participatory management practices that accompanied the employee ownership schemes led to employees improving their communication skills and learning management skills, which had helped them make better financial decisions at home (Boguslaw & Schur, 2019).

4.3 If You're So Clever, Why Aren't You Rich?

This raises what I call the "If you're so clever, why aren't you rich?" question—namely, if research over the years has found that employee ownership is a successful corporate model, why, if this makes companies more successful, is it not more widely adopted?

Most obviously, current company owners may wish to retain their ownership, regardless of how much better their employees might prove to be as co–owners. Moreover, for most public listed companies, the real owners of the company are institutional shareholders such as pension funds and the like, in which case there is no easy mechanism for bringing about employee ownership. Even where there is a single owner, such as Richer, the advice from banks and legal advisers would be to consider floating on the stock exchange or selling up to a bigger firm. Corporate institutional culture is largely ignorant about employee ownership, or otherwise outright hostile towards it would emerge.

4.4 Dropped Political Pledges

The UK Coalition government of 2010–2015 pledged to banish that ignorance and hostility. Liberal Democrat leader Nick Clegg announcing they would establish a centre to research and promote the benefits of employee ownership, including succession planning. The then Deputy Prime Minister told a 2012 event hosted by the City of London Corporation and Centre Forum think tank:

> We don't believe our problem is too much capitalism - we think it's that too few people have capital. We need more individuals to have a real stake in their firms. More of a John Lewis economy, if you like. And what many people don't realise about employee ownership is that it is a hugely underused tool in unlocking growth. I don't value employee ownership because I believe it is somehow 'nicer' - a more pleasant alternative to the rest of the corporate world. Those are lazy stereotypes. Firms that have engaged employees, who own a chunk of their company, are just as dynamic, just as savvy, as their competitors. In fact, they often perform better. Lower absenteeism. Less staff turnover. Lower production costs. In general, higher productivity and higher wages. They weathered the economic downturn better than other companies. (BBC, 2012)

The promised Centre was never established. While less well known than Clegg's U-turn on student university fees—which he had promised to abolish, and instead tripled—it was probably more damaging to the long-term success of the economy. While employee ownership can be more effective and such companies tend to have better outcomes, these benefits do not follow automatically: they require a considerable and sustained effort from management. This includes managers getting used to the idea that they are answerable to the employees rather than to shareholders. Research has found this can be a major hurdle, not so much for the senior management who will generally appreciate the potential gain, but for middle management, who will have got used to the old, adversarial ways of giving orders (see Michie, 2002).[4]

---

[4] Available at: https://www.theguardian.com/politics/2002/dec/03/economy.comment.

It also requires the support of government, in the form of legislation and regulation. That is largely lacking in most countries, for years. The key to the success of John Lewis over the decades has been not just the positive effects of employee ownership on employee motivation, commitment, innovation and productivity, but also that the employee trust is committed to promoting the interests of current *and future* employees. This has allowed them to sustain a more long-termist outlook; for example in rejecting takeover bids that might provide current employees with a windfall, but offer bleaker prospects for future generations of employees. However, UK company law governing employee ownership trusts includes a rule against perpetuity: such trusts are limited to 125 years (previously 80). The law 'has its origins in 17th Century common law and was developed in order to restrict a person's power to control perpetually the ownership and possession of his property after death and to ensure the transferability of property.'[5]

In the case of John Lewis, an 'Employee Benefit Trust' (EBT) has held all the shares of the company on behalf of employees, current and future, since 1950. The trust is governed by three trustees and the John Lewis chairperson; the trustees hold 60% of the shares, the chairperson the remaining 40%. Trustees are elected through a system of representative councils. The John Lewis trust uses a specific version of the perpetuity rule 'dating back to the era of the Crusades' that fixes the longevity of the EBT at 'twenty-one years after the death of the last survivor of the descendants then living of the British monarch at the time – King George V' (Erdal, 2011, p. 212). In this case, this means that the John Lewis trust shall continue until twenty-one years after the death of the current monarch, Queen Elizabeth. This creates a potential problem for John Lewis, with its legal team looking for alternatives to the projected dissolution of the trust.

The 2012 Nuttall Review[6] recommended that the rule against perpetuities be re-evaluated in relation to EBTs due to the additional risk and uncertainty that the rule introduces; such a change has been made in

[5] Available at: http://www.fieldfisher.com/publications/2014/01/employee-ownership-one-year-on.

[6] The full Nuttall report can be found here: https://www.gov.uk/government/uploads/system/uploads/attachment_data/file/31706/12-933-sharing-success-nuttall-review-employee-ownership.pdf.

both Jersey and Guernsey. The Department for Business, Innovation and Skills (BIS) began this review process in 2013. The John Lewis Partnership made a submission complaining that 'banks may also be less willing to lend to companies approaching the end of their term, so stultifying growth'.[7] Despite such arguments, the review concluded in 2014 against changing the rule. But this does have to change. Otherwise, all gains from employee ownership that are won will prove temporary.

4.5 Governance Arrangements: Workers on the Board?

In 2016 the UK Prime Minister Theresa May called for workers on company boards, and denounced company directors who take exorbitant dividend payments at the expense of company pension plans. She praised the idea of more interventionist government, criticised quantitative easing as benefitting the wealthy and pointed instead to expansionary fiscal policies and infrastructure investment, and reintroduced class politics to the political debate, seeking to promote 'working class' interests.

Regarding workers on company boards, this is seen by Germany as an important component of their post-war economic recovery, applied firstly in the coal and steel industries, and then extended to other sectors, now regulated by the Codetermination Act (Mitbestimmungsgesetz) 1976.[8] The idea of codetermination is to give an opportunity for 'voice' in governance—in the case of German codetermination, the voice of the employees and their trade union representatives. The UK has never had a general policy of employee representation at the micro level, but at the macro level, the National Economic Development Office brought together management, trade unions and government to seek to improve the country's economic performance. It was established in 1962 by

---

[7] BIS findings here, John Lewis comment on page 11: Available at: https://www.gov.uk/government/uploads/system/uploads/attachment_data/file/337988/bis_14_963_bis_response_to_call_on_amending_the_rule_against_perpetuities_2.pdf.

[8] In the UK, the earliest examples of codetermination in management were codified into the Oxford University Act 1854 (Cambridge University followed two years later).

the Conservative Government, and survived the Thatcher governments, albeit rather ignored, before the John Major government abolished it in 1992. At a micro, organisational level, there have been and still are various British examples of employee representation on Boards. The UK's Ownership Commission argued that the economy is stronger with a range of ownership and governance forms—which should include mutually owned companies such as John Lewis, alongside shareholder-owned, privately—and family-owned, and ownership through local, regional and national governments.

The historical and international evidence is that having workers on the Board can be beneficial both to the individual firm or organisation and to the development of the wider economy. However, this requires the employee representatives to have some degree of authority—unlikely with no ownership stake underpinning their position. Sweden had plans for rolling out such a system nationally through wage-earner funds, but it was not implemented. In the U.S. there is a widespread use of employee share ownership, supported across the political spectrum, and in some cases such share ownership is used to provide and support employee voice. In Britain, such share ownership schemes are weak—and tend to be limited to individual holdings, which provide no support for collective voice. For workers on the Board to be effective, such ownership stakes need to be pooled into Employee Trusts, along the lines of the John Lewis Partnership.

5 Social Finance

This section considers the potential role of mutuals and co-operatives with regards to finance. Whether the owners of mutuals can benefit financially is an interesting question for a range of reasons. Firstly, the members of mutuals do of course expect to gain financially in that they expect the company to be able to charge lower prices, or lower premiums on insurance policies, and to pay higher interest on savings if they are financial mutuals, so there is an economic benefit to not having to pay dividends to external shareholders. But this is a different meaning to the term 'financial gain' from the one used in the context of shareholders—who will receive a return on their investment, and the amount of money received will increase both with the size of their financial stake and with the profitability of the company. Hence, they have a direct material interest in the profitability of the company being maximised; this maximises the personal financial return that they as owners will receive. In contrast, the purpose and objective of the John Lewis Partnership is to make *sufficient* profits for the attainment of their other more important corporate objectives—of serving their customers and benefiting the current and future employees of the company—rather than the maximum possible amount of profits.

The other way in which shareholders in non-mutual companies achieve personal financial gain is through capital gains from increases in the value or price of the shares that can then be sold. Shareholders who are in a position to influence—or even manipulate—the share price can thus make personal financial gains from so doing, as is the case, potentially, with managers and directors who are rewarded in part through share options. Indeed, this is the whole purpose of designing such remuneration packages, to align the interests of the senior management with the shareholders so that the company would indeed be managed in ways that maximise the financial return to the shareholders; rather than in the pursuit of other interests or purposes—such as managerial goals that might include increasing the growth rate of the company rather than its financial return. The problem with such an approach is most apparent when actions are taken to manipulate the price of shares so that their price will be at a maximum at just the time when the Chief Executive and other senior executives are able to cash in their share options.[9]

The more general problem with this approach to corporate ownership and governance is that it engenders a short-term attitude to investment and the development of the company, focussing on short-term returns rather than long-term sustainability. One potential reason for such short-termism is the fear that if long-term decision-making results in a lower

[9] "Companies where executives are disproportionately compensated in stock options are more likely to report earnings that meet or beat analysts' forecasts" (Tabb, 2012, p. 48). The mechanisms whereby this is achieved, and the evidence regarding the scale of such activity, is provided by Tabb (2012, pp. 48–49).

share price in the short-term, then the company may be subject to a hostile take-over from private equity or other outside interest with a view to taking whatever short-term actions might cause a rise in the share price. This would enable the firm to be sold on again at a profit.

These incentives and mechanisms are generally absent, or at least quite different, in a member-owned mutual. Firstly, mutuals are generally run on a 'one member, one vote' principle, whereby each member has the same influence and say regardless of how much money they may have with the company. In the case of, say, a mutually-owned bank where a member can invest savings, or in the case of any mutual that might raise capital by issuing a bond, which might enable members to invest in the company. In such cases, the bond will pay a certain rate of interest, which is unlikely to be linked to the profitability or performance of the company. Even were the bond to be designed to include any such link of interest payments to corporate performance, the ownership of that bond (or the relative size of the investment in the bond) would not bring with it any greater say in the governance of the organisation, as does shareholding in a shareholder-owned company.

There is one instance, however, where the issue of financial returns to individual members of mutuals can be relevant. This is in the situation of 'demutualisation', where a mutual is converted into a shareholder-owned company with shares floated on a stock exchange and the revenue from the sale of those shares is distributed to the existing or former members of the mutual. In other words, the members of a mutual 'cash in' the value of the company or organisation, sharing the proceeds amongst themselves. This is what happened to many of the major mutual building societies in the UK during the 1980s and 1990s following a change in the legislation governing such societies made by the Thatcher government. The members gained financially, as did, in general, the Directors of the mutual building societies who recommended demutualisation to their members, and as did, also, the financial and other advisors who advised in favour of this course of action and oversaw the process. This process also led to the phenomenon of 'carpetbaggers' who would join a mutual for the sole purpose of voting that it ceases to be a mutual, so that they could benefit financially from the distribution of the proceeds from demutualisation.

5.1 The Historical Experience

Mutuals as a corporate form tended to arise in response to the development of privately-owned and shareholder-owned companies during and following the industrial revolution, where there was a mistrust of the quality being delivered by such companies as a result of their corporate purpose and their incentive to maximise profits at the expense of the customer, which in many cases led to practices of dishonesty, and in general to inferior products and services than would have been the case had the corporate purpose been to maximise the quality of service to the customer. Cox (2010), for example, details the various ways in which dishonest practice in the retail trade was commonplace in the pursuit of higher profits and financial returns.

This led to the 'Rochdale pioneers' in the north of England, who founded the co-operative movement, and to the development of co-operative and mutual corporate forms owned by their customer members with the purpose of delivering good quality and trusted food and other commodities, including financial services. The mutual building societies served as trusted financial institutions in which local people—and they did tend to be local, with a building society being formed to serve its members in the locality, with the names of the building societies often reflecting the town or locality in which they were formed and were based and operated from and for. They could entrust their savings, receiving interest payments in return, and from which they could then borrow money subsequently with which to purchase a house, paying back in the form of a mortgage. Receiving that large loan—or a mortgage—with which to purchase a house, was generally dependent on being already a member of the organisation—the mutual building society—and having saved with it over a number of years; that is, conditional on being a 'loyal' member.

The history of mutuals within the UK and indeed across most of the advanced capitalist economies is that they were generally overshadowed by the shareholder-owned limited liability (or 'Public Limited Company', PLC) corporate form, but that they nevertheless managed to survive as a small but resilient sector of the economy. Within the UK, the mutual building societies continued to have a dominant role in that market until legislative change under the Thatcher governments opened them up to demutualisation, enabling current members to cash in on the value that had been built up in the companies over years and indeed across generations. Within ten years or so, the majority of the market had been transferred from member-owned companies to being PLCs owned by external shareholders. These demutualisations withdrew around 70% of assets from the mutual building society and insurance sectors, thus substantially reducing their critical mass.

The UK's 2010 Coalition Government was committed to introducing a greater degree of corporate diversity into the financial services sector, including through supporting mutuals:

> We want the banking system to serve business, not the other way round. We will bring forward detailed proposals to foster diversity in financial services, promote mutuals and create a more competitive banking industry. (HM Government, 2010, p. 9)

The consultation document on 'financing a private sector recovery' that was issued jointly by the Department for Business, Innovation & Skills and HM Treasury stated that:

> Mutuals play a strong role in local communities, building long-term relationships with members and often operating in areas of economic and social deprivation. The range of services offered by building societies and other mutuals has expanded as the legal framework has been updated, and in response to changes in technology and customer demand. The Government is interested in views on the role that mutuals could play in facilitating access to finance for businesses and providing greater choice in financial services. (Department for Business, Innovation & Skills, 2010, p. 32)

Likewise, the Treasury White Paper on 'a new approach to financial regulation' stressed:

> The need to maintain diversity in the financial services sector (for example, by removing barriers to entry where possible, and ensuring that its rules do not disadvantage mutually owned financial institutions). (HM Treasury, 2010, p. 32)

And in the House of Commons on 16th June 2010, the Chancellor of the Exchequer reinforced this message by stating that 'Building societies and mutuals have an important role to play in the future. We want to strengthen them and support those who want to create mutuals'.

Achieving this policy goal appeared to be an easy win, being able to transfer Northern Rock back into the mutual sector. Instead, the Coalition Government sold it at a knock-down price to Richard Branson and a consortium of New York hedge funds, despite UKFI, the ownership vehicle for the Government who were in charge of its sale, having received advice on how it could have been transferred back to the mutual sector on favourable financial terms to the Government and taxpayer. Indeed, the Government Minister misled Parliament by claiming that they had received no such advice, despite knowing that this statement was false—although he was of course protected by Parliamentary immunity from challenge.[10]

5.2 International Experience

The United Nations has for some time argued that co-operatives contribute significantly to economies across the world—and has urged governments to encourage and facilitate 'the establishment and development of co-operatives, including taking measures aimed at enabling people living in poverty or belonging to vulnerable groups to engage on a voluntary basis in the creation and development of co-operatives' (UN Resolution 56/114 adopted in 2001). The UN declared 2012 to be the International Year of Co-operatives, with the following goals:

i. increasing public awareness about co-operatives and their contributions to socio-economic development and the achievement of the Millennium Development Goals;
ii. promoting the formation and growth of co-operatives; and

[10] For a detailed analysis and discussion of the case of Northern Rock, including why and how it could have been remutualised (Michie & Llewellyn, 2010). The Oxford Centre though, presented the specific mechanics of the proposed process in a separate briefing document for Mutual and Employee-owned Business to UKFI at a meeting in Oxford convened for that purpose.

iii. encouraging governments to establish policies, laws and regulations conducive to the formation, growth and stability of co-operatives.

The International Co-operative Alliance sought to build upon that year's activities to have the co-operative form of business acknowledged as leading in sustainability (ICA, 2012). In 2012 the membership of co-operatives reached one billion across 96 countries, with the world's 300 largest co-operatives having a combined turnover of US$1.6 trillion a year. This included significant co-operative and mutual companies in most of the advanced economies, including in the financial services sector: the proportion of national output generated by co-operatives in Sweden being then 13%, in Switzerland over 16%, in New Zealand over 17% and in Finland 21% (Worldwatch Institute, 2012).

The Centre for European Policy Studies (CEPS) produced two in-depth studies of the European financial services sector, following the 2007–2009 global financial crisis, which concluded that there are important advantages in having a degree of corporate diversity in banking structures and models (Ayadi et al., 2009, 2010). These reports include case studies of several European economies, which the authors argue to illustrate the advantages that derive from a degree of corporate diversity:

> The most important conclusion is that the current crisis has made it even more evident than before how valuable it is to promote a pluralistic market concept in Europe and, to this end, to protect and support all types of ownership structures. (Ayadi et al., 2009, p. 3)

The 2007–2009 financial crisis was caused by years of financial deregulation, globalisation and financialisation, fuelled in addition in the UK by demutualisation. Banks pushed for ever-higher rates or return, as 'shareholder value' became the business ethic, epitomised by the 'greed is good' philosophy, fuelled by ever-larger bonus payments and increased inequalities in income and wealth. The dominance of the shareholder ownership model, whose purpose is to maximise financial returns to the shareholders, proved a lethal combination with the deregulation over the previous twenty years, which led to the creation of new financial instruments, rising debt levels and a bloated financial sector—generally referred to as a process of financialisation. Ever greater risks were taken to drive up financial returns and 'shareholder value', culminating in the global financial crisis of 2007–2009, which included the first global recession since the 1930s during 2008–2009. As a Bank of England Financial Stability Report noted:

> Policy action is needed to reduce the structural problems caused by banks that are too important to fail (TITF). Larger UK banks expanded much more rapidly than smaller institutions in the run-up to the crisis and have received disproportionate taxpayer support during the crisis. That reflected a misalignment of risks on TITF banks' balance sheets, due to implicit guarantees on their liabilities. (Bank of England, 2010, p. 11)

Alongside the macroeconomic costs, managers who were primarily focussed on shareholder value sacrificed the interests of individual consumers. One of the former champions of shareholder value, Jack Welch, in 2009 called it 'the dumbest idea in the world'.

The financial crisis, which was largely caused by the activities of private sector banks, and shadow banks, resulted in the UK Government giving them a bailout of perhaps £80bn. In addition, the Government borrowed in order to provide the fiscal boost that was co-ordinated internationally to prevent a slide into global depression. These costs, along with the additional hit to Government finances that a recession causes, as tax receipts fall and unemployment benefits and other such payments rise, combined to create a fiscal deficit and accumulated debt that led to a subsequent decade of austerity. Given the financial, economic and social costs of the financial crisis and concomitant recession, a key priority for policy does indeed need to be to put in place measures to prevent a reoccurrence in the future. Otherwise, such problems may well recur, whether that be in ten, twenty, or thirty years' time (there is evidence that the incidence and frequency of bank crises around the world had already increased over time—see for example Eichengreen & Bordo, 2002; Laeven & Valencia, 2012). The 2020–2021 covid-19 pandemic thus hit a world economy that was not as resilient as it could or should have been.

A major contribution to ensuring the necessary systemic resilience is to create a more diverse financial services sector. Diversity of ownership and business models is also good for customers because of the resulting increased competition and choice, quality of service and fairness. Andrew Haldane, ex-Chief Economist at the Bank of England, has described well the way in which one of the factors that lay behind the 2007–2009 global financial crisis was that individual institutions had been diversifying. While this might be thought to reduce risk, it does not do so if all are diversifying in the same way, so instead the system becomes more concentrated (Haldane, 2009, pp. 18–19). It is a classic fallacy of composition, that what is good for an individual institution acting alone does not apply when you consider all of them together. In addition to increasing risk through reduced diversity, this process also had the effect of shifting risk from the shareholder-owned banks that moved into investment banking, to the public sector, on account of the Bank of England's obligation to act as Lender of Last Resort and the Government's obligation to support systemically important banks.

In a situation of uncertainty and unpredictability, we cannot know which corporate model will prove to be superior in all possible future circumstances—and the chances are that as they all react differently to events, they will each have various strengths and weaknesses as compared with each other. Therefore, we ought to be rather cautious about destroying any successful corporate forms. The global economy is a complex system. An important point about complexity is that many complex systems are intrinsically unpredictable, even if we know everything else about them. Thus, the problem is not just that the economic future is uncertain, but that it is fundamentally unpredictable. As The Economist notes: "Just as an ecosystem benefits from diversity, so the world is better off with a multitude of corporate forms" (*The Economist*, 2010, p. 58). While The Economist's 'Schumpeter' column focuses on government ownership and partnerships, the same logic would apply to including stakeholder corporate forms.

5.3 Public Services

The UK's 2010 Coalition Government was committed to extending the role of mutuals not only to create a more corporately diverse financial services sector but also in delivering public services; for example in the health service. The potential benefits of such a move are discussed and analysed in Ham et al. (2010), including in particular the potential for generating additional employee commitment, motivation, effort and innovation. This relates to the long-standing academic literature and history of corporate practice and public policy relating to employee commitment and motivation, and the role of a 'feeling of ownership'—and hence the potentially beneficial influence of including a measure of actual ownership. In the literature, this relates to the idea of 'high commitment work systems' (on which, see Michie & Sheehan, 2005). The evidence suggests that such policies deliver the best results when employees feel that they really do have an ownership stake. The role of participatory management practices is also significant, and this is more likely to play a major and significant role if employees have a genuine ownership stake. Without such a stake there is a risk that employees will regard any participatory management practices as just a fad, or not necessarily likely to endure when the current manager or managers move on (as found and reported by Michie & Oughton, 2003).

Such are the potential benefits to be had from 'contracting out' current public services to employee-owned mutuals. The big question, though, is what happens to the contracts when they come to be tendered. The problem for any newly formed mutuals is that the big multinational companies that operate in these sectors would be able and willing to make whatever bids are necessary to win the contracts, so that the newly-formed mutuals lose the contracts and hence, presumably, go out of business.[11] This proved largely to be the case, with little sustained support for—or growth of—the mutual sector. There needs to be an appreciation of and support for the idea of a 'double bottom line', where mutual (and not for profit) organisations have to break even financially but have other objectives as well – see for example Stanley et al. (2021).

[11] For an analysis and discussion of this 'public sector mutuals' agenda, see Michie (2012).

5.4 Corporate Diversity

There has been a long-standing recognition that the UK's industrial system suffers from a bias towards short-termism, along with a peculiar dominance of the City of London, with financial capital being in charge of industrial interests. From Keynes to Churchill, through to successive Chancellors of the Exchequer, this has been highlighted as a problem that needs to be tackled. There are three main arguments in favour of having a significant co-operative or mutual sector of the economy—where 'significant' is meant sufficient critical mass, in terms of market share, to be able to make a difference to how the sector as a whole functions.

Firstly, it can be argued that there are certain potential advantages in the member-owned mutual form, as against the shareholder-owned or other corporate models, because of the trust that members can have that 'their' firms would operate in their interests, given that this is their corporate purpose. So having such member-owned organisations with which to do business is in itself in the interests of at least those customers who choose to become members.

Secondly, customers who choose instead to do business with shareholder-owned firms would also benefit if there is a critical mass of mutual businesses operating in the market, as these would provide competitive pressure for the shareholder-owned businesses who may reduce their prices or improve their service in some other way in order to meet this additional competitive pressure. There is evidence that shareholder-owned firms improve their performance in terms of customer service, when faced with competition from mutual financial providers, specifically in terms of the spread between charges made for loans and interest rates offered on savings.[12]

Thirdly, mutuals have different ownership and governance structures, different corporate purposes and objectives, and different management structures and behaviour as compared with shareholder-owned companies. They therefore tend to behave differently, including in the face of some new event or incentive, such as from an external shock to the system. Having different corporate models would thus tend to make the

[12] This evidence is reported and discussed by Cook et al. (2003).

system as a whole more resilient—less likely to suffer a domino effect, with all companies reacting in the same way to an external shock.

In addition to these three reasons—or categories of reasons—why co-operative and mutual financial firms may deliver improved outcomes, there is an additional factor that combines the first and third; namely that the nature of decision-making that mutuals would tend towards, would itself be supportive of economic stability and resilience; being inherently less risky than would be the case with private and shareholder-owned companies. This is partly because the aims and interests of the members of mutual organisations would tend to receive goods and services on a stable and sustained basis. And partly because of the regulatory regimes that tend to be in place for the sector, which in general do not permit the more risky and unsustainable activities that private and shareholder-owned companies are permitted to pursue.

These arguments are set out and analysed in Michie (2011a), but the key point here is to appreciate that there are potential benefits to be had from the co-operative and mutual model, both to individual consumers and to the economic system as a whole. The degree to which this potential is actually realised would vary from country to country and over time, and depends crucially on the national legislative and regulatory system.

5.5 A Market for Mutual Finance

Given these various potential benefits from having co-operative and mutual companies in the financial services market, what in practice is undertaken in terms of promoting such corporate forms? The answer varies from country to country, as the crucial factors are what the legislative and regulatory regime is for such companies, as compared to firms with different corporate forms such as shareholder-owned companies. Shareholder-owned companies will tend to lobby for their own interests, and given that this is the dominant corporate form in most economies, the business organisations generally would tend to favour such corporate forms, if only by default, and would tend to oppose legislation or regulation, which is seen as favouring some alternative corporate form such as co-operative and mutual companies. The result is that whether for this explicit reason, or just because the private and shareholder-owned companies are seen as the norm; most legislation and regulation tends to assume that this is the 'natural' corporate form, and legislation and regulation thus tend to be designed for such entities, often hampering the ability of mutuals to operate, even if inadvertently. There tends to be a pro-PLC culture, which can be damaging to the operation of alternative corporate forms.

Thus, to promote a market for mutual finance, this cultural problem needs to be addressed, and action needs to be taken to ensure that regulators pay proper attention to the effect that their actions would have on mutuals, and change their ways accordingly so as to at least avoid putting barriers in the way of mutual organisations inadvertently.

The nature of corporate ownership was analysed in detail by the Commission on Ownership that ran from 2010 to 2012 in the UK, although taking evidence globally. Their Report, published in 2012, argued that a more diverse ownership structure would indeed be beneficial for the economy as a whole, including for the financial services sector (Ownership Commission, 2012). That Report argued that a single corporate form, namely the large shareholder-owned firm, to the detriment of corporate diversity, dominates the UK economy. 'Plurality of ownership forms', the Commission's Report argues, "should be viewed as an economic good in its own right, increasing both choice and the variety of corporate forms available for varying business models and their investors while spreading risk more effectively" (p. 9). Gagliardi (2009) also argues, "A plurality of ownership types and business models creates a corresponding diversity in forms of corporate governance; risk appetite and management; incentive structures; policies and practices; and behaviours and outcomes. It also offers a wider choice for consumers through enhanced competition that derives in part from the juxtaposition of different business models. Variety is the evolutionary fuel in economic development as well as in biology. Diversity is desirable across the economy, and diversity within the financial sector itself – both a variety of corporate forms and geographical dispersion, with stronger local presence – tends to support a broader variety of corporate forms in the rest of the economy which in turn enhances competition and consumer choice" (p. 19).

The Commission was also concerned that short-term pressures and decision-making increasingly influence private share ownership. The Commission therefore made various suggestions for reforming the PLC model to engender more long-term thinking and behaviour—but it also made recommendations for strengthening the operation of co-operatives and mutuals to enhance that sector, thereby creating a more corporately diverse economy.

Two of the proposed reforms were perhaps particularly important, namely enhancing the ability of mutuals to raise capital, and the need to be able to create permanent mutuals so as to give voters and local citizens the confidence that transferring public services from the public sector to mutual organisations will not result, in time, in those services being taken over by profit-maximising shareholder-owned companies. Possibly from overseas, with little intrinsic interest in maintaining and indeed enhancing the quality of those public services. This requires legislation.

Shareholder-owned firms can raise capital by issuing additional shares. Indeed, this is often the reason that a company will become shareholder-owned in the first place—in order to raise capital for necessary investment and expansion. Mutuals on the other hand cannot raise funds in this way, as they have no private shareholders. Were they to issue shares, then the shareholders who bought them would want a say on how the business was run, and they would want it to aim to maximise profits so that the dividends paid to the shareholders would be as high as possible. Hence, then, would the price of the shares themselves be maximised over time, enabling the shareholders to enjoy financial benefits not only from the receipt of dividends but also from the capital gain realised from the sale of the shares at some point in the future? Mutuals are largely limited to raising funds through debt, with interest paid at some fixed amount or rate. Perhaps varying according to some exogenous factor or variable such as the bank rate, but not varying in relation to the profitability of the company itself, as this would inject into the business an incentive to focus on profitability rather than serving the trading interests of the members of the mutual.

However, mutuals do need to raise capital for investment and expansion, and the constraint of only being able to do so through debt—from bank loans, issuing of bonds, or other such mechanisms—can be a limiting factor. Whether and how this conundrum can be tackled, even if only to a certain degree, is not a simple or straightforward issue, but nevertheless there are probably ways in which progress could be made, but again it might require legislative or regulatory change. Certainly, there may be some investors who would be happy to provide 'patient' capital in return for some ownership stake, whilst still accepting some degree of safeguards to enable the mutual nature of the organisation to be maintained.

There is another way in which a larger market for co-operative and mutual capital would strengthen the economy, and this is by providing an alternative—and often very appropriate, robust and sustainable—option for business succession. When the next generation of a family no longer wish to devote their time and energies to continuing to operate the family business, what are the options for the owners to divest themselves of the company? Financial advisors will generally point to a trade sale, or floating on a stock exchange. If neither are feasible there may be a danger of the business failing. There is another option, and that is to sell to the existing stakeholders—the employees, customers, suppliers, or local community—or possibly to some combination of these stakeholders. Such stakeholders are far more likely to continue to operate the company over time for the corporate purpose for which it was founded. Indeed, the motivation of a private buyer may be precisely to asset strip and close down a competitor—buying the company for the purpose of shutting it down and removing it as a competitor, whilst making as much money as possible through the process. From the point of view of the private or family owner, one of their main motivations for the sale might, however, be precisely to see the company taken forward on a sustainable basis, with this being part of their legacy.

A famous example of such a sale was that of Spedan Lewis, selling the chain of department stores that his father, John Lewis, had established. The mechanics in that case was for the Trust—that was established to own the company on behalf of its current and future employees—to pay the owner over time from the profits generated on an annual basis. Nevertheless, many owners—private or family—may want payment up front, rather than being prepared to wait, as Spedan Lewis was prepared to do. In that case, it will be important for funding to be made available up front for the Trust to borrow to pay the owner. However, private and shareholder-owned banks would tend to be biased against such arrangements, and thus reluctant to assist. Therefore, a stronger mutual finance sector will also create a more robust set of options for business succession. Davies and Michie (2012) argue this in detail for the case of the Welsh economy.

5.6 The Scope for Mutual Corporate Forms

Given the minority status that co-operative and mutual finance has in most economies, it is not immediately obvious which phenomenon is in need of explaining; that is why mutuals hold only a minority market share, or why they have nevertheless managed to continue to operate for over a century without being squeezed out of the market entirely? With a market share of only a few percent, one might expect co-operatives and mutuals to be regarded with some suspicion, or at least with a degree of uncertainty, such that at least when it came to important transactions, the more well-known PLC form of company would be more trusted. However, the most important transaction that most people will make in their lifetime is likely to be borrowing the money to purchase their house, and yet it is for this that many people have for years been happy to deal with companies organised along with this atypical form of member-owned mutuals. The reason must surely relate to the above point regarding trust. Thus, although the corporate model is a very minor one in terms of market share or number of companies, there is an understanding that their corporate purpose is indeed to deliver good service to their members. There is therefore a degree of trust that this will be achieved, whereas for privately or shareholder-owned companies there may always be the fear that profit maximisation would influence the company's behaviour for the benefit of the owners at the expense of the customers. Survey evidence tends to support this theory, that co-operative and mutual companies are more trusted than other corporate forms.[13]

---

[13] For a detailed discussion of these issues of trust as regards co-operative and mutual firms in the financial services sector, see Michie (2011b).

As discussed above, this positive aspect of the mutual corporate form is one of the reasons for wanting to encourage the growth of the mutual sector, along with the benefits delivered by the additional competitive pressure that is provided from a critical mass of mutuals, and the systemic stability from having a greater diversity of corporate forms, enriching the 'ecosystem'.

Of course, co-operative and mutual organisations may not be suitable for all types of financing, and large-scale infrastructure projects, for example, may be better suited to publicly-owned state or regional banks, or sovereign wealth funds. The key question is whether the members—or potential members—of the mutual organisations perceive a market need that they would like to have delivered by an organisation that would be dedicated, through its corporate purpose, to delivering on that market need to its members, whether this be savings, mortgages or any other financial products. The ability of such mutuals to deliver will then depend in part, on how well the country's legislative and regulatory system is at supporting such corporate forms.

Reference has been made above to the historic origins of co-operative and mutual finance, and it might be thought that its importance has waned over the past few decades. We would argue that the mutual form of ownership remains crucially important, and to the extent that we have over the past few decades witnessed a degree of demutualisation, which is to be regretted—not least because this demutualisation contributed towards the 2007–2009 financial crisis. This is argued in detail in Michie and Labao (2012): "The era of globalisation from the 1980s was one that prioritised the interests of private ownership of productive assets. It was fuelled by privatisation, demutualisation and deregulation. It was always a false dichotomy to suggest that the critics of such globalisation were opposed to international economic activities – it was not globalisation per se that was being contested, but rather the particular *laissez faire*, neoliberal form that was being promoted. This is not just being wise after the event. Andrew Glyn had warned of this on the very eve both of his own death and of the global collapse of what proved to have been a massive Ponzi scheme – literally in the case of Bernie Madoff, and figuratively in the case of the UK and US 'greed is good' variant of capitalism"[14] (p. 320).

Thus, in addition to the points made above about financial co-operatives and mutuals being appropriate for delivering financial products and services for their members—and providing healthy competition for the private and shareholder-owned sector of the economy—a strengthened mutual sector nationally and globally would be supportive of a renewed era of economic development. This should be on a more sustainable and resilient basis than that experienced since the 1980s.

6 The Great Reset?

The 51st World Economic Forum in 2021—held virtually because of the pandemic—sought to respond to the apocalyptic events of the previous 12 months. 'A crucial year to rebuild trust' was the theme, built around the 'great reset' that World Economic Forum (WEF) founder Klaus Schwab and HRH the Prince of Wales launched in 2020. This recognised that the effects of the Covid-19 pandemic are likely to be increasingly compounded by other major global threats—including the climate crisis, financial crises, and social and economic inequality. So, how successful is the WEF's mission likely to be?

6.1 Lessons from History

This is not the first time that global crises have required global action, but there have been mixed results in the past. After the First World War, the UK played a pivotal role in forming the League of Nations on the international stage. However, this ultimately failed to deliver, with the UK's insistence on post-war reparations undermining Germany's economic recovery and political stability. When the world next sought to prevent

[14] Bernie Madoff is a former American businessperson and non-executive chairperson of the NASDAQ stock market, who admitted operating a Ponzi scheme that is considered to be the largest financial fraud in US history. In 2009 Madoff pleaded guilty to defrauding thousands of investors of billions of dollars, estimated by the court at $18bn. He was given a 150-year jail term, and died in prison (in the Butner Federal Medical Center) on 14th April 2021.

future conflicts towards the end of the Second World War, the lessons were to some extent learned from last time around. The allies met at Bretton Woods, New Hampshire, in the U.S. in 1944 to develop policies for economic stability. This led to a new system of interlinked exchange rates organised around a gold-backed US dollar, as well as new institutions to help manage it, including the International Monetary Fund and what later became the World Bank. The United Nations and the forerunner followed this in the next couple of years to the World Trade Organization. The Bretton Woods system endured until the early 1970s when the U.S. came off the gold standard, but much of the system created in the 1940s survives in one form or another today. The 2007–2009 financial crisis, which involved the first global recession since the 1930s, led to many calls for action to prevent similar crises in future. There was some tightening of regulation, but the threat of instability remains, due to continued high levels of debt combined with huge speculative flows, and industrial-scale tax avoidance and evasion globally. With only the 1940s seeing an adequate response to global crises, what might make the difference this time?

The World Economic Forum's vision of a 'great reset' recognises that what is needed to tackle these crises goes far beyond economic reforms, or climate measures, or tackling a pandemic—it is all of these combined, and more. It is the idea that global action needs to be underpinned by a mission to change society, to make it more inclusive and cohesive to match environmental sustainability with social sustainability. The WEF seeks action across seven key themes: environmental sustainability; fairer economies; 'tech for good'; the future of work and the need for reskilling; better business; healthy futures with fair access for all; and 'beyond geopolitics'—national governments collaborating globally. At the time of writing (June 2021) the next step is the 2021 UN Climate Change Conference (COP26). 'COP' refers to 'conference of parties', and this is where governments need to agree on more ambitious actions.

The main cause for optimism is that today's crises are so great that they may provoke action. Future financial crises look likely. The climate crisis is increasingly accepted to be an existential threat. Now the pandemic is a huge economic and human disaster, with further such pandemics recognised as likely—due to everything from the rise in global travel, through to the effects of climate change.

6.2 The Need for a New International Settlement

There was a free-market form of globalisation leading up to the First World War, then a retreat during the inter-war period. Bretton Woods led to an era of regulated globalisation from 1945 until the 1980s. But since then, the 'global elite' has pushed back regulatory restrictions on everything from speculative financial flows across borders to mergers and acquisitions. A new era is required, building on the Paris Agreement to limit climate change, around a global Green New Deal geared towards achieving net zero emissions and making the world economy truly sustainable. We need bold initiatives to tackle the threat of future pandemics, financial speculation, tax evasion and avoidance, and the threat of financial crises; and to reduce the unsustainable inequalities of wealth, income and power across the globe.

Will corporate and political decision-makers rise to the challenge? There needs to be sufficient popular pressure—from citizens, voters, consumers, workers, educators and activists—to push governments and business to change course fundamentally. These past few years have witnessed the 'occupy movement', the 'me too movement', 'Black Lives Matter', and countless climate crisis groups. Calls for action have been coming from business leaders at Davos and elsewhere for years. The hope is that this time, the scale of the emergency will finally make radical change unavoidable.

7 The Need for a Global Green New Deal[15]

Blair (1995) declared that: "Globalisation is changing the nature of the nation state as power becomes more diffuse and borders more porous. Technological change is reducing the capacity of government to control a domestic economy free from external influence".[16] Blair was mistaken. The current international economic and political arrangements that are

[15] On the need for a Green New Deal, see also Pollin (2021) and Michie (2021).

[16] For a discussion and critique of this speech by Tony Blair, and his associated policy agenda, see for example Cole (1998).

generally referred to as constituting globalisation are the result of policy decisions taken by politicians such as Blair, as well as the actions of companies and others, and those decisions can be reversed and other decisions and approaches can and should be taken; governments are in any case not entirely constrained even by the current 'capitalism unleashed' form of globalisation, although certainly a more democratic form of international economic arrangements could and should be brought about.

Thus, the concept of globalisation needs to be seen in its historical context. Capitalism as a system has always sought to make money by operating across borders—trading, and if necessary moving capital, and people. Thus, Sutcliffe and Glyn (2003) argue that although today's economy is by any measure 'globalised', that has not been the result of some natural one-way evolution over time. Quite the contrary, when capitalism as an economic system was first developing, it generated in many ways a similar degree of globalisation, before that process led to the First World War, the Great Depression of the 1930s, and the Second World War. We have perhaps returned to a similar sort of era to the one, which preceded the First World War; that may be an unnerving comparison, but there are certainly parallels. One thing is certain: 1989 did not represent the end of history.

Indeed, Chang (2019) argues that the 'principle' of free trade and free-market capitalism internationally—that the developed countries espouse today—is, in effect, hypocritical and cynical, in that those same countries used quite different, interventionist policies to develop their own economies, generally developing behind barriers to trade and free capital movements. Only when their economies had developed, giving them a comparative advantage over others, did those countries advocate the scrapping of such barriers, as they were now in the best position to exploit such free trade, at the expense of others.

The current 'capitalism unleashed' form of globalisation—which included the abolition of exchange controls, in turn leading to a huge increase in global financial speculation—was to blame for creating the 2007–2009 global financial crisis. Famously, it was left to Queen Elizabeth II when visiting the London School of Economics to ask why economists had failed to foresee the crash. The response that was sent to the Queen some weeks later failed to admit that the economics profession had not only failed to foresee the disastrous and hugely costly crash, but also had indeed been cheerleaders for the sort of free-market policies that actually created the financial crisis. Those economists who had for years been questioning the mainstream economics consensus—and had been warning against its free-market policy prescriptions—were generally side-lined by the economic orthodoxy, including through appointments and promotions procedures, acceptances (or rather the lack of them) to publish in mainstream journals, and so on.

The crisis, and the questions posed by Queen Elizabeth and others, has however opened up some space for alternative thinking and reform proposals. This is to be welcomed. But there is a long way to go, as the various attempts at reform that have been pursued both nationally and globally have not as yet succeeded in moving the international economy beyond its 'capitalism unleashed' era. What is needed is globalisation for a purpose. Moreover, that purpose needs to be above all to promote environmental and social sustainability and resilience. The point is not, therefore, to pose nationalism versus globalisation, but, rather, to pursue these goals of sustainability and resilience at local, regional, national and global levels, as appropriate. At the heart of this needs to be to ensure that companies have a clear corporate purpose, with concomitantly appropriate corporate ownership models, and corresponding values, policies and practices that promote long-term stewardship and sustainability.

7.1 The Need for Environmental Sustainability

The need for environmental sustainability must surely be the most vitally and urgently important issue that faces humanity, because if globalisation were to continue along its current trajectory, the world's future, and the prospects for the survival of the human race itself, may become increasingly uncertain. Current production and trade patterns threaten catastrophic climate change, with unknowable impacts upon oxygen levels in the atmosphere and other such developments, which could threaten the very survival of human life on earth. The old ways of organising production and trade need to be abandoned. The environment needs to become central to all decision-making. This means overcoming the idea that the 'free market' can solve the problem, whether combined with carbon pricing or not. Whether goods and services should be produced—and if so how, where, and when—are questions that should be decided upon in relation to what the impact would be on climate change. The world is complex, and mainstream economics needs to accept that it does not and cannot have all the answers. We need multidisciplinary and interdisciplinary research. This in turn requires a more open approach from economists, both to other disciplines, and to those from within economics who take an approach different from the mainstream—evolutionary and institutional economists, for example, as well as environmental.

The various authors collected together by Dietz et al. (2011) make this case, on the need for environmental sustainability, and set out the policy framework required across the range of key actors—companies and managers, politicians and practitioners, consumers and producers. In addition, they argue that all this needs to be underpinned by a proper understanding of the political economy of the environment. At a corporate level, we need an approach based on the long-term stewardship—rather than the short-term exploitation—of assets, and this needs to be pursued at all geographical levels, from the local to the global. On the need for good governance to be pursued at the global level, and the interaction of globalisation on the one hand and democratic processes on the other, see the various authors brought together in Michie (2017a), where I argue that: "There could hardly be a more appropriate time in world history to be revising the issues of globalisation and democracy. After almost two centuries of what might be regarded as globalisation in the current usage of the term, two world wars followed by an era of regulated globalisation, we had thirty years of unregulated globalisation leading up to the 2007–2008 global financial crisis and subsequent 2009 global financial recession, followed by what will soon have been a 'lost decade' of stagnation, austerity, instability, and inequality. The previous consensus, that 'globalisation was the only game in town', promoted by all mainstream political parties, has fallen into disrepute. Voters have used the ballot box to reject both the concept of globalisation and the mainstream parties that promoted it. The UK voted to leave the EU, in the 2016 'Brexit' referendum, and the US elected Donald Trump as President" (p. *xiii*).

So, where did it all go wrong? Hodgson (2019) argues that the failure of the globalised economy also represented a failure of mainstream economics, which had backed the 'Washington Consensus', and either turned a blind eye or even applauded the 'capitalism unleashed' form of globalisation which wreaked such havoc on the environment, created inequality and instability, and may even cause its own collapse.

Thus, as argued above, we need a change in policy—towards a global green new deal—and we need a new economics: more pluralist, realistic, and open to working with other disciplines. The failed 'capitalism unleashed' form of globalisation needs to be replaced. The Washington Consensus needs to be rejected. We need a global green new deal that will prioritise the future of our planet, seeking to halt the disastrous climate change. And we need a more realistic and open form of economic analysis in order to focus on these real-world issues, and to recognise that we do not just need changes 'at the margin'. In response to 'price signals', we need major step-change action, with the use of legislation, regulation, public ownership, and the promotion of greater corporate diversity, with cooperative and other member-owned forms of organisation, focusing on local and regional economies. Such an approach could rejuvenate economic analysis, revitalise democratic engagement, and promote an environmentally and socially sustainable future.

8 Summary and Conclusion: Biodiversity and Corporate Diversity

Keynes's (1936) *General Theory of Employment, Interest and Money* is generally remembered for making the point that effective demand drives economic activity, and that governments can therefore tackle problems of unemployment by boosting effective demand through active fiscal policy. Nevertheless, it is worth recalling that what drove Keynes to write the book was not simply to make that technical point, but, rather, to change the way that people thought about economics. We face a similar need today—to change the way people think about the economy and economics. In part, this is to continue the task that Keynes himself was undertaking, as his attempt at overthrowing the old 'Treasury' view has still not been fully achieved. Indeed, the economic policies of austerity that have been pursued by governments over the past few years rely heavily on exactly those pre-Keynesian 'Treasury' views that Keynes had sought to overcome.

We also need a more open, interdisciplinary approach to analysing and tackling the great issues of our time. In the case of climate change, it should be self-evident that we need climate change scientists along with social scientists who understand issues of consumer behaviour and behavioural change, management decision-making, and so forth. Here I should declare an interest, as I have long argued that interdisciplinary research needs to be promoted, incentivised and rewarded, including through the UK's 'Research Assessment Exercises' and now the 'Research Excellence Framework' (REF)—through which the quality of university research is measured in the UK, on the basis of which decisions are made on funding allocations to universities. And it is great to be welcomed that at last there is a serious attempt to make this so in the current such exercise, REF2021, with the appointment to the REF assessment panels of members with an explicit remit of advising specifically on the interdisciplinary aspects of research (and I am pleased to have been appointed to such a role for the 'Management and Business' panel). It is to be hoped that this development will encourage a more realistic approach to economic analysis and policymaking, with proper account taken of institutional and behavioural factors, and of the complexity of economic processes.

The Great Depression of the 1930s led to Keynes's 1936 attempt to change the way that people thought about the economy. This led to the development referred to now as the Golden Age of Capitalism, from 1945 through to the early 1970s. We now need to replace the era of 'capitalism unleashed', which spread across the globe from the 1980s—and which caused the first global recession since the 1930s, in 2009 following the 2007–2008 global financial crisis. This will require a more realistic approach to analysing the workings of the economy; a policy agenda to promote new corporate forms and greater corporate diversity, greater regional resilience and reduced inequality; and above all the tackling of climate change, to deliver environmental and social sustainability.

References

Ayadi, R., Llewellyn, D. T., Schmidt, R. H., Arbak, E., & De Groen, W. P. (2010). *Diversity in European banking: Why does it matter?* Centre for European Policy Studies (CEPS).

Ayadi, R., Schmidt, R. H., Valverde, S. C., Arbak, E., & Fernandez, F. (2009). *Investigating diversity in the banking sector in Europe: The performance and role of savings banks*. Centre for European Policy Studies (CEPS).

Bank of England. (2010, June). *Financial Stability Report*, Issue No. 27. Bank of England.

BBC. (2012, January 16). *Nick Clegg plans more employee ownership*. https://www.bbc.co.uk/news/uk-16570840

Blair, T. (1995, July 17). *Speech at newscorp leadership conference*. Hayman Island, Australia.

Blasi, J. R., & Kruse, D. L. (2017). An American historical perspective on employee ownership. Chapter 8 in Michie, Blasi and Borzaga (Eds.), *Oxford handbook of mutual, co-operative and co-owned business*. Oxford University Press.

Boguslaw, J., & Schur, L. (2019). *Building the assets of low and moderate income workers and their families: The role of employee ownership*. Rutgers.

Carroll, L. (1872). *Through the looking glass: And what Alice found there*. Macmillan.

Chang, H. J. (2019). Kicking away the ladder—Globalisation and economic development in historical perspective. In J. Michie (Ed.), *The handbook of globalisation* (3rd ed., pp. 392–399). Edward Elgar Publishing.

Christopherson, C., Michie, J., & Tyler, P. (2010). Regional resilience: Theoretical and empirical perspectives. *Cambridge Journal of Regions, Economy and Society, 3*, 3–10.

Cook, J., Deakin, S., Michie, J., & Nash, D. (2003). *Trust Rewards: Realising the mutual advantage*. Mutuo.

Cox, P. (2010). *Spedan's partnership: The story of John Lewis and Waitrose*. Labatie Books.

Cole, M. (1998). Globalisation, modernisation and competitiveness: A critique of the new labour project in education. *International Studies in Sociology of Education, 8*(3), 315–333.

Davies, W., & Michie, J. (2012). *Employee ownership: Defusing the business succession time-bomb in Wales*. The Wales Co-operative Centre.

Department for Business, Innovation & Skills. (2010). *Financing a private sector recovery*. TSO.

Department for Business, Innovation & Skills. (2014). *On amending the rule against perpetuities: BIS Response*. TSO.

Dietz, S., Michie, J., & Oughton, C. (Eds.). (2011). *The political economy of the environment: An interdisciplinary approach*. Routledge.

Eichengreen, B., & Bordo, M. (2002). *Crises now and then: What lessons from the last era of globalization* (NBER Working Paper 8716). National Bureau of Economic Research.

Erdal, D. (2011). *Beyond the corporation*. Bodley Head.

Gagliardi, F. (2009). Financial development and the growth of co-operative firms. *Small Business Economics: An Entrepreneurship Journal, 32*(4), 439–464.

Glyn, A. (2006). *Capitalism unleashed: Finance, globalization, and welfare*. Oxford University Press.

Haldane, A. G. (2009). *Rethinking the Financial Network*. Speech delivered at the Financial Student Association, Amsterdam.

Ham, C., Michie, J., & Mills, C. (2010). *A mutual health service*. Kellogg College, University of Oxford.

HM Government. (2010). *The Coalition: Our programme for government*. Cabinet Office.

HM Treasury. (2010). *A new approach to financial regulation: Judgement, focus and stability*. TSO.

Hodgson, G. M. (2019). The great crash of 2008 and the reform of economics. In J. Michie (Ed.), *The handbook of globalisation* (3rd ed., pp. 439–455). Edward Elgar Publishing.

International Co-operative Alliance. (2012). *Blueprint for a co-operative decade*. ICA.

Keynes, J. M. (1936). *The general interest of employment*. Macmillan.

Laeven, L., & F. Valencia. (2012). *Systemic banking crises database: An update* (IMF Working Papers, WP/12/163).

Lysandrou, P. (2019). Global inequality and the global financial crisis: The new transmission mechanism. In J. Michie (Ed.), *The handbook of globalisation*, Chapter 27 (3rd ed., pp. 419–438). Elgar: Cheltenham.

Michie, J. (2002, 3 December). Inside the productivity gap. *The Guardian.*
Michie, J. (2011a). Promoting corporate diversity in the financial services sector. *Policy Studies, 32*(4), 309–323.
Michie, J. (2011b). Mutual financial firms. In J. Springford (Ed.), *A confidence crisis? Restoring trust in financial services*, Chapter 7 (pp. 125–131). The Social Market Foundation.
Michie, J. (2012, March). Mutual advantage? *The future implications of mutualism for employment relations.* Acas 'Future of Workplace Relations' (*Discussion Paper*). London.
Michie, J. (Ed.). (2017a). *Globalisation and democracy*, three volume set. Edward Elgar.
Michie, J. (2017b). *Advanced introduction to globalisation.* Edward Elgar.
Michie, J. (Ed.). (2019). *The handbook of globalisation* (3rd ed.). Edward Elgar.
Michie, J. (2021). Interpreting the world, in various ways—And changing it. *International Review of Applied Economics, 35*(3 and 4) (double issue).
Michie, J., Blasi, J. R., & Borzaga, C. (Eds.). (2017). *The Oxford handbook of mutual, co-operative, and co-owned business.* Oxford University Press.
Michie, J., & Labao, L. (2012). Ownership, control and economic outcomes. *Cambridge Journal of Regions, Economy and Society, 5*(3), 307–324.
Michie, J., & Llewellyn, D. T. (2010). Converting failed financial institutions into mutual organisations. *Journal of Social Entrepreneurship, 1*(1), 146–170.
Michie, J., & Oughton, C. (2003). HRM, employee share ownership and corporate performance. *Research & Practice in HRM, 11*(1), 15–36.
Michie, J., & Oughton, C. (2014a). *Measuring diversity in financial services markets: a diversity index* (Working Paper 097_DP113). The Centre for Financial and Management Studies, The School of Oriental and African Studies, University of London.
Michie, J., & Oughton, C. (2014b, November). *Corporate diversity in financial services—An updated diversity index.* Building Societies Association.
Michie, J., & Sheehan, M. (2005). Business strategy, human resources, labour market flexibility, and competitive advantage. *International Journal of Human Resource Management, 16*(3), 448–468.
Ownership Commission. (2012). *Plurality, stewardship and engagement: The report of the ownership commission.* Mutuo.
Oxford Centre for Mutual & Co-owned Business. (2011). *Mutuals yearbook 2011: Leading mutuals together—The definitive guide to the mutual sector.* Mutuo.

Pollin, R. (2021). The industrial policy requirements for a global climate stabilization project. *International Review of Applied Economics, 35*(3 and 4) (double issue).

Stanley, S., Hogg, T. L., Leviston, Z., & Walker, I. (2021). *From anger to action: Differential impacts of eco-anxiety, eco-depression, and eco-anger on climate action and wellbeing*. https://doi.org/10.1016/j.joclim.2021.100003

Sutcliffe, R., & A. Glyn. (2003). Measures of globalisation and their misinterpretation. Chapter 3 of Michie (Ed.), *The handbook of globalisation* (pp. 61–78). Edward Elgar, Cheltenham.

Tabb, W. K. (2012). *The restructuring of capitalism in our time*. Columbia University Press.

The Economist. (2010, August 21). The eclipse of the public company. *The Economist*, p. 58.

van Treeck, Till. (2015). Inequality, the crisis, and stagnation. *European Journal of Economics and Economic Policies: Intervention, 12*(2), 158–169.

Worldwatch Institute. (Ed.). (2012). *State of the world 2012: Moving toward sustainable prosperity*. Washington: Worldwatch Institute.

4

Equality, Resilience and Sustainability: Rebalancing Commercial Rights and Economic and Social Rights to Create More Equal Economies

Diane Elson

1 Introduction

This chapter explores concepts of equality, resilience and sustainability, and their interlinkages, in the light of the Covid-19 syndrome, and makes proposals for creating more equal economies. It is argued that equality should be understood as substantive equality, paying attention not only to opportunities but to outcomes, as is done in the UN system of human rights treaties and monitoring.

Evidence is discussed on inequalities in income, wealth and economic power globally and in the UK, adopting an intersectional approach that goes beyond class (as proxied by inter-household inequalities) to also consider inequalities related to gender and race/ethnicity. It is argued that ultimately what matters is inequality in wellbeing, which is linked to, but is not reducible to, income and wealth. Indicators of wellbeing

D. Elson (✉)
Colchester, UK
e-mail: drelson@essex.ac.uk

P. Arestis and M. Sawyer (eds.), *Economic Policies for Sustainability and Resilience*, International Papers in Political Economy,
https://doi.org/10.1007/978-3-030-84288-8_4

are discussed and unpaid care work and health outcomes are chosen for particular attention. The chapter argues that inequalities in income and wealth and wellbeing are rooted in unequal divisions of labour, both paid and unpaid; and unequal control over systems of production and consumption.

Ways in which inequality in income has been taken into account in discussions of resilience to financial shocks are explored. It is argued that some aspects of inequality are increased by processes that provide resilience to financial shocks (for instance through monetary policy that employs Quantitative Easing). Regressive resilience should be avoided through measures to reduce the likelihood of financial shocks and use of fiscal policy to sustain progressive resilience.

To address the climate emergency there must be a transition to sustainable patterns of production and consumption. While the UN Sustainable Development Goals include this goal, and also the goal of reducing inequality within and between countries, no explicit link is made between them. The chapter discusses the evidence that high inequality in income and wealth is a barrier to sustainability.

The chapter notes that the Covid-19 pandemic has intensified existing inequalities and highlighted inequalities in health and in unpaid care work. However, it has also led to a new willingness to address inequalities in policies to 'build back better'. This chapter argues that to be effective for the long run, such policies should not only focus on tax and transfer (redistribution of income) but also on the institutions and configurations of economic power that give rise to incomes and wealth and wellbeing pre-tax and transfer (predistribution). In particular, policies must rebalance the relationship between on the one hand commercial rights-regimes governing property, companies, and contracts; on the other hand rights set out in the International Covenant on Economic, Social and Cultural Rights (the right to work and just and favourable conditions of work, the right to an adequate standard of living, the right to social security, the right to education, the right to the highest attainable standard of health), rights which are critical to wellbeing. The limitations of the UK government plan to 'level up' are discussed and it is argued that more fundamental changes to rights are required that will directly reduce the power of wealthy companies and people, increase the bargaining power of workers, and reduce gender and racial inequality. Public spending and taxation should be used to reinforce this rebalancing of rights. However, money metrics are insufficient to ensure appropriate attention to wellbeing. The chapter concludes by discussing proposals to create a sustainable and equitable economy in the UK, focussed on well-being, by creating a caring economy, in which care services are treated as vital infrastructure, and everyone has time to care and time free from care.

2 Inequalities

There are many inequalities between people, and their form and extent are linked to the forms of inequalities between countries which have been shaped by imperialism and colonialism (Pomeranz, 2000). Contemporary inequalities between countries[1] constrain the policy space that many governments have for creating an equitable economy (UNCTAD, 2019).

Equality between people should be assessed not just in terms of formal legal equality but in terms of substantive equality, paying attention to outcomes, such as income and wealth and wellbeing, and not only to opportunities, such as access to education and jobs. Substantive equality encompasses the recognition that equality not only requires equal treatment, such as equal pay for work of equal value, but also support for different needs, such as the provision of maternity services to pregnant women, and often requires fundamental transformation, such as action to share unpaid care more equally between women and men (Fredman, 2016). Similarly, it encompasses recognition that there is entrenched racism throughout many economies, so that low-income people who belong to a more powerful ethnic group are in a more advantageous position in some respects than low-income people from other ethnic groups. Extending the same provisions to them all will not produce equal results—what is needed is 'targeted universalism', which is inclusive of the needs of both the dominant and the marginal groups but

[1] While noting inequalities between countries, for reasons of space these will not be explored in detail.

pays particular attention to the situation of the marginal group (Powell, 2012).

Substantive equality is the standard adopted in the UN system of human rights (Fredman, 2016); for instance, by the UN Committee on Economic, Social and Cultural Rights in relation to the principle of non-discrimination in the International Covenant on Economic, Social and Cultural Rights. Similarly, it has been adopted by the UN Committee on the Elimination of All Forms of Discrimination Against Women in monitoring compliance with the Convention on the Elimination of All Forms of Discrimination Against Women. Likewise, the International Convention on the Elimination of All Forms of Racial Discrimination "reaches beyond formal equality towards equality in fact" (Thornberry, 2005, p. 255).

Substantive equality does not imply that everyone should have the same income and wealth, but it does imply that inequalities in income and wealth should not be so large as to impede the realisation of economic and social rights on an equal basis for all: the right to work and just and favourable conditions of work, the right to an adequate standard of living, the right to social security, the right to education, the right to the highest attainable standard of health, rights which are critical to wellbeing. The high levels of inequality in income and wealth that now prevail do create obstacles to realisation of equality in enjoyment of economic and social rights (Balakrishnan et al., 2016; MacNaughton, 2021).

In the decade before the Covid-19 pandemic that struck the world in 2020, high inter-household/inter-personal inequalities in income and wealth within countries were revealed in research by economists in academic institutions, NGOs, and international organisations. Piketty's (2014) book examining trends in the concentration of income and wealth in the century since 1910 in the hands of the top 1% of people[2] in USA, UK, France, Germany and Japan, became an international bestseller. In the period from the early 1980s to around 2010, Piketty shows that on this measure inequality intensified, especially in the USA

[2] Strictly speaking, the data refers to inequality between tax units, which may be individuals or households. Piketty, like many writers on inequality, tends to blur the distinction between individuals and households, ignoring inequalities within households.

where the top percentile's share of national income rose to nearly 20%, compared to around 14% in UK, around 9% in France and Japan, and 11% in Germany (Piketty op. cit., pp. 316–317).

A global report from Oxfam showed that while all income groups experienced positive growth in their real income between 1988 and 2011, the incomes of the poorest 10% of people increased by $65, while the incomes of the richest 1% increased 182 times as much, by $11,800 (based on household survey data, assuming no inequalities within households) (Oxfam, 2016). This report also found evidence of how the wealthy shape rules and institutions to their benefit, including tax systems, corporate governance structures and laws (including intellectual property rights); and use personal connections to secure access to lucrative contracts. It argued that the social and political power of the wealthy are key drivers of increases in inequality.

Evidence of growing inequality in the distribution of income between rich and poor households was also highlighted by mainstream organisations. In 2015 the OECD published a report on inequality in household disposable income (measured after taxes and benefits), noting that in the mid-1980s, the Gini coefficient stood at 0.29, on average, across OECD countries. By 2013, it had increased to 0.32, rising in 17 of the 22 OECD countries for which long-time series are available (OECD, 2015, p. 23). Of course, the average conceals variations between the most unequal countries (Chile, Turkey and USA) and the least unequal (Slovenia, Norway, and Denmark) (OECD, 2015, p. 56). Inequality in the UK was somewhat above the OECD average, at 0.34 in 2011, having risen since the mid-1980s (OECD, 2015, p. 24).

IMF researchers have described widening economic inequality as "the defining challenge of our time" (Dabla-Norris et al., 2015, p. 4). Their analysis found that if the income share of the top 20% increases, then GDP growth declines over the medium term; whereas an increase in the income share of the bottom 20% is associated with higher GDP growth. They suggest that high levels of inequality dampen investment by fuelling economic, financial and political instability.

There has also been renewed attention to the functional distribution of income between capital and labour. The United Nations Development Programme (UNDP) reports that in 16 developed countries for which data is available, the labour share of national income declined from about 75% in the mid-1970s to 65% in the mid-2000s; and in 16 developing and emerging economies for which data are available, average labour shares declined from around 62% of gross domestic product (GDP) in the early 1990s to 58% in the mid-2000s (UNDP, 2013). The functional distribution of income points to inequalities in the system of production that underpin inequality in household or personal income and wealth; inequalities founded in the exclusion of workers, except the most highly paid, from ownership and control of the means of production (land, machines and systems), in which class inequality intersects with gender and race/ethnicity since the control of the means of production, is predominantly in the hands of elite men. Moreover, empirical evidence shows that in recent decades, increases in productivity have not been matched by increases in wages. In 91 of 133 countries between 1995 and 2014, wages did not grow as fast as productivity (Vázquez Pimentel et al., 2018). Power in workplaces and in markets underpins the distribution of income and wealth, and the market power of large companies in advanced economies has increased. IMF researchers found that between 1980 and 2015 their mark-ups increased on average by 39% (Diez et al., 2018).

There has also been widening inequality between different types of labour classified in terms of skills. For instance in G20 countries, the combined labour share of low- and middle-skilled labour fell by more than 10 percentage points from 1995 to 2009, while that for highly skilled labour rose by more than 5 percentage points in 'emerging G20' countries and by 10 percentage points in 'advanced G20' countries (IMF, 2017, p. 14). We should, however, be wary of accepting skill classifications at face value, as they do not simply reflect the kinds of skills actually called upon to do a job, but also the differential power of different groups to extract high wages. Corporate profits have been translated into strikingly high executive salaries and bonuses (Dabla-Norris et al., 2015).

Some international reports on income inequality have included discussion of a variety of systems of stratification beyond class. For instance, a report by UNDESA (2013) considered inequalities based on age, rural–urban location, disability, migration status, and inequalities faced by indigenous people. A report by UNDP (2013) on inequality in developing countries had a special chapter on gender inequality, which highlighted that reducing gender gaps in education had not been translated into reductions in gender gaps in labour markets. Unequal power in households means that it is important to examine the distribution of income, consumption and wealth within as well as between households (Albelda & Tilly, 1999; Doss, 2021). Unfortunately, much of the empirical evidence on distribution of income and wealth conflates households and people, and implicitly assumes equal distribution of income and assets within households.

There is a huge literature on gender employment and wage gaps, but little that analyses the interaction of these gaps with the inter-household distribution of income. An exception is OECD (2015) which estimates what the Gini coefficient would have been in 2007 (or latest available year before the financial crisis) if households had the same female employment characteristics as in the mid-1980s, and finds that overall, more women in paid work means less income inequality between households than would otherwise have been the case. However, the OECD report (op. cit.) does not examine whether the mitigating impact of the decrease in gender inequality in paid work is at the cost of more work in total for women, an extension of their total working day, adding paid work to their unpaid work caring for their families. Data on time use reveals that in Australia, Canada, the Netherlands, Norway and UK, women's total hours of work went up. This suggests that in at least these countries the mitigating impact on inter-household income inequality of reductions in gender equality in the labour market—which was particularly strong in UK and Netherlands—came at the cost of more work in total for working-age women on the average (Elson, 2018). To get a full picture of inequality, it is important to examine unpaid care and domestic work as well as paid work.

Gender inequality in employment has been taken into account in an analysis of the functional distribution of income by Guschanski and Onaran (2017), who analysed the share of labour compensation in 14 OECD countries in the periods 1970–2007 and 2008–2014, and included female share of hours of employment as one of the variables. They found a decline in labour's share of income, mainly attributable to offshoring production, a decline in the bargaining power of labour (as measured by union density, i.e. union members as proportion of workforce) and a rise in female share of hours of employment (which is seen as a marker of lower bargaining power, given the disadvantaged position of women in the labour market). Guschanski and Onaran (2017) conclude that an increase in the female share of employment in the absence of strong collective representation of women workers is associated with a fall in the wage share. This study highlights the role of different forms of power in the determination of growing inequality in the functional distribution of income.

It is important to recognise that structures of inequality are not separate but intersect, so that class is experienced differently by people of different ethnicities and genders and in different countries; and race/ethnicity is experienced differently by people of different classes, genders and countries; also, gender is experienced differently by people of different classes, race/ethnicities and countries. Economies are racialised and gendered, as well as being divided by class (Banks, 2021; Folbre, 2021). Racism, sexism, and class privilege mean that millions of people face harassment and violence in their daily lives, having to endure this to get a living and make provision for their families. Inequality leads to harassment and violence, which in turn deepens inequalities. It is difficult to capture all of this through the metrics of income and wealth. A metric of well-being, using a wider variety of indicators comes closer to grasping the multidimensional way in which people experience inequality.

The OECD (2020) has developed a wellbeing framework in which wellbeing has 11 dimensions. These dimensions relate to economic conditions (Income and Wealth, Housing, Work and Job Quality); quality-of-life factors that encompass how well people are (and how well they feel they are), what they know and can do, and how healthy and safe their places of living are (Health, Knowledge and Skills, Environmental Quality, Subjective Well-being, Safety); and how connected and engaged people are, and how and with whom they spend their time (Work-Life Balance, Social Connections, Civic Engagement). Here there is no space to consider all these dimensions, so I have chosen to consider, in addition to income and wealth, inequalities in health and in time spent in unpaid care and domestic work (reported by OECD, op. cit., under the heading of work-life balance).

Not surprisingly the OECD (2020) finds that people with higher income also report better health. On average, 79% of those in the top income quintile in OECD countries say their health is good, compared to only 60% in the bottom quintile. There are also gender inequalities: life expectancy at birth is higher for women (83.2 years, on average) than for men (77.9 years) in all OECD countries. However, 70% of men report their health to be good, but only 66% of women do. No data are provided on inequalities by race and ethnicity. Under the heading of work-life balance, the OECD considers how people divide their time between leisure and personal care, unpaid care and domestic work, and paid work. Women spend longer hours in unpaid work (around 2 hours more per day, for the OECD on average), while men have more time off for leisure and personal care (OECD, 2020). Some governments have already begun to take steps towards integrating wellbeing into their approach to economic policy, including Iceland and New Zealand, and also Scotland and Wales.[3]

3 Inequalities in UK

Joyce and Xu (2019) found that inter-household income inequality as measured by the Gini coefficient is higher in UK than in most European countries, though not as high as in the USA. On this measure, income inequality (measured after taxes and benefits) rose steeply in the 1980s but has not changed much since early 1990s. However, the Gini coefficient does not capture the vastly diverging fortunes of the richest and poorest. The share of income going to the 1% richest households has risen sharply through the 1990s to 8% in 2017; in part reflecting a big increase in earnings among the highest earners. In 2017, the average pay of CEOs of FTSE 100 companies in the UK was 145 times the pay of the average worker, up from 47 times in 1998. Household earnings

[3] Wellbeing Economy Alliance (2020).

of the poorest have stagnated, with the lowest-earning working households earning little more than such households earned in the 1990s. After benefits, the gap between the lowest household and those in the middle and at the top of the earnings distribution has been reduced, but income from benefits can carry a stigma and is vulnerable to austerity policies, so it is vital to look at underlying inequalities in earnings.

Joyce and Xu (2019) note there is gender and race inequality in earnings in the UK. The gap between male and female hourly earnings had been falling but progress has stalled and the gap was still 18% in 2018. Though there is undoubtedly some outright discrimination against women in labour markets, a very important factor is structural inequalities in the division of unpaid care work. Andrew et al. (2020) found that gender gaps in employment, working hours and wages really open up after workers become parents. Many more mothers than fathers stop paid work altogether or switch to part-time paid work while taking on the majority of the childcare. This has long-lasting, cumulative impacts on women's hourly wages well into the future. Even in families where the mother had a higher wage than the father before the first child arrived, fathers' working patterns are largely unaffected by childbirth whereas mothers reduce their hours of paid work substantially. There is a motherhood penalty that persists into the future. Moreover, the gender gap in average total earnings (including those with no earnings, i.e. those not in paid work) is much wider than the gender gap in average hourly earnings. Feminist economists point to the way in which women's decisions are shaped by the pressure of social norms, the practices of employers, and the lack of affordable good quality childcare.

Gender inequality intersects with class: for instance, falls in mothers' labour market participation are greatest for mothers with the lowest education (Costa Dias et al., 2018). It also intersects with race: for instance, women of Bangladeshi and Pakistani ethnicity earn less on average than white British women, and the gap has been widening (Joyce & Xu, 2019).

Around 80% of the population of England reports as being from the White British group; the largest minority groups are White Other, Indian, Pakistani, Bangladeshi, black African and black Caribbean (Platt & Warwick, 2020). The gap in 2019 between the median hourly pay for those in the White British ethnic group and the those in ethnic minority groups was 2.3%, its narrowest level since 2012, but this simple comparison between White and ethnic minority groups masks a wide variety of experiences among different ethnic minorities. While most minority ethnic groups earned less on average than White British people in 2019, a few groups[4] earned more than their White British counterparts (ONS, 2020a, pp. 3–4). Rates of unemployment faced by Black groups are particularly high at over double those for the White majority, and the gaps are even larger among youth. Tests of applications sent to employers show that there continues to be systematic racial discrimination within the labour market across ethnicities (IFS, 2020).

Wealth is much more concentrated than income (D'Arcy & Gardiner, 2017). In 2012–2014 the distribution of wealth between households, as measured by the Gini coefficient was 0.66, which was almost twice as high as the household income Gini coefficient in the same period of 0.34; with wealth comprising net property wealth, private pension wealth and net financial wealth. The distribution of net financial wealth was much more unequal than other kinds of wealth, with a Gini coefficient of 0.93. Many adults own very little or no net wealth, while adults in the top 10% accounted for nearly half (49%) of all Britain's wealth in 2012–2014, with the top 1% alone owning 14% of the wealth. Since 2006–2008, the trends in the inequality of these different asset types have varied. While inequality between households has risen in relation to both property (from 0.67 to 0.71) and financial wealth (0.91–0.93), the Gini coefficient for private pension wealth has fallen (from 0.78 to 0.75). D'Arcy and Gardiner (2017) use individual measures (rather than household measures) to provide a snapshot of gender inequality in wealth. They report that median total net wealth of women (£71,000) is 13% lower than for men (£81,000).

The ONS (2020b) has compared median wealth by race/ethnicity of household head for the period 2016–2018. It reports that the median total wealth for all households in Great Britain was £286,600, ranging from £34,000 among those with a household head from the Black African group to £314,000 for the White British group. Households

[4] ONS (2020a) distinguishes 17 different ethnic groups.

from the Indian ethnic group had median wealth almost the same as the White British group. Race intersects with class in the distribution of wealth: with exception of the White British and Indian ethnic groups, households from all other groups are more likely to be in a lower wealth quintile than average. Households with a White British head were approximately nine times as likely to be in the top quintile of total wealth (wealth above £865,400) as those of Black African ethnicity and 18 times as likely as those of Bangladeshi ethnicity. Nevertheless, controlling for age, sex, housing tenure, household composition, socio-economic group and educational attainment, ONS (2020b) found that there remain statistically significant differences in the total wealth of a household, depending on the ethnicity of the household head, and concludes "This suggests that the inequality in wealth by ethnicity is not explained by differences in the factors that we have adjusted for" (p. 3).

There is substantial inequality in health and life expectancy and inequalities widened between 2010 and 2020. Poorer communities, women and those living in the North have experienced little or no improvement since 2010 (Marmot, Allen, Boyce et al., 2020, p. 33).[5] There are also persistent inequalities in the distribution of unpaid work caring for families. ONS (2016) provides data on unpaid time spent on 'active'[6] care for children and adults in 2000 and 2015. In 2015, mothers spent, on average, 1 hour and 57 minutes per day providing childcare compared to 2 hours and 4 minutes per day in 2000. Despite this fall, mothers were still providing 74% of total childcare. On average, both males and females over 50 increased the amount of time devoted to unpaid caring of adults, by 15 and 21% respectively between 2000 and 2015. Women accounted for 59% of the time spent in 2015. Women's much higher contribution to unpaid care work underpins their inequality in paid work.

There are also substantial and widening economic inequalities between different parts of the UK (UK 2070 Commission, 2020). The UK is the

---

[5] This report does not examine inequalities between different race/ethnic groups.

[6] 'Active care' is distinguished by ONS from being 'on call' which is known as 'passive care'. Active care can include feeding a child or washing an adult as opposed to passive care which may include time when a responsible person is on call if they are needed but perhaps engaged in their own activity.

most inter-regionally unequal large high-income country. In the period just before Covid-19, while the London region was the richest region of Europe, the UK also had six of the ten poorest regions. Per capita income in London was 43% above the national average compared with 18% in 1985. In England the greatest concentration of the most deprived neighbourhoods is in the north.

Underpinning inequalities between people and places is the concentration of economic power in the hands of a few big companies. In the period just prior to the Covid-19 pandemic, six energy companies had 82% of the retail energy market; four supermarkets had 69% of the grocery sales; five banks had 85% of retail bank accounts; four mobile phone companies had 89% of customers; and a few firms like Carillion held a very high proportion of outsourced contracts to deliver publicly funded services (IPPR Commission on Economic Justice, 2018). The companies operating the major digital platforms dominate the UK market, as they do in almost all the countries in which they operate: in UK Facebook had 74% of the market for social networks, Amazon was responsible for around 80% of online sales of books, and Google enjoyed 90% of the search engine market (IPPR Commission on Economic Justice, 2018).

4 Inequalities and Resilience

The global financial crisis of 2008/2009 led to a focus on resilience in the face of financial shocks. A review paper by economists in the OECD Economics Department (Sánchez et al., 2015) considers a body of research that defines a resilient economy as one that better withstands an adverse shock and returns back faster to the pre-shock trend growth rate (i.e. minimising the cumulative GDP loss relative to potential output). This definition includes no consideration of environmental sustainability (only of financial sustainability) or of inequality. The findings of the paper reflect conventional neo-classical thinking prior to the Covid-19 pandemic. Thus, it notes that expansionary monetary policy helps shorten recessions by boosting demand but warns there are limits about how long expansionary monetary policy, especially unconventional monetary policy measures, can be kept in place to support recoveries, without fuelling additional risks, such as inflation. The possibility of such policies leading to increased wealth inequality is not mentioned. On the fiscal side, the study reports that effective countercyclical policy responses require sufficient fiscal space, but does not mention that fiscal space is constrained by refusal of the rich to pay fair taxes; or that failure to spend may lead to long-lasting falls in economic potential, for instance via adverse health impacts. It commends automatic stabilisers that cushion the impact on household disposable incomes, but does not explore how the strength of these stabilisers may be lower in more unequal economies in which political pressure from the rich for low taxes may starve the social security system of adequate funding. It suggests that stringent employment protection can cushion the impact of adverse shocks, but also slow the recovery by hampering labour reallocation. Active labour market policies are recommended to facilitate the retraining of workers and their reallocation to new jobs, but there is no concern that this process may be structured by gender and race inequalities, with new jobs going mainly to white men; or that the new jobs may have worse pay and conditions than the old ones.

It is important to recognise that some sources of resilience are regressive, intensifying inequalities even as they assist in the recovery of aggregate production, income and consumption. Quantitative Easing (QE) since 2008 has helped stabilise financial markets and without it, the fall in output and employment would have been higher (given the decisions on fiscal policy), but it has led to asset price inflation. Evgenidis and Fasiano (2021) find that QE has had significant and lingering effects on wealth inequality in Great Britain, raising wealth inequality across households, as measured by both their Gini coefficients and percentile shares. Mumtaz and Theophilopoulou (2017) find that QE worsened income and consumption inequality in the UK. Montecino and Epstein (2018) find that QE is dis-equalizing in the USA, and the ECB (2016) has recognised that the effects of QE benefitted wealthier households more than poorer households. QE has been argued to benefit men more than women in the Eurozone, given the men predominate among the holders of high levels of wealth (Metzger & Young, 2020). Another regressive source of resilience is an extension of women's unpaid care and domestic work to provide a safety net that to some extent cushions children, husbands, and other family members against external shocks, as women strive to make falling incomes go farther and try to safeguard the health and education of their children (for examples see Elson, 1995). But this is often at the expense of women's own health, leading to a depletion of women's own capacities and an increase in gender inequality (Elson, 2012).

Progressive forms of resilience maybe provided by redistributive systems of social security and public service provision. Sánchez et al. (2015, p. 11) report that the strength of such 'automatic stabilisers' depends on the size of the public sector, the design of the social security system, and the progressivity of the tax system. Among OECD economies, automatic stabilisers tend to be particularly strong in Denmark, Belgium and Germany. The UK was not among the weakest with respect to automatic stabilisers but was found to be considerably weaker than those three countries. Moreover, the austerity policies that were adopted in UK after 2010, with the aim of stimulating private sector investment by reducing the budget deficit and public debt, weakened automatic stabilisers and failed to produce the anticipated recovery. These austerity policies had the greatest incidence on the poorest, on women and on ethnic minorities (Women's Budget Group, 2017).

5 Inequalities and Sustainability

In 2015 the governments of the world adopted an Agenda for Sustainable Development (UNDESA, 2015), accompanied by 17 goals and 169 targets. Goal 10 calls on governments to reduce inequality within and among countries, while Goal 12 calls on governments to ensure sustainable consumption and production patterns. However, no explicit link was made between the reduction of inequality and the achievement of sustainability goals.

A review in 2020 of progress made across the world on the Agenda give little indication of effective action on either inequality or sustainability. It found that in the period 2012–2017, while real incomes of the poorest within the majority of countries are rising, the rich still prosper disproportionately; workers are receiving a smaller share of the output they helped produce, comparing 2017 with 2004; and while income inequality (as measured by the Gini coefficient) has been falling in some countries between 2010 and 2017, levels generally remain high (UNDESA, 2020).

The review also found that the world continues on a path of using natural resources unsustainably; growth in the generation of electronic waste far outpaces its rate of recycling. Despite the growing urgency of the climate crisis, governments are still subsidising the fossil fuel industry; and the world is way off track to meet the Paris Agreement target for reduction in greenhouse gas emissions, signalling 'cataclysmic changes ahead' (UNDESA, 2020).

Oxfam (2015) addressed the link between inequality and the climate emergency, pointing out that the climate emergency impacts disproportionately on the poor and is generated disproportionately by the rich. While the poorest people live in areas most vulnerable to the climate emergency, the poorest half of the global population are responsible through their consumption[7] for only around 10% of total global emissions. The average carbon footprint of the richest 1% globally could be as much as 175 times that of the poorest 10% (Oxfam, 2015).

As well as inequalities between rich and poor, inequalities between countries are important. As Harvey (2021, p. 151) notes, countries with higher per capita incomes produce higher per capita emissions. Though in the aggregate, China is the country that produces the most emissions of CO2; the average Chinese person generates two and a half times less CO2 than the average American; and the average person living in the EU generates CO2 emissions that are less than half those of the average American.

It is the richest people in the richest countries that are responsible for the highest levels of CO2 emissions. The majority of the world's richest 10% high emitters live in OECD countries; around a third are from the U.S. The per capita consumption emissions of the richest 10% of

[7] In comparison between people and between countries, it is more appropriate to focus on the emissions generated by consumption than by production because richer consumers in richer countries are more able 'off-shore' emissions associated with manufactures to producers in other countries and import the finished goods.

Chinese citizens are considerably lower than the richest of their OECD counterparts (Oxfam, 2015).

Harvey (2021) notes that the data produced by Oxfam suggest that the more unequal the society, the larger the per capita emissions of the top 10%. For instance, the USA is more unequal than the UK, France and Germany; and the UK is more unequal than France and Germany. In the USA the consumption of the top 10% generated 50 tonnes of CO2 emissions per capita per year. The UK's top 10% consumers generated less than half that of the top 10% in the USA per capita, at 24 tonnes, with Germany at 14 and France at 13 tonnes CO2 per capita per year.

The inequalities in emissions generated by unequal purchasing power are not simply determined by consumer choices, but are inscribed in the unequal ownership and control of productive resources, and the decisions of governments about what kinds of energy, transport, housing, and food production to support (Harvey, 2021). For instance, Oxfam (2015) draws attention to the 'carbon baron billionaires', the CEOs of multinational fossil fuel companies, whose lobbying has secured subsidies and tax breaks that are much larger than support to the renewables sector. The climate emergency does require that fossil fuel be left in the ground, but the geographical distribution of reserves is very unequal: "...for the world to meet the current IPCC global warming targets, the United States and the Former Soviet Union would each be required to leave well over 200 billion tonnes of coal underground, with China and India locking-down over 100 billion tonnes each. Given their coal dependence, China and India face a starkly unequal loss of potential wealth and energy compared with other nations" (Harvey, 2021, p. 163).

Sustainable consumption and production will not be achieved unless these kinds of resource inequalities between countries are more effectively addressed.

Inequality in income and wealth does not only structure consumption and production, it also shapes the politics of change. UNCTAD (2019) has pointed to the links between political trust, inequality and ability to address the climate emergency, arguing that even after the global financial crisis, the rules of the game that had generated high levels of inequality, insecurity and indebtedness prior to that crisis have remained largely intact, further eroding trust and often directing blame to 'outsiders' of various kinds. "This breakdown in trust has occurred at the very moment the collective actions needed to build a better future for all depend on a greater sense of shared responsibility and solidarity" (p. iv).

UNCTAD (2019) called for a Global Green New Deal that would mobilise public investment and industrial policies to establish low-carbon growth paths, as well as addressing problems of pollution and environmental degradation more generally. This would incorporate substantial international transfers of finance and technology to address inequalities between countries. It is argued that this would also reduce inequality within countries by creating millions of new skilled jobs in both developed and developing countries. However, job creation does not directly address inequalities of gender and race, as given the current patterns of occupational segregation, most of those jobs would probably go to men of the dominant ethnic group, unless special measures are taken to recruit more women and men from marginalised ethnic groups. Nor does it directly ensure that the rich do not benefit more than the poor.

A group advocating a Green New Deal for the UK was formed as early as 2007 (Pettifor, 2020) and the idea has been adopted by a wide range of think tanks, NGOs and political parties. The core idea is a public investment to tackle climate change and create thousands of new 'decent jobs' in 'clean' energy and transport and housing (see for example New Economics Foundation, 2019). Some versions focus mainly on the UK and do not address the issue of how we can decarbonise our consumption without assisting in the decarbonising of the economies from which we import manufactures, food and raw materials, many of which have a lower GDP per capita than the UK. However, Ann Pettifor, a founding member of the UK Green New Deal Group, argues that this group always had an internationalist perspective and called for the UK government to help build a different international economic system to support sustainability, especially focusing on international finance. Pettifor (2020, p. 13) contrasts this with the later, and perhaps better known, American Green New Deal, which is primarily focused on the US economy (Pettifor, 2020, p. 13). However, the American Green New

Deal has more focus on the reduction of inequalities within the USA than the UK Green New Deal has on inequalities within UK (Pettifor, op. cit., p. 19).

6 The Impact of Covid-19 on Inequalities

There is widespread agreement that the impact of Covid-19 on health throughout the world has been worse for poorer people than for the rich. The IMF Fiscal Monitor reports that cross-country analysis shows that both infection and death rates are higher, the higher the share of the population living below 50% of a country's median income (IMF, 2021). Minority groups have been experiencing even worse health outcomes than predicted on the basis of income alone, reflecting inequities in access to basic services and in the labour market. For instance, Sze et al. (2020) find a higher risk of COVID-19 infection for Black and Asian people than for White people in USA and UK. Oxfam (2021) reports that in Brazil, people of Afro-descent have been 40% more likely to die of COVID-19 than White people.

Women are particularly at risk through their employment in health care: more than three-quarters of the world's medical doctors and nursing personnel combined are women (Boniol et al., 2019). But they also have a substantial presence in sectors that have been closed by Covid-19 related lockdowns. Losses in working hours are estimated at an average of 8.8% in 2020 relative to the fourth quarter of 2019 (ILO, 2021). This far exceeds the impact of the global financial crisis of 2009. Global labour income (before taking into account income support measures) in 2020 is estimated by the ILO to have declined by 8.3%, which amounts to US$3.7 trillion, or 4.4% of global gross domestic product (GDP). However, while there have been massive job losses in hard-hit sectors (such as accommodation and food services, arts and culture, retail, and construction), there has been a growth in jobs in a number of higher-skilled services sectors (such as information and communication, and financial and insurance activities). This divergence will tend to increase inequality within countries (ILO, 2021).

Research by Oxfam (2021) suggests that, while both men and women have been doing more unpaid care work especially because of the Covid-19 related closures of schools and nurseries, women continue to do the most; and have experienced increased mental and physical illness because of this increased workload.

Comprehensive data on the impact of Covid-19 on personal income and wealth inequalities is not yet available, but it is clear that there have been Covid-19 related increases in inequalities in income and wealth. For instance, Oxfam (2021) notes that while over two million people have died, and hundreds of millions of people are being forced into poverty, many of the richest individuals and corporations are thriving. The fortunes of the top-thousand billionaires, mainly white men, returned to their pre-pandemic highs in just nine months, as after an initial fall, stock markets have been booming, supported by QE policies of leading central banks. However, 103 countries went into the pandemic with at least one in three of their workforce lacking labour rights and protections such as sick pay.

The response to the pandemic has drawn on similar forms of resilience as the response to the 2009 financial crisis: both regressive forms of resilience such as that provided by QE and an expansion of unpaid work; and progressive forms of resilience, notably the introduction of cash transfers and loans in many countries to support businesses and workers through the lockdown. However, the scope of the latter has been limited in many countries by the amount of fiscal space available, and they have not been as effective in supporting the self-employed as employees (ILO, 2021). Whereas rich countries have been able to borrow unlimited amounts in their own currencies at very low rates of interest, the same is not true for low and middle-income countries. As the United Nations Special Rapporteur on extreme poverty has noted, Covid-19 has revealed "a world where poverty, extreme inequality and disregard for human life are thriving, and in which legal and economic policies are designed to create and sustain wealth for the powerful" (Alston, 2020, p. 2).

The relation between Covid-19 and inequalities in the UK is consistent with the global picture. The health impacts of Covid-19 have correlated with pre-existing inequalities, with particularly negative outcomes for those already disadvantaged. In spring 2020, age-adjusted Covid-19 death rates in the most deprived tenth of areas in the UK were more than double those in the least deprived areas. People in the bottom three deciles of the income distribution were 50% more likely to have a pre-existing illness that put them at heightened risk than people in the top two deciles (Blundell et al., 2020). There have also been much larger health impacts on minority ethnic groups relative to White people, which cannot be reduced to differences in age and location (Blundell et al., op. cit.). These are related both to prevalence of under-lying ill health conditions and to occupational exposure (Platt & Warwick, 2020). The social determinants of health inequalities in the experience of Covid-19 are also examined by Marmot, Allen, Goldblatt et al. (2020), who conclude that "It is structural racism that means minority ethnic groups suffer from disadvantage in each of the social determinants highlighted" (p. 7). There is also evidence that much of the Black and Minority Ethnic workforce in highly exposed occupations were not sufficiently protected with PPE and safety measures (Marmot et al., op. cit. p. 14).

People designated as 'Key Workers' (including not only health and social care workers but also workers in a number of other sectors such as public transport and food retail, wholesale and processing) were particularly exposed to infection and death rates in these occupations were higher than among the general population (Blundell et al., 2020). Key workers were disproportionately women and members of ethnic minorities.

Large sectors of the economy were shut down, with a bigger impact on poor people than on rich people. Excluding key workers, 80% of people in the bottom tenth of the earnings distribution had jobs in shut down sectors or were unlikely to be able to work from home, compared to only 25% of the highest earning tenth (Blundell et al., 2020). The ability to work in a safe environment by working from home was much higher for high earners than for low earners.

Those who could not earn money because of lock down were supported by special schemes. Almost one-quarter (24.2%) of self-employed people had received support from the Self-Employment Income Support Scheme (SEISS) in the period up to October 2020. In comparison, 17.6% of employees were receiving or had at some point received support from the Coronavirus Job Retention Scheme (CJRS) (ONS, 2021). The self-employed accessing the SEISS were more likely to report reduced income compared with those on the CJRS. SEISS payments were based on a proportion of average historical trading profit, while employers could choose to 'top-up' wages above the government's contribution. However, they were more likely to do this for high earners. People who were in the bottom quintile of the income distribution (as measured by their income in the same period of the previous year), were much more likely to be paid in part (60.9%) than in full (27.8%), while over half (52%) of people in the top quintile of the income distribution were paid in full (ONS, 2021). Nevertheless, the support measures seem to have ensured that the hit to household incomes taking into account benefits was similar across the income distribution (Handscomb & Judge, 2020).

However, other dimensions of inequalities increased. Women were called upon to increase their unpaid work caring for others, as schools shut down, and risk of infections lead to reluctance to send small children to nurseries and frail elderly relatives to care homes. A study of heterosexual couples with school-age children found that both mothers and fathers had substantially increased the time they spent on unpaid care, but more was being done by mothers, even if they had a paid job. Moreover, mothers were more likely to have lost their jobs (either temporarily or permanently) than fathers, with women with the lowest levels of education at the most disadvantage (Andrew et al., 2020). After the onset of Covid-19 numbers of unpaid carers for adults increased in 2020 by 4.5 million to over 13.6 million, nearly 58% of them women, nearly 3 million of whom combine paid work with care. A survey of almost 5900 carers in October 2020 found nearly two thirds had no respite from their caring responsibilities; three quarters reported feeling exhausted and worn out; two thirds said that their mental health has worsened. 11% of carers reported they had reduced their hours of paid work to manage their caring responsibilities, and 9% had given up paid work because of caring (Carers UK, 2020). These increases in the unpaid care contributed by women mean that progress on reducing gender inequality in incomes has been put at risk.

There was a marked divergence between different income groups with respect to wealth. In 2020 many lower-income people had to borrow more money than usual and were unable to save (ONS, 2021). However, household savings increased overall, as the lockdown restricted consumption opportunities. The accumulation of savings was greatest for high-income households: 42% of high-income employed households saved more during the pandemic, compared with 22% of low-income employed households. About 70% of those who saved more planned to continue to hold the savings in their bank accounts. Others planned to use their savings to pay off debts, invest, or top up their pensions (Bank of England, 2020).

Home-owners benefited from a surge in house prices in 2020, encouraged by reductions in taxes on property sales. They also benefited from mortgage payment holidays and a ban on repossessions. However, many tenants in the private and social rented sector have struggled to keep up rent payments and have fallen into arrears. Unpaid arrears remain liabilities of tenants, even if they get evicted (Macfarlane & Berry, 2020). Owners of financial assets benefited from increases in value of shares boosted by QE.

The power of many large companies, especially those operating online and delivering to homes, increased. A notable example is Amazon whose UK sales rose 51% to almost £20 billion. UK online fashion retailers have also benefited: ASOS saw profits soar from £25 million in 2019 to £113 million in 2020, and Boohoo saw profits increase from £47.5 million to £72.8 million. All three companies have been widely criticised for exploitative employment practices, so the jobs they create are unlikely to combat widening inequality. There were outbreaks of Covid-19 in summer 2020 in Leicester garment factories that supply Boohoo and claims that pressure to produce fast and cheap led to failure to maintain a Covid-19 secure working environment (Macfarlane & Berry, 2020).

Other companies benefited from a rapid increase in Covid-19 related public sector outsourcing, mostly awarded without an open competitive public tender, as the standard rules were suspended, often to companies with no track record in producing the required goods and services. An investigation by an international anti-corruption NGO found that 27 contracts worth £2.1 billion for Protective Personal Equipment and Coronavirus testing were awarded to firms with political connections to the governing Conservative Party (Transparency International, 2021). There has been much criticism of the effectiveness of delivery by outsourced suppliers (British Medical Association, 2020). For instance, the parliamentary all-party public accounts committee found that the £37 billion test and trace programme (costing three times as much as the high performing NHS vaccination programme) could not point to a measurable difference it had made to the progress of the pandemic (Rawnsley, 2021).

Some large companies have taken advantage of the disruption caused by the pandemic to slash the pay and conditions of workers using so-called 'fire-and rehire' tactics. The TUC found that nearly 1 in 10 workers in Britain have been told to re-apply for their jobs on worse terms and conditions since the first lockdown in March 2020. Minority ethnic and young workers were particularly affected (TUC, 2021). An investigation published by *The Observer* found that some companies using these tactics were at the same time raising executive pay and claiming support from the furlough scheme (Wall, 2021).

7 Towards Greater Equality

There is widespread agreement that without effective responses the post-Covid-19 world could see inequalities worsening further (IMF, 2021). However, the disruptions caused by Covid-19 may create opportunities to build support for action by governments to reduce inequality, as seems to be happening in the USA where the President Biden administration has been putting forward bold new policies that are being compared to Roosevelt's New Deal. They include not only investment in physical infrastructure but also new income transfers, higher taxes on corporations and rich people, support for workers' rights and wages, and investment in health and care services.

In the UK the government produced a plan to Build Back Better (Treasury, 2021) that emphasised reducing geographical inequalities in England, primarily through 'levelling up' via special funds for investment in new physical infrastructure in low productivity towns and cities, plus some additional funding for skills development. This was supposed to increase productivity, and it was assumed that this would improve living standards. It was reported that the criteria for allocating the new funding did not include the index of multiple deprivation, and the funding was distributed disproportionately to towns that had Conservative Party MPs (The Observer, 2021). The plan was supported by substantial tax breaks for corporations but funding for local public services was projected to continue to fall in the 2021 UK budget (Johnson, 2021).

Much of the discussion among researchers about how to create a more equal economy has focused on redistribution of income and wealth through taxes and benefits. However, more recently there has also been a focus on 'predistribution'. For instance, researchers at the World Inequality Lab (including Piketty) argue that "public policies can also affect the pre-tax distribution of income (what we will call 'predistribution')" (Bozio et al., 2020, p. 1). They point to the education system (particularly the inequality in education spending across social groups), labour market regulations (e.g., the level of the minimum wage and the various legal rules affecting the role of unions and the bargaining power of workers), and other policies affecting the distribution of primary assets and capabilities (including the health care system, the inequality of wealth and inheritance, etc.) (Bozio et al., 2020). However, they do not maintain a clear distinction between pre-distribution and redistribution, because "The tax system has also an influence on pre-tax income: first, because taxes are needed to pay for publicly funded education and other public policies, second because taxation can lead to behavioral responses affecting labor and capital income, and third because progressive taxation of income and wealth can also affect the formation of top end compensation packages and wealth inequality" (Bozio et al., 2020, p. 33). Their empirical research found that both changes in pre-tax inequality and redistribution have had a significant impact on the historical reduction of inequality in France and the USA, but the former is quantitatively about three times as large as the latter. However, it is not clear how to interpret 'pre-tax inequality', given the claim that the tax system has an impact on pre-tax income.

IMF researchers have also distinguished between predistributive and redistributive policies but assume that predistributive policies reduce market income inequality (before taxes and transfers), whereas Bozio et al. (2020) leave open the possibility that they may increase inequality. The IMF (2021) points to policies to enhance opportunities and increase human capital before individuals enter the labour market; and policies to support participation in labour markets. IMF (op. cit.) categorises public spending in health and education as 'predistributive', but unlike Bozio et al. (2020) do not specifically recognise that taxation is required to fund this and therefore has an impact on 'pre-tax income'. Moreover, rather than referring to labour market regulations and the way they shape the bargaining power of labour, the IMF report refers to the need for investment in active labour market policies—vocational training, job search assistance, wage subsidies, or public work programmes. The IMF researchers do identify reducing gender gaps in labour markets as an important 'predistributive policy', through making childcare more widely available and affordable, increasing the transparency of pay, decreasing gender gaps in salaries, and providing more parental leave. However, there is no reference to feminist critiques of the terms on which most women are 'included' in growth which lead to a very unequal distribution of the fruits of their labours between them and those who employ or subcontract them (Elson & Seth, 2019).

The perception that inequality is shaped by policies other than tax and transfers is important, but neither the World Inequality Lab nor the IMF include as part of 'predistribution' the laws and systems that underpin corporate power, though these are surely critical. UNCTAD does not use the term 'predistribution', but it does argue in the 2020 Trade and Development Report that the lack of appropriate regulation of corporate power is a key determinant of inequalities. "Increase in market concentration, proliferation of anti-competitive practices, abuse of dominant market position, and corporate tax avoidance and evasion have become ubiquitous features of today's rentier economy, made possible by deregulations and absence of appropriate state actions. This has become widespread in both financial and non-financial sectors but has so far reached a pinnacle in the digital economy by platform monopolies that have further strengthened their positions since Covid-19. Accordingly, the power of corporations to influence and rig the rules of the game, not only on the national, but also on the international level, has increased" (UNCTAD, 2020, p. 129).

The increase in corporate power also enables CEOs and other senior executives to extract very high pay (salaries plus bonuses). Shareholders must approve these pay deals, but in the UK only a minority of shareholders are willing to vote against them (The Observer, 16. May 2021, p. 56).

UNCTAD (2020) also points to the ways in which the bargaining power of workers has been reduced and calls for raising minimum wages, and strengthening collective bargaining institutions while suggesting some degree of international coordination will be critical to induce all countries to adopt the necessary policies.

I suggest that a clearer and more telling definition of pre-distribution is in terms of the structure of rights: on the one hand commercial rights-regimes governing property, company, and contracts; on the other hand rights set out in the International Covenant on Economic, Social and Cultural Rights (the right to work and just and favourable conditions of work, the right to an adequate standard of living, the right to social security, the right to education, the right to the highest attainable standard of health). The system of commercial rights is very strong; the fulfilment of economic, social rights is very weak. Commercial rights are disproportionately in the hands of elite men, with the majority of women and minority ethnic groups excluded from ownership of large businesses. The upholding of current systems of commercial rights is often at odds with the fulfilment of economic, social and cultural rights, on which women and minority ethnic groups are more reliant for their wellbeing. This imbalance underpins the growth of inequality and must be redressed if we are to create more equal societies. As IFS researchers recognise, "The post pandemic world could provide an opportunity to rethink competition policy and re-examine the balance of power between firms and workers in wage setting" (Blundell et al., 2020, p. 23). This would not only address class inequalities but also gender and race inequalities. For an equitable, resilient and sustainable recovery, the incomes, wealth and power of rich people and corporations need reducing.

UNCTAD (2020) notes that anti-trust measures are now very much on the agenda at the national and regional levels. It calls for existing multilateral agreements, such as the UN's Equitable Principles and Rules for the Control of Restrictive Business Practices, adopted by the General Assembly in 1980 to be strengthened and operationalised with new institutional support such as a global competition authority. It argues that urgent action is required to address "the price gauging, patent abuse and other anti-competitive practices of pharmaceutical giants and digital platforms" (p. xi), to ensure the recovery is both fair and resilient.

Competition policy in UK should be reformed. The remit of the Competition and Markets Authority (created in 2013) is narrow, concerning only price, quality and choice for consumers and not the wider public interest. Between 2012 and 2014 it issued fines worth only £65 million (in 2015 prices) compared to the fines of almost £1.4 billion issued by the equivalent body in Germany (IPPR Commission on Economic Justice, 2018). Attention should be focused on limiting market share and reviving tools previously used to reign in excessive market power, such as prohibition of price discrimination and of vertical integration. Corporate takeover rules in the UK have meant that takeovers are more common in the UK, more likely to be hostile, and more likely to be successful than in other advanced economies. The rules need to be changed so that government can block takeovers that may be in the short-term interests of shareholders but are against the long-term public interest (IPPR Commission on Economic Justice, 2018). Proposals for a fair and comprehensive competition law that limits unfair mergers, enforce accountability and redistributes power through stakeholder governance are set out by Meagher (2020).

Weak corporate governance has led to soaring executive pay. In response, pay ratio disclosures have been mandatory in annual reports of companies listed on the London stock exchange since 2020, and the High Pay Centre (2021) has called upon the biggest institutional investors to use this information to vote against disproportionate pay awards for executives in future. However, companies have proved reluctant to do this; and it is clear that changes are needed in the governance of companies, including reform of the Companies Act to end the primacy of shareholders' interests, ensure representation of workers on boards, and oblige companies to take into account not only the interests of shareholders but also workers, consumers, wider society and the environment. One suggestion is that 45% of a company board should be elected by the workforce, 45% by the shareholder body, with the remainder representing social and environmental interests and mandatory profit-sharing for workers in companies above 50 employees as in France (Lawrence et al., April 2020.) The TUC has called for company law to require that worker directors comprise one third of the board in companies with 250 or more staff (TUC, 2020).

In addition, researchers at the High Pay Centre suggest establishing sectoral governance bodies to monitor fair pay, made up of stakeholders including representatives from business, unions, workers and government in a similar fashion to the Wages Councils, which were in place in the UK until the 1990s. Their remit could include setting guidelines for minimum wages and pay ratio limits across the sector, using pay ratio disclosures to inform recommendations (Kay & Hilyard, 2020).

Limiting the pay of CEOs and other executives could free up resources to protect at-risk jobs or raise the pay of the low wage workers (High Pay Centre, 2021). The think tank Autonomy has argued for a 'maximum wage' with incomes capped in the low hundreds of thousands. A maximum wage of £100,000 could increase the annual median wage by £3,535 and this cap would only affect 2.85% of earners in the UK (Autonomy/High Pay Centre, 2020).

These measures to limit profits and pay should be complemented by more effective taxation of profits, wealth and high incomes. Such taxes have been reduced across the world and this has been supported with arguments that this will benefit the rest of the population by stimulating economic growth and employment. However, Hope and Limberg (2020) find that while reducing taxes on the rich has led to higher income inequality as measured by the top 1% share of pre-tax national income, such reductions have not served to boost economic growth and reduce unemployment.

Corporation tax rates have fallen substantially across the world. In 1980, OECD statutory corporate rates were rarely less than 45% but by 2020 this had fallen to 23.3% (US Department of the Treasury, 2021, p. 11). In addition, multinational corporations are able to shift profits and hide income offshore in tax havens. As UNCTAD (2020) emphasises more effective multilateral cooperation is required. A lead on this has been given by US President Biden, who has proposed raising the US corporate income tax rate from 21% to 28%; and encouraging global adoption of a minimum rate of corporation tax (US Department of the Treasury, 2021).

Reforms are also needed to end the unfairness by which personal income from wealth—for instance, in the form of dividends and capital gains—is taxed more lightly than income from work. In the UK the highest capital gains tax rate was 40% between 1988 and 2008 but by early 2021 this had been substantially reduced, with capital gains on most assets taxed at 10% for basic rate taxpayers, and 20% for higher and additional rate taxpayers; and capital gains on residential property taxed at 18 and 28% respectively. The returns to owners of these assets are 'economic rents' rather than returns for taking risks. To reduce inequality, capital gains should instead be taxed under the income tax schedule—in early 2021 this was 20% for basic rate taxpayers, 40% for higher rate taxpayers, and 45% for additional rate taxpayers (Nanda & Parks, 2019). Reforms to other wealth taxes are proposed by Roberts et al. (2018) including abolition of inheritance tax and introduction of a lifetime gift tax paid by recipients of gifts; abolition of council tax and introduction of a property tax which is proportional to the contemporary value of homes; and a land value tax to replace business rates. Wealth is disproportionately owned by white men, so these proposals would reduce gender and racial inequality in the enjoyment of wealth (Palmer, 2020).

The combination of these measures to restructure commercial property rights and tax profits and high incomes more effectively, would reduce inequalities in income and wealth, and help to change patterns of production and consumption to make them more sustainable. Changes to corporate governance could support more effective regulation of production to end fossil fuel production. The demand for private jets, luxury yachts, large 'gas-guzzling' cars, and large houses with high energy costs would decline, and revenue would be available to support public investment in green public transport, and affordable energy-efficient housing.

Measures to limit the power and incomes of large corporations, and those who run them, as well as hold shares in them, must be complemented by measures to strengthen labour rights. All workers should be able to access the support of a union and speak with co-workers through a union to negotiate with their employer. The TUC (2020) has called for unions to have access to workplaces to tell workers about the benefits of union membership and collective bargaining (following the system in place in New Zealand); new rights to make it easier for working people to negotiate collectively with their employer; a broadening of the scope of collective bargaining rights to include all pay and conditions; reform of the Central Arbitration Committee (CAC) that adjudicates on union recognition requests, requiring it to take account of the benefits of collective bargaining in its decisions; the establishment of new bodies for unions and employers to negotiate across sectors, starting with hospitality and social care; the abolition of the Trade Union Act of 2016 and unions to be permitted to use electronic balloting in votes including all internal elections and votes on industrial action. A new law protecting union rights is part of the American Jobs Plan put forward in early 2021 by President Joe Biden in the USA, who began his launch speech with the words: "I am a union guy. I support unions" (Sainato, 2021).

Enhanced rights are also needed to combat precarious work. Prior to Covid-19, 3.7 million people were in insecure work, one in nine of the workforce, including 20% of those classed as occupying elementary roles, including kitchen assistants, security guards and farm workers; 17% of those in caring and leisure roles, and 19% of those working in skilled trades. Black workers, women and disabled workers were all disproportionately represented in insecure work (TUC, 2020). Their rights could be strengthened by measures including a ban on zero-hours contracts and bogus self-employment; the return of protection against unfair dismissal to millions of working people; robust rules on notice of shifts and compensation for cancelled shifts, a statutory presumption that workers are employed (to combat bogus self-employment) and penalties for misleading workers on their employment status (TUC, 2020). The question of employment status is vital to the millions who work in the growing 'gig' economy operated by owners of digital platforms that claim to be simply connecting customers to 'self-employed' workers. Some of those workers are getting unionised and, in the case of Uber drivers, have succeeded in obtaining a court order that they are workers with rights to a minimum hourly wage and holiday pay. However, there is still a dispute about how working hours are to be counted: Uber is insisting that only time actually spent driving a passenger should be counted, not the hours from clocking on for work (via the Uber app) to clocking off (The Observer, 21 March 2021).

Workers are diverse, and specific rights are needed to address gender and race inequalities. Equal Pay legislation is necessary but not sufficient. UK-wide gender pay gap reporting was instituted into law in 2017 for British private sector employers with at least 250 employees. The legislation was weak compared to many other EU countries, which have thresholds lower than 250, and require more detailed data and a corrective action plan (Fawcett Society et al., 2020). The government decided to suspend the requirement for businesses to report in 2020, citing the coronavirus crisis. UK gender pay gap reporting needs to be reinstated and strengthened; and ethnicity pay gap reporting needs to be introduced on the same basis. In addition, laws are needed to strengthen the rights of workers with caring responsibilities, who are disproportionately women. These should be designed to support the more equal sharing of unpaid care and domestic work between women and men: equal legal entitlements to paid caring leave for all employees and self-employed people (male and female), including equal sharing of parental leave in the first year of a child's life, and leave for caring for elderly/disabled people and older children when required.

As well as new laws, stronger rights for workers can be supported by ensuring state support for businesses, including through procurement contracts, is made conditional on upholding these rights. However, stronger rights to and at work though necessary are insufficient for creating an equitable economy because workers are always at risk from unemployment due to ill-health and lack of jobs; participation in paid work varies over the lifecycle; and people enter the labour market with different capacities, due to inequalities in educational achievement and health status, mainly linked to the income and wealth of their parents (UNDP, 2019). Stronger rights to and at work must be buttressed by stronger rights to social security, health, education and an adequate standard of living (including housing and food). These rights are best fulfilled through public provision, since individual purchase in the market is an ineffective way of accessing services that have large externalities, as these will be undersupplied and unaffordable to the majority. However, higher public expenditure, though necessary, is not sufficient. The ways in which public money is used is critical. Social security and public services must be organised on the basis that people have a right to good quality provision caringly delivered in ways that are consistent with human dignity and are responsive to people's needs. This means that cost minimisation is not an appropriate goal, as this so often results in poor quality services that do not meet these criteria. Instead the focus should be on fulfilling the rights of both recipients and providers of services (Balakrishnan et al., 2016).

Outsourcing of the delivery of public services must be comprehensively rethought. The TUC (2020) calls for all service provision to be brought 'in-house' and only outsourced where there is a strong public interest for doing so, with existing contracts renegotiated or terminated where this is demonstrably in the public interest. Others argue that there is a role for some outsourcing to cooperatives, community businesses and social enterprises; and for a system of social licensing, which would supersede the weak rules currently governing social value in procurement, giving companies or sectors the right to trade in public sector markets only if they accept reciprocal obligations to offer social returns, such as being a living wage employer that offers decent progression and training routes for its staff (Lloyd Goodwin et al., 2020).

An overarching vision of how to rebalance rights and change priorities to achieve greater equality in income and wealth and wellbeing in a sustainable economy has been set out by recent Commission on a Gender Equal Economy (Women's Budget Group Commission on Gender Equal Economy, 2020). This calls for the creation of a caring economy, which prioritises care of one another and the environment. Care, rather than financial targets, takes priority for all businesses, large or small, owned by shareholders, employees or members of cooperatives, for all levels of government (local, regional, national) and all kinds of public agencies; for all non-governmental organisations and community groups, and for all families, neighbours and friends. In a caring economy, there is substantial equality in care, as everyone gives and receives care on the basis of their capacities and needs, supported by well-resourced high-quality public care services, and time off from paid work, including a shorter working week.

Good-quality care services, such as adult social care, healthcare, and childcare are critical for a caring economy. But a caring economy extends beyond provision of care services. It means caring about the pay and conditions of workers, especially the low paid, and acting together to ensure that all workers have decent work. It means caring about deprivation and poverty and acting together to bring them to an end. It means caring about tackling domestic violence and sexist and racist abuse, supporting those who have been subjected to it, and acting together to eliminate it. It means caring about our planet and acting together to ensure we do not pollute and degrade our air, water and soil. It means acting together to improve wellbeing rather than to maximise economic growth.[8]

The Covid-19 pandemic has given us some glimpses of what a caring economy might look like, in the ways that neighbourhood groups sprang up in many places to support people especially vulnerable to the virus, and in the way air pollution levels drastically fell in some locked down cities. But it has also showed us the many ways in which we have an uncaring economy, such as the lack of personal protection equipment for health and social care workers, the lack of adequate financial support for those asked to quarantine, the low pay and poor conditions for so many key workers, many of whom are from migrant and ethnic minority communities, and the ways in which mothers, more than fathers, have been expected to take on most of the home-schooling and extra child care, when schools are closed in lockdowns, with detrimental impacts on their own wellbeing.

Substantial public investment in child and adult care services, to extend and insource provision, and improve quality of services for recipients and pay, conditions and training could make a major contribution to the creation of a more equitable economy in the UK and to post Covid-19 recovery. Empirical research on UK, USA and selected European Union countries has found that a care-led, rather than construction-led,

[8] A similar vision is put forward by Marmot, Allen, Goldblatt et al. (2020).

recovery programme creates more jobs and reduces gender inequality in employment (largely because the care sector employs mainly women and the construction sector mainly men). More jobs would be created even when employment conditions for care workers are improved, improving gender inequality in wages (De Henau & Himmelweit, 2021). As well as reducing gender inequality in the economy this investment in the UK would also reduce inequality based on class, race and migration status, as the workforce is also disproportionately low wage, and from Black and Minority Ethnic groups and recent migrants. In addition, a more caring economy, employing more people in care jobs, is also a greener economy, since the production of care services generates lower emissions than most sectors (De Henau & Himmelweit, 2020). Creation of public universal child and adult care services, with strong rights for workers and for those who need care, and strong regulatory frameworks, should accompany any investment in a Green New Deal. However, currently the plans of the UK government to reduce inequalities in a post-Covid-19 economy include neither a Green New Deal nor a Care New Deal.

8 Summary and Conclusions

This chapter has reviewed evidence on inequalities in UK and other countries and concluded that for an equitable, resilient and sustainable recovery, the incomes, wealth and power of rich people and corporations need reducing. It focuses the attention on two contrasting structures of rights: on the one hand commercial rights-regimes governing property, company, and contracts; on the other hand rights set out in the International Covenant on Economic, Social and Cultural Rights (the right to work and just and favourable conditions of work, the right to an adequate standard of living, the right to social security, the right to education, the right to the highest attainable standard of health). The system of commercial rights is very strong; the fulfilment of economic, social rights is very weak. Commercial rights are disproportionately in the hands of elite men; and current systems of commercial rights are at odds with the fulfilment of the economic and social rights, on which women and minority ethnic groups and poor people are more reliant for their wellbeing. This imbalance underpins the growth of inequality and must be redressed if we are to create more equal and more sustainable economies. Necessary legal changes are identified, together with transformation of social security and public services. This can be given substance through action to create a caring economy, aimed at improvements in wellbeing rather than economic growth.

References

Albelda, R., & Tilly, C. (1999). Income distribution. In J. Peterson & M. Lewis (Eds.), *Elgar companion to feminist economics.* Edward Elgar.

Alston, P. (2020, July 11). Covid-19 has revealed a pre-existing pandemic of poverty that benefits the rich. *The Guardian.* https://www.theguardian.com/global-development/2020/jul/11/covid-19-has-revealed-a-pre-existing-pandemic-of-poverty-that-benefits-the-rich.

Andrew, A., Bandiera, O., Costa Dias, M., & Landais. C. (2020). *The careers and time use of mothers and fathers.* Institute for Fiscal Studies.

Autonomy/High Pay Centre. (2020). *Paying for Covid: Capping excessive salaries to save industries.* Available at: https://autonomy.work/wpcontent/uploads/2020/10/2020OCT_SalaryCap_Ameneded.pdf.

Balakrishnan, R., Heintz, J., & Elson, D. (2016). *Rethinking economic policy for social justice: The radical potential of human rights.* Routledge.

Bank of England. (2020). *How has Covid affected household savings?* Available at: https://www.bankofengland.co.uk/bank-overground/2020/how-has-covid-affected-household-savings#:~:text=The%20accumulation%20of%20savings%20was,them%20had%20increased%20their%20savings.

Banks, N. (2021). Intersectional identities and analysis. In G. Berik & E. Kongar (Eds.), *The Routledge handbook of feminist economics.* Routledge.

Blundell, R., Costa Dias, M., Joyce, R., & Xu, X. (2020). *Covid-19 and inequalities.* Institute for Fiscal Studies.

Boniol, M., McIsaac, M., Xu, L., Wuliji, T., Diallo, K., & Campbell, J. (2019). *Gender equity in the health workforce: Analysis of 104 countries* (Working Paper 1). World Health Organization.

Bozio, A., Garbinti, B., Goupille-Lebret, J., Guillot, M., & Piketty, T. (2020). *Predistribution vs. redistribution: Evidence from France and the U.S.* (World Inequality Lab—Working Paper N° 2020/22). Available at: https://wid.world/document/predistribution-vs-redistribution-evidence-from-france-and-the-u-s/.

British Medical Association. (2020). *The role of private outsourcing in the Covid-19 response*. Available at: https://www.bma.org.uk/media/2885/the-role-of-private-outsourcing-in-the-covid-19-response.pdf.

Carers UK. (2020). *Caring behind closed door*. Available at: http://www.carersuk.org.

Costa Dias, M., Joyce, R., & Parodi, F. (2018). *Wage progression and the gender wage gap: The causal impact of hours of work* (IFS Briefing Note 223). Available at: https://www.ifs.org.uk/publications/10358.

Dabla-Norris, E., Kochhar, K., Ricka, F., Suphaphiphat, N., & Tsounta, E. (2015). *Causes and consequences of income inequality: A global perspective* (IMF Staff Discussion Note). Available at: https://www.imf.org/external/pubs/ft/sdn/2015/sdn1513.pdf.

Doss, C. (2021). Intrahousehold decision-making and resource allocation. In G. Berik & E. Kongar (Eds.), *The Routledge handbook of feminist economics*. Routledge.

D'Arcy, C., & Gardiner, L. (2017). *The generation of wealth. Asset accumulation within* and *across cohorts*. Intergenerational Commission. Resolution Foundation. Available at: https://www.resolutionfoundation.org/publications/the-generation-of-wealth-asset-accumulation-across-and-within-cohorts/.

De Henau, J., & Himmelweit, S. (2020). *A care-led recovery from Coronavirus*. Available at: https://wbg.org.uk/wp-content/uploads/2020/06/Care-led-recovery-final.pdf.

De Henau, J., & Himmelweit, S. (2021). A care-led recovery from Covid-19: Investing in high quality care to stimulate and rebalance the economy. *Feminist Economics, 27*(1–2), 453–469.

Diez, F., Leigh, D., & Tambunlertchai, S. (2018). *Global market power and its macroeconomic implications* (IMF Working Paper 18/3). Available at: https://www.imf.org/en/Publications/WP/Issues/2018/06/15/Global-Market-Power-and-its-Macroeconomic-Implications-45975.

Elson, D. (2018). Intersections of gender and class in the distribution of income. *The Japanese Political Economy, 44*, 7–24.

Elson, D. (1995). *Male bias in the development process* (2nd ed.). Manchester University Press.

Elson, D. (2012). Social reproduction in the global crisis: Rapid recovery or long-lasting depletion? In P. Utting, S. Razavi, & R. Buchholz (Eds.), *The global crisis and transformative social change*. Palgrave Macmillan.

Elson, D., & Seth, A. (Eds.). (2019). *Gender equality and inclusive growth*. UN Women.

European Central Bank. (2016). *Annual report*. Available at: https://www.ecb.europa.eu/pub/pdf/annrep/ar2016en.pdf.

Evgenidis, A., & Fasiano, A. (2021). Unconventional monetary policy and wealth inequalities in Great Britain. *Oxford Bulletin of Economics and Statistics* 83(1:1), 15–175.

Fawcett Society and Global Institute for Women's Leadership, Kings College. (2020). *Gender pay gap reporting: A comparative analysis*. Available at: https://www.kcl.ac.uk/giwl/assets/gender-pay-gap-reporting-a-comparative-analysis.pdf.

Folbre, N. (2021). Conceptualising patriarchal systems. In G. Berik & E. Kongar (Eds.), *The Routledge handbook of feminist economics*. Routledge.

Fredman, S. (2016). Substantive equality revisited. *International Journal of Constitutional Law, 14*(3), 712–738.

Guschanski, A., & Onaran, Ö. (2017). *The political economy of income distribution: Industry level evidence from 14 OECD countries* (Greenwich Papers in Political Economy, University of Greenwich, #GPERC51).

Handscomb, K., & Judge, L. (2020). Caught in a (Covid) trap. Incomes, savings and spending through the coronavirus crisis. Resolution Foundation Briefing. Resolution Foundation.

Harvey, M. (2021). *Climate emergency: How societies create the crisis*. Emerald.

Harvey, M., & Geras, N. (2018). *Inequality and democratic egalitarianism*. Manchester University Press.

High Pay Centre. (2021). *Briefing: Using pay ratio disclosures to inform ESG strategies and stewardship practices*. Available at: https://highpaycentre.org/wp-content/uploads/2021/05/AGM-season-investor-briefing-draft-for-circulation.docx.pdf.

H. M. Treasury. (2021). Build Back Better: our plan for growth. CP 401.

Hope, D., & Limberg, P. (2020). *The economic consequences of major tax cuts for the rich* (Working Paper 55). International Inequalities Institute, LSE, London.

Institute for Fiscal Studies. (2020). *Race and ethnicity*. Available at: https://www.ifs.org.uk/inequality/themes/race-and-ethnicity/.

ILO. (2021). *ILO Monitor: COVID-19 and the world of work* (7th ed.). Available at: https://www.ilo.org/global/topics/coronavirus/impacts-and-responses/WCMS_767028/lang--en/index.htm.

IMF. (2017). *Fostering inclusive growth. Note prepared for the G20 Leaders' summit, Hamburg*. IMF. Available at: https://www.imf.org/external/np/g20/pdf/2017/062617.pdf.

IMF. (2021). *Fiscal monitor 2021: A fair shot*. Available at: https://www.imf.org/en/Publications/FM/Issues/2021/03/29/fiscal-monitor-april-2021.

IPPR Commission on Economic Justice. (2018). *Prosperity and justice: A plan for a new economy*. Policy Press.

Johnson, P. (2021). *Opening remarks: Spring budget 2021*. Available at: https://www.ifs.org.uk/budget-2021.

Joyce, R., & Xu, X. (2019). *Inequalities in the 21st century. Introducing the IFS Deaton review*. Available at: https://www.ifs.org.uk/inequality/wp-content/uploads/2019/05/The-IFS-Deaton-Review-launch.pdf.

Kay, R., & Hildyard, L. (2020). *Pay ratios and the FTSE 350: Analysis of the first disclosures*. High Pay Centre. Available at: https://highpaycentre.org/wp-content/uploads/2020/12/0.1_MUL1564-FOUNDATION-Pay-ratios-report.pdf.

Lawrence, M., Buller, A., Baines, J., & Hager, S. (2020). *Commoning the company*. Available at: http://www.common-wealth.co.uk.

Lloyd Goodwin, T., Bilsborough, B., & McInroy, N. (2020). *Restoring public values: The role of public procurement*. Centre for Local Economic Strategies. Available at: www.cles.org.uk.

Macfarlane, L., & Berry, C. (2020). *Who is winning from Covid-19?* Available at: http://www.stuc.org.uk/files/Policy/Research-papers/Who_is_winning_from_covid.pdf.

MacNaughton, G. (2021). Is economic inequality a violation of human rights? In M. Davis & M. Kjaerum (Eds.), *Research handbook on human rights and poverty*. Edward Elgar.

Marmot, M., Allen, J., Boyce, T., Goldblatt, G., & Morrison, J. (2020). *Health equity in England: The Marmot Review 10 years on*. Institute of Health Equity.

Marmot, M., Allen, J., Goldblatt, G., Herd, E., & Morrison J. (2020). *Build back fairer: The COVID-19 Marmot review. The pandemic, socioeconomic and health inequalities in England*. Institute of Health Equity.

Meagher, M. (2020). *Competition is killing us*. Penguin Business.

Metzger M., & Young, B. (2020). *No gender please, we're central bankers: Distributional impacts of quantitative easing* (IIPE Working Papers 136). Berlin School of Economics.

Montecino, J. A., & Epstein, G. (2018). *Did quantitative easing increase income inequality?* (PERI Working Papers, 407). University of Massachusetts, Amherst.

Mumtaz, H., & Theophilopoulou, A. (2017). The impact of monetary policy on inequality in the UK: An empirical analysis. *European Economic Review, 98*, 410–423.

Nanda, S., & Parkes, H. (2019). *Just Tax*. Institute for Public Policy Research, Centre for Economic Justice.

New Economics Foundation. (2019). *A green new deal in the UK.* Available at: https://neweconomics.org/about/our-missions/green-new-deal.

OECD. (2015). *In it together: Why less inequality benefits all*. OECD.

OECD. (2020). *How's life 2020? Measuring well- being*. Available at: https://www.oecd-ilibrary.org/sites/9870c393-en/1/3/10/index.html?itemId=/content/publication/9870c393-en&_csp_=fab41822851fa020ad60bb57bb82180a&itemIGO=oecd&itemContentType=book .

Office of National Statistics. (2016). *Changes in the value and division of unpaid care work in the UK: 2000 to 2015.* Available at: https://www.ons.gov.uk/releases/changesinthevalueanddivisionofunpaidcareworkintheuk2000to2015.

Office of National Statistics. (2020a). *Ethnicity pay gaps: 2019.* Available at: https://www.ons.gov.uk/releases/ethnicitypaygaps2019.

Office of National Statistics. (2020b). *Household wealth by ethnicity, Great Britain: April 2016 to March 2018.* Available at: https://www.ons.gov.uk/peoplepopulationandcommunity/personalandhouseholdfinances/incomeandwealth/articles/householdwealthbyethnicitygreatbritain/april2016tomarch2018.

Office of National Statistics. (2021). *Personal and economic well-being in Great Britain: January 2021.* Available at: https://www.ons.gov.uk/peoplepopulationandcommunity/wellbeing/bulletins/personalandeconomicwellbeingintheuk/january2021.

Oxfam. (2015). *Extreme carbon inequality: Why the Paris climate deal must put the poorest, lowest emitting and most vulnerable people first*. Oxfam. Available at: http://oxf.am/Ze4e.

Oxfam. (2016). *An economy for the 1%.* Oxfam. Available at: http://policy-practice.oxfam.org.uk/publications/an-economy-for-the-1-how-privilege-and-power-in-the-economy-drive-extreme-inequ-592643.

Oxfam. (2021). *The inequality virus*. Oxfam. Available at: https://oxfamilibrary.openrepository.com/bitstream/handle/10546/621149/bp-the-inequality-virus-250121-en.pdf.
Palmer, R. (2020). *Wealth, tax and gender*. Paper for Commission on a gender equal economy. Available at: https://wbg.org.uk/wp-content/uploads/2020/03/Paper-2-Wealth-tax-and-gender.pdf.
Pettifor, A. (2020). *The case for a green new deal*. Verso.
Piketty, T. (2014). *Capitalism in the twenty first century*. Harvard University Press.
Platt, L., & Warwick, R. (2020). *Are some ethnic groups more vulnerable to Covid-19 than others?* Institute of Fiscal Studies.
Pomeranz, M. (2000). *The great divergence: China, Europe, and the making of the modern world economy*. Princeton University Press.
Powell, J. A. (2012). *Poverty and race through a belongingness lens*. Policy Matters.
Rawnsley, A. (2021, March 14). The record-beating cost to the tax-payer of this shockingly wasteful government. *The Observer*.
Roberts, C., Blakely, G., & Murphy, L. (2018). *A wealth of difference. reforming the taxation of wealth*. IPPR Commission on Economic Justice.
Sainato, M. (2021, April 3). The fuse has been lit': Union leaders hope Amazon effort will boost support across US. *The Guardian*. Available at: https://www.theguardian.com/technology/2021/apr/03/amazon-bessemer-union-leaders-labor-movement-us .
Sánchez, A.C., Rasmussen, M., & Rohn, O. (2015). *Economic resilience: What role for policies?* (OECD Economics Department Working Papers No. 1251). OECD.
Sze, S., Pan, D., Nevill, C., Gray, L., Martin, C., Nazareth, J., Minhas, J., Divall, P., Khunti, K., Abrams, R., Nellums, B., & Pareek, M. (2020). Ethnicity and clinical outcomes in COVID-19: A systematic review and meta-analysis. *EClinicalMedicine* (pp. 29–30) (100630).
The Observer. (2021, March 14). *Unlevelling down is the Tories new vote-winner*.
Thornberry, J. (2005). Confronting racial discrimination: A CERD perspective. *Human Rights Law Review, 5*(2), 239–269.
Transparency International. (2021). *Track and trace*. Available at: https://www.transparency.org.uk/sites/default/files/pdf/publications/Track%20and%20Trace%20-%20Transparency%20International%20UK.pdf.

TUC. (2020). *A better recovery. learning the lessons of the corona crisis to create a stronger, fairer economy.* Available at: https://www.tuc.org.uk/sites/default/files/TUC%20Report%20'A%20Better%20Recovery'%20(2).pdf.
TUC. (2021). *'Fire and rehire' tactics have become widespread during pandemic—Warns TUC*. Available at: https://www.tuc.org.uk/news/fire-and-rehire-tactics-have-become-widespreadduring-pandemic-warns-tuc.
UK 2070 Commission. (2020). *Make no little plans. Acting at scale for a fairer and stronger future*. Available at: http://uk2070.org.uk/wp-content/uploads/2020/02/UK2070-FINAL-REPORT.pdf.
UNCTAD. (2019). *Trade and development report 2019: Financing a global green new deal.* UN.
UNCTAD. (2020). *Trade and development report 2020: From global pandemic to prosperity for all.* UN.
UNDESA. (2013). *Inequality matters. Report on the world social situation*. UN.
UNDESA. (2015). *Transforming our world: The 2030 agenda for sustainable development*. Available at: https://sdgs.un.org/2030agenda.
UNDESA. (2020). *The sustainable development goals report.* Available at: https://sdgs.un.org/publications/sustainable-development-goals-report-2020-24686.
UNDP. (2013). *Humanity divided: Confronting inequality in developing countries*. UNDP.
UNDP. (2019). *Human development report 2019: Beyond income, beyond averages, beyond today: Inequalities in human development in the 21st century*. UNDP.
US Department of the Treasury. (2021). *Made in America tax plan*. Available at: https://home.treasury.gov/system/files/136/MadeInAmericaTaxPlan_Report.pdf.
Vázquez Pimentel, D. A., Macías Aymar, I., & Lawson, M. (2018). *Reward work, not wealth.* Oxfam International. Available at: https://www.oxfam.org/en/research/reward-work-not-wealth.
Wall, T. (2021, April 18). 'Fire and rehire' tactics rife at workplaces that are in profit…. and claiming Covid cash. *The Observer.*
Wellbeing Economy Alliance. (2020). *Our work: Wellbeing economy governments*. Available at: https://bit.ly/3kHqC6E.
Women's Budget Group. (2017). *Intersecting inequalities: The impact of austerity on BAME women.* Women's Budget Group and Runnymede Trust. Available at: http://www.intersecting-inequalities.com/.

Women's Budget Group Commission on Gender Equal Economy. (2020). *Creating a caring economy: A call to action.* Available at: https://wbg.org.uk/wp-content/uploads/2020/10/WBG-Report-v10.pdf.

5

Society Must Transform the International Financial System in Order to Stabilise the Ecosystem

Ann Pettifor

1 Introduction

> As a rule, a society does not become conscious of the true nature of the institutions under which it lives until those institutions have already passed. (Polanyi, 1940)

Today's private international financial system is dependent on public resources and institutions for its capital gains. These include resources provided by central banks; the valuable collateral that is the sovereign debt of OECD governments; and taxpayer-backed bailouts. Yet despite

Relevant recent own publications are: Pettifor (2017 and 2019)

A. Pettifor (✉)
Policy Research in Macroeconomics (PRIME), London, UK
e-mail: ann.pettifor@primeeconomics.org

P. Arestis and M. Sawyer (eds.), *Economic Policies for Sustainability and Resilience*, International Papers in Political Economy,
https://doi.org/10.1007/978-3-030-84288-8_5

its dependence, the sector is not governed by *public authority*—regulatory democracy. Instead, it is governed by the *private authority* of markets, based on Wall Street and other financial entrepots. Alan Greenspan shed light on that private sector independence when he remarked that: "Thanks to globalisation, policy decisions in the US have been largely replaced by global market forces. National security aside, it hardly makes any difference who will be the next president. The world is governed by market forces" (as reported in Tooze, 2018).

Can the scale, size and power of the capitalist international system, of global financial institutions and Silicon Valley platforms, be moderated by the regulation and oversight of nation states? Can that be achieved in the interests of both societies but also the ecosystem? Is it possible 'to turn the clock back?'.

In this chapter I will argue that what is at stake is the survival of democracy, and of the ecosystem on which human civilisation depends. Transformation of the international financial system, therefore, is vital.

For humanity to survive on a liveable planet there is an urgency to what we must, and can, do. Earth's complex life support systems of atmosphere, oceans, land surface and life forms are at the point of breakdown, according to the world's top scientists. As George Mobiot has warned, "Only one of the many life support systems on which we depend – soils, aquifers, rainfall, ice, the pattern of winds and currents, pollinators, biological abundance and diversity – need fail for everything to slide" (Pettifor, 2019 p. ix).

We live in a new age of anti-democratic nationalism and authoritarianism. US President Donald Trump's 2016 'America First' election campaign echoed the slogan of the 1930s fascist sympathiser, William Randolph Hearst, publisher of bylines by Hitler and Mussolini. (Rauchway, 2015, p. 114.) Far right parties have made gains in Europe. In October 2019, the AfD party won more votes in the eastern state of Thuringia than Mrs Merkel's conservative Christian Democrats. In 2021, Mrs Le Pen's far right National Front gained ground in France, with indications that many young people would vote for the party in the 2022 presidential elections.

Fascism, as Polanyi (2018) explained, "is merely the most recent and most virulent outburst of the anti-democratic virus which was inherent in industrial capitalism from the start....fascism is no more than the most recent form of the recurrent attack of capitalism to popular forms of government" (p. 108).

Democracy worldwide has been weakened by capitalism's "pernicious influence of corruption, kleptocracy, and illicit finance" as the authors of a recent US report remind us (Sutton & Judah, 2021, p. 1). They show that the emergence of kleptocracy as a threat to global democracy has occurred in tandem with the growth of poorly regulated and ungoverned spaces in the international financial system. This system has in turn birthed a vast 'shadow' financial economy that shields immense flows of dirty, anonymous wealth.

The more the de-regulated international system is seen to annihilate "the human and natural substance of society" (Polanyi, 1944, p. 3) the more likely society will take measures to protect itself from the market by turning to strong leaders and anti-democratic political parties. "Inevitably" Polanyi (op. cit.) wrote, "...whatever measures (society) took impaired the self-regulation of the market, disorganized industrial life, and thus endangered society in yet another way." (p. 3).

And so it has proved in the United States, Brazil, India and Russia where kleptocratic leaders exacerbate global political tensions, stoke war, and promote nationalist and protectionist policies. These in turn endanger the market, the ecosystem and ultimately society itself.

1.1 Restoring Public Authority Over the International System

If societies are to tackle the grave crises of economic failure and ecological collapse, restoration of public authority over the international system is central to the vital task of re-embedding global corporations, capital markets and the shadow banking system in society's democratic regulatory frameworks. By restoring public authority over the international system, societies as disparate as those of Europe, Africa and the United States can hope to restore both ecological and economic stability, but also public faith in democratic regulatory institutions.

However, too often, the *systemic* cause of corporate power is overlooked and the focus shifted to individuals leading companies, or to their activities. Society's perspective is often narrowed to specific corporate activities (including tax evasion) in the domestic economy. This chapter instead focuses on the need to transform *the international system* in order to address challenges and crises in domestic economies because, as President Roosevelt's Treasury Secretary Henry Morgenthau once explained, it is imperative to.

> …recognize that the wisest and most effective way to protect our national interests is through international cooperation – that is to say, through united effort for the attainment of common goals. (Morgenthau, 1944, p. 2)

Today's international system inhibits cooperation and coordination between states to protect national interests and attain common goals—as the experience of the 2019–2021 Coronavirus pandemic amply demonstrated. Instead, the international system of government by markets (in the case of COVID19, pharmaceutical markets) divides and disrupts, even as it enables, enriches and empowers the 1%-corrupt oligarchs, Silicon Valley bosses, global tax-avoiding corporations, and those active in the vast shadow banking system.

1.2 There Is Hope of Transformation

It is important to understand that things have not always been so, nor need always to be so in the future. Power exercised over the international system has shifted between democratic states and finance corporations over the period discussed in this chapter. Earlier in the twentieth century, financial capitalism and the nineteenth century, form of globalisation (the gold standard) suffered several major setbacks. This was in part a result of the monetary theory, actions and policies of John Maynard Keynes, President Franklin D. Roosevelt, their supporters and voters.

As early as 1919, after a catastrophic World War, Keynes proposed internationalist, cooperative, and progressive monetary policies for the restoration of prosperity to the nations of Europe. He was a capitalist, determined to protect capitalism from itself. His efforts were to be defeated by a Wall Street-friendly American president at the Versailles Peace Conference who cloaked his arguments in the guise of the US national interest. Nationalism provided the cover for what were effectively Wall Street interests. That victory extinguished any hope of cooperative internationalism to defend national interests and resolve common threats. It ensured the interests of the wealthy that were made paramount through the 1920s, and wider society (labour) subordinated to the governance of Wall Street and the City of London. The consequences were catastrophic—characterised by financial and economic crises, social and political upheaval. These culminated in the US Depression of 1920–1921, the 1929 Great Crash (Galbraith, 1955) the 1931 Great Depression (Straumann, 2019) and World War II.

The antagonism of finance capital to policies for the subordination of the market to the interests of society i.e., democracy—led to the rise of fascism. "After having utterly and completely destroyed all democratic institutions" (Polanyi, 2018, p. 110) fascism nevertheless protected titles to property, and left "capitalism untouched" (Polanyi, op. cit., p. 129).

However, financial capitalism was not successful everywhere. In the US in 1933 an elected, and internationalist politician, Franklin D. Roosevelt succeeded in dismantling the gold standard, snatching victory from Wall Street, and once again subordinating finance to the interests of labour and the ecosystem (the 'Dust Bowl'). The system that had been reconstructed after 1919 was quickly dismantled by Roosevelt's democratically accountable government, and plans were laid for a more cooperative, progressive internationalist system. Then in 1945 internationalism came to the fore again, and more progressive, if imperfect policies prevailed during the 1945–1971 Bretton Woods era.

Since 1971 and up until the present day, markets are once again in the driving seat of the international system; safely 'encased' (Slobodian, 2018, p. 13) from intervention by regulatory democracy. It is my contention that this is largely due to the deliberate distortion and marginalisation of the internationalist economic theory and policies of John Maynard Keynes. Instead, actors in private markets have used neoliberal economic theory and power to incite nationalism, while inflating the wealth and interests of 'the 1%'. Once victory over the internationalism of Bretton Woods was secured, politicians in key markets were lobbied and bribed to legislate in favour of financial deregulation. Deregulation included policies to remove barriers to the gains made from the global mobility of capital and trade; policies that condoned tax havens and tax dodging; that raised interest rates; and inflated credit and expanded rent seeking. Ultimately these deflationary economic policies enriched creditors and investors and lowered the incomes, living standards and security of all those who worked by hand and brain—the majority.

Policies that promoted government by globalised financial markets inevitably led to economic imbalances including wealth inequality, vast mountains of debt relative to global income, recurring financial crises, trade imbalances and geopolitical tensions. These in turn led to the election of nationalist, protectionist and disruptive regimes, including those of Presidents Trump, Modi, Bolsanaro, Oban and Putin—to name but a few.

What of the future? Can another struggle by progressive internationalists defeat nationalism fundamental to today's model of financialised globalisation and rentierism? Alternatively, are we doomed to endure the inevitable collapsing dominoes of financial crises, economic failure, earth systems breakdown and another global war?

This author is confident that transformation is not only possible, but given the threats posed by climate breakdown and biodiversity collapse, urgent. This chapter reviews and revives policies that once before successfully subordinated global capital markets to the interests of society and the ecosystem; and considers whether they can again be deployed to tame the financialised corporate sector. The rest of this chapter is as follows.

Section 2 looks back over the twentieth century and analyses Keynes's confrontation with Wall Street over the internationalist economic policies promoted at the 1919 Versailles Peace Conference. His *Grand Scheme* was to be side-lined and subsequently misrepresented by historians but provided a template for future progressive gains in economic policy making in the 1930s and 1940s.

Section 3 briefly reviews the 1933–1971 era and Roosevelt's successful confrontation with Wall Street. Particular attention is paid to the internationalism of the 1933–1945 Roosevelt administration, the dismantling of the gold standard, and the restoration of policy autonomy to a democratically elected US government. That victory, over Wall Street effectively, extended into the Bretton Woods era—and was to be subsequently defeated in the post-war period.

Section 4 covers the post-second world war era, 1945–1971, the expansion and dominance of private capital markets over policymaking, the return of the rentier, the rise of inequality and the recurrence of crises.

Section 5 discusses the era from the 1970s until today and notes the massive inflation of credit and periodic deflations of debt that provide parallels with the 1920s and early 1930s.

Section 6 deals with the suggestion that tackling earth systems breakdown requires vast, but sustainable sources of finance, and the kind of urgent action that governments would take to build a steady state economy and protect human civilisation from grave threats. We use the history outlined above to map out a policy route to new internationalist, cooperative and steady state economies.

Section 7 briefly summarises and concludes.

2 1919: A Struggle for Power Over the International Financial System

How western economies constructed a globalised and financialised international system is understood in part by excavating one of the hidden, distorted, and yet most revealing chapters of financial history. These events continue to have a bearing on today's financial system and the world's economies, but historians have often misunderstood and misinterpreted them (Macmillan, 2003, Tooze, 2014). The events took place at, and after the Versailles Peace negotiations in Paris, in 1919. The negotiations represented a herculean struggle over monetary theory and policy between the young economist, John Maynard Keynes, and a man dubbed by his grandson biographer as the '*Ambassador from Wall Street*' (Lamont,

1993)—an adviser to America's President Wilson, and a powerful figure at the negotiations.

During the Versailles negotiations, John Maynard Keynes began to apply his monetary theory to policies needed to help Europe recover from the catastrophe of war; but more importantly to support the international economy. The consequence of adopting these policies would have led to the dismantling of the gold standard and would have limited the power of Wall Street and the City of London over the economies of Europe and beyond.

This was the first of twentieth-century struggles for power over the international system, and they were to presage the economically transformational events of 1933 and 1945. Because of their later significance, the next section examines Keynes's proposal in some detail.

2.1 Keynes's 1919 'Scheme' for the Transformation of the International System

John Maynard Keynes, unlike many of his peers now and then, understood money properly—as social technology—rather than as 'real exchange' based on barter. Dependent on a social construct, money originates everywhere as credit—'the promise to pay'. If managed well and at a low rate of interest, Keynes was to argue in his *General Theory of Employment, Interest and Money* (1936), the world's credit and monetary systems could help finance and create conditions of full employment and prosperity.

His understanding of money was enhanced by his almost accidental posting to the India Office in 1906, and by his 1913 membership of the Royal Commission on Indian Finance and Currency. That experience helped him see what many economists had missed: that India had adopted a currency policy that did not conform to the then dominant international financial architecture, defined as the gold standard. Instead, the Indian authorities simply (and wisely) declined to convert their currency to gold. They had moved to a gold-exchange standard that allowed their public authorities to maintain a stable exchange rate, while foregoing the expense of holding large quantities of gold.

As Professor Eric Rauchway explains: Keynes began his monetary writing not so much by assailing the international gold standard, but by discovering that it barely existed. "For Keynes, from the first of his many books, the future of international monetary affairs required leaving the gold standard behind and finding some better way of assuring international liquidity than depending on a scarce yellow metal, inconvenient to manage and expensive to hold" (Rauchway, 2016, p. 14).

This experience was to be formative for Keynes and as Robert Skidelsky notes in his biography of Keynes, from thereon: "international monetary reform, based on the gradual elimination of gold, was a constant in Keynes's thought" (Skidelsky, 1983, p. 275).

Keynes (2013a, CW, VOL. XVI, p. 436) was acutely aware of the dangers posed to capitalism in 1919. He set about producing a simple, but revolutionary plan for the rehabilitation of Europe (op. cit.). Given the absence of formal and rigorous public accounting systems, his was a back-of-an-envelope plan, refined by constantly checking and amending his understanding of the assets and liabilities of the German and Allied economies. (This checking and accounting went on after 1919, notably in his 1922 book *A Revision of the Treaty*).

Getting the numbers right, was important. However, more important was Keynes's reconceptualization of the world's economic and financial structure. His *Scheme for the Rehabilitation of European Credit and for Financing Relief and Reconstruction* proposed a new international financial order based not on the gold standard, but on the economic activity and public authority of states. (Keynes, 2013a, CW, Vol. XVI, p. 429). It was a plan that would have financed recovery in Europe, permitted policy autonomy to domestic economies—and enabled officials and politicians to respond to democratic mandates. It set out to restore stability and prosperity to national economies within a sound, stable, and very necessary international framework. That insight alone was profound: that a national economy could be helped to recover from a cataclysmic world war by the deliberate actions and policies of a cooperative international financial system. For Europe to recover, he argued, its economies required a stable international financial system to help countries attain full employment, social and economic stability.

His *Grand Scheme* was a radical departure from the chaotic "architecture" of the gold standard, that "fantastic machinery of global self-regulation by international bankers and financiers" to quote Fred Block (Block, Introduction, Polanyi, 2001, p. XXX). A system in which the 'invisible hand' played a pivotal role in cross-border capital mobility, in the allocation of finance, in the determination of a nation's interest and exchange rates, and in investment and employment.

The revolutionary element of Keynes's *Scheme* was that it replaced a system governed by the *private authority* of unaccountable financial markets with one governed by *the public authority* of democratically accountable governments.

His scheme was to be rejected effectively by the narrow nationalisms of Presidents Wilson, Prime Minister Lloyd George and by France's Georges Clémenceau.

In his opposition to Keynes, Wilson was aided by 'the money interest' or as J. P. Morgan's biographer Ron Chernow, describes it, 'Yankee Wall Street'.

'Yankee Wall Street' was present at Versailles in part because the First World War had been a 'bonanza' for the Street, as Chernow (2010, p. 195) explains. The biggest foreign loan in Wall Street history—a $500 million Anglo-French loan—"five times as big as the previous record holder, the $100 million loan to Great Britain for the Boer War", had been syndicated in 1915 by J. P. Morgan (Chernow, 2010, p. 197). No surprise then that J.P. Morgan was not just present at Versailles, but according to one of the bank's competitors, Bernard Baruch of Kuhn Loeb bank, "J. P. Morgan and Company was running the show" (Chernow, op. cit, p.197).

Many years later, in 1942, Dr. E. Rosenbaum sent Keynes a list of 'fascinating reminders' of events and participants that encountered in Versailles in 1919. Responding, Keynes (1942) reminded his correspondent of the City financiers' present at the conference. And as Keynes (op. cit.) argued: "Some of the lists you sent me remind me of the distinguished …financiers whom I collected in Paris with a view to discussing a general project of international financial reconstruction, which, in the event, never came off. How much subsequent evil might have been avoided if only they had! They were the most distinguished financiers of each country that I could get track of. Yet of those concerned in these negotiations, no less than four ultimately ended in prison on well-justified charges of fraud...Rydbeck, Glückstadt, Manz-Fê and Klotz" (p. 416).

2.2 Nationalism vs Internationalism

Michael Cox correctly points out in his new introduction to the latest edition of *The Economic Consequences of the Peace* that Keynes was an internationalist and loathed President Wilson's overt nationalism (Keynes, 2019, p. 3). In a 1922 sequel to *The Economic Consequences Keynes* elaborated the point: "The Wilsonian dogma, which exalts and dignifies the divisions of race and nationalism above the bonds of trade and culture, and guarantees frontiers but not happiness, is deeply embedded in the conception of the League of Nations as at present constituted. It yields us the paradox that the first experiment in international government should exert its influence in the direction of intensifying nationalism" (Keynes, 2013c, CW, Vol. III, p. 11).

Wilson's nationalism, like today's rising nationalism, blocked the possibility of a shared, internationalist resolution of the crisis.

2.3 The Economic Mechanism of Europe Is Jammed

Keynes's closest political friend in Paris was the South African leader, Jan Christian Smuts. He had travelled widely around Europe in the early months of 1919 and spent his evenings with Keynes describing the pitiful plight of Central Europe. Millions of Europeans starved, mutinied and revolted while, the two friends agreed, while world leaders engaged in 'arid intrigue' at the Palace of Versailles. That was not because the facts of widespread suffering were hidden from the four leaders. Almost hourly, wrote Keynes in *The Economic Consequences of the Peace* they received,

> .... reports of misery, disorder and decaying organisation of all Central and Eastern Europe, allied and enemy alike, and learnt from the financial representatives of German and Austria unanswerable evidence of the terrible exhaustion of their countries.... (Keynes, 2013a, CW, Vol. XVI, p. 435)

While the two friends talked in the spring of 1919, Paris was in turmoil. Unemployment and hunger had led to unrest and violence on the streets of the city and to the declaration of a French general strike on the 1st of May. There was what Skidelsky (1983) called "a sense of the fragility of capitalist civilization" (p. 401). In Germany the defeat had led to a rise in social tensions; the navy had mutinied, and the angry, starving population resorted to food riots. The November revolution, a civil conflict that erupted in late 1918, led to the dismantling of Germany's constitutional monarchy and the departure of the Kaiser. Meanwhile Russia's Bolshevik revolution proved popular with German workers and revolutionaries.

Despite that evidence, Keynes wrote in *The Economic Consequences of the Peace,* "The future life of Europe was not their concern; its means of livelihood was not their anxiety. Their preoccupations...related to...revenge, and to the shifting by the victors of their unbearable financial burdens on to the shoulders of the defeated" (Keynes, 1920, p.57).

The economic problem Keynes (2013a, CW, Vol. XVI, p. 429) addressed was this: vast swathes of the European economy had been destroyed and had to be rebuilt—which required financing. The Germans owed the British money but had no capacity to pay nor capital to invest in reconstruction of new assets that would generate income for repayment of foreign debts.

British owed the Americans money, but they too had no capacity to pay unless the Germans paid—which they could not. His 'cunning plan' can be briefly summarised as follows.

Germany would issue bonds to the present value of £1bn and to a face value of £1.2bn bonds that would pay interest of 4%. These bonds would be guaranteed 'jointly and severally' by the "principal allied and associated governments, by the three Scandinavian governments and by the governments of Holland and Switzerland" (Keynes, 2013a, CW, Vol

XVI, p. 429). These were the strongest economies of the world, represented by the four leaders at Versailles. The bonds issued under this Scheme would have "priority over all other German obligations whatever" (ibid.). Allied guarantees would make the bonds attractive to capital markets, so that the 'prostrate Reich' could raise the finance needed to pay most of what was owed to the Allies in reparations and debt. In brief, Keynes proposed that "there would be a 1% sinking fund to retire (repay the principal) by 1925 70% of the money raised would go to reparations" (Rauchway, 2015, p. 11). The proposal can be summarised as:

- 30% for reconstruction.
- The Bonds would have priority over all other German obligations.
- Enemy nations would guarantee them jointly & severally.
- The US, UK and France would guarantee 20% each.
- The League of Nations would impose penalties or foreclosure if Germany defaulted.

His *Grand Scheme* included provisions for the other Central Powers and new nations to issue similar bonds, also secured by their richer allies.

Keynes's plan was even more ambitious. It evolved into a strategy for the transformation of the post-war international financial system. The bonds issued by Germany would be accepted at par value plus accrued interest in payment of all indebtedness between any of the allied and associated governments, but would have a second, more important purpose. They would become an international financial asset—accepted as payment between Allied governments and as first-class collateral at central banks. The bonds could act as a form of inter-governmental money—backed not by gold, but by economic activity within, and between Allied nations. The Germans could use the bonds to raise finance for debt repayment to the allies and could convert the purchasing power of the bonds into finance for reconstruction. The French could use the bonds to pay debts to the British and the British could use them to pay debts to the Americans.

In a briefing sent to Prime Minister Lloyd George outlining his Scheme, Keynes (2013a, CW, Vol. XVI) explained that it was, "an attempt to deal simultaneously in as simple a way as possible with several distinct problems. The countries that have been the victims of devastation are enabled to convert the bonds of the enemy into immediate purchasing power for the purpose of early restoration….The acute problem of the liquidation of inter-ally indebtedness, while not disposed of, is sensibly ameliorated. The governments of the new states are enabled to prepare definite economic programmes which will consolidate their, at present precarious positions and inspire confidence in their peoples" (p. 435).

Keynes was not solely concerned with Germany. He worried also about the impact of the war on the Allies and pointed out in his briefing "that France was probably the greatest gainer from the scheme and was offered a way out from her almost overwhelming financial difficulties" (Keynes, 2013a, CW, Vol. XVI, p. 435). His concern was to alleviate the suffering of the citizens of Europe, and to give them a way of discharging a part of their obligations and a reasonable measure of security for their economic existence in the immediate future. His concern was not for individual nationalisms, but for Europe: "The good faith of the world as a whole is pledged for the carrying out of a scheme the sole object of which is to set on its feet the new Europe" (Keynes, op. cit. p. 435).

Aware of the need to assuage the suffering of both the Allied and enemy nations, while reassuring the world's most powerful creditor, he continued as follows. "It could not be supposed that two great continents, America and Europe, the one destitute and on the point of collapse and the other overflowing with goods which it wishes to dispose of, can continue to face one another for long without attempting to frame some plan of mutual advantage." (Keynes, 2013a, CW, Vol. XVI, p. 436).

Keynes's conceptualisation of the new system was revolutionary, the first step in drawing away from the gold standard and restoring a degree of public authority over the international system. It was necessary he asserted, because "the problem of restoring Europe is almost certainly too great for private enterprise alone" (Rauchway, 2015, p. 13).

Keynes had sent his proposal to the British Treasury and to the Prime Minister, David Lloyd George. They enthusiastically backed the Scheme and proposed it to their ally, President Woodrow Wilson of the United States.

2.4 Wilson and JP Morgan's 'Ambassador' Thomas Lamont

"If Wilson worried about the fragility of civilization, he did not show it" notes Rauchway (2015, p. 15). The American President rejected Keynes's proposal outright and did not suggest an alternative for fear, it was said, that the Americans might be left "holding the bag" (op. cit., p. 12). The war, he argued had been a very heavy burden "even for our well-to-do commonwealth" (op. cit., p. 13).

Keynes agreed that might indeed be so but added two points: America had not incurred foreign debts to finance the war. Second, the US had profited immensely from the war, ending the war richer than in 1914 thanks to both profitable Wall Street loans to the belligerents, and increased exports to the warring parties. Finally, if the American economy was to remain buoyant, it was vital for American goods to find export markets abroad—and for those to be financed so that Americans could be remunerated (Keynes, 2013a, CW, Vol. XVI, p. 436).

The president disagreed because he did not believe he could persuade Congress "to place a Federal guarantee upon bonds of European origin" (Rauchway, 2015, p. 15).

Unknown to Keynes, but recently revealed by Rauchway (op. cit., p.15), Wilson's letter of rejection was drafted not by the President, but by a senior Executive of J P Morgan's bank, Thomas W. Lamont.

Back in Washington, Lamont had 'dazzled' Wilson with his diplomatic skills, according to Jack Morgan's biographer (Chernow, 2010, p. 195). His political beliefs had dovetailed nicely with Wilson's and with the bank's financial requirements, for as it expanded its foreign lending, it looked for stable governments, global security, and free trade. According to Chernow (2010), Lamont was "ideologically flexible, able to hint to politicians of both parties that sided with them. He was a man of many masks who played his parts so masterfully that he sometimes fooled himself" (p. 197).

In Versailles, Lamont ran 'the show' for President Wilson, right down to drafting his letters.

That is why a President's response to Prime Minister Lloyd George's recommendation of Keynes's Grand Scheme was drafted by the Wall

Street banker. When the president seemed to object to priority being given to loans backed by the Allies and expressed his preference for the desirability of post-war lending going through 'the usual private channels' it was, Rauchway (2015) reminds us, "the voice of the usual private channels speaking about its own desirability" (p. 15).

2.5 Looking Back: The Perspective of Historians

Fast forward to 2003 and Lloyd George's great-grand daughter, the historian Margaret Macmillan, asserts in her book, Paris, 1919, that Keynes wrote *The Economic Consequences of the Peace* "as something of an act of atonement" (Macmillan, 2003, pp. 478–479) for the supposedly destructive part he played at the international peace conference. To emphasise her point she draws on Thomas Lamont, whom she describes as "the American expert on reparations" and quotes his view that "Keynes got sore because they (world leaders) wouldn't take his advice, his nerve broke, and he quit" (ibid.).

Adam Tooze in *The Deluge, 2014,* argues that "No single individual did more to undermine the political legitimacy of the Versailles peace than Keynes with his devastating book *The Economic Consequences of the Peace*". Tooze then asserts that "generations of economists have picked apart the flaws in Keynes's argument" and notes pointedly that Keynes "was welcomed with open arms in Germany (although) it was far from obvious, even from a German standpoint, whether he did not do more harm than good" (p. 295).

We can guess who those "generations of economists" were and should not be surprised by the hostility to Keynes's *Grand Scheme*. Nor should he have been so naïve as to believe Wall Street would accept it. Keynes's proposal for the preferencing of *public* bond repayments over subordinated *private* foreign debt repayments due to bankers like J.P. Morgan—was anathema to Wall Street, its friends in the media and in the economics profession.

2.6 The Aftermath

The failure to adopt Keynes's *Grand Scheme* in 1919 gave financiers the whip hand and allowed Wall Street and the City of London to restore the gold standard to its international role of effectively governing the economic policies of states. The restoration was followed, predictably, by bouts of credit inflation and debt deflation. The 1920s and early 1930s witnessed mass unemployment, instability and industrial unrest in both Europe and the USA.

Post-war industrial production in the USA peaked in January 1920. In part because of Europe's weakness, the American economy then moved into a major depression, with production levels dropping by 32.5% by March 1921. After the bust, Wall Street churned out new credit, financed the 'Roaring Twenties' boom, which led to the massive inflation of debt. This was followed by a spectacular debt deflation, the 1929 Wall Street Crash and The Great Depression.

In Europe, the restoration of the gold standard deepened austerity and led to economic instability, unemployment, deflation, and, ultimately to the rise of Fascism (Straumann, 2019). These sorry consequences culminated in a devastating Second World War.

Worldwide there were further consequences. Monetary hegemony passed to the United States. Central Bankers reasserted their independence from political authority. Capital markets were liberalised. High, real rates of interest on Wall Street—loans prevailed. Moreover, a colossal and crippling War Loan of £2bn issued at 5% burdened the UK. Like the financial globalisation of the 1980s, the 1920s was an era of dear money. The interests of wealthy elites were made paramount while those of labour were disregarded, as Tily (2016) explains.

Perhaps the greatest vindication of Keynes's internationalist approach emerged at the end of the Second World War, when world leaders gathered at the Yalta Summit between 4 and 11 of February 1945. Josef Stalin and Russian diplomats wanted Germany 'dismembered' writes Professor David Reynolds (2020a) of Cambridge University. Churchill and the British Foreign Office disagreed, as they were "haunted by John Maynard Keynes's polemic about the 'Carthaginian Peace' of 1919 – (and) were determined not to repeat what they considered the mistakes of the Versailles Treaty. They wished to avoid another territorial settlement that would fuel German vengeance and feared that punitive reparations could again destabilise the international economy" (Reynolds, 29 January 2020b).

Keynes had failed to persuade world leaders to rescue Europe and stabilise the international economy after the catastrophe of the First World War. Nevertheless, if Professor Reynolds is right, his polemic helped restore prosperity to Germany; also, to stabilise the international economy after the Second World War.

Most economists and historians fail to recognize that extraordinary feat.

3 Keynes's 1919 Failed *Scheme* and the *New Deal*

The consequence of the American decision to reject Keynes's *Grand Scheme* in 1919 was to cause him great personal as well as professional anguish; anger that was to motivate his controversial and in places, intemperate book: *The Economic Consequences of the Peace*. Drawing on the experience of Versailles, Keynes published his *Tract on Monetary Reform* in 1923 and the *Treatise on Money* in 1930. In a speech to the Liberal Party in December 1923 Keynes (1923) reminded his audience that: "…there is no part of our economic system which works so badly as our monetary and credit arrangements; none where the results of bad working are so disastrous socially; and none where it is easier to propose a scientific solution" (pp. 158–159).

Keynes was then a senior civil servant in HM Treasury, and involved in monetary arrangements that modified both Britain's internal gold standard, and the government's foreign exchange policy (Tily, 2012). Foreign exchange policy became exchange management. From 1915 JP Morgan was instructed to buy and sell sterling in order to preserve an exchange rate of $4.76. The JP Morgan arrangements meant that the short-term rate of interest was freed from its role in preserving the exchange parity and could, in theory at least, be operated more in accord with the requirements of domestic wartime policy. Later in 1930, he played a key role in the Macmillan Committee on Finance and Industry, which came to the following important conclusion. "In the case of our financial, as in the case of our political and social, institutions we may well have reached the stage when an era of conscious and deliberate management must succeed the era of undirected natural evolution" (Tily, 2012, p. 3).

These developments were noticed in Washington and New York, where Franklin D. Roosevelt was state governor and oversaw the fallout, and impact on unemployment, of the 1929 Wall Street Crash. Fourteen years after the Versailles conference ended, and by now the President of the United States, Roosevelt, pivoted away from the economic orthodoxy of the gold standard imposed by his predecessor President Hoover. Instead, he adopted the monetary approach first outlined in Keynes's *Grand Scheme for the Rehabilitation of European Credit.*

So convinced was Roosevelt by Keynes's monetary theory that on the night of his inauguration he began dismantling the fantastic machinery of the gold standard. In the first weeks of the administration, Rauchway (2015) notes, and while Keynes's newspaper columns circulated among the Roosevelt group, the banker and Roosevelt confidante James Warburg grumbled that Keynes provided "a scientific backing, if Keynes can be called 'scientific' for Roosevelt's policies" (p. 51).

The adoption of Keynes's approach 'proved spectacularly successful' for the newly elected President. As the president later reminded others, the bank holiday, "was an emergency measure, but it was also the first of the steps in transferring to the Federal Government the more effective control and regulation of the monetary system, including monetary gold, and restricting the private profits of a privileged few out of the Government's action" (Rauchway, 2015, p. 54).

Roosevelt was forced to defend his decision before an unsympathetic Supreme Court in 1935. He submitted evidence on his reasons for withdrawing from the gold standard—the effect of deflation and its impact on debtors and noted the recovery under way. He also predicted mass bankruptcies, and the resurgence of both 'America First' protofascists and elements that are more radical. Fortunately, the Court voted by just 5–4 to uphold his policy decisions. If the Court had restored the gold standard, it would, as Rauchway (2015) notes, "have undone the administration's measures to prop up the banks and undercut the fragile recovery, inducing widespread defaults and ruin. As it was, the Court left Roosevelt's dollar intact while dismantling much else. With politics preventing the adoption of an adequate public works plan and the justices striking down price-fixing policies, the dollar policy became ever more important as the major remaining tool for recovery" (p. 108).

The Roosevelt administration's regulatory initiatives combined with monetary policy were fundamental to the success of the New Deal. For the world economy as a whole, Roosevelt's adherence to Keynes's scorned monetary theory and policies established the terms for what became, after the Second World War, a new age of international prosperity.

3.1 The Grand Scheme and the Road to Bretton Woods: A New International System

By 1940, Keynes had already drafted a plan for the post-war world—an updated and expanded version of the 1919 *Grand Scheme.* He had taken it to the United States and discussed it with President Roosevelt—and shared it widely with colleagues. The plan drew on the experience of the lend-lease system that had created an international system of moneyless accounts and that proved that a high level of production and trade could operate without the dollar/Wall Street (Rauchway, 2015, p. 54).

Harry Dexter White was appointed to the US Treasury and was mandated by Roosevelt's Treasury Secretary, Henry Morgenthau, to develop a plan for the post-war international order. White and Keynes, in preparing for the Bretton Woods conference, shared a commitment to internationalism—to build a "more prosperous world" (that) would be better for the "healthy development of democratic institutions" (Rauchway, 2015, p. 162). Nevertheless, there were differences. White was close to the leaders of the world's swiftly rising power in Washington, "whereas Keynes was born to a dying empire" (Rauchway, op. cit., p. 152).

White's plan for an International Stabilisation Fund (ISF) differed from Keynes's International Clearing Union (ICU) in one important respect; the creation of two USA-based institutions: The International

Monetary Fund and World Bank. White argued that both would be funded with gold and various currencies contributed by member nations on a pro rata basis.

Keynes's plan by contrast did not need members to contribute gold or currency; the money would be created by accounting for trade denominated in an international currency, his named 'bancor'—literally 'bank gold'. It would have a fixed value in gold, but like the USA dollar could not be converted to gold. It could only be used for exchanging and settling international trade transactions in a system of multinational clearing. It was a system to ensure that money earned by selling goods to one country could be spent on buying the products of another. Bancor quotas would grow and shrink with the expansion or contraction of international trade; as Rauchway (2015) notes: "Bancor did not need digging up; it was created by the commerce it funded" (p. 163).

An International Clearing Union and a neutral international currency, independent of any imperial state, was never accepted. Instead, at the 1944 Bretton Woods Conference, Harry Dexter White, backed by the power of the US economy, proposed the US dollar be made the world's international reserve currency.

Despite this setback, and despite solid opposition from Wall Street to the new system, the 1945 Bretton Woods agreement launched the 'golden age'. In the same year, radical changes in Britain led a Labour government to nationalise the Bank of England. That decision effectively ended an era in which unaccountable central bankers 'independently' deployed the Bank's great powers. Public—that is, democratic—agency over the international financial system was restored by Bretton Woods.

4 1945 and After: The Rate of Interest, Inequalities of Wealth, and Extractivism

Nevertheless, not all proceeded as well as Keynes (who died in 1946) had hoped for and expected. We need not search far to find the institutions that hastened to restore *private authority* over the international system.

In the development of his monetary theory during the inter-war years, Keynes had laid great store by his new theory of interest. High rates of interest represented Keynes high rates of return for wealthy rentiers. These rates contrasted with the returns (wages) paid to labour. As he concluded in the final chapter of the General Theory, "There is…a much more fundamental inference from our argument which has a bearing on the future of inequalities of wealth: namely our theory of the rate of interest" (Keynes, 1936, p. 375).

Keynes understood that because money is not a commodity, or based on a commodity, but is instead a social construct (a 'promise to pay') it could not become scarce. Low rates of interest (across the spectrum of lending, not just the central bank rate) would therefore, he optimistically surmised: "mean the euthanasia of the rentier, and consequently, the euthanasia of the cumulative oppressive power of the capitalist to exploit the scarcity value of capital. Interest today rewards not genuine sacrifice, any more does the rent of land. The owner of capital can obtain interest because capital is scarce, just as the owner of land can obtain rent because land is scarce. But whilst there may be intrinsic reasons for the scarcity of land, there are no intrinsic reasons for the scarcity of capital" (Keynes, 1936, p. 376).

The return of policies for high *real* interest rates after his death set the stage therefore, for a return to the obscene levels of wealth inequality that had prevailed in the 1920s and 1930s. Inequality posed a threat to social, economic, and political stability.

Second, Keynes understood that low rates of interest were essential to the maintenance of adequate levels of investment and economic activity—i.e., full employment. It is often overlooked that the *General Theory*, is in fact *The General Theory of Employment, Interest and Money*. As Tily (2012) notes, for Keynes "the rate of interest was the cause, not the passive consequence, of the level of economic activity" (p. 34).

In Chapter 13 of *The General Theory*, Keynes had turned the classical theory on its head, arguing that the rate of interest was not determined by the demand for savings, but by the demand for *assets,*—both illiquid and liquid assets (Keynes, 1936, p. 165). Given that savings were *a consequence* (not a source) of investment financed by credit ('the promise to pay'), the real demand was for a place (asset) in which to store profits, savings or surpluses accumulated from investment.

Investors he reckoned, have different preferences for their savings. Some (pension funds) need to deposit savings for long-term safety. Others speculate and make capital gains effortlessly and a third group need their savings to be liquid—to be available effectively, as cash (Keynes, 1936, p. 165).

How to meet such demands? Keynes's revolutionary theory of liquidity preference led to policies for the management of government bond issuance designed to satisfy the full range of investor preferences, and thereby to strongly influence commercial market rates. This would be achieved by Treasury working with the Debt Management Office to issue bonds that would meet the varied investor demands for assets (collateral) across a spectrum of preferences—for safety, for speculation or for cash (Keynes, 1936, p. 166).

Under the Bretton Woods system, Treasury officials operated in an international monetary environment that made it possible to issue debt over different time periods, to set rates of interest for the *domestic* economy as a whole. The rate of interest at home could not be exchanged for a higher or lower rate abroad, in say Australia. By this means, Keynes ensured that monetary policy was used to lower rates of return within the domestic economy; to encourage investment and employment; and to discourage both rentiers and the build-up of debts.

Keynes's abhorrence of wealth inequality and the injustice of debt burdens were not novel. The theory of usury had preceded his work by two thousand years—at least. Today, in the midst of climate break-down and the threat of biodiversity collapse, high rates of interest take on an additional menacing dimension: extractivism. High rates of interest demand increased extraction (returns) of both ecosystems assets (forests, the seas, and the land) and the intensified exploitation of labour—to earn the means for debt repayment.

4.1 1951: The Return of High Rates, Rentierism and Extractivism

Keynes had not long been dead when in 1951, under a Conservative government, the Bank of England rate was raised for the first time in twenty years. Interest rate policy determination, based on the theory of liquidity preference was moved away from HM Treasury and the Debt Management Office—i.e., the government. Instead, decisions on the bank rate were determined by the judgement and decisions of unaccountable technocrats at the Bank of England. Commercial (market) rates for the wider economy were to be determined by 'the invisible hand'.

In Britain, the removal of controls over credit creation and interest rates led to the massive expansion of credit ('easy money') and to the 'Barber Boom' (1971–1974) during which inflation flared upwards. This was largely the result of the introduction by the Bank of England of a framework defined as '*Competition and Credit Control*' (CCC) but often parodied as 'all competition and no control'. In the words of Duncan Needham (2014), "Credit rationing by cost replaced rationing by control. What followed was one of the most intense periods of monetary chaos in recent British history. By the time the policy was de factor abandoned in December 1973, the broad money supply had grown by 72%. Britain's highest-ever inflation, and the worst banking crisis since the nineteenth century, followed hard on the heels of CCC" (p. 46).

At the same time, and probably under the influence of rentiers in both the City of London and Wall Street, the 1951 USA Federal Reserve-Treasury Accord achieved the same result. The power to conduct monetary policy and influence interest rates across the spectrum of lending via the issue of a range of assets was no longer conducted by the Treasury and its Bureau of Fiscal Service. Instead, the power to set the Fed Funds Rate was transferred to technocrats at the Federal Reserve with close relationships to Wall Street. Rates of interest on commercial loans and on Treasury bonds were to be determined by 'the market'.

Keynes's theory of interest rates as a social construct, with central bank rates determined by 'liquidity preference,' was abandoned. Instead, rates as the price of commodity money, determined by the theory of supply and demand, was restored. Central bankers were empowered to determine the central bank rate. The 'invisible hand' of the market would determine rates for loans made to those active in the real economy.

This theory granted unaccountable central bankers immense public authority over the lives of millions of people. In the years since 1951, technocrats have made catastrophic errors in the determination of rates—and suffered very little accountability for the real-life consequences of their decisions. On the contrary, as Dean Baker commented in *The Guardian,* after the Great Financial Crisis of 2007–2009, some were rewarded with substantial pensions and with elevation within the ranks of the establishment: "The economies of the United States and Europe are seeing their worst downturn since the Great Depression. Tens of millions of people are unemployed or underemployed. This has led to millions losing their homes, their access to health care, and, in some cases, their lives. Remarkably, the two individuals who bear the greatest responsibility for this disaster, former Federal Reserve Board chairman Alan Greenspan former president of the European Central Bank Jean-Claude Trichet, do not appear to be suffering at all for their failure. Both are living comfortably and continue to be sought out for their expertise on economic policy. This should infuriate reasonable people everywhere" (Baker, 2013).

Governor Alan Greenspan's and the Federal Reserve board's rate rise decisions in the run-up to the Great Financial Crisis, combined with financial deregulation policies, helped precipitate catastrophic failures of heavily indebted investors, bankers and borrowers. The crisis inflicted intense economic pain and losses on millions of Americans and citizens across the world. Before the European Union could recover from the crash of 2007–9, the ECB's 2011 decision to increase the benchmark rate by 25 bps in two consecutive quarters, deepened the slump, and caused Portuguese sovereign debt to be downgraded to junk. In less than a year, Greece's creditors were forced to restructure the country's sovereign debt to remain in the currency union. (Morris, 2016). As Keynes would have expected even in 'robust northern Eurozone' private investment activity continued to trend downward after Trichet's rate hike (Morris, op. cit.).

In 1997 in Britain, the 'independence' of central bankers was announced to much fanfare by the Chancellor of the time, the Right Honourable Gordon Brown MP. However, while it was more of a PR exercise, and a successful one at that, the Chancellor was only formally acknowledging a transfer of power that had taken place way back in 1951.

The inordinate power now enjoyed by technocrats at central banks has, in conjunction with deregulation, led to the expansion and shaping of private capital market activities—in both the traditional and the vast $200 trillion shadow banking sectors (see FSB, 2020).

These developments were exacerbated by the dominance of the US dollar, through which the United States continued to impose its will on the post-war world. Keynes's Clearing Union would have been neutral as between deficit and surplus sovereign states and would have prevented the vast imbalances that have grown up between trading nations, in part because of the levels of inequality within nations. The spirit of internationalism that informed Keynes's Clearing Union and the establishment of the 'bancor' currency would have encouraged cooperation and coordination. Instead, the world is riven with capital and current account imbalances that have led to trade wars, and to rising, and increasingly grave, geopolitical divisions and tensions.

Moreover, as Jane D'Arista explains in her book, *All Fall Down: Debt, Deregulationand Financial Crises* (2019, p. 1) the dollar-denominated key currency system required all countries whose currencies were not accepted for cross-border payments to adopt an export-led growth model that relied on trade surpluses to acquire the means of payment needed to engage in international trade and investment. This requirement suited those active in the increasingly globalised financial system, where the export revenues of poor countries financed dollar-denominated debt issued in rich countries.

The requirement for export-led expansion was also a consequence of rising inequality and imbalances at home. Deflationary policies lowered demand, incomes, and living standards for the many in domestic economies and resulted in the production of gluts on the one hand, and on the other, the under-consumption of domestically produced goods and services. Because the rich consumed less of their income, export markets became an outlet for surplus capital and production, which enabled the wealthy to find new opportunities for profitable investment and speculation abroad. Inequality at home exacerbated class wars, and the dumping of surpluses abroad led in turn to trade wars as Matthew Klein and Michael Pettis argue in their book, *Trade Wars are Class Wars* (Klein & Pettis, 2020). Ironically, and contrary to widespread perceptions, the authors argue that the United States' 'exorbitant privilege' as an issuer of the world's reserve currency has made the country 'the largest single victim' of the system. Instead, they write: "Absorbing the rest of the world's excess output and savings – at the cost of deindustrialization and financial crises – has been America's exorbitant burden" (p. 221).

5 The 1970s Onwards: Victory for Private Authority over the International System

Eric Helleiner in his distinguished account of the post-war era, '*States and the Re-emergence of Global Finance*' (Helleiner, 1994) draws on deep historical research to provide a comprehensive overview of moves by states and the private sector to dismantle the Keynes-White international architecture and construct a new international system of deregulated financial globalisation. Helleiner (op. cit.) examines, in much greater depth than can be undertaken here, key episodes in the re-construction of the system: the restoration of high real rates of interest after 1951; the creation of the Euromarket in the 1960s; the failure to restore management of global capital flows in the 1970s; the deregulation of capital controls in the 1980s; the expansion and the recurring international financial crises of the decades from 1970.

Until the 1970s, UK bank assets had been equal to roughly half the value of UK GDP for a century. Following changes, by the mid-2000s, they had risen to five times the value of GDP (Haldane, 2010). As with size, the effects of liberalisation on banking concentration were immediate and dramatic. The share of the top three largest US banks in total assets rose fourfold, from 10 to 40% between 1990 and 2007 (Haldane, op. cit., Chart 2).

A similar trend is discernible internationally: the share of the top five largest global banks in the assets of the largest 1000 banks has risen from around 8% in 1998 to double that in 2009. This degree of concentration, combined with the large size of the banking industry relative to GDP, has produced a pattern, which is not mirrored in other industries. The largest banking firms are far larger, and have grown far faster, than the largest firms in other industries. (Haldane, 2010, Chart 3).

With the repeal of the McFadden and Glass-Steagall Acts, the too-big-to-fail problem has not just returned but flourished.

By the time of the financial crisis in 2007–8, the UK's financial sector relative to its economy was bigger than that of any other G7 nation. In contrast, UK industry has suffered a faster decline than all its economic rivals in that same period. From 1979 to 1989, investment in financial services grew 320.3% next to investment in manufacturing, which rose only 12.8% (Coates, 1995, p. 6).

From 1979, the global monetary system reverted to the foundation of a real exchange economy on which the interwar restoration of the gold standard was based. While the contemporary globalised regime differs in form from that of the 1920s, ongoing global economic and financial crises are a testament to the similarity in substance.

5.1 The Shadow Banking System

Nowhere is the commodity basis of the financial system clearer than in the shadow-banking sector, or, as the Financial Stability Board (FSB) prefers to call it *The Non-Bank Financial Intermediation* (NBFI) sector.

This sector comprises mainly pension funds, insurance corporations and other financial intermediaries (OFIs). As the FSB reports, the shadow banking sector has grown faster than the banking sector over the past decade, including in 2019. The financial assets of the NBFI sector amounted to an astonishing $200.2 trillion in 2019, accounting for nearly half of the global financial system in 2019, up from 42% in 2008 (FSB, 2020).

Today the vast shadow banking system operates in the equivalent of the financial stratosphere. In this sphere, companies engage in collateralised lending—where cash is exchanged for assets. One of the biggest players is Blackrock, the asset management fund that controls nearly $9 trillion of the world's savings (assets). The shadow-banking sector has expanded in part because it is not viable for companies like Blackrock to safely deposit trillions of dollars in Main—Street banks.

Companies in the sector use repurchasing agreements (repos) to increase (leverage) liquidity in capital markets. This sector has expanded (a) because of the 'encasement' of capital markets beyond the oversight of regulatory democracy; (b) because of the support and engagement of publicly backed central banks; and third because of a flawed, conventional understanding of money. That understanding is of a collateral-based medium of exchange, which lubricates the provision of goods and services. A system that treats money at essence as a commodity, like oil or soya beans, subject to the market forces of supply and demand. That is the orthodox or neoclassical understanding of the nature of money and explains the explosion in the shadow banking sector and the rise of crypto currencies, including bitcoin. It is a theory of money that has caused considerable confusion within the economic profession, as Claudio Borio, head of the Monetary and Economic Department at the Bank for International Settlements has argued: "Few issues in economics have generated such heated debates as the nature of money and its role in the economy. What is money? How is it related to debt? How does it influence economic activity? The recent mainstream economic literature is an unfortunate exception. Bar a few who have sailed into these waters, money has been allowed to sink by the macroeconomics profession. And with little or no regrets" (Borio, 2019, p. 1).

In contrast to today's macroeconomics profession, Keynes understood money as a system based not on a commodity, or on 'exchange' but on the social technology of credit, and its associated regulatory institutions designed to engender trust. For, as Borio (op. cit.) explained, a, "well-functioning system also requires trust that it will deliver price and financial stability. Ensuring trust is difficult and calls for strong institutions – an appropriate 'institutional technology'" (p. 1).

Once again, the global system is unstable. Any variation in the valuation of highly leveraged collateral (securities) in the shadow banking sector is liable to cause panic and financial crisis. Many believe that the Great Financial Crisis of 2007–2009 was caused by a sudden collapse in the value of mortgage securities, widely used as collateral in the shadow-banking sector. This collapse led to runs on repo markets, to bankruptcies, and to financial chaos.

To stabilise the market-based international financial system requires a sound understanding of the nature of money and its possibilities and constraints. That understanding is still beyond the grasp of the most mainstream and orthodox economists, and therefore of many in the finance sector. However, it can be revived.

Second, banking and the financial intermediation of the shadow banking sector, needs to once again be drawn down into the real democratic world of banking regulation. This matters if credit or finance needed by the state is to be mobilised for a transformation of the economy away from dependence on fossil fuels.

5.2 The Return of the Rentier and Wealth Inequality

Keynes, while sound on monetary theory, could be starry-eyed in his political judgements. In the 'concluding notes' of *The General Theory* he predicted that "the rentier aspect of capitalism (is but) a transitional phase which will disappear when it has done its work…the euthanasia of the rentier, of the functionless investor, will be a gradual continuance of what we have seen recently in Great Britain, and will need no revolution" (Keynes, 1936, p. 376).

Beginning in the 1950s, the rentier sector fought back vigorously against that delusion. The policies Keynes had advocated were quickly abandoned. Instead, the sector once again burdened the global economy with debt; wealth inequality; economic, political, and social instability; ecological imbalances; and geopolitical tensions—not unlike those that led to World War II.

Disregarding his warning that dear money should be avoided "as we would hell-fire" (Keynes, 1937, p. 389) real interest rates from the 1980s matched almost exactly those of the 1920s, as Tily (2012) shows in the relevant chart (p. 77).

Radical changes to monetary policy had the distributional impact that Keynes had feared, as this US Federal Reserve data visualisation of March 2021 on the wealth of the top 1% vs the bottom 50%, illustrates so clearly (FED, 2021).

We now inhabit an international system of "economic production and reproduction in which incomes are dominated by rents, and economic life is dominated by rentiers" (Christophers, 2020, p. xvii).

Brett Christophers (op. cit.) calls this system *proprietorial rentier capitalism* rather than *entrepreneurial capitalism*—a form of capitalism structured not around making or providing but around 'having'—assets. Economies have been rigged to favour rentiers: wealthy owners of assets (bonds, stocks and shares, property, racehorses, works of art etc.,).

The most lucrative assets with high real rates of return are debts. In a largely deregulated financial system, there can be no shortage of credit; and because credit effortlessly generates capital gains in the form of interest, the total sum of global credit or debt, relative to the world's income, has exploded. In February 2021, the worldwide debt-to-GDP ratio was at 355%—a record $281 trillion according to the Institute of International Finance's global debt monitor (Reuters, 17 February 2021). At the same time, the global economy, weakened by the Global Financial Crisis, has failed to generate sufficient income (in the form of wages, profits, and tax revenues) needed to repay debts—both public and private. Low rates of investment have resulted in weak economic activity, unemployment, and the expansion of low-paid precarious employment. In addition, looking ahead, there is not much to cheer. 2020 was exceptional because of the pandemic, but according to UNCTAD, global foreign direct investment (FDI) collapsed, falling 42% from $1.5 trillion in 2019 to an estimated $859bn (UNCTAD, 2021). Such a low level was last seen in the 1990s and is more than 30% below the investment trough that followed the 2008–2009 global financial crisis.

The extraordinary level of private and public debt, the low levels of both public and private investment are evidence of dangerous imbalances. The international system has been reconstructed and re-engineered to bolster the 'cumulative oppressive power' of the rentier—and to accelerate the extraction of both labour's and the earth's assets; exploited to repay and reward the rentier.

6 Capitalism and the Climate

A hundred years after the catastrophe of World War I, the global economy is faced with the grave threat of climate breakdown and biodiversity collapse. The Paris climate agreement of 2015 sought to limit global temperature rises to 2 C. That outcome will cost the US alone $36tr in climate damages, according to an important study in Nature

(Martinich, 2019). In a highly indebted world, global warming would lower the income of affected nations as well as damage human health.

In 2017, disasters triggered by weather and climate-related hazards led to global losses of US$320bn. Devastating floods in South Asia took more than 1,200 lives, while communities in the Caribbean struggled to recover from the unprecedented and dangerous hurricane season (Pettifor, 2019, p. 151). For 2018, the insurance giant AON estimated global economic costs of extreme weather at $215bn in the wake of hundreds of cyclones, floods, wildfires, and other relevant episodes. Rival insurer Munich Re set the bill for extreme weather in 2018 at $160bn. AON suggests that 2017–2018 was the costliest two-year period on record for extreme weather disasters, reaching $653bn (as Pettifor, op. cit. clearly demonstrates).

"Climate change is pain," said the top climate scientist, Michael Mann in testimony to the US Congress. "Anyone who tells you differently is selling something – most likely fossil fuels" (Mann, 2019, June 25).

Added to these costs are the subsidies and tax breaks that countries provide to private fossil fuel-extracting corporations. The IMF estimates that "globally, subsidies remained large at $4.7tn (around 6.3% of global GDP) in 2015 and are projected at $5.2tn (and around 6.5% of GDP) in 2017." The largest subsidizers in 2015 were China ($1.4 trillion), the United States ($649bn), Russia ($551bn), the European Union ($289bm), and India ($209bn). About three-quarters of global subsidies are due to domestic factors—energy-pricing reform thus remains largely in countries' own national interest—while coal and petroleum together account for 85% of global subsidies. Efficient fossil fuel pricing in 2015 would have lowered global carbon emissions by 28% and fossil fuel air pollution deaths by 46%, and increased government revenue by 3.8% of GDP (Pettifor, 2019, p. 152).

6.1 'Cathedral Thinking'

Tackling the threat of climate breakdown and biodiversity collapse on human populations and on the economy requires what Greta Thunberg (2019) calls 'cathedral thinking'. Governments will have to mobilise and deploy finance to compensate fossil fuel companies for losses; to retrain workforces and to invest in new more sustainable forms of energy, transport and land use. There will need to be an investment in extreme-weather-event protection; in alternative surface transport, in the power sector. There will have to be improvements to building insulation; in agriculture and land use, by for example, reforesting and sequestering carbon in soils, peatlands, and salt marshes. These mitigation and adaptation measures will be financially costly. Economies will need to undertake a 'great transformation' to end the addiction to fossil fuels. As in the case of war, the scale of this task—to guarantee the security of the nation—is not one the private sector has the financial capacity or motivation to undertake alone.

Given the developed nature of monetary systems in the OECD economies, it is possible to raise large quantities of finance for these purposes. In addition to the role that monetary institutions can play in mobilising credit/finance, the world has accumulated vast quantities of savings that can be deployed for this purpose.

Data collected by the Financial Stability Board (FSB, 2020), set up by the G20 to monitor the global financial system following the crisis, provide estimates of the level of global savings. As noted earlier, the financial assets of the Non-Bank Financial Institutional (NBFI) or shadow-banking sector, amounted to $200.2tn in 2019, accounting for nearly half of the global financial system in 2019, up from 42% in 2008. Furthermore, according to an OECD annual report, "pension funds held retirement savings in pension funds, pension insurance contracts and in other vehicles that exceeded the USD 50 trillion mark worldwide for the first time, with USD 49.2 trillion in the OECD area and USD 1.7 trillion in other reporting jurisdictions at the end of 2019" (OECD, 2020, p.7). Norway holds the biggest sovereign wealth fund in the world, estimated at $872bn.

This vast quantity of savings must be compared to global GDP in current prices, which, according to the World Bank (2021), amounted to only $87.375tn in 2019.

We can therefore safely conclude that there are potential supplies of both public and private *credit* for the purposes needed, and, secondly, there are staggeringly large supplies of both public and private *savings* that could be released to the same end.

We can afford what we can do. However in order to mobilise stable sources of finance, governments will once again have to subordinate capital markets to *public authority*, to guarantee public/private partnerships in mobilising finance, and to serve the interests of society and the ecosystem—as Keynes and Roosevelt partially succeeded in doing in the 1930s and 1940s.

To devise that international system in which markets act as servants, not masters of the global economy, we can draw on the experience, wisdom, and policies of both Keynes and Roosevelt.

6.2 How to Re-purpose the Global Economy?

The first key purpose of a new, more internationalist system must ironically be to re-orient economic activity away from the external stimulus of private actors in the invisible, unaccountable 'encased' globalised economy—and towards the domestic economy. This purpose will be twofold. First, to fulfil democratic mandates to protect the security of a nation's population. Second, to build international peace and cooperation to meet common goals, *by creating full employment at home.* There will be, as a result, no need to compete for economic resources abroad, thereby setting the interests of one country against those of its neighbours. We must, "…recognize that the wisest and most effective way to protect our national interests is through international cooperation – that is to say, through united effort for the attainment of common goals" (Morgenthau, 1944, p. 2).

However, how is this extraordinary transformation to be achieved? That task—of subordinating the private finance sector to the interest of domestic economies—appears insurmountable, given the power and detachment of the sector from the regulatory frameworks of states. However, while the sector appears vast and unstoppable that will change in the event of another global financial crisis, a major ecological catastrophe, or some other transformational event.

Societies will continue to object to the power of the sector (as they do now) and will likely seek protection from markets in a flight to protectionism and authoritarianism. The return of populist, fascist governments that leave globalised, financialised capitalism intact, is not unthinkable. To build and sustain renewed confidence in democracy, governments must prepare and have a plan for an alternative, cooperative, coordinated and more stable international system to draw upon, if they are to address common threats.

The transformation to a more stable system that addresses human needs should be led, not by politicians, but by people power. We know that for change to occur, there is truth in the saying 'the people must lead, so that leaders can follow'.

The first of many steps that must be taken, if societies are to harness the latent power of the population, is to spread public understanding. People cannot act to transform that which they do not understand. Much about the *international* financial system is deliberately clouded and made abstruse by language designed to protect private capital markets operating internationally, from public scrutiny. Instead, the public is encouraged by the economics profession among others, to focus on the nation, the firm, and the individual. That must change and a broader understanding of the international financial order explained.

The most important fact to be shared is this: taxpaying citizens in prosperous economies with sound institutions have immense, potential power. This is an understanding that Keynes deployed when he proposed to use public power—public authority—to revive not just the devastated European economy of 1919, but also the international economy.

Millions of honest, law-abiding citizens may not be aware, but they help to uphold the private, globalised financial system. They do so by regularly paying taxes. The certainty and predictability of tax revenues in OECD economies make the issue of their sovereign bonds safe. OECD bonds are used by the finance sector as highly valuable collateral to back borrowing, speculation, and investment. Taxpayer-backed treasuries and central banks simultaneously help to expand, guarantee and de-risk the activities of the private financial sector.

Public borrowing, or public debt, is not only of great value in mobilising resources for tackling climate change, creating good jobs, and essential infrastructure. It is also of immense importance to the private, globalised 'shadow banking' sector in generating capital gains, and leveraging additional finance. To Wall Street and the City of London, the safe public debt of Britain, Europe and the United States is a truly awesome and even phenomenal gift. (Pettifor, 2019, p. 159). Shadow banks operate by making temporary loans of cash in exchange for, or guaranteed by, collateral—an exchange known as a re-purchase agreement. As Daniela Gabor (2015) has argued, the US and European repo markets, the largest in the world, are built on this most valuable collateral. The state has become 'a collateral factory' for shadow banking.

Despite this backing, the risks the unregulated shadow banking market poses to the global economy are grave. Shadow bankers can use a single unit of collateral to re-leverage a number of times. Manmohan Singh (2017) of the IMF has estimated that, by late 2007, the same collateral 'churned' or was used roughly three times to leverage additional borrowing in speculative markets. That is like using the value of a single asset—one's property—to guarantee additional borrowing from three different banks.

The public is largely unaware of these grave risks to their economic security and stability. Nor is the public aware of the reliance of the finance sector on public institutions like central banks.

A recent interview throws light on Wall Street's dependence on the public debt of the United States—or US 'treasuries'. R. Martin Chavez, a retired Goldman Sachs executive, explained that US Treasuries "are the beating heart of the global financial system ...... the core of the (private) financial system." He went on to express concern about a possible cyberattack on Treasuries—99.9% of which exist purely in electronic form—and explained:

> There's just a computer somewhere that's keeping track of who owns them. And if someone could get into that record and cause us to lose confidence in who owns the Treasuries, that would be, I mean—it's so hard to even think about that outcome—it would be so extreme and so dire. (Bloomberg, 12 January 2021)

Mariana Mazzucato wrote that the 'timid mouse' that is the private finance sector needs the 'roaring lion' of the public sector. (Mazzucato, 2018 p. 5). The fact is private financial markets cannot function without the backing of public institutions: central banks, government treasuries, their taxation systems and institutions, and the safety of public debt. Yet guarantees and subsidies that derisk private investments are granted without the explicit consent of taxpaying citizens.

Until societies fully grasp the importance of public debt to the finance sector, then we will lack the ability to leverage power over immensely wealthy, globalised corporations and individuals. If we turn a blind eye to the value they attach to public assets—central bank resources, tax revenues, and government debts—then the sector will continue to parasitically extract rent from public assets, and to weaken both the economy and society.

To reiterate, taxpayers have agency over global financial markets.

Around the world, taxpayers subsidise, embolden and enrich centres of financial power such as Wall Street, Frankfurt, Tokyo and the City of London. The bank bailouts after the 2008 crisis demonstrated that citizens and publicly financed institutions could protect capitalism's rentiers from the discipline of the 'free market'. Thanks to the backing and firepower provided by millions of taxpaying citizens, central banks deployed immense financial might to bail out the globalised banking system. Those actions protected corporations from the market's power to discipline risk-taking and excess with bankruptcies, debt deleveraging and collapse. A Great Depression was avoided. It was a great power deployed by central bankers but without the authority—or even the knowledge—of many citizens.

Citizen power over the financial system lies in abeyance, suppressed by the dominant moneyed class—and by many in the economics profession. Suppressed also by the narrow, myopic view that politicians and citizens have of their potential economic power.

6.3 There is Hope: Keynes's Grand Scheme Revived in Europe

Recent developments provide hope for a necessary transformation. Just over hundred years after Keynes produced his *Grand Scheme* in October 2020, the European Union, after extensive debate and argument, issued a joint plan to fund economic recovery across the Union from the coronavirus pandemic. Given the neoliberal nature of the Eurozone, it was an implausible initiative driven by countries worst hit by the coronavirus pandemic, Italy and Spain. The then Italian Prime minister, Giuseppe Conte and Spanish PM Pedro Sanchez, made a proposal for European Commission-backed 'corona bonds' in April, 2020. This proposal required the issue of *joint public debt* at the EU level, creating a solidarity mechanism for the redistribution of debt between the European states (EU Stability Mechanism, April 2020). As the European Commission explains on its website: "this initiative is part of a concerted European response, which includes the European Commission with its safety net for workers called SURE and the European Investment Bank with its safety net for businesses. The Commission's SURE initiative provides funding to Member States of up to €100tn by covering part of the costs related to the creation or extension of national short-time work schemes" (EU Stability Mechanism, April 2020).

The Eurozone system had been constructed as a single unified monetary system—effectively detached from oversight by the regulatory democracy of European states. The Eurozone's primary aim was to remove any friction to the mobility of capital across the union. The zone's unified monetary policy was not complemented by the solidarity of a shared fiscal policy—not even during the Eurozone crisis of 2008–2012. However, the burden of losses caused by the Great Financial Crisis were borne by taxpayers across the continent, particularly those in the poorer states. In just the same way as First World War debts and the burden of adjustment had been imposed on defeated nations in 2019.

The global pandemic of 2019 brought dramatic change. At an extraordinary and historic meeting on 21 July 2020, European leaders overcame the resistance of Hayekian-influenced economists, and agreed to the creation of the temporary recovery instrument. It was to be dubbed 'Next

Generation EU' (EU Commission, NGEU, and 27 May 2020). What was unprecedented about the instrument was that it crossed previous red lines. Red lines that had prevented the more prosperous countries from using their economic power to mobilise finance for weaker EU nations. The 2020 decision to jointly issue and back EU common debt and central transfers, echoed a central tenet of Keynes's 1919 *Grand Scheme*. It would enable the bloc of EU states to 'jointly and severally' use their collective power to raise finance to alleviate the social and economic consequences of the COVID-19 pandemic—across the union.

As would have been the case for the proposed 1919 bonds, the decision granted the EU preferred creditor status—with debt repayment to the EU taking priority over funds owed to private or other bilateral creditors.

In launching the new monetary instrument, the President of the European Council, Charles Michel—the ex-prime minister of Belgium—said, "I truly think this is a historic moment. ... the decision to borrow together for the sake of investment and reform, is to renew our European marriage vows for the next 30 years. European unity has won through, and more than ever I think that the message we are sending to European citizens is one of confidence, of solidity, of strength" (EU Council, 23 July 2020).

Back in 1919 there was no continent-wide central bank to support a bond issuance by European states. A hundred years later, in 2020, the board of the European Central Bank (ECB) had already agreed to an asset purchasing programme and collateral framework dubbed the 'pandemic emergency purchase programme' (ECB 18 March, 2020). Launched in March 2020 with an initial envelope of €750bn it permitted the ECB to purchase jointly issued Euro bonds, as well as the sovereign bonds of individual states of the EU. By so doing, the PEPP helped, at a time of severe economic crisis, to counter a rise in the yields of the sovereign bonds of EU states.

These radical steps towards the use of the collective power of the EU's richer states to support the recovery of weaker states may just be a temporary aberration and may even benefit richer countries of the EU more than lower income countries. However, they indicate a shift in thinking that reflects both the radical ideas of the 1919 *Grand Scheme* and raises the possibility of transformation.

7 Summary and Conclusions

The nineteenth-century gold standard, like today's financial globalisation, represented "the internationalism of wealth - of the 1%" (Tily, 2020). We need to build, as Keynes and Roosevelt attempted to do in the 1930s and later at Bretton Woods, an 'internationalism of labour' to tackle the grave crises of economic failure and climate breakdown.

That particular task is urgent. The 1979 Charney Report from the US National Academy of Sciences calculated that doubling the stock of atmospheric carbon would increase global temperatures by 3 degrees centigrade (Policy Tensor, 23 May 2019). At the time, the world was dumping 5bn metric tons per annum into the atmosphere. Now we are dumping 10bn metric tons every year. We are riding what some scientists are calling 'the hockey stick of doom'. In order to protect life's support systems and to achieve a radical and urgent transformation, society must escape from capitalism's globalised, carbon-belching financial system—designed and engineered to issue trillions of dollars of unregulated credit to fund supposedly limitless speculation, consumption and production; and in turn to fuel toxic emissions.

For humanity to survive, we can no longer afford to bend to the will of the gods of finance.

Indeed, by escaping from the inexorable control of the masters of the financial universe, we will find we can afford to create a new, more balanced system of international economic and ecological justice. We can, and to survive, we must, transform and end the failed globalised system of capitalism that now threatens democracy, the earth's life support systems and human civilisation. We know we can do that, because, as this chapter shows, we have done it before.

References

Baker, D. (2013, June 3). Recession culprits? Start with Alan Greenspan and Jean-Claude Trichet. *The Guardian.*

Block, F. (2001). *Introduction* to Polanyi, K. *The Great Transformation* (p. XXX), Beacon Press.

Bloomberg, B. S. (2021, January 12). Wall Street visionaries provide chilling views on next big risk. *Bloomberg News.*

Borio, C. (2019, January 11). *On money, debt, trust and central banking* (BIS Working Papers, No 763). Available at: https://www.bis.org/publ/work763.htm.

Coates, D. (1995). UK underperformance: Claim and reality. In D. Coates & J. Hillard (Eds.), *UK economic decline: Key texts* (pp. 3–24). Prentice Hall.

Chernow, R. (2010). *The house of Morgan: An American banking dynasty and the rise of modern finance.* Grove Atlantic Publishers.

Christophers, B. (2020). *Rentier capitalism: Who owns the economy and who pays for it?* (p. xvii). Verso Publishers

D'Arista, J. (2019). *All fall down: Debt, deregulation and financial crises* (p. 1). Edward Elgar Publishers.

European Commission: *Recovery plan for Europe.* Available at: https://ec.europa.eu/info/strategy/recovery-plan-europe_en

European Commission: *Next generation EU, 27 May, 2020. Europe's moment: Repair and prepare for the next generation.* Press Release. https://ec.europa.eu/commission/presscorner/detail/en/ip_20_940

European Council. (2020, July 23). *Speech by President Charles Michel, at the European Parliament.*

ECB. (2020). *ECB announces €750 billion Pandemic Emergency Purchase Programme (PEPP).* Available at: https://www.ecb.europa.eu/press/pr/date/2020/html/ecb.pr200318_1~3949d6f266.en.html.

European Stability Mechanism. (2020, April). *Pandemic crisis support.* Available at: https://www.esm.europa.eu/content/europe-response-corona-crisis; https://ec.europa.eu/info/strategy/recovery-plan-europe_en.

Federal Reserve. (2021, March 9). The distribution of household wealth in the U.S. since 1989! Available at: https://www.federalreserve.gov/releases/z1/dataviz/dfa/distribute/chart/#quarter:125;series:Assets;demographic:networth;population:1,7;units:levels;range:1990.1,2020.4.

Financial Stability Board (FSB). (2020, December 16). *Global monitoring report on non-bank financial Intermediation 2020.*

Gabor, D., & Cornel, B. (2015). *Banking on bonds: The new links between states and markets*. UWE Bristol and Boston University. Available at: https://doi.org/10.1111/jcms.12309.

Galbraith, J. K. (1955). *The great crash 1929*. Pelican Publishers.

Haldane, A. (2010). *The $100bn question*. Speech. Available at: https://www.bankofengland.co.uk/-/media/boe/files/speech/2010/the-100-billion-question-speech-by-andrew-haldane.pdf?la=en&hash=97C2693961C85F58D9071131BBF61AED1B9E777C.

Helleiner, E. (1994). *States and the re-emergence of global finance*. Cornell University Press.

Keynes, J. M. (1920). *The economic consequences of the peace*. Palgrave Macmillan.

Keynes, J. M. (1923, December). Speech to the liberal party. CW, Vol. XIX, pp. 158–159.

Keynes, J. M. (1933). *The means to prosperity*, CW IX. (E. Johnson & D. Moggridge, Eds.). Royal Economic Society.

Keynes, J. M. (1936). Edition published by the Royal Economic Society, 1973

Keynes, J. M. (1937, January 13). Article in *The Times*, CW. XXI, p. 389.

Keynes, J. M. (2013a). *Draft for an explanatory letter to be addressed by the Prime Minister to the president, M. Clemenceau, and Signor Orlando*, CW, Vol. XVI, p. 436.

Keynes, J. M. (2013b). Activities 1914–1919: The treasury and versailles. Letter to Dr E Rosenbaum, 11 April 1942, CW, Vol. XVI, p. 416.

Keynes, J. M. (2013c). *The revision of the treaty*, CW, Vol. III, p. 8.

Klein, M. C., & Pettis, M. (2020). *Trade Wars Are Class Wars: How Rising Inequality Distorts the Global Economy and Threatens International Peace*. Yale University Press.

Lamont, E. (1993). *The ambassador from Wall Street: The story of Thomas W. Lamont, J.P. Morgan's chief executive: A biography*. Madison Books.

Macmillan, M. (2003). *Paris 1919: Six months that changed the world*. Penguin Random House.

Mann, M. (2019, June 25). *Oral opening statement. Testimony to U.S. house oversight committee hearing on climate change & natural disasters*. Available at: https://michaelmann.net/content/oral-opening-statement-michael-mann-testimony-us-house-oversight-committee-hearing-climate.

Martinich, J., & Crimmins, A. (2019). Climate damages and adaptation potential across diverse sectors of the United States. *National Climate* (pp. 397–404). Available at: https://doi.org/10.1038/s41558-019-0444-6.

Mazzucato, M. (2018). *The entrepreneurial state: Debunking public vs. private sector myths* (p. 5). Penguin.

Morgenthau, H. (US Treasury Secretary). (1944, July 22). *Address at closing plenary session.* Bretton Woods Conference. Available at: https://www.cvce.eu/en/obj/closing_address_by_henry_morgenthau_jr_22_july_1944-en-b88b1fe7-8fec-4da6-ae22-fa33edd08ab6.html.

Morris, E., & Pitchfork, van B. (2016, February 18). *The ECB hiked rates into a crisis in 2011: 4 charts looking back on European private markets.* Available at: https://pitchbook.com/news/articles/the-ecb-hiked-rates-into-a-crisis-in-2011-4-charts-looking-back-on-european-private-markets.

Needham, D. (2014). *UK monetary policy: From devaluation to Thatcher, 1967–82* (p. 46). Palgrave Macmillan.

OECD. (2020). *Pension markets in focus.* Available: https://www.oecd.org/pensions/private-pensions/pensionmarketsinfocus.htm.

Pettifor, A. (2019). *The case for the green new deal*. Verso. Available at: https://www.versobooks.com/books/3102-the-case-for-the-green-new-deal.

Polanyi, K. (1940). *The passing of 19th century civilisation, PRIME economics* (Bennington Lecture 1). Available at: https://www.primeeconomics.org/articles/the-1940-polanyi-bennington-lectures-series-in-one-go/.

Polanyi, K. (1944). *The great transformation: The political and economic origins of our time* (p. 3). Beacon Press, 1957.

Polanyi, K. (2018). *Economy and society: Selected writings* (M. Cangiani & C. Thomasberger, Eds.). Polity Press.

Policy Tensor. (2019, May 23). *Fear and loathing on the hockey stick of doom.* Available at: https://policytensor.com/2019/05/23/fear-and-loathing-on-the-hockey-stick-of-doom/.

Rauchway, E. (2015). *The money makers: How Roosevelt and Keynes ended the depression, defeated fascism, and secured a prosperous.* Peace. Basic.

Rauchway, E. (2016). Keynes's early work on monetary policy. *Challenge Magazine, 59*(1), 12–21.

Reuters, M. J. (2021). *COVID response drives $24 trillion surge in global debt*. Available at: https://www.reuters.com/article/us-global-debt-iif-idUSKBN2AH285.

Reynolds, D. (2020a, January 31–February 6). Between toughness and talking. *New Statesman* (p. 30).

Reynolds, D. (2020b, January 29). Between toughness and talking: 75 Years since Yalta. *New Statesman.* Available at: https://www.newstatesman.com/world/2020/01/between-toughness-and-talking-75-years-yalta.

Singh, M. (2017). *Collateral reuse and balance sheet space*. IMF Working Paper. imf.org.

Skidelsky, R. (1983). *John Maynard Keynes, Volume 1, Hopes Betrayed, 1883–1920* (p. 401). Viking.

Slobodian, Q. (2018). *Globalists: The end of empire and the birth of neoliberalism* (p. 5). Harvard University Press.

Straumann, T. (2019). *1931: Debt, crisis, and the rise of Hitler*. Oxford University Press.

Sutton, T., & Judah, B. (2021, February). *Turning the tide on dirty money: Why the world's democracies need a global kleptocracy initiative*. Center for American Progress. Available at: https://www.americanprogress.org/issues/security/reports/2021/02/26/495402/turning-tide-dirty-money/.

Thunberg, G. (2019). Speech to the British parliament. *The Guardian*. Available at: https://www.theguardian.com/environment/2019/apr/23/greta-thunberg-full-speech-to-mps-you-did-not-act-in-time.

Tily, G. (2012, May 29). *Keynes's monetary theory of interest* (BIS Papers No. 65). Available at: https://www.bis.org/author/geoff_tily.htm

Tily, G. (2016). *As if Keynes had never lived. TalK on 80th anniversary of publication of Keynes's general theory in King's College*. Cambridge. Published by Policy Research in Macroeconomics. Available at: https://www.primeeconomics.org/articles/geoff-tily-presents-at-cambridge-keynes-conference/.

Tily, G. (2020). *From the globalisation of wealth, to the internationalism of labour*. Unpublished but shared with the author in June 2020.

Tooze, A. (2014). *The deluge: The great war and the remaking of global order* (p. 295). Penguin.

Tooze, A. (2018, July 29). Politics don't matter; market forces shape our world. So ran the dominant ethos before 2008. Adam Tooze, the author of a landmark book, says it was always an illusion. *The Guardian*. Available at: https://www.theguardian.com/commentisfree/2018/jul/29/city-of-london-desperate-gamble-china-vulnerable-economy.

UNCTAD. (2021, January 24). *Investment trends monitor*. Available at: https://unctad.org/news/global-foreign-direct-investment-fell-42-2020-outlook-remains-weak.

US Federal Reserve. (2021). *Distributional financial accounts. distribution of household wealth in the U.S. since 1989*. Available at: https://www.federalreserve.gov/releases/z1/dataviz/dfa/distribute/table/.

World Bank. (2021). *GDP: current US$*". Available at: https://data.worldbank.org/indicator/NY.GDP.MKTP.CD.

6

Exploring the Case for Universal Services

Anna Coote

1 Introduction

The Social Guarantee has been developed in the UK as a contribution to policy debates about sustainable welfare systems. Launched in 2021, its primary purpose has been to develop and communicate the idea that everyone has a right to life's essentials or, put another way, to get what they need to participate in society and live a life that they value. It reflects a growing interest in the concept of universal basic services (UBS) that represent a virtual or social income alongside money income. Indeed, UBS grew out of a concern with an increasingly widespread endorsement of 'universal basic income' (UBI) as an alleged solution to problems of poverty, unemployment and deteriorating welfare states. During the COVID-19 pandemic, support for UBI grew more vociferous, on the ground that it would ease the process of economic recovery. The Social

A. Coote (✉)
New Economics Foundation (NEF), London, UK
e-mail: Anna.Coote@neweconomics.org

P. Arestis and M. Sawyer (eds.), *Economic Policies for Sustainability and Resilience*, International Papers in Political Economy,
https://doi.org/10.1007/978-3-030-84288-8_6

Guarantee offers an approach that shares some of the goals of progressive advocates of UBI, but is embedded in a different ideology and has widely different practical implications. It seeks to reclaim and develop the collective ideal that inspired the creation of welfare states in the post-war era. It embodies transactions that are public, shared and largely decommodified, rather than private, individual and marketised.

The Social Guarantee encompasses both cash income and social income, as Fig. 1 indicates. On the left-hand side is income, derived from earnings and an income guarantee. On the right-hand side are universal services: these are key examples, rather than a definitive list.

My focus for this chapter is the right-hand side of the diagram, where social income is derived from in-kind benefits in the form of services and other collectively generated activities that are intended to secure life's essentials for all. While I use the term UBS throughout to describe these services and activities, this is not to imply that 'basic' means minimal.

I explore the hypothesis that the Social Guarantee—as a framework for policy and practice—can make a vital contribution to sustainability and resilience by helping to create what Raworth identifies as a 'safe and just space for humanity' between a social foundation and an ecological ceiling (2017, p. 44).

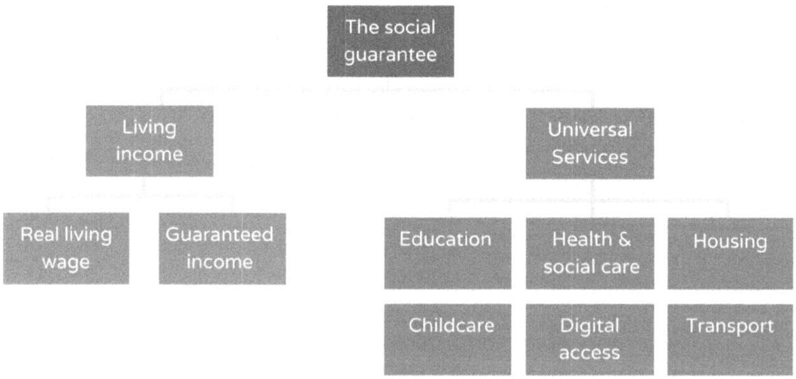

Fig. 1 The Social Guarantee (*Source* Own Construction)

I consider the component parts of UBS and how—taken together—they relate to the objective of improving and maintaining human well-being within these parameters. I examine the practical implications of applying this approach generically across service areas and specifically in four areas: childcare, housing, transport and food. I explore the likely impact of UBS in terms of equity, efficiency, solidarity and sustainability. I address challenges to the case for UBS and end by considering the relationship between the two sides of the Social Guarantee, how cash and in-kind benefits are interdependent and how they can best support each other.

1.1 The Emerging Case for UBS

The first prospectus for UBS was produced by the Institute for Global Prosperity at University College London in 2017 (Portes et al., 2017). The ideas in the original report were further developed through a indicative literature review published in 2019 (Coote et al., 2019), a book published in 2020, *The Case for Universal Basic Services* (Coote & Percy, 2020), and a range of papers and blog posts available via the Social Guarantee website launched in 2021 (The Social Guarantee, 2021).

Proposals for UBS have been closely informed by the experience of public services in the UK, where government policies since the 1970s have chipped away at the post-war consensus and at the value of benefits in kind. Changes have been driven by a vision of economic success based on personal choice, private ownership, a small state and a free market, blaming the jobless and poor for their own troubles and urging individuals to help themselves. Many services, including care for children and disabled adults, as well as housing and transport, have been outsourced to for-profit corporations, stripped down to the bare bones, abolished altogether or left to the vagaries of voluntarism and philanthropy. Combined with cuts to the value of social security benefits, the effects have greatly exacerbated social and economic inequalities, and left more than a million living in destitution (Fitzpatrick, 2018). This was before the Covid-19 pandemic, which has made matters a great deal worse.

The UK experience has been echoed across Europe, where many other countries have travelled a similar path. In most of them, however, there seems to have been a slower deterioration and I have noted below some of the many examples of better practice, which offer useful lessons for developing UBS.

1.2 Component Parts of the Concept

The term 'universal basic services' (UBS) is defined as follows. Taking its components in reverse order, *'services'* are defined as collectively generated activities that serve the public interest. A service can be distinguished from a 'good' as being a type of activity that is not separable from the producer and where production and consumption occur simultaneously. However, material goods and infrastructure are intrinsic to services in all areas of need, as we shall see below. Services are described as '*basic*' to distinguish activities that are essential and sufficient to enable people to meet their needs. They are not simply the bare minimum for survival, but what is required to participate and flourish. *'Universal'* conveys the idea that all citizens and/or residents are entitled to services that are sufficient to meet their needs, regardless of ability to pay (Coote & Percy, 2020, p. 4).

Defined in this way, UBS includes services that already exist in many countries, such as education and healthcare. More importantly, it conveys an ambition to expand the approach in practice both by improving the quality of existing services, and by reaching into new areas such as housing, care and transport, to enable everyone to have access to life's essentials.

1.3 Satisfying Human Needs

The case for UBS rests on two key principles: *shared needs* and *collective responsibilities*. It recognises that all human beings have the same set of basic needs that must be satisfied in order to survive and thrive, think for one's self and participate in society. Theories of capability and human need converge around this point. Nussbaum (2000) describes three 'core' capabilities: of affiliation, bodily integrity and practical reason. Doyal and Gough (1991) identify health and critical autonomy as basic human needs that are prerequisites for social participation. The theme is echoed in more recent work on 'protected needs', as in Di Giulio and Defila (2020).

Several factors distinguish human needs from wants or preferences. They are universal across time and space. While the detail of how they are met will vary widely, they always require certain generic 'satisfiers' that remain fairly constant, although the list may evolve over time. These have been identified by need theorists in the following ways: as water, nutrition, shelter, secure and non-threatening work, education, healthcare, security in childhood, significant primary relationships, physical and economic security, and a safe environment (Doyal & Gough, 1991; Miller, 2012). More recent efforts to identify "a set of universal, irreducible and essential material conditions for achieving basic human wellbeing" have found that access to motorised transport and to information and communications should be included (Rao & Minn, 2017). There is a strong case for including *care*, which is only implied in the list above, as a generic satisfier (The Care Collective, 2020).

Needs are intrinsically satiable: there are limits beyond which more food, more work or more security are no longer helpful and could even do one harm. There comes a point where *sufficiency* is reached in the process of meeting needs: this helps to constrain a tendency towards excessive use of resources that is associated with satisfying consumer wants, threatening to breach planetary boundaries. The focus on needs and sufficiency aligns UBS with sustainable development, aiming to meet current needs without compromising the ability of future generations to meet their own needs (Brundtland Commission, 1987).

1.4 The Spectrum of Life's Essentials

The means of satisfying human needs (life's essentials) range across a spectrum that is generated by history and cultural expectations as well as by the specifics required to secure access in each case. At one end of the spectrum, there are needs that few can meet on their own, where most people depend on collective systems of provision. Trying to access and pay for them individually is likely to be ruinous if not fatal: examples include education and healthcare. Childcare and adult social care may belong to this category or be closer to the centre of the spectrum: this will vary between countries and household types, depending on how far uncommodified care is available within families and on the social and financial implications for informal carers.

Towards the centre of the spectrum, there are needs that many, but by no means all, are able to meet through direct payment: housing and transport are some examples. These tend to involve a considerable amount of material infrastructure and it is most unlikely that unregulated markets will ensure fair and adequate distribution. The higher the costs passed on to the user, the more people will find that life's essentials are beyond their reach. Public policies are crucial for making them universally affordable, accessible and of sufficient quality.

At the other end of the spectrum there are needs most people expect to meet for themselves directly through market transactions—food is a relevant example. Even so, public policies are required to safeguard quality and availability for all (Benton et al., 2019; Sharpe & Barling, 2019).

Figure 2 suggests how different areas of need satisfaction are distributed across the spectrum. It is purely indicative, reflecting what tends to happen in most societies for historical and cultural reasons. It is not normative, nor is it inclusive: it could also cover other essentials, such as utilities. The left hand side is where life's essentials tend to be met by individual market transactions; on the right they tend to be met through collective measures. Those in the centre are often met by private payment but require collective measures such as investment and regulation, to ensure access is universal, equitable and sufficient.

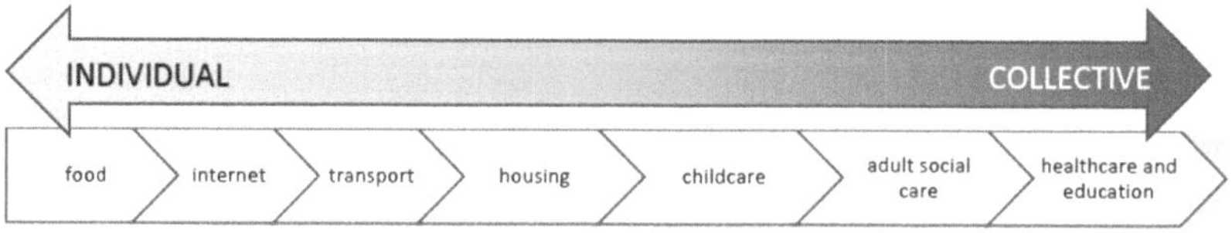

Fig. 2 Individual-collective spectrum for securing life's essentials (*Source* Own Construction)

The Social Guarantee includes a living income to ensure that everyone has enough disposable cash to secure part or all of those essentials that occupy the 'individual' end and centre of the spectrum. In every case, however, exercising a degree of collective responsibility is the only way to ensure that everyone has access to life's essentials, according to need, not ability to pay. This is the 'fundamental basis' of social life, as Durkheim observed: people "cannot live together without agreeing and consequently without making mutual sacrifices, joining themselves to one another in a strong and enduring fashion" (Durkheim, 1984, pp. 154–159). The goal of a safe and just space for humanity can only be realised through societal responsibility, to enable universal "access to a minimum level of ecological and social resources necessary to be able to live a good life" (Fuchs, 2020, 296).

UBS is about exercising collective responsibility to meet shared needs, with a focus on services rather than money and goods. It involves pooling resources, sharing risks and investing collectively—through government institutions—in social and material infrastructure to serve the public interest. As such, this agenda relates chiefly to resource use that is public or social, rather than private: services that are used by all who need them and funded wholly or partly through taxation.

The collective provision of services to meet shared needs amounts to a social income that replaces out-of-pocket expenditure. This leaves individuals and households with more disposable cash (all else being equal) that may be spent on meeting needs at the 'individual' end of the spectrum.

In the rest of this chapter, I describe the principled framework that underpins the Social Guarantee and show how this can be applied to existing universal services as well as to childcare, housing, transport and food. The potential benefits of this approach, in terms of equity, efficiency, solidarity and sustainability, are explored. A number of challenges are addressed, including questions about costs and funding sources. I end by considering how the case for universal basic income (UBI) relates to the Social Guarantee and how a cash income guarantee can be combined with a social income in the form of universal services.

2 Putting UBS into Practice: A Customised Approach Within a Shared Framework

The idea of universal services is not new. It builds on the spirit of Roosevelt's New Deal and post-war welfare states. Since most rich countries have health and education systems that are free at the point of use, there is plenty to learn from past experience. For example, concentrating power in the hands of large, centrally controlled institutions has been found to diminish the autonomy of citizens and service users; contracting out services to for-profit organisations rarely serves the public interest well; and there is no one-size-fits-all model for service delivery. A key lesson is that there can be no return to the traditional top-down model of 20th-century state services. Instead, the UBS agenda seeks to transform the ways in which services are organised, delivered and controlled.

Services differ from each other because of the specific functions they perform to meet needs. This requires a customised approach to planning and organisation in each case. Yet all areas within the UBS agenda have certain features in common because they are all engaged in enabling people to have fair and sufficient access to life's essentials. Thus, an acknowledgement of the specific characteristics and provisioning systems associated with different areas of need is combined with a generic approach shaped by shared values. Together, they constitute the Social Guarantee as a framework for policy and practice.

Summarised briefly, this framework involves collective responsibility for ensuring that shared needs are met, exercised through democratically elected governments. Power is devolved to the lowest appropriate level. Services are delivered by a range of organisations with different models of ownership and control, all sharing a clear set of enforceable public interest obligations. These obligations include giving workers decent pay and conditions.

There is meaningful participation in planning and delivering services by residents and service users, working in close partnership with professionals and other service workers. In addition, there are clear rules and procedures for fair and inclusive eligibility and entitlement. People have access according to need, not ability to pay. Access is conditional on need.

Who decides who needs what will vary from one service to another: eligibility may depend on professional judgement, locality or age, or on a claim by the individual—or a combination of these. Decisions about the scope of UBS and who is eligible should be subject to democratic dialogue, through citizens' assemblies and juries or similar models (Coote & Percy, 2020, pp. 111–112).

In some cases and settings, reflecting the right-hand side of the spectrum in Fig. 2, it may be appropriate for a service to be free to all at the point of use. In others, the critical factor may be a realisable entitlement to a service, rather than free provision: here, there may be a strong element of collective funding, combined with low-cost charges for users and partial or total exemptions to ensure that they are genuinely accessible for all income groups.

Access to life's essentials as an entitlement rather than a concession or privilege follows Marshall's view of 'social citizenship'. This holds that every member of society should have *positive* economic and social rights as well as the more traditional '*negative*' rights that protect us from harm and maintain our civil liberties (1965, pp. 261–272). 'Positive' social rights enable people to claim the means that are essential for participating fully in society, and for realising their civil and political rights. They feature in the constitutions of some countries, including Finland, Sweden and Belgium, among others. While there is often quite a distance between what is written in a constitution and what happens in practice, declarations of this kind set out what is agreed to be desirable and help to create a favourable climate of opinion. As such they can serve as a touchstone and support for progressive policymakers, local initiatives and social movements.

Most declarations of social rights need further development, including legislation backed up by strong political support, to put them into practice. For social rights to be realised fully, they would ideally be codified in law and be accompanied by a robust framework of 'procedural rights', that is, systems and protocols that enable people to know and claim what they are entitled to by means that are fair, accessible, timely and affordable (Galligan, 1992, pp. 55–68).

Once entitlements are established, they have to be upheld. This implies corresponding duties and duty-bearers who are clearly identified and suitably resourced and supported to fulfil their duties. The role of the state is crucial in this regard. In some areas of need and in some settings, it will be appropriate for the state to be a direct provider of services, often working through local authorities. The Social Guarantee involves a shift in power towards localities (including local councils and locally-based non-government organisations) and people who use services. It favours diverse models of ownership and control, coupled with a changing dynamic between 'bottom-up' and 'top-down' politics, and a transformation of the culture and practice of public authorities.

Against this background, the national state retains four essential functions. The first is to ensure equality of access, between and within localities. The second is to set and enforce ethical and practical standards. The third is to collect and invest the necessary funds, distributing them to maximise inclusion and fairness. The fourth is to encourage diverse models of delivery and to coordinate functions across the different areas of need, in order to maximise positive impacts.

3 Extending UBS into New Areas

The Social Guarantee aims for radical improvements in healthcare, schooling and other services, such as policing and social work, which are already (in theory, if not always in practice) in the public realm and universally available according to need, not ability to pay. It also seeks to extend the approach to areas such as housing, transport and childcare as well as to adult social care, and to access to digital information and communications. Here, I focus on four of life's essentials ranging from the collective to the individual end of the provisioning spectrum outlined in fig 2. I consider what would constitute a package of measures consistent with the principled framework of the Social Guarantee, examples of good practice that could be built upon to implement the framework and possible impacts in terms of human and planetary wellbeing.

3.1 Childcare

Education, security in childhood and access to paid work are recognised as generic 'satisfiers' of basic human needs and childcare is a means of meeting those needs; this is by providing early education and care for pre-school age children and enabling parents to go out to work. It can only be made available and affordable for all by exercising collective responsibility. Poor children and families have more to gain from it—and are more disadvantaged without it—than those who are better off (Lloyd & Potter, 2014, p. 78). Childcare is therefore an obvious candidate for inclusion in the UBS agenda. 'Childcare' is the term used throughout this section to denote early childhood education and care, for pre-school children. The period it covers varies between countries,.

Many countries have well-developed childcare systems. The challenge almost everywhere is to ensure that a sufficient quality of childcare is universally accessible. Factors that contribute to quality in childcare include training and qualifications of staff, ratios of children to staff (lower is generally better), a good mix between children with different social and ethnic backgrounds, suitably warm, consistent relationships between children and staff, parental involvement in managing childcare centres, and opening times to suit parents' working lives.

Norway, which sets an enviable example, has well-qualified staff, relatively high staff-child ratios, a consistent form of childcare setting (the kindergarten) and continuity of care from age one to six as the norm. It combines "a legal guarantee to a place for all children with fees that are both low overall and income-related" (Ellingsaeter, 2014, pp. 53–76).

In most countries childcare is provided by a mix of for-profit, public and voluntary organisations. The role of for-profit providers has a bearing on both cost and quality, where resources are "siphoned off for shareholders rather than invested in staff wages and other quality inputs" (Stewart et al, 2014, pp. 19–42; also, pp. 209–226). Where for-profit provision is combined with a demand-led, fee-paying system, the observed effects are "a rise in the fees charged by providers, a drop in standards in poorer areas, and an increase in inequalities of access" (Penn, 2014, pp. 453). However, Norway has reportedly managed to expand provision, open it up to private businesses and still maintain quality. This is attributed to the fact that government covers 85% of childcare costs, caps fees, imposes tight regulations on staff qualifications, limits profit to what is 'reasonable' and ensures that parents sit on kindergarten boards.

To make sure children from disadvantaged backgrounds participate, research suggests that "the most effective strategy is universal access plus outreach to vulnerable groups, not one or the other" (Stewart, 2013, p. 223).

Few governments have been willing to provide entirely free universal childcare for all pre-school children, in spite of strong evidence about the benefits it can bring. In Denmark, which is typical of more generous state funders, local authorities are expected to cover no less than 75% of costs, while parents pay no more than 25%. For a lone parent in the US, childcare costs are over half of average net income and in Ireland that figure is 42%. Couples in the UK and New Zealand spend around a third of their income on childcare (OECD, 2016). This highlights the value of social income delivered through the SG framework.

Total public spending on childcare (including care, pre-school education and related in-kind benefits) as a percentage of gross domestic product (GDP) ranges from 1.7% in France, 1.5% in Norway and 1.4% in the Netherlands, to 1.1% in the UK, 0.8% in Germany and 0.7% in Australia, leaving the US at the lower end with spending worth 0.6% of GDP (Stewart, 2013).

Spending and quality are inevitably intertwined. In the UK campaigners have argued that in order to achieve high quality care, childcare workers should have training and salaries comparable to primary school staff. They have calculated, accordingly, that free universal provision for children aged from six months to the start of compulsory schooling, would cost 3% of GDP. They also estimate that nine-tenths of the costs would be recouped through employment gains, increased tax revenues and reduced income support payments (De Henau, 2017; Himmelweit et al., 2014).

Childcare can play a substantial role in enabling children and families to stay within Raworth's "safe and just space for humanity". The OECD has identified a range of social benefits that can be derived from "high quality early childhood education and care", including better health, reduced likelihood of individuals engaging in risky behaviour and stronger ‘civic and social engagement’, with positive ‘spill-over effects’ for society as a whole (OECD, 2011, p. 4). Enabling parents—especially mothers—to undertake paid employment can also bring considerable social benefits, including greater financial security, personal autonomy and development, and the avoidance of harms associated with unemployment, such as poverty, ill-health, low self-esteem and depression.

There are three ways in which childcare can contribute to ecological sustainability. While these are not quantifiable, they help to illustrate the potential contribution of a range of public services (such as education, healthcare and adult social care), which could have a significant combined effect. First, childcare can help to prevent various kinds of harm that would otherwise impair people’s wellbeing and require costly and resource-intensive interventions by a range of public agencies. Secondly, a well-regulated and securely funded system can be brought within a shared set of protocols for sustainability, covering for example the way childcare centres are constructed, equipped and maintained, how much energy and non-renewable resources they use, and how children travel to and from home. Thirdly, they can encourage children from a very young age to value, enjoy and safeguard the natural environment. In commercial settings, where childcare is a commodity supplied by competing and profit-seeking providers it would be far more difficult to achieve such results.

3.2 Housing

Housing is widely acknowledged as one of life’s essentials and is central to the SG agenda. It occupies the centre of the spectrum, where the aim of collective intervention is not to give everyone free accommodation, but to ensure that everyone has access to accommodation that is secure, sufficient, accessible and affordable.

Delivering housing as a universal basic service involves a lot more than bricks and mortar. It must take account of the quality of housing, neighbourhoods and local amenities, how far residents are engaged in planning and managing their homes and surroundings, the quantity and affordability of housing supply, fair access and distribution, and sustainability. None of this can be achieved through markets alone, but requires a combination of individual and collective action.

The collective element involves intervention through public authorities, to invest, regulate and distribute so that everyone has access to housing that is secure, sufficient and affordable. Only such collective measures can ensure that housing is constructed (or retrofitted), equipped and managed in ways that are ecologically sustainable.

The politics and capacity of bodies exercising collective responsibility, and the extent of residents' control over their homes and neighbourhoods are intertwined to create conditions for security and sufficiency in housing. How far a dwelling is sufficient is partly a matter of objective measures such as floor space per capita, fittings, outdoor space and amenities; it is also determined by subjective judgements shaped by history and culture. For example, home ownership is highly desirable in the UK but in Vienna, 80% of the population rent their homes and more than half pay social rents. Residents' views about sufficiency will be influenced by the quality of their surroundings, relationships with neighbours, and how easily they can find their way to transport, jobs, schools, public services, shops, leisure facilities, and open spaces. All these things can spell the difference between a living environment that enables people to meet their needs, and one that is experienced as inadequate or debilitating, making life a struggle.

Ghettos of deprivation are common in the UK, but elsewhere, some municipal authorities have set out to integrate residents from different backgrounds. Vienna has its Wohnsfond Wien policy that supports mixed tenure of housing blocks, with the explicit aim of maintaining a social balance across the city. In the new town of Ørestad near Copenhagen, social and private housing have been developed side by side, sharing enviable transport links, shops and amenities. Neighbourhoods where people from different backgrounds live side-by-side are more likely to generate mutual understanding and respect, and a sense of shared responsibility for the community as a whole.

Where residents have some control over their day-to-day living conditions, they tend to be healthier and happier: this stems not only from being able to influence what happens to their homes and surroundings, but also from the very experience of control (Marmot et al., 2018, p. 98). Indeed, 'political voice' is recognised as integral to the social foundation that underpins Raworth's 'safe and just space for humanity' and having 'a say in shaping society' is included in Di Giulio and Defila's list of 'protected needs' (2020, p. 108). Residents can exercise control by being engaged in decision-making and this can range from being consulted as part of a residents' association, to co-producing decisions with landlords, to joining co-operative structures for owning and managing local housing. Housing co-ops flourish in many countries, including Austria, Denmark, Germany, Spain and Switzerland, where they run a considerable chunk of the housing stock. In parts of Copenhagen, up to 40% of housing units are owned and managed as cooperatives (Falk & Rudlin, 2018, p. 9). Where co-ops function well, it is usually because governments provide firm and enduring political and practical support.

In a universal service no one is excluded for want of money. Scarcity drives up prices, so increasing supply is an early goal wherever there are housing shortages. Supply can be increased by building more dwellings, but it may be equally important to refurbish and redistribute existing stock, using regulation, taxation or compulsory purchase to discourage or eliminate empty dwellings and multiple home ownership (Dorling, 2014, p. 114).

Markets are unlikely to produce sufficient and affordable housing unless they are shaped and managed by local and national governments, using regulation, public investment and partnerships between commercial, state and other non-profit bodies. Public Asset Corporations in Copenhagen and Hamburg, and Montpellier's Special Purpose Vehicles for pooling and developing land are examples. The cost of supplying more homes can be kept in check by investing public funds in infrastructure, land acquisition, building and retro-fitting, by legislating to prevent speculation on land and property values, and by limiting profits extracted by private developers. Public funds can be raised by issuing government bonds, by taxing land and property as well as income, by generating revenue from local shops and amenities, and by reinvesting revenues from rent and sales. There is also a case for taking land into collective ownership through municipal authorities or civil society vehicles such as

Community Land Trusts, so that it becomes a shared asset managed in the public interest, rather than a barrier to affordable housing.

In Vienna the city government has kept housing affordable by owning most of the land, using municipal developments and supply-side subsidies to keep costs down. Denmark levies a tax on land, based on one-thousandth of the market value of the land, reviewed every two years, which is collected nationally and distributed to local government for reinvestment in housing and infrastructure. In England and Wales, a growing network of Community Land Trusts, set up by local people, develop and manage affordable housing and other local assets. There are countless initiatives in cities across Europe that aim in these and other ways to boost the supply of affordable housing (Falk & Rudlin, 2018).

Affordability is of course a relative notion and even the least expensive homes are beyond the means of some. Poorer households generally pay a much larger slice of their income in rents or mortgages (OECD, 2019). So further measures are needed if housing is to be genuinely affordable for all. These may take the form of demand-side benefits, such as housing benefit in the UK (widely considered a poor use of public funds) or supply-side measures, whereby prices, including rents and purchase deposits, are capped or subsidised, as is common in parts of Austria, Denmark, Germany and the Netherlands.

Housing accounts for a substantial share of GHG emissions and resource use, which means that the sector has considerable potential to maintain or breach planetary boundaries. This is reflected in policy proposals such as the European Union's 'Green Deal', which calls for doubling the rate of renovating private and public buildings to improve energy efficiency, climate proofing and compatibility with the circular economy; it also stipulates that particular attention should be paid "to the renovation of social housing, to help households who struggle to pay their energy bills" (European Commission, 2019, 2.1.4). The UK's Green New Deal Group has proposed large-scale investment in energy efficient and affordable homes (Green New Deal Group, 2013).

The town of Freiburg in South West Germany is claimed to be the 'solar capital of Europe' but that involves 'far more than simple technological conversion'. The Frieburg model reportedly promotes "urban eco-living, facilitated by a strong long-term vision, national policy frameworks and a focused commitment to change and community engagement" (Falk & Rudlin, 2018, p. 13). There are many other developments across the world—although, still far too few—that adopt similar approaches. Where housing is designed and managed to maximise ecological sustainability, it will help to safeguard natural resources and the capacity of future generations to meet their own needs.

3.3 Transport

Motorised transport is said to belong to "a set of universal, irreducible and essential material conditions for achieving basic human wellbeing" (Rao & Min, 2017, pp. 138–225). As such, it fits within the Social Guarantee, in which services are available to all according to need, not ability to pay. Like housing, it occupies the centre of the spectrum, where universal access may be achieved through a range of measures including free services.

The ultimate goal of transport as a universal basic service is a well regulated, inter-connected, frequent, reliable and adequately funded scheme that also discourages car use and encourages safe walking and cycling alongside public transport. Free bus travel has been proposed as a first step in the right direction (Coote & Percy, 2020, p. 88).

A universal transport service could help to maintain both lower and upper boundaries of Raworth's (2017) 'safe and just space for humanity'. No one would be denied access to essential travel because of inability to pay. According to a 2016 evaluation of free bus travel for older and disabled people in England, pass holders found it easier than others to access services such as healthcare, had more opportunities for social interaction and were left with more disposable income; all this disproportionately benefited those on lower incomes (Department of Transport, 2016). Other studies have found that free bus travel leads to better health as a result of more physical activity (because bus travellers walk longer distances than people travelling by car), easier access to jobs, increased independence, reduced isolation, a greater sense of belonging to one's local area, and contributing more to society (Jones et al., 2013, pp. 202–209; KPMG, 2017, p. 12; Macket, 2015, p. 12).

At the same time, free bus travel could help to maintain ecological sustainability by discouraging car use and reducing air pollution and greenhouse gas emissions. A UK study found that GHG emissions from use of cars and taxis were more than seven times higher than from use of buses (Department of Transport, 2017, p. 6). Accessible, co-ordinated public transport across a large conurbation, even without free fares, has been estimated to reduce car traffic by 9%, resulting in better air quality and lower carbon emissions (Sloman & Hopkinson, 2019, p. 6). Free bus fares could reasonably be expected to accentuate that effect.

For their full potential to be realised, research suggests that free buses would have to be coupled with strong disincentives for private vehicles, such as a road user charge (Storchmann, 2003, pp. 89–105). No less important, they would have to be genuinely useful to as many people as possible, so that they are widely adopted as a preferred form of travel.

There are free local transport schemes (mainly buses) in more than 100 towns and cities worldwide, including more than 30 in the USA and 20 in France, as well as in Poland, Sweden, Italy, Slovenia, Estonia, Australia, and elsewhere. Some are restricted to certain social groups and times of the day. Frequency and connectivity vary between countries. In the UK, for example, adults over 65 and disabled people are entitled to free bus travel. Since 1985 most local buses have been deregulated (though not in London). Four large corporations now dominate the market, producing a patchwork of poorly connected and/or infrequent services with no shared system of ticketing; prices have risen as government subsidies have diminished (Bayliss & Mattioli, 2018, pp. 13–14).

Most other European countries have regulated bus services with better co-ordinated routes and timetables, as well as better links between town and country, and higher levels of public subsidy. Compared with the UK, they are found to be more affordable and their users more satisfied (Bayliss & Mattioli, 2018).

Costs of developing transport as a universal basic service will vary between countries, and will depend on what is already available, how far services are entirely free and the extent of public investment required to ensure that they are genuinely affordable for all. A huge variety of taxes are levied by local authorities around the world to pay for their public transport systems, ranging from local income and property taxes, to sales and tourism taxes, corporation tax and road user charges (Taylor & Sloman, 2016, pp. 115–116). In France, for example, public transport is funded through a payroll levy called Versement Transport (VT), whereby more than 80% of France's urban transport authorities apply the levy, which pays for more than half of their infrastructure investment and subsidies to operators. For the UK, analysis by the Institute for Global Prosperity found that extending free bus passes to the whole population would cost around £5.2 billion a year (0.26% GDP), and the cost of extending London's level of public transport service, which includes underground and local rail travel, across the UK would be £12.3 billion (0.63% GDP) (Portes et al., 2017, pp. 35–36).

Moving from free buses to a more comprehensive public transport service could eventually include trains, trams and underground railways (as well as safe cycling and pedestrian routes), making them as widely accessible and affordable as possible. Indeed, frequent, well-connected and affordable train services (along with long-distance buses) offer an important opportunity to reduce short-haul flights, which are a major source of GHG emissions. Public investment in the necessary material infrastructure such as vehicle fleets, stations, routing systems, railways and tramlines would be a crucial prerequisite. Collective control of investment and the capacity of public authorities to impose public interest obligations on suppliers could help to ensure that all aspects of the transport system were ecologically sustainable.

3.4 Food

Everyone needs adequate nutrition. Food is one of life's essentials and arguably every society has a responsibility for ensuring that everyone has enough to eat. It is uncontroversial to assert that no child should go to school hungry and no family should have to choose between heating and eating. Yet these things happen routinely in poor countries. In rich countries food poverty and hunger are on the rise and food banks—provided by charities to supply free food to the needy—are multiplying.

Applying the SG framework to food does not mean that governments have a duty to supply free food to everyone or to subsidise more food banks. Indeed, most charities agree that food banks should be an emergency response only (Perry et al., 2014, pp. 7–13). They are not the answer to the problem of food poverty, which is linked to a complex web of factors including income insecurity and corporate profiteering, as well as poor housing, ill health, unemployment, family breakdown and social isolation.

Typically, people buy food for themselves. It sits at the 'individual' end of the spectrum and is widely regarded as a matter of personal choice (including specific dietary requirements). A radically improved social security system that establishes a guaranteed income floor would certainly help. However, food choices are severely edited by material and cultural factors. These have to be addressed in order for everyone to have sufficient and affordable nutrition—and it is here that collective measures are called for.

One example of a service that reflects the SG approach is the provision of free meals for all schoolchildren, regardless of family income. In the United Kingdom, free school meals are provided to all pupils in reception and years one and two, but thereafter the service is means-tested, although some local authorities provide free school meals to all primary school pupils. Finland has provided universal free school meals since 1943, and children can now get free hot lunches in Helsinki's parks during the summer months. The point of universal provision is not only to make good the failings of the means-tested system, which has been found to stigmatise and exclude too many, but also to improve the wellbeing and educational performance of all children.

This rests on the assumption that meals provide a decent quality and quantity of food, which is not always the case. A UK government scheme to give weekly food parcels to children during a Covid-related lockdown in January 2021 turned out to be scandalously inadequate (BBC, 2021). Whether meals are free or individually purchased, it matters what quality of food people can obtain and afford, and whether it is sufficiently nutritious to enable them to flourish.

Systems for producing food have multiple impacts on the natural environment. Growing, processing, packaging, storing, transporting, marketing, selling, cooking and wasting food variously determine the quality and sustainability of land, air and water, biodiversity, use of fossil fuels and plastics, and GHG emissions (among much else). In the food sector, unlike childcare and far more than housing, the implications are global. What people eat in rich countries will affect the diets and life-chances of people in poor countries, as well as the carrying capacity of the planet (Willett et al., 2019). The challenge for a sustainable welfare state is therefore to ensure that healthy diets are universally accessible, globally sufficient and sustainable over time.

This requires a whole-systems approach. It would include policies for trade and agriculture that support sustainable food production, regulation of business to promote healthy, affordable food, and statutory controls of advertising and sales to restrict foodstuffs that are harmful. There would be policies to reduce 'food miles' with high emissions, to support local initiatives that promote collective food production and consumption, and to make sure good food is available everywhere so that there are no more 'food deserts' in disadvantaged neighbourhoods. Health and education services would encourage healthy and sufficient diets; they would work together to build knowledge across the population about what's good and sustainable to eat and why it matters. Schools, hospitals, childcare centres, care homes and other public institutions would supply appetizing, nutritious and ecologically sustainable meals for all who use their services. Under this scenario, food banks would be history.

The impacts of diet on health are extensively documented (GDB Diet Collaborators, 2017). So are ways in which food systems affect the environment. According to the Lancet, adopting healthy and sustainable eating habits worldwide (with dietary changes differing widely between regions) could "substantially benefit human health, averting about 10.8–11,6 million deaths per year" (Willett et al., 2019, p. 448). At a global level, today's food supply chain is estimated to create 26% of anthropogenic GHG emissions (Poore & Nemecek, 2018). The world's current eating habits are neither healthy nor sustainable, but alternative diets have been identified that offer substantial health benefits and "could, if widely adopted, reduce global agricultural greenhouse gas emissions, reduce land clearing and resultant species extinctions, and help prevent diet-related chronic non-communicable diseases" (Tilman & Clark, 2014, p. 1).

4 Potential Benefits of UBS

Protagonists claim that improving and extending universal services (or UBS) would bring substantial benefits in terms of equality, efficiency, solidarity and sustainability. These claims are not definitive because the concept is new and there has so far been little opportunity for scrutiny and debate. There is nevertheless some evidence, drawn from studies of existing public services, which support them. In this section I look at each area of benefit in turn.

4.1 Equality

Public services are known to reduce income inequalities by providing a virtual income, made up of in-kind benefits, which is worth much more to people in low-income groups. A study of OECD countries (Verbist et al., 2012) suggests that poor people would have to spend three quarters of their income on essential services. Table 1 below shows in-kind benefits—education, health care, social housing, ECEC (early childhood education and care), and elderly care—as a share of disposable income per quintile.

The 75.8% share for the lowest income quintile compares with a 13.7% income share for the highest quintile. Indeed, the study shows that inequality in OECD countries is reduced by one fifth when the measure is extended from money incomes to a combination of money and social income (Verbist et al., 2012). Without in-kind benefits,

Table 1 In-kind benefits as a share of disposable income by Quintile, average over 27 OECD countries, Late 2000s

	Q1	Q2	Q3	Q4	Q5	Total
Education	30.6	18.5	14.2	10.4	5.6	11.8
Health care	34.9	22.2	15.8	11.8	7.2	13.9
Social housing	1.8	0.7	0.4	0.2	0.1	0.4
ECEC	4.5	3.0	2.4	1.5	0.8	1.8
Elderly care	4.0	1.9	0.7	0.4	0.2	0.9
Total	75.8	46.4	33.5	24.3	13.7	28.8

Source Verbist et al. (2012)

many individuals and families would be unable to meet their needs and flourish. They are important for all families, and especially for those on lower incomes, not only directly through the services they offer (education, care, housing), but also indirectly through their preventative effects. Those who can rely on getting an education, a decent home and care when they need it are better protected over time against accumulating risks and vulnerabilities.

4.2 Efficiency

Measures of efficiency in the public sector are usually complex and contested. Public services have been accused of inefficiencies, to justify introducing market rules. But privatisation, competition between multiple providers and customer choice for service users have largely failed to improve outputs let alone outcomes. These failings have been greatly exacerbated by public spending cuts.

Non-profit, collective forms of provision avoid inefficiencies that routinely arise from market processes: inflexible contracts, higher transaction costs and moral hazards that are encountered when profit incentives combine with unequal knowledge in markets. A non-profit system does not need to extract funds to pay dividends to shareholders.

A 2016 study compared spending on health care and average life expectancy in OECD countries. It found the USA, which is a mainly market-based system, outspent the UK in 2014 by the equivalent of £6,311 per person, compared with £2,777, yet had an average life expectancy at birth of 78.8 years, compared with 81.4 in the UK (ONS, 2016).

Calculations of efficiency must take account of the multiple dimensions of value, the many ways in which value is experienced and how it accrues. This calls for social value analysis to take account of longer-term, indirect effects across social and environmental dimensions. Expenditure on UBS can be seen as an investment in social infrastructure, which can be expected to yield significant returns over time.

Social Return on Investment (SROI) is one approach that has been adopted by the UK government, which formally requires public authorities to consider whether their procurement practices "improve the economic, social and environmental well-being of the relevant area, and how, in conducting the process of procurement, it might act with a view to securing that improvement" (DCMS, 2014, p. 2). Bauwens and Niaros (2017) have called for a major 'Value Shift': instead of rewarding 'extractive' practices "that enrich some at the expense of the others", we should reward 'generative' practices that enrich the social and environmental resources to which they are applied (p. 3). Building support for UBS and the Social Guarantee will partly depend on redefining efficiency along these lines, by asking how far universal services lead to outcomes that renew local assets, safeguard planetary boundaries and nurture human flourishing.

4.3 Solidarity

The concepts of shared needs and collective responsibilities embody the idea of solidarity, and implementing UBS, as defined here, has potential to develop and strengthen it in practice. Solidarity is taken to mean feelings of sympathy and responsibility between people that promote mutual support. It is an inclusive process, not just within well-acquainted groups but also, crucially, between people and groups who are 'strangers' to each other. It involves collective action towards shared objectives (Wilde, 2013, p. 1).

Pursuing the UBS agenda not only require solidarity but may also contribute to it—in three main ways. First, it can develop an experience of shared needs and collective responsibility, which builds understanding of how people depend on each other and a commitment to retaining those interconnections. Secondly, where services bring people together from different social groups, they can provide opportunities for developing mutual sympathy and responsibility. Thirdly, the combined effects of more and better services, as I have noted, bring benefits to society as a whole and have a redistributive effect, reducing inequalities that otherwise create barriers to solidarity.

By contrast, there is a rich literature on the ways in which systems based on individualism, choice and competition weaken the values of social citizenship and undermine solidarity (Brodie, 2007; Jayasuriya, 2006, p. 15; Lynch & Kalaitzake, 2018, pp. 1–20).

4.4 Sustainability

Sustainability involves, at its simplest, an inherent 'capacity for continuance', as Ekins (2014) observes: a sustainable system is one that can function in ways that continue to achieve its desired goals over time (p. 56). Here, I reflect briefly on the potential of UBS to affect this capacity through prevention of harm, through economic stabilisation and through helping to mitigate climate change and the depletion of natural resources. The urgent necessity to move away from unsustainable economic, social and environmental practices provides a new justification and impetus for extending universal services.

As noted above, services that help people to stay well and flourish are directly beneficial to individuals and society; they can also reduce demand for a range of services required to cope with problems that are otherwise likely to occur. For example, unemployment, anti-social behaviour, and many forms of crime have roots in poverty and deprivation, which can be significantly reduced by a more generous 'social income'(Coote, 2015, p. 19). By helping to maintain and improve social wellbeing, UBS can not only support the capacity of society to continue to flourish; they can also prevent harm and thereby mitigate the risk of services becoming overwhelmed by rising demand, enabling them to continue to function effectively (Gough, 2013, pp. 1–21).

Where the economy is concerned, public services can help to stabilise fluctuations by generating relatively stable employment and providing security through meeting everyday needs. In these ways, they can act as a counter cyclical buffer, helping to offset the effects of market downturns and recession, contributing to the economy's 'capacity for continuance'.

A move towards more and better universal services is considered likely to prove more environmentally sustainable than leaving the process of meeting needs to transactions in a market-based system. There are three main reasons for this. First, the SG framework focuses on sufficiency for all, rather than on satisfying wants and preferences, which can escalate without constraint. This helps to put a brake on excessive consumption that would otherwise threaten to breach planetary boundaries.

Secondly, by promoting collective action to pool resources and share risks so that everyone's needs are met, universal services can play a part in changing the way economic success is measured—favouring a concern for human wellbeing within planetary limits rather than simply focusing on GDP growth.

Thirdly, provisioning systems that are democratically controlled with the purpose of serving the public interest have greater potential than market-based systems to promote sustainable consumption. Through their networks of employees, service users and suppliers, they can coordinate sustainable practices such as active travel, resource-efficient buildings and local food procurement, avoid duplication and waste, minimise excessive demand, and implement national strategies for reducing GHG emissions. Where governments issue guidance, public sector organisations are more likely to comply because they share public interest values. Where public bodies work with non-government partners or subcontractors, they can spread sustainable practices among a wider range of institutions.

There is evidence that collectively provided services have a smaller ecological footprint than privately funded alternatives. For example, the direct carbon footprint of the NHS amounts to 3% of the UK total compared to an estimated 8–10% from the private-sector-dominated US health care system. Put another way, the carbon footprint of health care in the USA is two and a half times greater than in the UK and three and half times greater than in several European countries. Figure 3 illustrates this by comparing the carbon footprint per capita of the healthcare system in eight OECD countries.

There is also some evidence that more extensive welfare states are generally better suited to adopting and implementing pro-environmental policies, especially where they embody ideas about shared needs and collective responsibilities (Gough et al., 2008, pp. 325–344).

Finally, universal services can play a vital role in 'greening' the economy in a just way. They constitute a social pillar for Green New

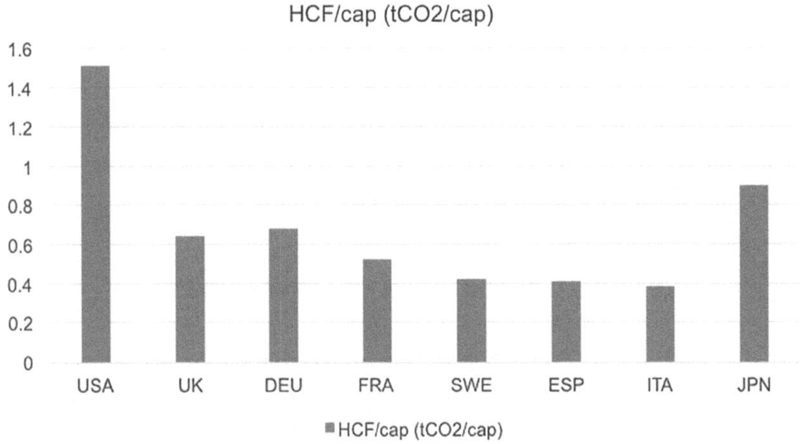

Fig. 3 Healthcare carbon footprints per Capita, selected countries, 2014 (*Source* Pichler et al. [2019])

Deal programmes. If accepted as such and fully integrated, measures to reduce emissions and resource depletion would be designed to comply with the principles of the SG framework, rather than simply focusing on ecological targets. This would help to ensure a 'just transition' to sustainable living, rather than one that will load costs onto the poorest people and communities.

5 Challenges to UBS

Because these proposals are relatively new, they have not yet attracted much in the way of direct challenge. Various critiques have begun to emerge and they can roughly be summarised as follows. UBS would lead to big government, centralised power, paternalism and social engineering; the state is not competent to realise the vision; there is a lack of clarity about how decisions would be made; it could lead to further accumulation by big business; it would run into strong resistance from those with an interest in the status quo; it is incompatible with capitalism and requires radical transformation, not piecemeal reform; and there are inevitably questions about how much it costs and whether it is affordable (Duffy, 2018; Foundational Economy Collective, 2018, pp. 123–30; Frankel, 2018; Standing, 2020).

There is clearly more work to be undertaken on the political economy of the Social Guarantee, on costs and benefits, and the nuts and bolts of implementation. There are nevertheless grounds for countering most of these challenges, as I hope to demonstrate.

5.1 Power and Competence of Government

The extent to which any UBS system would enhance the power of central government will depend on partly how far power is devolved to localities. But localism is not in itself a recipe for better policy or practice. That depends on the structures and political strategies that operate locally and nationally (Born & Purcell, 2006, pp. 195–207).

The SG framework acknowledges that services can be provided by a range of organisations with diverse models of ownership, rather than always being directly provided by government. With more devolution and a reformed tax system, it is possible to envisage more localised power to raise money for investment in services. However, it will be crucial for central government to retain key functions—not least to ensure that everyone has access to sufficient services, wherever they live, on the basis of need, not ability to pay. This points to a system of central government investment to supplement local funds, adjusted for equitable distribution between localities.

As for the competence of government to implement the SG, it would be futile trying to graft this proposal on to unchanged systems and structures. Integral to the idea, as noted earlier, is a new kind of relationship between local, regional and national governments, and significant changes in the culture and practice of public authorities. The aim is to transform those authorities so that they generate and support different ways of delivering services and enabling people to meet their needs. There are lessons to be learned from cities such as Barcelona in Spain, Bologna in Italy, Ghent in Belgium, Cleveland in Ohio, USA and Preston in Lancashire, UK, where authorities have committed themselves in various ways to enabling local people to gain more control over access to life's necessities.

In Barcelona, for example, Barcelona En Comú, described as a 'citizen platform', has led the city government in promoting what it calls a collaborative economy, including many hundreds of co-operatives and other community-led and public-interest organisations. In Bologna, the city government has introduced a pioneering regulation for 'the care and regeneration of urban commons' and has entered into more than 90 different 'pacts of collaboration' with citizen groups, including collaborative services, shared enterprises and co-production. The Flemish city of Ghent has endorsed an ambitious 'commons transition plan', which promotes a model of 'poly-governance', with state, markets and civil society working together to support and scale up locally generated social and economic initiatives. In Cleveland, Ohio, the Evergreen Co-operative Initiative works with local businesses, foundations and public sector organisations to transform poor neighbourhoods by creating living wage jobs in local co-operatives. Inspired by this approach, council leaders in Preston, UK, began to lift the city out of apparently irreversible decline by encouraging new co-operative ventures and credit unions, and persuading public bodies operating in the area to spend their money locally.

All these ventures have encountered criticism, even from local progressive organisations, and it would be foolish to idealise them. This is work in progress. What they all show is a willingness to transform relationships between local government and local residents, shifting power outwards to a wide variety of groups and organisations, many of which could—or already do—play a part in designing and delivering services under local control.

5.2 Decision-Making

A democratic framework for making decisions would be essential. The New Economics Foundation (among others) has proposed "a dialogue that combines lay people along with professionals (in service delivery, for example) and other experts, and with democratically elected representatives" (Coote, 2017, pp. 14–15). This approach could be used at local, regional or national level to determine what needs should be met collectively and to design services and other appropriate activities. It combines elements of participatory and representative democracy, and builds on experience of citizens' juries, deliberative polling, people's forums, town hall meetings and similar initiatives in the US, Europe and elsewhere.

Among notable examples is Ireland's citizens' assembly convened between 2016 and 2018 to consider a range of questions including the law on abortion. Lay members were selected to represent a broad cross-section of the population. They considered evidence and discussed relevant questions with experts, as well as among themselves and drew conclusions through consensus. Their conclusions led to a referendum that legalised abortion. This kind of framework for three-way deliberative dialogue is not intended to replace representative democracy but to revive and enrich it by drawing closer to the views, values and everyday experiences of the people it is supposed to represent.

The French Convention Citoyenne pour le Climat is noteworthy because the French government committed from the start to put forward its proposals for legal adoption—without changes—via referendum, parliamentary vote, or executive order. This makes it a leading example of introducing dialogic democracy into determining policy.

5.3 Profiteering by Big Corporations

There is a risk of maximising profits for big corporations if they were allowed to dominate an expanding market in service provision. This can be avoided if service delivery is embedded in a well-regulated system with multiple providers and measures to encourage and support public bodies and other non-profit organisations. It would mean bringing for-profit and non-profit organisations within a shared framework of values, goals and expectations, and at the same time strengthening the role of non-profits in the economy. The EU's Commission for Sustainable Equality recommends new measures to build and support the 'social and solidarity economy', so that it ceases to be merely an 'add-on' or limited alternative to the dominant profit-seeking model; but instead becomes a "long-term mainstream model for a truly sustainable economy" in social, environmental and democratic terms (Mersch, 2018, p. 75).

The Foundational Economy Collective proposes a system of *social licencing* that would make the right to trade dependent on "providing a service, plus meeting negotiated criteria of community responsibility on issues such as sourcing, training and payment of living wages" (2018, p. 111). This follows the current practice in many European countries and could lend force and definition to the otherwise woolly concept of 'corporate social responsibility'.

5.4 Meeting Political Resistance

How to meet the challenge of winning and sustaining electoral support for universal services? Establishing a framework for democratic dialogue would certainly help, as I have noted above. An important characteristic of the Social Guarantee is that it is not a 'silver bullet' demanding sudden wholesale change. It is both radical and pragmatic in that it is designed to enable changes to be introduced gradually, to iron out mistakes along the way, demonstrate successes where possible and give people opportunities to learn from experience. It builds incrementally on what already exists without sudden shocks to the system.

If the process of change is incremental, service contracts can be altered as they come up for renewal, to improve access and quality and to strengthen public participation. Incumbent providers are bound to resist such changes. The larger and richer they are, the heavier their influence is likely to be. How far they prevail will depend on the political and economic environment in which changes are introduced.

The question of whether the Social Guarantee is compatible with capitalism is worth asking. Capitalism is not intrinsically antithetical to exercising collective responsibility to meet shared needs, as the post-war settlements have shown. The current neoliberal phase of capitalism prefers a small state and a free market, which are not conditions in which universal services can flourish. But varieties remain—both of capitalism and of welfare regimes in different countries across the world—some less hostile and more conducive to the SG framework than prevailing models in the Anglosphere. It is likely that some of these would co-exist comfortably with universal services. It is also possible that implementing the SG framework could begin to reshape welfare capitalism so that universal sufficiency, collaboration and human flourishing became the measures of success rather than cost efficiency, accumulation and growth.

5.5 How Much Would It Cost and is It Affordable?

This is an ambitious proposal and it is reasonable to ask whether services we wish to make universally affordable for individuals can also be collectively affordable.

Costings for all proposed new services, plus the improvements that should be made to existing universal services are bound to vary widely between services and between countries. A great deal depends on the quality and scope of what is provided, which services already exist and how much has to be built up from scratch, the balance between collective and individual contributions—what is free at the point of use and what is deemed affordable—and how gradually changes are introduced. Roughly calculated, the additional annual cost of five services (childcare, adult social care, housing, transport and digital access) has been estimated at between 4 and 5% of GDP in a typical OECD country (Coote & Percy, 2020, pp. 115–116).

The main options for generating public funds for universal services are through taxes, borrowing and redistributing funds from other areas of government spending. Conventional ways of thinking about limits to public spending were thoroughly disrupted by governments' responses to the COVID-19 pandemic. As never before since wartime, spending became a matter of political choice rather than submission to preordained rules. A real-life experiment demonstrated that, if a government wanted to do something—however costly and out of the ordinary—it could find the money. Questions remain, however, since universal services are proposed as part of a long-term settlement rather than an ad-hoc emergency. What are the best ways to raise funds that are consistent with creating a safe and just space for humanity?

The London School of Economics' Wealth Tax Commission (2020) proposed a one-off wealth tax to be paid by any UK resident (including 'non-doms' and recent emigrants) with personal wealth above a set threshold, at a rate of 1% of all assets such as main homes and pension pots, as well as business and financial wealth, but minus any debts such as mortgages, payable in instalments over five years. Assuming a threshold of £500,000 per person, this was estimated to yield £260 billion or the equivalent of 2.6% GDP a year for five years. The Commission concluded that the tax could recoup costs incurred during the COVID crisis in a manner that was fair, efficient and hard to avoid. As a one-off levy, it would not fund universal services, but it offers a plausible alternative to a renewed 'austerity' drive, leaving the way clear to expand rather than reduce access to life's essentials.

The wealth tax proposal can be seen as part of a widespread re-evaluation of the nature and purpose of the economy, which predates the pandemic and may well have been enhanced by it. As the Netherlands-based coalition Our New Economy (ONE) points out, there are many longer running issues to be tackled, including "climate change, rising inequality, financial instability, biodiversity loss, increasingly precarious and stressful working lives, growing power concentrations, and resource depletion" (p. iii)'. There is a growing recognition that conventional economics is implicated in causing these problems and must be fundamentally reformed to solve them. Arguably, a paradigm shift is underway, which is agnostic about GDP growth and instead focuses economic thinking on sustainably creating and maintaining human and planetary wellbeing.

Our New Economy proposes a renewed welfare system based on job guarantees, extended services and rights to benefits, which "could be financed through (higher) taxes on (net) wealth, land, data, inheritance, unhealthy consumption, financial transactions and pollution as these would contribute to making the economy more stable, fair, and sustainable" (Muijnck et al., 2021, pp. 29–30). For example, 'smart VAT' would target consumption tax on items that are harmful to human and planetary health, which could range from sugar to SUVs (Fell, 2016, pp. 106–110 Gough, 2017, p. 162); a frequent flyer levy would help curb the growing demand for air travel, based on analysis showing that 15%

of the population take 70% of all flights (Harrabin, 2019); a progressive property tax and a land value tax would redistribute assets and power (Monbiot et al., 2019, ch. 3). Designed to generate social and ecological value, rather than merely to boost growth, these proposals can be seen as part of the paradigm shift noted above.

Universal services do not just cost money: they can also save and generate resources in a number of ways. There are likely to be economies of scale where needs are met collectively rather than individually. Where transaction costs and profit extraction are minimised, collective services produce better value for money than private procurement. Furthermore, under the SG framework services would be organised to enable people to co-produce—as far as possible—the ways in which their needs are met. This brings uncommodified human resources into the process. Provided the individuals concerned are adequately supported, this enables them to take more control over their lives and have a say in how their needs are met, which can not only improve their wellbeing but also improve the quality and scope of the services without a corresponding increase in the overall cost. Co-production as envisaged in the SG framework is about devolving power and transforming the policies and practices of public institutions, rather than 'dumping' state responsibilities on poor communities (Boyle et al., 2010).

Where collective action is taken earlier enough to meet needs, it can prevent harm that would otherwise require more costly interventions later on. I have noted above how applying the Social Guarantee to child-care, housing, transport and food can safeguard human wellbeing and avoid a range of social and environmental problems occurring: this is a well-documented process that too seldom informs or shapes political decision-making (Coote, 2012; Early Action Task Force, 2011).

Universal services support employment in two main ways. As noted, they help people to get and keep jobs, by providing life's essentials: education, health and social care, decent housing, public transport and digital access all contribute to a person's employability. In addition, services themselves generate a considerable amount of employment—across all skills levels, in different sectors and across all parts of the country. The Social Guarantee stipulates that service workers should have fair pay and conditions, with adequate training and career progression, which in turn can generate social and economic benefits. When jobs are in public services and employers are subject to public interest obligations (covering pay and conditions for workers), they are likely to be a lot less precarious than many jobs in the private sector. A recent analysis of the costs and benefits of care work in New York State found that public funding for improved pay and conditions for care workers "is an eminently safe investment, ensuring both job creation and economic spillover while being less sensitive to economic fluctuations than industries like tourism and gaming" (Jabola- Carolus et al., 2021, p. 25).

Many jobs in universal services—in caring and teaching for example—depend on human relationships that cannot be usurped by robotics or artificial intelligence. And most have a relatively small ecological footprint, either because they are primarily relational or because they are embedded in organisations committed to sustainable practice. Although today's politics is dominated by different imperatives (most notably climate emergency) the Social Guarantee shares aspirations of Roosevelt's New Deal of the 1930s and the Beveridge Plan of the 1940s in seeking to generate secure jobs to support a flourishing economy.

For all these reasons (and more), meeting the costs of universal services represents an investment that is likely to yield substantial returns. Some of this is an investment in material infrastructure (bricks and mortar for homes, schools and hospitals, roads, railways, cables, masts and so forth), which is generally regarded as suitably financed through public borrowing. Beyond that, it is increasingly recognised that the success of a society depends on investing in the social infrastructure of care and human development, which ultimately determines the quality and sustainability of life on earth. Reflecting on President Biden's plans in 2021, the *Financial Times* observed that, while investment in rich and poor countries alike still focused primarily on physical capital, it was "time to recognise that, perhaps more than any other form, human capital is the infrastructure of the twenty-first century" (Foroohar, 2021).

Arguably, then, borrowing (by issuing long-term government bonds) is a suitable option for meeting the costs of universal services. But in any case, public attitudes towards taxation appear to be shifting. While support is strongest for higher taxes on wealth and corporations, people are less reluctant to pay more taxes themselves to fund healthcare and other public services (Tax Justice UK, 2020). In the UK in 2009, 52% of people preferred spending cuts to tackle the deficit, with only 30% favouring tax rises, but the balance reversed by 2020, when only 27% opted for spending cuts, compared with 47% for tax rises (Johnson, J. 2021).

6 Cash and Services: Getting the Balance Right

When the case for universal basic services (UBS) was set out by the Institute for Global Prosperity in 2017, it was a challenge to the burgeoning campaign for universal basic income (UBI), meaning regular, unconditional cash payments to all (Portes et al., 2017). UBI supporters claimed it as a solution to problems of poverty, powerlessness and ungenerous, stigmatising social security systems. UBS supporters argued that universal cash payments were prohibitively expensive and represented an individualised, monetised strategy for addressing a shared, systemic set of problems; meeting the costs of UBI would wipe out the chance of investing in collective measures, leaving individuals to fend for themselves in the marketplace and doing nothing to reduce GHG emissions or safeguard natural resources.

The Social Guarantee combines universal services with a living income. The question then is how such a combination can best be achieved. As noted, public funds can be increased substantially if governments choose to do so, but there is bound to be a trade-off between money devoted to cash payments and money devoted to public services. What matters is the level at which the budget for cash payments begins to divert funds that could otherwise be spent on improving and extending services. This in turn hinges on the political motivation for favouring cash over in-kind benefits.

Regular, unconditional cash payments to every individual, regardless of income and status, which are set at or near the poverty line in any country would, according to the International Labour Office (ILO), cost on average "for most world regions … in the range of 20 to 30% of

GDP" (Ortiz et al., 2018, p. 13). This would render cash payments fiscally incompatible with UBS.

Furthermore, a system that supports market-based consumption may not be best placed to address problems such as poverty, precarious employment and inequality which themselves have emerged from free-market practices. Some champions of UBI see cash payments as an alternative to public services and a route to recommodifying welfare states. More progressive advocates usually acknowledge that cash payments should be underpinned by a strong framework of public services, but do not explain how both could be sufficient and affordable at the same time—let alone how sufficient payments could be funded alongside an ambitious programme to improve and extend universal services.

There is no room here for a detailed discussion of UBI. But it is worth reflecting briefly on how the approach to cash payments envisaged by protagonists (as summarised above) compares with UBS across the four dimensions of equality, efficiency, solidarity and sustainability.

If you give cash payments to people who have little or nothing, it is bound to make at least a small improvement in their lives. But cash payments on their own cannot reduce inequalities. As the ILO observes, this can never amount to "a stand-alone solution to redress an ever more unequal primary distribution of incomes". People need power and access to a range of social and material resources that cash payments could not enable them to buy. Without a coherent policy framework that takes these broader factors into account, says the ILO, "a UBI may exacerbate inequality" (Ortiz et al., 2018, p. 29). There is simply no conceivable scenario where funding a sufficient UBI scheme would be compatible with funding the full range of public provision needed to achieve social justice rather than minimal poverty relief. If the balance of investment in any country were to swing away from services towards cash payments, the value of the social wage delivered through services would be bound to fall, hitting the poor hardest and widening inequalities.

If a UBI scheme replaced all means-tested benefits, it could arguably simplify and reduce the administrative costs of income support. But, as most UBI protagonists admit, it would have to be topped up by conditional payments—for example, for people with physical or mental disabilities and (depending on the level at which it is set) for most people who are already on low incomes. At the same time, the tax system would have been overhauled to claw back part or all of the payments for people on higher incomes. One critic, envisaging a small and affordable UBI, describes a "powerful new tax engine [that] will pull along a tiny cart" (Gough, 2016). It is hard to see how this would be more efficient than the status quo. Certainly, cash transfers should not be increased without a proper assessment of whether the same goals could be achieved more effectively through public services.

If a UBI scheme were to replace public services as well as income support, people would be left to buy themselves out of any trouble that happened to befall them. As noted, market-based systems are less efficient than collective services for meeting many of our shared needs because of higher transaction costs, greater risk of moral hazard and the pursuit of profit. Efforts to generate value through a UBI scheme and return it to the source of input (the people who receive and spend the cash payments) will very likely be outweighed by extractive practices in the marketplace.

Giving money to individuals to spend as they wish does nothing to bring them together or build a sense of common purpose. On the contrary, it plugs them into a market system that feeds on choice and competition. It erodes the relational base of services and the ethos of shared interest and collective responsibility. In the words of Francine Mestrum, the radical Belgian writer and analyst, basic income is an individualist solution to a set of shared problems: "progressives will look for other solutions, based on solidarity, reciprocity and collective action" (2018, pp. 97–8).

Ed Whitfield, founder of the US-based Fund for Democratic Communities, argues that a guaranteed basic income would "only help people have more access to consumption without altering anything about how production is organised" (2018, pp. 109–112). Such a scheme can do nothing to change patterns of consumption, to encourage more sustainable use of resources, or to create the conditions for a collective approach to climate mitigation at local or national levels. Cash payments may prevent starvation, but they have nothing to offer that is strategically preventative over time, nothing to build the 'capacity for continuance' in social, economic or environmental terms.

7 Two Sides of the Same Coin

Debates about the relative merits of UBI and UBS may continue. But of course both cash and in-kind benefits—money income and 'virtual income'—are needed, as the Social Guarantee makes clear. They are two sides of the same coin (Coote & Lawson, 2021). The more that people have access to life's essentials through collective services, the less cash they will require to meet their needs. If services are depleted, they will need more money. These two dimensions of the Social Guarantee must complement and support each other, not compete for funds or political capital. That means developing a system for cash payments that is as generous and non-stigmatising as possible without absorbing funds needed to improve and extend services. This could be achieved if the 'universal' dimension were a guarantee, rather than an automatic payment: in other words, everyone would be entitled to a sufficient income and when that fell below an agreed level, it would be topped up by a benefits system funded through taxation. The New Economics Foundation has proposed a minimum income guarantee, which avoids the indignities of means-testing by paying money automatically to those who claim it, with over-payments recouped if necessary through taxation the following year (Stirling & Arnold, 2020). This approach is far more compatible with universal services, fiscally and ideologically, than UBI as defined by many of its leading protagonists.

8 Summary and Conclusions

The Social Guarantee offers a principled framework for ensuring that every individual has access to life's essentials. Most people cannot meet all their needs through individual market transactions. Collective measures are required, funded through taxation and delivered partly or wholly through public institutions. The Social Guarantee seeks to improve and extend collectively provided services, sometimes known as 'universal basic services' (UBS), to meet a range of needs—most obviously healthcare and education, but also childcare, adult social care, housing, transport, digital access and other essentials. These services represent a virtual or social income that complements money income. Investment in this social infrastructure will yield a range of benefits in terms of equality, efficiency, solidarity and sustainability. Universal Basic Income (UBI), by comparison, is prohibitively expensive, risks widening inequalities, achieves less value for money and promotes individual consumption rather than ecological sustainability. An income guarantee, which ensures that no-one's income falls below an agreed level of sufficiency, can be combined with UBS to provide the foundations for a sustainable and resilient economy.

References

Bauwens, M. & Niaros, V. (2017). *Value in the commons economy: Developments in open and contributory value accounting.* Heinrich Boll Foundation and P2P Foundation.

Bayliss, K., & Mattioli, G. (2018). *Privatisation, inequality and poverty in the UK: Briefing prepared for UN Rapporteur on extreme poverty and human rights* (SRI Working Paper Series, no.116).

BBC. (2021). *Free school meals: Mother's 'sadness' at 'mean' food parcel*. Available at: https://www.bbc.co.uk/news/uk-55641740

Benton, T., Froggatt, A., Wright, G., Thompson, C. E., & King, R. (2019) *Food politics and policies in post-Brexit Britain.* Royal Institute for Public Affairs.

Born, B., & Purcell, M. (2006). Avoiding the local trap: Scale and food systems in planning research. *Journal of Planning Education and Research, 26*(2).

Boyle, D., et al. (2010). *Right here, right now: Taking co-production into the Mainstream.* Nesta.

Brodie, J. M. (2007). Reforming social justice in neoliberal times. *Studies in Social Science, 1*(2).

Commission, B. (1987). *Our common future*. Oxford University Press.

Coote, A. (2017). *Building a new social commons.* New Economics Foundation.

Coote, A. (2015). *People, planet power: Towards a new social settlement*. New Economics Foundation.

Coote, A. (2012). *The wisdom of prevention.* New Economics Foundation.

Coote, A. Kasliwal, P., & Percy A. (2019). *Universal basic services: Theory and Practice—A literature review*. UCL Institute for Global Prosperity.

Coote A and Lawson, N. (2021). Post-Covid Britain needs a new social guarantee. *The Guardian*. https://www.theguardian.com/commentisfree/2021/mar/11/post-covid-britain-new-social-guarantee-universal-basic-income-pandemic

Coote, A., & Percy, A. (2020). *The case for universal basic services*. Polity Press.

DCMS, Department for Digital Culture Media and Sport. (2014). The Public Services (Social Value Act) 2014, *Introductory guide*, UK Government.

Department for Transport. (2017). *Transport statistics great Britain 2017: Energy and environment*. Department for Transport.

Department for Transport. (2016). *Evaluation of concessionary bus travel: The impacts of the free bus pass*. Department for Transport.

De Henau, J. (2017). *Costing and funding free universal childcare of high quality*. Women's Budget Group Childcare Briefing.

Di Giulio, A., & Defila, R. (2020). The 'good life' and protected needs. In A. Kalfagianni, D. Fuchs, & A. Hayden (Eds.), *The Routledge handbook of global sustainability governance* (pp. 100–114). Routledge.

Dorling, D. (2014). *All that is solid: How the great housing disaster defines our times and what we can do about it*. Allen Lane.

Doyal, L., & Gough, I. (1991). *A theory of human need*. Palgrave Macmillan.

Duffy, S. (2018). *Basic income or basic services*. Centre for Welfare Reform;

Durkheim, E. (1984). *The division of labour in society*. Palgrave Macmillan.

Early Action Task Force. (2011). *The triple dividend*. www.community-links.org/uploads/documents/Triple_Dividend.pdf

Ekins, P. (2014). Strong sustainability and critical natural capital. In G. Atkinson et al. (Eds). *Handbook of sustainable development*. Edward Elgar.

Ellingsaeter, A. (2014). Towards universal quality early childhood education and care: the Norwegian model. In L. Gambero, K. Stewart, & J. Waldfogel. (Eds), *An Equal Start? Providing quality early education and care for disadvantaged children*. Policy Press.

European Commission. (2019). *The European Green Deal*. https://eur-lex.europa.eu/legal-content/EN/TXT/?qid=1596443911913&uri=CELEX:52019DC0640#document2

Falk, N., & Rudlin, J. (2018). *Learning from international examples of affordable housing*. Shelter.

Fell, D. (2016). *Bad habits, hard choices: Using the tax system to make us healthier*. London Publishing Partnership.

Fitzpatrick, S., Bramley, G., Sosenko, F., Blenkinsopp, J., Wood, J., Johnsen, S., & Watts, B. (2018). *Destitution in the UK 2018.* Joseph Rowntree Foundation.

Foundational Economy Collective. (2018). *The foundational economy*. Manchester University Press.

Foroohar, R. (2021). The US infrastructure most in need of investment is human. *Financial Times,* April 18.

Frankel, B. (2018). Fictions of sustainability: The politics of growth and post capitalist futures. Greenmeadows.

Fuchs, D. (2020). Living well within limits: The vision of consumption corridors. In A. Kalfagianni, D. Fuchs & A. Hayden. *The Routledge handbook of global sustainability governance*. Routledge.

Galligan, D. (1992). Procedural rights in social welfare. In A. Coote (Ed), *The welfare of citizens: Developing new social rights*. IPPR/Rivers Oram Press.

GBD 2017 Diet Collaborators. (2019, May 11). Health effects of dietary risks in 195 countries, 1990–2017: A systematic analysis for the global burden of disease study 2017. *Lancet*.

Gough, I. (2017). *Heat*. Edward Elgar.

Gough, I. (2016). Potential benefits and pitfalls of a UBI. *The Guardian.* https://www.theguardian.com/politics/2016/jun/10/potential-benefits-and-pitfalls-of-a-universal-basic-income

Gough, I. (2013). The political economy of prevention. *British Journal of Political Science* (pp. 1–21). ISSN 1469–2112.

Gough, I. et al. (2008). Climate change and social policy: A symposium. *Journal of European Social Policy, 18*(4).

Green New Deal Group (2013). *A National Plan for the UK.* New Weather Institute. https://greennewdealgroup.org/wp-content/uploads/2013/09/Green-New-Deal-5th-Anniversary.pdf

Harrabin, R. (2019, September 24). Introduce frequent flyer levy to fight emissions, government told. *BBC.* https://www.bbc.co.uk/news/business-49808258

Himmelweit, J. M., et al. (2014). *The value of childcare.* New Economics Foundation.

Jabola-Carolus, I., Luce, S., & Milman, R. (2021). *The case for public investment in higher pay for New York state home care workers: Estimated costs and savings*. CUNY Academic Works.

Jayasuriya, K. (2006). *Statecraft, Welfare and the politics of inclusion.* Palgrave Macmillan.

Johnson, J. (2021). *Tax rises are no longer taboo in the UK: The party that grasps this could reap huge rewards.* https://www.theguardian.com/commentisfree/2021/feb/25/tax-rises-party-uk-rewards-voters-pandemic

Jones, A., Goodman, A., Roberts, H., Steinbach, R., & Green, J. (2013). Entitlement to concessionary public transport and wellbeing: A qualitative study of young people and older citizens in London, UK. *Social Science & Medicine, 91.*

Kellas, J. (1992). *The Scottish Constitutional Convention.* The Scottish Government Yearbook. University of Edinburgh.

KPMG. (2017). *The 'true value' of local bus services: A report to Greener Journeys.* Greener Journeys.

Lloyd, E. & Potter, S. (2014). *Early childhood education and care and poverty* (Working paper for Joseph Rowntree Foundation). University of East London.

London School of Economics. (2020). *Wealth commission report.* https://www.lse.ac.uk/News/Latest-news-from-LSE/2020/L-December/Wealth-Commission-report

Lynch K., & Kalaitzake, M. (2018). Affective and calculative solidarity: the impact of individualism and neoliberal capitalism. *European Journal of Social Theory, 23*(2).

Mackett,R. (2015). Improving accessibility for older people—Investing in a valuable asset. *Journal of Transport & Health. 2*(1).

Marmot, M., et al. (2018). *Strategic review of health Inequalities in England post 2010.* Institute of Health Equity.

Marshall, T. (1965). The right to welfare. *The Sociological Review, 13*(3).

Mersch, M. (Ed). (2018). *Wellbeing for everyone in a sustainable Europe.* Independent Commission on Sustainable Equality.

Mestrum, F. (2018). Why basic income can never be a progressive solution. In A. Downes & S. Lansley (Eds), *It's basic income: The global debate.* Policy Press.

Miller, S. C. (2012). *The ethics of need: Agency, dignity and obligation.* Routledge.

Monbiot, G., Grey, R., Kenny, T., Macfarlane, L., Powell-Smith, A., Shrubsole, G., & Stratford, B. (2019). Land for the many. *The Labour Party.*

Muijnck, S. Bogliaccini, E., & Surie, J. (2021). Towards the wellbeing economy: implications for public, environmental and financial policy. *ONE.* https://www.ourneweconomy.nl/wp-content/uploads/2021/04/2021.04.10_Towards-the-Wellbeing-Economy.pdf.

Nussbaum, M. (2000). *Women and human development: The capabilities approach*. Cambridge University Press.
OECD Affordable Housing Database. (2019). *Housing costs over income.* https://www.oecd.org/housing/data/affordable-housing-database/housing-conditions.htm
OECD. (2016). *Society at a glance 2016: OECD social indicators 2016*. OECD.
OECD. (2011). *Investing in high-quality childhood education and care (ECEC).* https://www.oecd.org/education/school/48980282.pdf
ONS. (2016). *How does UK healthcare spending compare internationally?* https://www.ons.gov.uk/peoplepopulationandcommunity/healthandsocialcare/healthcaresystem/articles/howdoesukhealthcarespendingcompareinternationally/2016-11-01
Ortiz, I., Behrendt, C., Acuña-Ulate, A., & Anh, N. Q. (2018). *Universal basic income proposals in light of ILO standards: Key Issues and global costing*. ILO.
Penn, H. (2014). The business of childcare in Europe. *European Early Childhood Education Research Journal, 22*(4).
Perry, J., Williams, M., Sefton, T., & Haddad, M. (2014). *Emergency use only: Understanding and reducing the use of food banks in the UK*. Oxfam.
Pichler, P. P., Jaccard, I. S., Weisz, U., & Weisz, H. (2019). International comparison of health care carbon footprints. *Environmental Research Letters, 14*, 6.
Portes, J., Reed, H., & Percy, A. (2017). *Social prosperity for the future: A proposal for universal basic services.* IGP.
Poore, J., & Nemecek, T. (2018). Reducing food's environmental impacts through producers and consumers. *Science, 360*.
Rao, N. D., & Min, J. (2017). Decent living standards: Material requisites for human well being. *Journal of Social Indicators Research, 138*(1).
Rayworth, K. (2017). *Doughnut economics: 7 ways to think like a 21st century economist*. Random House.
Sharpe, R. & Barling, D. (2019). The right thing to do': ethical motives in the interpretation of social sustainability in the UK's conventional food supply. *Agriculture and Human Values, 36*(2).
Sloman, L., & Hopkinson, L. (2019). *Transforming Public transport: Regulation, spending and free buses for the under 30s.* Friends of the Earth.
Standing, G. (2020). *Battling eight giants.* I. B. Taurus.
Stewart, K., Gambero, L., Waldfogel, J., & Rutter, J. (2014). Common challenges, lessons for policy. In Gamero et al. (Eds), *An equal start? Providing quality early education and care for disadvantaged children.* Policy Press.

Stewart, K. (2013). *Labour's record on the under 5s: Policy spending and outcomes 1997–2010*. Centre for Analysis of Social Exclusion. LSE.
Stirling, A., & Arnold, A. (2020). *Building a minimum income guarantee for the UK.* New Economics Foundation. https://neweconomics.org/2020/03/building-a-minimum-income-protection
Storchmann, K. (2003). Externalities by Automobiles and fare-free transit in Germany—A Paradigm Shift? *Journal of Public Transportatio,. 6*(4).
Taylor, I., & Sloman, L. (2016). *Building a world class bus service for Britain.* Transport for Quality of Life.
Tax Justice UK. (2020). https://www.taxjustice.uk/blog/new-poll-reveals-concern-about-the-state-of-public-services-and-support-for-higher-taxes-on-wealth
The care collective. (2020). *The Care Manifesto*. Verso.
The Social Guarantee. (2021). https://www.socialguarantee.org/
Tilman, D., & Clark, M. (2014). Global diets link environmental sustainability and human health. *Nature, 515*(7528).
Verbist, G., Förster, M. F., & Vaalavuo, M. (2012). *The impact of publicly provided services on the distribution of resources: Review of new results and methods* (OECD Social, Employment and Migration Working Papers No. 130). OECD Publishing.
Whitfield, E. (2018). Why basic income is not good enough. In A. Downes & S. Lansley (Eds), *It's basic income: The global debate*. Policy Press.
Wilde, L. (2013). *Global solidarity*. Edinburgh University Press.
Willett, W., Rockström, J., Loken, B., Springmann, M., Lang, T., Vermeulen, S., Murray, C. J. (2019). Food in the Anthropocene: The EAT-Lancet commission on healthy diets from sustainable food systems. *The Lancet* , *393*(10170), 447–492

7

A Green New Deal: Opportunities and Constraints

Katie Kedward and Josh Ryan-Collins

1 Introduction

The Covid-19 crisis has seen governments intervening in market economies on a scale not seen since wartime. Previously unthinkable levels of peacetime public spending and borrowing have been undertaken to maintain the productive capacity of economies, prevent mass unemployment as well as support healthcare sectors stretched to their limits. These developments open the door to a wider reset of macroeconomic policy. A number of politicians and economic commentators have

K. Kedward (✉) · J. Ryan-Collins
Institute for Innovation and Public Purpose, University College London, London, UK
e-mail: k.kedward@ucl.ac.uk

J. Ryan-Collins
e-mail: j.ryan-collins@ucl.ac.uk

P. Arestis and M. Sawyer (eds.), *Economic Policies for Sustainability and Resilience*, International Papers in Political Economy,
https://doi.org/10.1007/978-3-030-84288-8_7

rallied behind the 'Green New Deal' as the policy framework best placed to realise such a shift.

Even before the pandemic, the world faced a confluence of interconnected social, environmental, and economic challenges, including rising inequality, stagnating global growth (IMF, 2019), increasing global temperatures, and more frequent natural disasters related to climate change (IPCC, 2018). The pandemic has exacerbated many of these trends: between 88 and 115 million more people were pushed into extreme poverty over the course of 2020, defined as living on less than $1.90 per day (World Bank, 2020); both corporates and households have become even more indebted (Tiftik & Mahmood, 2021), undermining the ability of the private sector to drive a global recovery. Meanwhile the environmental outlook remains grave: temperature rises are on track to reach 3–5 °C above pre-industrial levels by 2100, based on current emissions levels (WMO, 2018); biodiversity and ecosystem health is declining at precipitous and unprecedented rates towards potentially irreversible tipping points (Dasgupta, 2021; IPBES, 2019). Yet initiatives to resolve these challenges remain woefully underfunded: investment for decarbonisation is some $480-billion short of the sum needed per year to meet the target of limiting global temperature rising to 1.5 °C (McCollum et al., 2018). The gap in annual investments needed to achieve the Sustainable Development Goals (SDGs) is estimated at $2.5 trillion (UNCTAD, 2020).

The original vision for a Green New Deal (GND), first articulated in 2008, in response to the Global Financial Crisis (GFC), offered a comprehensive action plan for these grand societal challenges (NEF, 2008). Recognising the intertwined nature of environmental, social, and economic crises, this GND vision emphasised the need for a more active role of the state, major systemic reform at both national and international levels, and redistributive policies to overcome climate injustice. Whilst the GND narrative has various interpretations in different nations and contexts, a major achievement has been to reframe sustainability goals as more than economy-versus-environment trade-offs, and towards an increasing acceptance of the potential synergies between green investment and better social and employment outcomes. However, since the GFC, the policy has been held back by concerns around public debt and deficits. The unprecedented policy response to the Covid-19 pandemic—itself a zoonotic disease linked to environmental degradation (Crow, 2020)—has shifted the macroeconomic consensus to create a more favourable stance for GND-style policies. Large-scale fiscal stimulus is back on the agenda, monetary policy has assumed a wider role than just price stability (Cavallino & De Fiore, 2020), and politicians are embracing the rhetoric of the GND with more urgency (Hepburn et al., 2020). US President Biden embraced the GND's green jobs narrative within his original $2 trillion infrastructure proposal; whilst in the EU, the European Commission has pledged 30% of its Recovery Plan—over half a trillion euros—to climate objectives. The European Green Deal, first announced in December 2019, has been reemphasised as the 'compass' of the EU's recovery package (Simon, 2020).

However, there is a danger that the emerging GND-style policy packages are framed too narrowly in terms of short-term demand-side recovery stimulus, instead of the broader context of the structural economic transformation—also requiring fundamental supply-side shifts—required to reach net-zero carbon emissions at an international scale. Indeed, there are a number of serious conceptual limitations within current GND proposals, which limit their potential to deliver a truly global green transition. Firstly, despite the above-mentioned consensus shift, policymakers continue to implicitly rely on private financial markets to lead the green recovery, with an ongoing assumption that higher public investment should be balanced against the risk of 'crowding out' the private sector (Blanchard, 2019) or inflation (Summers, 2021). Accordingly, the emphasis in many major economies has been on addressing market failures and 'de-risking' policies to ensure sufficient private investment flow into green capital projects. Secondly, and relatedly, current GND strategies suffer from limited industrial policy ambition and policy coherence. They focus too narrowly on government investment and neglect the full range of public policy tools able to steer markets in the desired direction and create sufficient demand to achieve cross-sectoral transformation, including public procurement, environmental and financial regulation, and monetary policy operations. Thirdly, current iterations of the GND have lost the internationalist dimension of the original GND, emphasising instead the narrative of domestic recovery packages focused on green jobs. Such an inward-looking agenda neglects the distributional and international macroeconomic challenges of ensuring that decarbonisation and ecological restoration is successful at a global level. This chapter tackles each of these critiques in turn and proposes alternative ways forward.

The rest of the chapter is laid out as follows. In Sect. 2, we trace the intellectual history of the GND, with its origins as a reaction to the GFC and its present-day incarnations as a means to rebuild economies post-Covid. Section 3 considers the current efforts of governments to stimulate economies in the aftermath of Covid-19 under the umbrella of a GND, with a particular focus on the EU. The remaining three sections examine the limitations of the current approach, focussing on the role of (private) finance (Sect. 4), the limited role of the state in driving forward industrial development and green innovation (Sect. 5) and the lack of a global approach to the net-zero carbon transition (Sect. 5). Section 6 summarises and concludes.

2 An Intellectual and Political History of the Green New Deal

The original rallying call for a GND appeared in a New York Times article at the beginning of 2007 (Friedman, 2007), but the onset of the GFC shortly after gave the idea of increased potency. Faced with a 'triple crunch' of global financial meltdown, climate change, and high oil prices, a group of British economists and campaigners developed an ambitious economic plan to address what it saw as overlapping crises (NEF, 2008). The group argued that the green transition required structural economic transformation both across sectors and between nations, including major government investments in green infrastructure that would create good quality jobs as well as supporting decarbonisation. This original GND could be described as a form of 'Green Keynesianism'—advocating huge fiscal stimulus, subordination of the global financial system to the interests of society, and redistributive policies towards the Global South, given the West's historic debt in terms of carbon emissions. As the anaemic recovery to the GFC persisted, the GND gained broader appeal among policymakers as a Keynesian strategy to restart ailing economies (Barbier, 2010). A 2009 United Nations Environment Programme report aimed to coordinate national economic stimulus plans towards a Global Green New Deal, recommending that high-income economies spend 1% of GDP on green initiatives (UNEP, 2009). President Obama's administration included an unprecedented $90 billion on clean energy and environmental initiatives within the American Recovery and Investment Act in 2009.

However, the GND narrative as adopted by governments in the aftermath of the GFC, placed less emphasis on structural economic change and regulations to curb carbon emissions. Instead, it embraced an 'ecological modernization' agenda that focused on investments in technical solutions to renewable energy, energy-efficiency initiatives, and market-based instruments to improve environmental incentives (Galvin & Healy, 2020; Mastini et al., 2021). The actual crisis stimulus fell far short of the 3–4% GDP achieved under Roosevelt's New Deal, with the G20 group spending only 0.8% of GDP ($513 billion) by the end of 2009 (Barbier, 2016). By 2010, the tide had turned against Keynesian demand-side macroeconomics, with the G20 meeting in Toronto heralding a new era of fiscal consolidation across high-income economies, and especially in the UK and Eurozone.

A decade later, the original GND vision, more focused on structural change, was re-galvanised by grassroots campaigning through the US-based Sunrise Movement. In 2019, US congressional representative Alexandria Ocasio-Cortez and Senator Ed Markey, introduced a non-binding resolution for an American Green New Deal, co-signed by 111 federal legislators. Reimagined for the US context, this 'GND 2.0' outlined an ambitious scope of programmes to accelerate decarbonisation within 10 years whilst tackling the US' structural inequality, poverty, and racial divides. The resolution reemphasised the need for deep economic transformation, advocating for public investment underpinned by ambitious industrial policy and a job guarantee scheme, and more command-and-control style regulation (e.g., a moratorium on fracking) rather than market-led solutions. Although revitalising the transformative agenda of the original 2008 GND, the US vision was less internationally oriented, with the particular social and racial context of the USA at the heart of the proposals, which placed a strong emphasis on domestic job creation (Pettifor, 2019).

Although the resolution ultimately failed to proceed in the House, the ambitious vision of GND 2.0 sparked international interest and inspired a wave of new policy proposals in the UK (Satow, 2019), Eurozone (DiEM25, 2019), and green government policy in South Korea (Lee & Woo, 2020). The US proposals have also sparked debate amongst macroeconomists, particularly over how the GND could be financed and its inflationary potential. Some scholars argued that a US GND would generate economic activity exceeding spare capacity, and hence require politically unpalatable levels of taxation or interest rate rises to control inflation (Palley, 2019). Others have argued that an ambitious GND was not just about injecting new demand but also reorienting resources from unsustainable to sustainable uses and that carefully targeted investment spending (towards under-utilised areas) could increase economic capacity by creating the conditions to boost confidence and enable further investment (Nersisyan & Wray, 2019). Using Senator Bernie Sanders' GND cost estimates, Galvin and Healy (2020) calculate that any excess inflation generated could be managed by tax increases on the wealthiest citizens similar to those levied in the second half of the twentieth century. The Biden administration's $1.9 trillion Covid-stimulus package, which did not have a particularly green angle, was worth around 9% of GDP, and was also subject to the heated debate around its inflationary potential (Summers, 2021), but has demonstrated the potential for large-scale government stimulus to gain legislative approval.

In December 2019, the European Commission introduced its own version of a GND: the European Green Deal (EGD) (European Commission, 2019a). Designed as a Europe-wide climate action plan and sustainable growth strategy, the EGD joins a variety of new and existing policy initiatives. These include: the target for net zero emissions by 2050; industrial strategy to decouple resource and energy use and promote a circular economy; a 'Just Transition' framework; strategies to restore biodiversity; and planned efforts to streamline and update fossil fuel subsidies and the EU Emissions Trading Scheme (EU-ETS). The EGD is supported by the Sustainable Europe Investment Plan (SEIP), which aims to mobilise at least €1 trillion of funding from private and public sources by 2030 (Claeys & Tagliapietra, 2020), and a new Horizon Europe programme for research and innovation, which is structured around a set of 'missions' to accelerate the development and diffusion of green innovation. Over 35% of the latter's €95.5 billion budget over 2021–2027 will contribute towards climate objectives.

Although the EGD is the world's largest and most comprehensive green transition programme, its ambition has been questioned. Critics note that €100 billion annually over 10 years is far less than the European Commission's own estimates of the €260 billion needed yearly to meet 2030 emissions targets.[1] Furthermore, the EGD's budgetary commitments largely represent existing pledged funds that have been reshuffled, rather than new funding (Claeys & Tagliapietra, 2020). Others have suggested the EU budget alone is insufficient; ambitious national fiscal policy is also needed but is currently 'straitjacketed' by fiscal rules that prioritise debt reduction and balanced budgets over ambitious investment spending (Lallemand, 2021; Pekanov & Schratzenstaller, 2020).

Like the US GND, the EGD positions the green transition as a regional green transition strategy more than a global-scale decarbonisation challenge. Yet it differs from its US counterpart in adopting the above-mentioned 'ecological modernization' approach predicated on steering markets towards green technical progress, rather than embracing an agenda for structural transformation. Whilst the US GND embeds social and welfare policies in the heart of its vision, the EGD treats the social implications of the green transition as an 'add-on' policy via the Just Transition mechanism. The EGD places greater emphasis on mobilising private finance through budgetary guarantees and 'blended finance' mechanisms that de-risk market investments rather than an active role for direct state investment, perhaps acknowledging the challenging Eurozone macroeconomic context. As critics have noted, this raises the problem of socialising the losses whilst privatising the gains of green investment opportunities and leaves the European policy framework at risk of capture by private interests—as has been seen by the

[1] Although even this estimate relates to the EU's former target of 40% emissions reductions from 1990 levels by 2030. The target has since been updated to a 55% reduction.

watered-down sustainable investment taxonomy (Varoufakis & Adler, 2020).

In summary, the intellectual and political development of the GND has shifted considerably across time and geographies. This is perhaps a weakness, and political strength, of the GND's appeal to a broad church of political agendas. The key contribution of the GND vision is its success in establishing the synergies between environmental and social justice policies and making a win–win case for green investment and decent jobs. As such, it remains an important unifying concept underpinning economic strategies for the green transition. The macroeconomic significance of the GND has only become more pressing and pertinent in the wake of the fallout generated by the COVID-19 global economic crisis.

3 Developments in Macroeconomics Since COVID—And Ongoing Limitations of Responses

The consensus approach to macroeconomics in both academia and policymaking since the 1970s considers that fiscal policy should be confined to short-term economic stabilisation, rather than longer-term structural economic development (Tobin, 1975). Whilst market rigidities and frictions may exist in the short run, market forces, via the price discovery mechanism, are seen to ensure the optimal allocation of resources in the long run (Woodford, 2003). Under assumptions of a limited supply of 'loanable funds' or savings, public investment runs the risk of distorting the price and allocation of capital by pushing up interest rates above their equilibrium or 'natural' rate (Spencer & Yohe, 1970). More recently, the macroeconomic consensus has evolved to acknowledge the benefits of expansionary fiscal policy benefits when monetary policy is at its effective zero lower bound (Ostry et al., 2016). This follows empirical evidence of high fiscal multipliers during downturns (Auerbach & Gorodnichenko, 2017) and the exacerbating consequences of excessive fiscal consolidation after the global financial crisis (Fatás & Summers, 2015).

This shift in thinking has been accelerated by the COVID-19 crisis where, amidst a global public health crisis and lockdown-induced demand and supply shocks, governments have been forced to deploy large-scale state support to protect jobs, incomes, and productive capacity. On average, fiscal deficits in high-income economies rose to 9% of GDP in 2020, whilst global public debt to GDP ratios reached record peacetime levels of 98% of GDP by the end of 2020 (IMF, 2021). Reversing 30 years of emphasising the importance of balanced public budgets, international organisations such as the IMF and the OECD have warned that fiscal retrenchment could derail the recovery (Giles, 2020, 2021). There have also been growing warnings that monetary policy alone is insufficient to ensure a sustained economic recovery in the post-Covid era (Constâncio, 2020; Lagarde, 2020). These arguments have been supported by a growing narrative, emerging even before the pandemic, that fiscal stimulus is justified and even warranted under economic conditions where (1) private demand is weak, output is substantially below potential, and monetary policy is at its effective lower bound, meaning multipliers are likely to be larger than usual, and (2) the interest rate on government debt is likely to remain below the rate of growth for a sustained period of time, removing the fiscal costs of deficit spending (Blanchard, 2019). In summary, there is now increased recognition of the importance of demand-side fiscal policy in ensuring economic stability in times of crisis and that monetary policy has limits—a major contrast with the post-2007–2008 crisis period.

A second shift in the macroeconomic consensus relates to policy coordination between fiscal and monetary policy. Since the emergence of inflation targeting in the 1990s, central banks in high-income economies have maintained that full independence from governments is key to the effectiveness of monetary policy as the key macroeconomic stabilisation policy. Yet central banks have played a key role in facilitating the above-mentioned fiscal stimulus via purchasing sovereign bonds in quantitative easing (QE) operations of unprecedented scale and speed and implicit or explicit versions of yield curve control (Kliesen &

Bokun, 2020). Whilst central bankers have vehemently denied accusations of monetary financing,[2] monetary policy interventions have undoubtedly created substantial fiscal space to aid pandemic spending—with sovereign borrowing costs declining across major economies even whilst deficits were rising (Wolf, 2020). Proposals for more explicit fiscal-monetary policy mixes are now seeing renewed interest among economists who previously adhered to a strict separation between fiscal and monetary spheres. Recent analysis has emphasised that coordinated policy may be more appropriate under current extraordinary circumstances, when both monetary and fiscal tools are short of policy space (Bartsch et al., 2020; Blanchard & Pisani-Ferry, 2020; Galí, 2020). Apart from government debt, central banks have also intervened far more extensively into other financial asset classes, and even into the real economy. The US Federal Reserve, for example, has created liquidity facilities to support not just corporate bonds, but also municipal debt, junk bonds, and Exchange Traded Funds; whilst the Bank of England, through its Covid Corporate Financing Facility, has used newly created reserves to lend directly to corporates (Cavallino & De Fiore, 2020).

Thirdly, and relatedly, the increased reach of central bank balance sheets had led to growing recognition of the potential long-run effects of monetary policy upon the real economy. This has become especially debated in regard to corporate asset purchase portfolios, which have been shown to have had the unintended consequence of disproportionately supporting incumbent unsustainable industrial sectors (Dafermos et al., 2020, 2021b; Kedward et al., 2021; Jourdan & Kalinowski, 2019). Some central bank officials have recently acknowledged that 'market neutrality' may need reconsidering as an operating principle for monetary policy operations where there is clear evidence of significant market failures, such as the failure of financial markets to price in environmental risks (Arnold, 2020; Schnabel, 2020). The significance of such a shift in consensus lies in the potential for monetary policy to be deployed to support broader government objectives. In the UK, for example, the

[2] Emphasising, for example, the temporary nature of asset purchase programmes and the fact that they have not been undertaken with the explicit objective of funding governments (BIS, 2020).

Treasury has recently updated the Bank of England's remit 'to be consistent with the transition to a net-zero economy', enabling the Bank to announce plans to decarbonise its corporate bond purchase portfolio (HM Treasury, 2021, p. 1; Hodgson et al., 2021).

Finally, as attention now turns from the immediate pandemic response to the longer-term economic recovery, green fiscal stimulus is increasingly being embraced by policymakers as the most effective strategy to accelerate not only the green transition, but also restart economic activity (Hepburn et al., 2020). Government spending oriented towards green projects such as insulation retrofits, electrification infrastructure, and renewable energy has been shown to have potentially high multiplier effects—generating high and geographically well-distributed additional employment whilst upskilling the workforce with urgently needed skills for the green economy (Hepburn et al., 2020; Krebel et al., 2020).[3] Infrastructure investment has been reembraced as an appropriate justification for deficit spending, given the risk-adjusted social returns exceed the interest rates on government debt (Blanchard, 2019). This is widely acknowledged to be the case with green infrastructure, given the enormous costs of failing to invest for climate mitigation and adaptation (IPCC, 2018). Modelling a range of growth scenarios, Ruiz and Stupariu (2021) conclude that green fiscal spending is compatible with public debt sustainability, provided there is sufficient medium-term growth relative to the rate of interest on government debt.

Drawing together these developments, the macroeconomic consensus is now shifting to a more favourable stance towards GND-style policies. Namely, large-scale fiscal stimulus is back on the agenda, monetary policy is assuming a wider role than just price stability and is actively creating fiscal space, and the high employment multiplier of green-oriented public investment is aligning a jobs-led recovery with the need for a net zero carbon transition. Politicians are accordingly embracing the rhetoric of the GND with more urgency. Despite not endorsing Sanders' GND plan during the presidential campaign, US President Biden embedded its green jobs narrative within his proposed $2 trillion

[3] Government investment in the care economy has also been shown to have superior employment outcomes relative to construction, with additional jobs created being both gender-balanced and compatible with the green transition (De Henau & Himmelweit, 2021).

infrastructure plan, originally pledging around $330 billion to environmental purposes (White House, 2021), although the bipartisan bill eventually passed pledged a substantially smaller amount for climate purposes. In the EU, the European Commission has pledged 30% of its Recovery Plan—over half a trillion euros—to climate objectives. South Korea has become the first nation in East Asia to commit to a net zero emissions target by 2050—pledging a US$144 billion GND investment programme (1.7% of GDP) over the first five years (Lee & Woo, 2020).

However, something of a gap has appeared between the rhetoric and reality of green stimulus. Even Biden's proposed infrastructure spending would have been spread over eight years, with its original climate investment amounting to only around 0.5% GDP annually (Tooze, 2021). Recent analysis has found that fiscal packages in 15 of the G20 economies will have a net-negative environmental impact (Vivid Economics, 2021), whilst leading European economies are expected to pour two thirds of pandemic recovery funding into unsustainable sectors (Finance Watch, 2021). More than half a trillion dollars of stimulus worldwide has supported high-carbon industries with no conditions to reduce emissions, whilst the comparative figure for low-carbon industries is just $12.5 billion (Harvey, 2020). Meanwhile, in addition to concerns over the carbon intensity of corporate asset portfolios noted above, a recent global review of 188 central banks and financial supervisors also found that less than 1% had directly embedded sustainability factors into their crisis responses (Dikau et al., 2020).

There is thus a danger that the GND is framed too narrowly in terms of a short-term demand-side stimulus instead of the broader, medium-term context of the structural economic transformation required to reach net-zero carbon emissions at an international scale. Indeed, there are a number of serious conceptual limitations within current GND proposals, which will limit the potential to deliver a truly global green transition. These are an over-reliance on private finance, a lack of ambition on industrial policy and policy coordination more generally, and finally insufficient focus on international action. The next three sections deal with these in turn.

4 Limits of Private Finance in Directing Structural Economic Transitions

One of the concerns within existing GND strategies, as well as emerging narratives on GND-style recovery packages, is the implicit reliance on private finance to fund the development and deployment of green innovation. Nowhere is this more evident than in the European Green Deal (EGD), the largest and most comprehensive GND strategy currently in play (Claeys & Tagliapietra, 2020; Storm, 2020). The EGD's Sustainable Europe Investment Plan (SEIP) aims to mobilise at least €1 trillion of funding from private and public sources by 2030. Tables 1 and 2 show the breakdown in sources of funding for the EGD, updated to include additional climate commitments extended under the latest EU budget for 2021–2027 and the temporary Recovery and Resilience facility. With fiscal policy at the member state level constrained by the strict fiscal rules of the Stability and Growth Pact, the European Commission's approach is to mobilise private funding through a *de-risking* strategy—i.e., by using the European Investment Bank (EIB) and national development banks to 'crowd in' private involvement through the creation of a loan facility backed by an EU budget guarantee.

Table 1 Annual sources of funding for the European Green Deal

Source of funding	Funding per year (€, billions)
EU budget 2021–2027 dedicated to climate[a]	46.0
Recovery and Resilience Facility dedicated to climate[a]	28.8
Invest EU (mobilized funds)[b]	27.9
National co-financing[b]	11.4
EU Emissions Trading Systems Funds[b]	2.5
Just Transition Mechanism[b] (mobilized funds)	15.0
Total	131.6

Notes [a]Yearly figure for 2021–2027, 30% of both the EU Budget and RRF have been committed to climate objectives

[b]Yearly figure for 2021–2030, based on European Commission's estimates for raised/mobilised funds

Sources Claeys and Tagliapietra (2020), Storm (2020) and European Commission (2020a; 2020b; 2020c); and own calculations

Table 2 Implied private investment required to meet annual investment shortfall

Source of funding	40% target €, billion share		55% target €, billion share	
EGD pledged and mobilised funds	131.6	51%	131.6	33%
Additional implied private investment	128.4	49%	268.4	67%
Total estimated annual investment requirement	260.0	100%	400.0	100%

Sources Claeys and Tagliapietra (2020), Storm (2020) and European Commission (2020a; 2020b; 2020c); and own calculations

Even with the estimated mobilised funds, the total investment estimated under the current EGD strategy falls short of the investment required to decarbonise the Eurozone. The European Commission has estimated that €260 billion is needed annually to reduce emissions by 40% from 1990 levels by 2030. Yet the EU's emissions reduction target has since been updated to −55% by 2030, which implies investment needs of closer to €400 billion per year, or 3% of GDP—assuming a linear relationship between decarbonisation and investment (Storm, 2020). As Tables 1 and 2 shows, even under the old target, the EGD's current pledges and estimated mobilised funds, only meet around half of the required investment needs, showing an implicit reliance on the private sector to step in to meet the shortfall.

The Sustainable Europe Investment Plan (SEIP) accordingly places significant emphasis on policies to create an enabling framework for green private finance. Great effort has been made to support the development of new green financial instruments and robust green product labelling (via the Sustainable Taxonomy instrument), as well as de-risking and blended finance mechanisms designed to make green sectors more 'investable' (European Commission, 2018). Similar market-led strategies for the green transition are being pursued in the UK (BEIS, 2019), as well as in emerging and low-income economies, where multilateral development institutions are strongly pushing de-risking and blended finance strategies, most notably through Public–Private Partnerships (PPPs), as the primary mechanisms of achieving the climate and other sustainability goals in the Global South (Dafermos et al., 2021a). As we expand in Sect. 6, initiatives such as the World Bank's *Next Generation Africa for Climate Business Plan* are conceived almost in direct opposition to progressive GND discourses, positioning global institutional investors, rather than domestic governments, as the leading actors in a global sustainable transition.

This approach to greening finance is predicated upon neoclassical welfare economics, which justifies government action in the short run in order to correct market failures such as information asymmetries, unpriced externalities, or other market rigidities. Government intervention, from this perspective, is seen as a second-best means of achieving

Pareto improvements in the absence of a short-run market equilibrium (Lipsey & Lancaster, 1956). The green investment gap is widely conceptualised to be one such market failure: environmental factors are not priced into existing markets, hence green investment remains underfunded because its returns are not attractive enough or financiers lack information on the viability of the investment opportunity (Jaffe et al., 2005). This perspective underpins the 'market-fixing' approach (Mazzucato, 2016) to mobilising green investment: once hidden environmental costs, benefits, and risks are internalised into market prices, it is presumed that the market mechanism will automatically shift investment flows towards more sustainable activities (Christophers, 2017; Ryan-Collins, 2019). Recently, central banks and financial supervisors have taken a leading role in developing this approach advocating for the measurement and disclosure of climate risks as the primary means of guiding financial markets to support the green transition (NGFS, 2020).

This market-fixing strategy has not had great success in shifting investment flows away from carbon-intensive industries and towards green innovation. Several years after the launch of the Taskforce for Climate-related Financial Disclosures (TCFD) in 2017, newly available climate investment information has yet to materially affect investment decisions for the majority of banks and investments (Ameli et al., 2019; Christophers, 2019; Hook & Vincent, 2020). Moreover, bank lending to fossil fuel companies has actually expanded since the Paris climate agreement in 2015 (BankTrack and Rainforest Action Network, 2020), even in the Eurozone, where climate policy and regulation has generally been the most ambitious (ECB, 2020, p. 73). A critical conceptual flaw contributing to this poor track record is the fact that the most prominent disclosure frameworks, most notably the TCFD, account only for the risks that climate change poses to the financial system, rather than also accounting for the impacts that the financial system has as an enabler of environmentally negative activities. By neglecting to recognise this 'double materiality' dynamic (European Commission, 2019b), market-fixing approaches fail to consider where and how the financial system may have to be structurally transformed in order to align with (rather than hinder) the financing requirements of a GND.

The failure of this market-fixing strategy is related to underlying conceptual flaws. Firstly, it presumes that environmental externalities are fully known, measurable, and able to be internalised into market prices. Secondly, the particular investment required to drive transition—in green innovation—is considered to be much the same as investment into established technologies. Thirdly, and most notably, it implicitly accepts the status quo economic structure as a given, with markets assumed to require only price corrections to ensure sustainable capital allocation. This static efficiency-optimisation approach is unsuited to the challenge of green transition, which involves dynamic change at a systemic level, with prices changing across multiple sectors and economic agents (Mazzucato & McPherson, 2018; Zenghelis, 2016). Importantly, there is no 'ready-made pathway' for the green transition: multiple outcomes may result from the endogenous interaction of policy and regulatory reform, shifting consumer preferences, technological innovation, and complex financial system dynamics; and yet the probabilities of these different outcomes are impossible to estimate in advance (Bolton et al., 2020; Chenet et al., 2021). In the presence of such incalculable 'unknown unknowns', market prices cannot be relied upon to reliably internalise environmental factors, implying a more proactive role for policymakers in shaping the shift to a net-zero carbon economy (Chenet et al., 2021; Ryan-Collins, 2019).

Scholars coming from an evolutionary tradition argue that investment in green innovation should be considered as qualitatively different to investment within established industries, because it is subject to intrinsic uncertainty over long-time horizons (Deleidi et al., 2020; Mazzucato & Perez, 2015). Path dependency is hence an important phenomenon shaping how new markets, sectors, institutions, green and consumer behaviours will evolve. Indeed, Aghion et al. (2014) show how the transition is characterised by powerful reinforcing feedback processes that can either accelerate or hinder the development, deployment, and adoption of green technology. These evolutionary dynamics include learning-by-doing and knowledge spillovers (Dechezlepretre et al., 2017), economies of scale and large switching costs (Eberle & von Helmolt, 2010), network externalities and coordination effects (Kemp-Benedict, 2018), and social and institutional feedbacks, including the role of expectations and narratives (Schiller, 2019). The uptake of green innovation is also hampered by a disadvantageous starting position (e.g., lack of electric vehicle charging infrastructure), which in turn affects the evolving expectations of relevant economic actors (Grubb et al., 2021).

Due to the non-linear effects induced by such evolutionary dynamics, the 'first best' option of carbon pricing mechanisms alone may be insufficient to drive investment into green innovation (Aghion et al., 2014; Hall et al., 2017). In addition, a uniform carbon price is too blunt to account for the different cost and innovation dynamics existing between sectors, where the price likely to act as a tipping point in system behaviour is likely to vary substantially between industries (Kattel et al., 2018) There is considerable evidence of inertia in technological diffusion which is typically not accounted for in conventional optimisation models (Grubb et al., 2021; Zenghelis, 2016). This means that greater emission reductions may be achieved by the deployment of a variety of different policy tools, to address both the price and non-price barriers to green technology diffusion (Mercure et al., 2014).

In summary, the structural transformation necessitated by the green transition generates significant economy-wide uncertainty. Market-led approaches alone are likely to be insufficient to ensure sufficient investment in green innovation. Substantial 'unknown unknowns' mean environmental externalities cannot accurately internalised into market prices. Investing in green innovation is also subject to intrinsic long-term uncertainty, and dependent upon powerful non-linear path-dependency effects that price-based mechanisms alone cannot overcome. Taken together, these insights indicate that GND strategies need to focus on more than just the provision of investment finance. The structural economy-wide nature of the green transition necessitates a broader suite of policies to shape new markets in the required direction.

5 A Mission-Oriented GND: The Market-Shaping Role of the State

5.1 From Market Fixing to Market Shaping

Market-shaping approaches to public policy stem from an alternative intellectual tradition to the neoclassical foundations underpinning market failure thinking, drawing instead from political economy, classical Keynesianism, institutional analysis, systems thinking, and evolutionary economics. As noted by Polanyi (1957), this tradition conceptualises markets as an outcome of the interactions between firms, individuals, and the state, rather than existing a priori. From these perspectives, value is not just generated by the private sector, but 'co-created' collectively by multiple economic stakeholders (Mazzucato & Ryan-Collins, 2019). Evolutionary and institutional scholars have reflected upon this alternative conceptualisation of markets in the context of structural economic change and the development and diffusion of innovation (Nelson & Winter, 1974; Schumpeter, 1983). Given that markets are constructs operating under conditions of fundamental uncertainty, it is argued that there is no *optimal* pathway to structural change, but a combination of possible outcomes that can be influenced by how the state interactions with other economic actors (Geels & Schot, 2007; Kattel et al., 2018). Governments and public institutions can therefore play a key role in steering and accelerating technological change (Freeman & Perez, 1988).

Mazzucato (2013) has shown how governments have played an entrepreneurial role in shaping and directing innovation throughout history; public investment led the way in the development of space flight, for example, as well as various hardware and software innovations within the iPhone. Governments are uniquely able to take on risky investments, whilst shaping the policy environment to strengthen the whole innovation chain, in effect 'tilting the playing field' to maximise chances of success (Block & Keller, 2011; Mazzucato, 2013). The strategy of long-term public investment together with coordinated public policy constitutes a 'market-shaping' role for public policy. It is able to not only mitigate uncertainty amongst private actors, but also generate substantial knowledge spillovers and positive network effects that benefit broader economic activity. For the development of new technologies characterised by significant uncertainty, therefore, strategic government investment and policy can mobilise—rather than 'crowd out'—further private investment. In doing so, it can accelerate structural economic transitions. From this perspective, sustainable economic growth not only has a rate, but also a direction. Table 3 summarises the key differences between market-fixing and market-shaping roles for public policy.

Drawing from these insights, we can recognise the green transition as a 'wicked problem' of dynamic structural change across multiple sectors, encompassing both supply and demand dynamics, and uniquely predicated upon the complex dynamics of developing and deploying green innovation. Accordingly, the GND needs to be understood as more than just a strategy to de-risk private investment or as a green-version of Keynesian demand-side stabilisation; instead, it needs to be conceptualised as a comprehensive industrial strategy aimed at nurturing the conditions for a green structural economic transition (Mazzucato & McPherson, 2018; Mazzucato & Perez, 2015).

Importantly, this is not about top-down economic planning, but rather about the state setting a clear direction within the long-term policy landscape and supporting bottom-up experimentation across different sectors to encourage economy-wide multiplier and innovation spillover effects. GND strategies therefore need to encompass all of the institutional features that influence market outcomes. This includes not just public investment, but also regulatory frameworks, incentive structures (e.g., tax policy, prize schemes), the development of labour force skills, and the creation of demand for new markets (e.g., through public procurement). This 'mission-oriented' approach to policymaking hence has two pillars: firstly, the provision of patient long-term public investment guided by democratically determined missions; and secondly, policy coordination between fiscal, industrial, financial, and regulatory spheres, in order to create the enabling conditions for markets to succeed (Kattel & Mazzucato, 2018; Mazzucato, 2016).

Table 3 Market-fixing versus market-shaping green transition policy frameworks

	Market-fixing	Market-shaping
Level of uncertainty	Low	High
Desired change	Incremental	Transformational
Cause-effect relationships	Proportionate	Disproportionate
Justification for the role of government	Market failures, e.g., public goods (a stable atmosphere), negative externalities (pollution, carbon emissions), imperfect information (lack of carbon risk disclosure)	Markets and institutions are co-created by public, private, and third sector stakeholders. Government role is to align markets in support of green transition
Policy appraisal frameworks	*Ex-ante* cost-benefit analysis, market failure, welfare economics	Systems thinking, dynamic efficiency, complexity economics, technological transitions
Underlying assumptions	Possible to estimate reliable future value using discounting. System is characterised by equilibrium behaviour	Future is radically uncertain because of the potential for structural change. System is characterised by complex behaviour, non-linear trajectories, feedback loops

(continued)

Table 3 (continued)

	Market-fixing	Market-shaping
Policy evaluation	Focus on whether the policy solves market failure and whether government failure is avoided (pareto-efficiency)	Ongoing and reflexive evaluation of whether system is moving in direction of mission via achievement of intermediate milestones and user engagement. Focus on interactions between the whole portfolio of policies
Approach to risk	Highly risk averse; optimism bias assumed	Failure is accepted and encouraged as a learning device

Source Adapted from Kattel et al. (2018)

5.2 Mission-Oriented Patient Finance

The green transition is often conceptualised solely as a problem of the *supply* of finance. Whilst access to finance is of course critical to firms seeking to innovate, increasing its availability alone will not ensure investment in green innovation. This is because finance is not neutral: different types of finance affect the qualities of investments that are chosen (Mazzucato & Semieniuk, 2018). As discussed in Sect. 4, innovation pathways are subject to dynamic complexities, fundamental uncertainty, and lengthy high-risk lead times. These factors mean innovation requires not just any type of investment, but patient, long-term, strategic investment, that has a high tolerance for risk (Lazonick & Mazzucato, 2013). Yet, over recent decades, the private sector has been a poor provider of such long-term capital: studies have shown advanced economy bank credit to have shifted away from the productive real economy and towards asset markets, in particular real estate (Bezemer et al., 2016). By contrast, in many countries, public investment has provided the early-stage high-risk capital needed to create and shape new markets, which then encourages private sector involvement.

There is a growing evidence-base showing these dynamics at play within the green transition. One recent study found that as much as 40% of investment into renewables between 2004 and 2014 had been financed by public institutions, with public actors more present than private investors in the higher risk technologies (Mazzucato & Semieniuk, 2018). A further study, using the same renewable energy dataset, found that direct public investment has consistently had the largest positive effect in stimulating private investment compared to feed-in tariffs and taxes—with the results holding for both renewable technology in general, as well as wind and solar sectors separately (Deleidi et al., 2020).

These results are consistent with what we might expect from the non-linear and path dependent nature of green innovation. If structured effectively, early-stage public investment and coordinated policy can have positive reinforcing effects, tipping complex systems towards a different state. This is now becoming more evident within the renewable energy space: the efficiency and productivity of solar photovoltaic and wind power have rapidly improved over recent years, to point of reaching cost parity with fossil fuel electricity generation (Carbon Tracker, 2020). Private investor interest has concurrently soared, with rapid growth in green bond issuance from US$ 2 billion in 2013 to US$ 38 billion in 2019 (IRENA, 2020). From this perspective, strategic public investment does not just resolve *supply* problems within green finance, but in addition the twin problem of *demand* for green investment, by actively supporting and nurturing the growth of new green markets.

Indeed, mission-oriented policy could have larger multiplier effects than normal fiscal stimulus because its targeted focus on strategic innovation increases productive capacity and 'crowds in' further private investment into R&D (Deleidi & Mazzucato, 2019). A recent study of different types of government spending in the US provides some empirical evidence for this 'super-multiplier' effect, finding that mission-oriented innovation policies generated multiplier effects 10 times larger than conventional public spending on consumption and capital investment (Deleidi & Mazzucato, 2021). The study also found mission-oriented policy to have the strongest effect on 'crowding in' private investment, rather than crowding it out. The 'super-multiplier' potential of a mission-oriented GND gives it obvious appeal as the basis for an effective green recovery package in the aftermath of the COVID-19 epidemic.

These examples, and others throughout the history of the twentieth-century innovation, articulate a specific role for the public sector as 'investor of first resort' for strategic high-risk activities that are under-provided by private markets (Macfarlane & Mazzucato, 2018; Mazzucato & Penna, 2016). Such an entrepreneurial role requires the public sector to embrace a range of funding instruments and to develop mission-oriented capabilities within public financial institutions to appropriately manage investments for public purposes. Diverse funding instruments allow public investment to be appropriately matched to the risk-return profile and innovation stage of the investment opportunity. Importantly, this means moving beyond the use of loan guarantees to consider direct public investment encompassing both debt and equity, as well as challenge-focused grants and prize schemes, mission-oriented conditionalities within state aid, and convertible instruments such as debt-to-equity structures. The latter two options have become particularly pertinent in the context of the COVID-19 epidemic, where a weakened and indebted corporate sector may increasingly require non-debt forms of public support to prevent a balance sheet recession (Detter et al., 2020). In the context of the green transition, aligning COVID-19 recovery packages with the emissions mitigation commitments, and other environmental goals, is essential in order to avoid infrastructural lock-in effects and the associated risks with potential future stranded assets.

Embracing a broader range of funding instruments is also warranted due to the need to ensure an appropriate balance of risk and reward across the mission-oriented public investment portfolio. Market-fixing policy approaches have focused upon de-risking strategies (e.g., loan guarantees and Public–Private Partnerships—PPPs) to incentivise private investment and to keep large capital expenditures from burdening public sector balance sheets. Yet these strategies essentially give the public sector considerable investment downside with no potential upside. Instead of socialising losses and privatising gains, mission-oriented policy approaches recognise that the public sector should receive returns on successful investments, in compensation for having assumed investment risk. This is as much an issue of prudent portfolio management as it is fairness: return-generating mechanisms are needed to offset the inevitable failures that will feature within a diverse and mission-oriented investment portfolio focused on innovation. Such mechanisms should include means for the public sector to recoup returns from investments as well as retain equity, royalties, or shares of intellectual property (Laplane & Mazzucato, 2020; Macfarlane & Mazzucato, 2018).

To be effective, this entrepreneurial function for public investment needs to be carried out within the right institutional framework. This has taken different forms: public wealth funds, such as Singapore's Temasek, and public venture capital funds, such as Israel's Yozma (Detter et al., 2020), as well as public investment banks, such as Germany's KfW, and multilateral banks, such as the European Investment Bank (EIB). Importantly, the mandate, governance, and economic role of such public financial institutions need to be structured in ways that support the achievement of policy missions (Kattel et al., 2018). In an analysis of eight-state investment banks, Macfarlane and Mazzucato (2018) find that 'mission-driven' state investment bank mandates are more likely to generate additionality (i.e., not 'crowding out' investments that would have happened anyway) and hence catalyse dynamic spillover effects.

5.3 Financial Policy Coordination

The market-shaping perspective recognises that a single policy or institution cannot bring about the profound transformation that characterises the green transition. A 'systems approach' is instead needed (Hafner et al., 2020), that involves policy coordination across fiscal, industrial, regulatory, and financial policy. Such coordination is especially warranted to manage the potential social consequences of green policies and to ensure that the structural transition is just as well as green. Coordination also becomes particularly important in order to ensure that industrial policy, and public investments that fall within it, interact favourably with the broader financial ecosystem.

Given the higher uncertainty and longer time horizons associated with innovation-focused industrial policy, active 'financial policy' has historically been coordinated with fiscal and industrial policy to ensure that private financial markets support—or at the very least do not undermine—strategic industrial priorities. In both high-income and emerging economies over the course of the twentieth century, financial regulation, credit policy, and monetary policy were commonly deployed to support economic development goals, steering or encouraging private finance towards priority sectors whilst also restricting or discouraging excessive activity in speculative or other undesirable sectors (e.g., real estate) (Amsden, 2001; Bezemer et al., 2018). Central banks, in close collaboration with state investment banks, were often explicitly tasked with carrying out such interventionist financial policy in support of government objectives (Epstein, 2006).

The need to deploy broader policies to manage the dynamics of private finance is particularly critical for the green transition. As discussed in Sect. 4, considerable sums of investment capital continue to flow to carbon-intensive industries whose current and future business strategies are incompatible with global decarbonisation trajectories. These financial dynamics pose a significant threat to the success of mission-oriented GND policies. Exposure to such industries leaves private financial actors vulnerable to the 'transition risks' of disorderly asset repricing as the green transition progresses (Carney, 2015). The adverse consequences of economy-wide 'stranded assets' could spread through the financial system (Battiston et al., 2017), impairing economic activity and undermining the business confidence needed to galvanise an economy-wide transition. But more than just financial stability risks, carbon-intensive capital flows also contribute to 'carbon lock-in' (Unruh, 2000). Given the path-dependent nature of the economy, investment decisions taken today determine the infrastructure pathways that define tomorrow's world. The continued deployment of carbon-intensive infrastructure hence embeds a persistently dominant position for high-emissions technologies in the economy, making decarbonisation more difficult and costly, despite the increasing profitability of green alternatives (Kemp-Benedict, 2018). 'Carbon lock-in' enabled by private finance hence threatens to severely delay and potentially derail the goals of GND policies.

Today, the financial stability risks of climate change and other environmental threats are widely recognised by central banks across the world to be relevant to their mandates (Bank of England, 2020; Brainard, 2021; ECB, 2020). However, concerns over potentially overstepping the limits of central bank independence have prevented the implementation of the sorts of more interventionist policies commonly used during the twentieth century. Yet, as discussed in Sect. 3, the COVID-19 pandemic has revealed the limitations inherent within the current institutional setup of central banks. To deal with the pandemic, monetary policy has had to become increasingly coordinated with fiscal policy, and central banks have had to put aside notions of market neutrality in delivering liquidity stimulus to targeted parts of the economy.

Given that climate change is poorly priced in by markets—a situation that may be impossible to resolve (Bolton et al., 2020; Chenet et al., 2021; Ryan-Collins, 2019), central banks should strive for *coherence* with government transition policy rather than *market neutrality* as the guiding operational principle for monetary, prudential, and regulatory policy-making for the green transition (Barkawi & Zadek, 2021; Robins et al.,

2021). The rationale is that (1) government transition policy is less likely to be successful if private financial dynamics are pushing against it; and (2) alignment with government transition policy is the most effective way for central banks to minimise systemic risks to financial stability. As per a market-shaping understanding of policymaking, this perspective recognises that central banks are not exogenous to the financial system, observing the emergence of transition risks like a weather forecaster reporting the likelihood of rain but being powerless to effect its occurrence. Rather, they are participating economic actors whose policy decisions help shape markets; their policy toolkits can hence be deployed to shape the direction of a smooth, orderly transition (Chenet et al., 2021).

A number of policy proposals have been put forward articulating how central bank policies can be 'greened' to encourage a green transition within private financial markets (Campiglio et al., 2018; D'Orazio & Popoyan, 2019). From the monetary policy perspective, asset purchase portfolios could be tilted towards purchasing green assets and/or exclude the assets linked to the most environmentally-damaging activities (Dafermos et al., 2020; Jourdan & Kalinowski, 2019). The collateral framework, which specifies how assets can be pledged as collateral in exchange for loans, could similarly be redesigned to align with government climate targets (Oustry et al., 2020). Funding and refinancing schemes, which provide the financial system with liquidity, could also be structured so as to incentivise lending to priority green sectors (van't Klooster & Van Tilburg, 2020). Many existing refinancing schemes already aim to selectively target such liquidity operations, as, for example, the Bank of England's Term Funding Scheme for Small and Medium Enterprises (TFSME) and the ECB's Targeted Long-Term Refinancing Operations (TLTROs), which aim to incentivise lending to the real economy.

These price-based credit guidance policies could also be complemented by policies to steer credit using quantity-based mechanisms, such as maximum lending ceilings (for undesirable sectors) and minimum lending floors (for strategic industries). Such 'green credit guidance' has already been implemented in emerging economies such as China, India and Bangladesh (Dikau & Ryan-Collins, 2017). Yet the highly globalised nature of market-based finance in the twenty-first century also likely requires reforms that are more comprehensive. Dafermos et al. (2021c) have argued that, to prevent regulatory arbitrage, green-supporting and dirty-penalising policies must also be extended to the currently under-regulated shadow banking architecture.

From the prudential and regulatory policy side, it has been argued that the current focus on environmental disclosures and stress-testing exercises is insufficient to either green capital flows or safeguard against risks to financial stability, due to the 'radically uncertain' nature of environmental risks, which cannot be precisely quantified (Bolton et al., 2020; Chenet et al., 2021; Ryan-Collins, 2019). Given the increasingly severe consequences of inaction, central banks could instead undertake discretionary policies on a precautionary basis—much like macroprudential policy, which is already implemented to manage the build-up of systemic risks in the housing market. Such measures could include punitive capital requirements on carbon-intensive sectors (Philipponnat, 2020); countercyclical capital buffers designed to restrict carbon-intensive exposures during expansionary credit cycles (D'Orazio et al., 2019); and large exposure limits for the most environmentally-damaging counterparties (Schoenmaker & Van Tilburg, 2016).

Many of the policy options presented in this section are actively being explored by central banks and financial supervisors (NGFS, 2021). For example, the Bank of England has announced plans to decarbonise both its corporate bond portfolio and its collateral framework. If led by clear, mission-oriented transition policy set out by the government, such policies do not need to contravene the notion of an operationally independent central bank (Robins et al., 2021). Indeed, many central banks such as the ECB already have secondary mandates to support the broader objectives of economic policy. Yet central banks can go beyond just *aligning* with government policy; they can also create more fiscal space for mission-oriented policy by buying green bonds issued by the government and other public entities such as municipalities and public investment banks. As discussed in Sect. 3, such fiscal-monetary coordination has seen in a revival in the post-COVID era, given the ineffectiveness of isolated monetary policy at the effective lower bound. Combined with the 'credit-steering' policy and regulatory measures outlined in this section, such a market-shaping approach to financial policy almost certainly heralds a distinct institutional framework for central banking in the context of the green transition. This is characterised not by inflation targeting and operational independence, but by a broader suite of policy tools more or less subordinated to the democratically determined 'missions' of the Green New Deal.

6 Towards a Truly Global GND

In the aftermath of the global economic crises caused by the COVID-19 pandemic, GND-style policy proposals have been reframed almost entirely as domestic recovery packages focused on green jobs. However, to be successful, the green transition and the recovery from Covid-19 must be coordinated at an international level—an argument also emphasised by the original GND proposal (NEF, 2008). Scholars and campaigners from the Global South have long emphasised the inevitable questions of equity and redistribution that must accompany policy proposals for a global green transition. Given that the global economy will face at some point hard ecological limits—a fact increasingly acknowledged within mainstream circles (e.g., Dasgupta, 2021; OECD, 2020)—how can we ensure a high quality of life for all without destabilising finite planetary processes?

Balancing the provision of basic social needs within planetary boundaries is the challenge that GND strategies need to focus upon (Raworth, 2012). A recent study found that no country meets basic social goals within a globally sustainable level of resource use, whilst many countries that do stay within planetary boundaries fail to achieve basic social provisioning (O'Neill et al., 2018). This suggests that some 'development space' should be reallocated to low-income nations to allow them to 'catch up', whilst high-income economies should bear the greater burden for reducing the resource intensity and absolute quantity of consumption (Kallis et al., 2012). Such a 'contraction and convergence' approach is justified by the fact that historic responsibility for climate change lies with the Global North: developed nations have emitted the lion's share of global cumulative emissions (Botzen et al., 2008;

Hickel, 2020). Furthermore, significant proportions of emissions and ecosystems damage that arises in the Global South is caused by consumption demand in the Global North (Brand & Wissen, 2013), where developed nations have effectively 'offshored' industrial production and its associated environmental consequences to export-oriented emerging economies such as India and China (Liddle, 2018; Peters et al., 2011). Despite this inequality in responsibility, however, the Global South is bearing the brunt of adverse physical effects of climate change both today and into the future (IPCC, 2018).

Most development narratives relating to green finance neglect the particular needs of low-income and emerging economies, revealing the structural power dynamics at play. The green finance movement has a clear bias towards climate mitigation: less than 5% of climate finance mobilised between 2015 and 2018, for example, focused on adaptation needs (Buchner et al., 2019). There has also been very little policy attention paid to 'loss and damage' financing needs, which relates to climate-related disasters materialising today—most often in low-income nations. 'Loss and damage' was ostensibly included in the 2015 Paris Agreement, but has been given no legal or enforceable weight as a necessary budget item (Gewirtzman et al., 2018). Most notably, carbon taxes—the favoured environmental policy tool of market-fixing approaches—do not account for the unequal legacy and consequences of climate change (Perry, 2020). They also have significant distributional implications: carbon taxes have been shown to be more regressive in countries with higher income inequality (Andersson & Atkinson, 2020), which characterises many low-income nations; and, in the absence of mechanisms to effectively recycle tax revenues, a global uniform carbon price is likely to be highly regressive towards developing nations (Sager, 2019).

Such environmental tax recycling is less likely to be easy within developing nations, many of whom remain beholden to rigid fiscal rules embedded within WTO-led trade and investment treaties signed with high-income economies from the 1990s onwards. More fundamentally, the neoliberal policy reforms pursued by the Washington Consensus of the WTO, the IMF, and the World Bank has also left many low-income nations at a structural economic disadvantage with regards to the green transition (UNCTAD, 2019). The emphasis on fiscal rectitude, the privatisation of public functions, and mechanisms such as 'investor-state dispute settlements' (ISDS) has restricted policy space and undermined the ability of governments to deploy transformational, GND or mission-oriented policy mixes. COVID-19 has worsened this situation, with collapsing export and tourism revenues, coupled with currency depreciation and sharp capital outflows, squeezing debt service capacity. Indeed, fiscal balances deteriorated in low-income nations over the course of 2020, increasing overall sovereign debt vulnerability (IMF, 2021). By December 2020, 45 countries had formally requested debt service suspension—more than 60% of eligible countries. The destabilising effects of COVID-19 demonstrate how financial liberalisation and the 'market disciplining' forces of footloose foreign capital have the potential to amplify the financial stability risks associated with climate events. Many low-income and emerging nations, thus, find themselves on the precipice of a vicious circle of financial instability: being vulnerable to both severe climate events and short-term international capital outflows, whilst simultaneously being unable to deploy the long-term development strategies that may help to mitigate those threats (Svartzman & Althouse, 2020).

To reach global net-zero carbon, *all* states must have sufficient fiscal space and empowered public sector capacity in order to implement proactive GND policy strategies. In the developing country context, for example, mission-oriented industrial policy could be targeted towards (1) 'leap-frogging' outdated fossil-fuel technologies in order to avoid costly technological lock-in effects; (2) infrastructure investment for climate adaptation; and (3) long-term investment into social provisioning and welfare systems for economic and social resilience. To be successful, this requires freely shared technology transfers (Popp, 2011) but also significant curbs on the destabilising dynamics and political influence of international private capital.

At present, the international policy consensus is on how to de-risk developing and emerging market economies to suit the needs of global institutional investors as the central financiers of sustainable development (Dafermos et al., 2021a; Gabor, 2021). Encapsulated by the World Bank's *Maximising Finance for Development* agenda and, more recently, its *Next Generation Africa for Climate Business Plan*, this 'Wall Street Consensus' (WSC) (Gabor, 2021) advocates for the creation of climate asset classes, especially climate-aligned Public–Private Partnership (PPP) infrastructure assets, as the primary means of financing development and climate infrastructure within the Global South. In the interests of attracting private investors with higher returns and lower risks, such investment vehicles require the public sector to assume significant contingent liabilities, including demand risk, currency risk, and even compensation for the effects of future government regulation, such as the introduction of minimum wages (Bayliss & Van Waeyenberge, 2018). Yet PPPs promise very little upside: not only are they increasingly acknowledged to be more costly than direct public investment (European Court of Auditors, 2018), but de-risking on this project-by-project basis offers none of the macroeconomic 'super-multiplier' effects of strategic mission-oriented policy. It also reinforces, rather than resolves, the vulnerability of low-income nation exposure to procyclical capital flows (Dafermos et al., 2021a). Overall, the WSC subordinates the notion of a proactive, entrepreneurial state to the prioritisation of profit-making investment opportunities for global finance.

A central goal for GND strategies, therefore, must be to recognise and address the current and historic injustices that have left many low- and middle-income nations with structural economic disadvantages and increasing vulnerabilities to climate impacts. Harnessing the spirit of the original GND (NEF, 2008), such an internationalist goal should have a three-pronged approach. Firstly, as Ann Pettifor expands upon in Chapter 5 of this book, the international monetary and economic architecture must be reformed to allow the Global South to reclaim urgently needed policy space. This should include multilateral mechanisms for restructuring sovereign debt, including debt owed to private creditors (Volz et al., 2020), and a renegotiation of free-trade agreements and other bilateral treaties that have severely curtailed the abilities of governments to pursue long-term strategic development policy (UNCTAD, 2019). Secondly, in order to account for the fact that developing countries would face the brunt of impacts from environmental impacts that are already locked-in, GND policies deployed in the Global North should include contributions to green transition finance in the Global South, through significantly larger grants and transfers. Importantly, this should be recognised not as 'aid' or 'charitable contributions', but as fair and just compensation for historic climate injustices (Kaur Paul, 2021; Perry, 2020). Such climate reparations could be delivered through existing but under-funded mechanisms such as a Green Climate Fund, which was established in the 2015 Paris Agreement (Táíwò & Cibralic, 2020).

Thirdly, low- and middle-income countries must be supported in their efforts to deploy mission-oriented industrial policy for a green transition. Both state investment banks (SIBs) and multilateral development banks (MDBs) could be critical actors in the provision of patient green finance, but many are currently embedded within the Wall Street Consensus strategy of commodifying public goods into derisked private financial assets (Dafermos et al., 2021a). In developing nations, where critical infrastructure is lacking and supply constraints are in play, the need to direct finance away from rent-seeking speculative activity and towards productive investment in the real economy is even more pressing. The particular transition and adaptation financing needs of developing countries should form specific missions around which SIBs and MDBs are redesigned, whilst also coordinating with broader strategic government transition policy.

There is a long history demonstrating the effectiveness of such market-shaping strategies in accelerating structural economic transitions within emerging economies. In several East Asian nations, for example, SIBs and coordinated government policy rapidly enabled the structural shift from agrarian to industrial economies after the 1960s (Amsden, 2001). Central banks also acted as 'agents of development' during this period, extending capital and credit to development banks and using credit guidance tools to steer finance towards strategic sectors and away from undesirable uses (Epstein, 2006). This legacy of coordinated, market-shaping policy is observable in green transition policies within some emerging and low-income economies today. Countries such as Bangladesh, Brazil, China, India, and Indonesia have led the way in green central banking, deploying green credit allocation and prudential policies long before advanced economy central banks began to address climate change (Dikau & Ryan-Collins, 2017). Importantly, the effectiveness of such interventionist financial policies has historically been dependent upon operating within a broader context of financial repression, particularly with regard to international finance. Given the destabilising effects of exposure to global capital markets, as made clear by huge outflows due to COVID-19, countries should consider the use of capital controls in some contexts, in order to nurture the development of domestic capabilities and strategic sectors for the green transition.

Taken together, the reforms suggested in this section run against the still dominant, neoliberal approach to sustainable development. Yet resolving both climate and economic injustices requires challenging the prevailing international architecture that continues to perpetuate those injustices. In its articulation of a proactive, empowered state, directing strategic public policy for public purpose, a mission-oriented GND should be understood as part of an alternative paradigm for sustainable development, embedded within the principles of a just transition. Most importantly, the green transition would not be successful in the sense of halting environmental breakdown unless it is truly global in scope. The Global North must therefore take responsibility for both its historic and current (offshored) environmental impacts through redistributive, compensatory mechanisms to the Global South.

7 Conclusion

The Covid-19 pandemic offers the world an unprecedented opportunity for a reset of macroeconomic policy. A mission-oriented approach to the GND differs from many existing green policy strategies in that it emphasises a far more active role for the state in determining the pathway for the transition. This is warranted due to the transformational nature of the structural change required, which is characterised by high uncertainty and complex system behaviour. Unlike private financial actors, governments can play a unique 'entrepreneurial' role in the development and deployment of innovation, coordinating the full suite of policies—including supply-side regulation, and monetary and financial policy—to shape the markets in which public investments will succeed. So far, only the European Green Deal has explicitly embraced a mission-oriented approach within its Horizon 2020 Research Programme (Mazzucato,

2018); yet even this initiative—though laudable—comprises only a fraction of the EGD budget and is not integrated fully into the broader strategy of the EGD. GND strategies must also address the current and historic injustices that have left many low- and middle-income nations with structural economic disadvantages and increasing vulnerabilities to climate impacts. This requires both widespread reforms to the international economic architecture as well as redistributive, compensatory mechanisms to the Global South. The green transition will not be successful in the sense of halting environmental breakdown unless it is truly global in scope. A mission-oriented GND offers an alternative policy paradigm for sustainable development, embedded in the principles of a just transition, which emphasises the need for a proactive, empowered state to direct strategic policy for public purpose.

References

Aghion, P., Hepburn, C., Teytelboym, A., & Zenghelis, D. (2014). *Path dependence, innovation and the economics of climate change* (Policy Paper). Centre for Climate Change Economics and Policy.

Ameli, N., Drummond, P., Bisaro, A., Grubb, M., & Chenet, H. (2019). Climate finance and disclosure for institutional investors: Why transparency is not enough. *Climatic Change, 160*, 565–589.

Amsden, A. (2001). *The rise of "the rest": Challenges to the west from late-industrializing economies*. Oxford University Press.

Andersson, A., & Atkinson, G. (2020). *The distributional effects of a carbon tax: The role of income inequality* (Working Paper No. 349). Grantham Research Institute on Climate Change and the Environment.

Arnold, M. (2020, October 14). ECB to consider using climate risk to steer bond purchases, says Lagarde. *Financial Times*.

Auerbach, A. J., & Gorodnichenko, Y. (2017). *Fiscal stimulus and fiscal sustainability* (Working Paper Series No. 23789). National Bureau of Economic Research. Available at: https://doi.org/10.3386/w23789.

Bank of England. (2020). *The Bank of England's climate-related financial disclosure 2020*. Available at: https://www.bankofengland.co.uk/-/media/boe/files/annual-report/2020/climate-related-financial-disclosure-report-2019-20.pdf.

BankTrack, Rainforest Action Network. (2020). *Banking on climate change.* Available at: https://www.banktrack.org/download/banking_on_climate_change_fossil_fuel_finance_report_2020/banking_on_climate_change__2020_vf_2.pdf.

Barbier, E. (2010). *A global Green New Deal.* Cambridge University Press.

Barbier, E. (2016). Building the green economy. *Canadian Public Policy, 42*, S1–S9. Available at: https://doi.org/10.3138/cpp.2015-017.

Barkawi, A., & Zadek, S. (2021). *Governing finance for sustainable prosperity* (Discussion Note). Council on Economic Policies.

Bartsch, E., Bénassy-Quéré, A., Corsetti, G., & Debrun, X. (2020). *It's all in the mix: How monetary and fiscal policies can work or fail together* (Geneva Reports on the World Economy No. 23). Centre for Economic Policy Research.

Battiston, S., Mandel, A., Monasterolo, I., Schütze, F., & Visentin, G. (2017). A climate stress-test of the financial system. *Nature Climate Change, 7*, 283.

Bayliss, K., & Van Waeyenberge, E. (2018). Unpacking the public private partnership revival. *The Journal of Development Studies, 54*, 577–593.

BEIS (2019), *Green finance strategy: Transforming finance for a greener future.* (Industrial Strategy). HM Government.

Bezemer, D., Grydaki, M., & Zhang, L. (2016). More mortgages, lower growth? *Economic Inquiry, 54*, 652–674. Available at: https://doi.org/10.1111/ecin.12254.

Bezemer, D., Ryan-Collins, J., van Lerven, F., & Zhang, L. (2018). *Credit where it's due: A historical, theoretical and empirical review of credit guidance policies in the 20th century* (Working Paper Series No. 2018-11). UCL Institute for Innovation and Public Purpose.

BIS. (2020). A monetary lifeline: Central banks' crisis response. In *BIS annual economic report 2020.* Bank for International Settlements.

Blanchard, O. (2019). Public debt and low interest rates. *American Economic Review, 109*, 1197–1229.

Blanchard, O., & Pisani-Ferry, J. (2020). Monetisation: Do not panic. *Blog,* VoxEU.org. Available at: https://voxeu.org/article/monetisation-do-not-panic.

Block, F. L., & Keller, M. R. (2011). *State of innovation: The U.S. government's role in technology development.* Routledge.

Bolton, P., Després, M., Pereira da Silva, L., Samama, F., & Svartzman, R. (2020). *The green swan: Central banking and financial stability in the age of climate change.* Bank for International Settlements. Available at: https://www.bis.org/publ/othp31.pdf.

Botzen, W. J. W., Gowdy, J. M., & Van den Bergh, J. C. J. M. (2008). Cumulative CO_2 emissions: Shifting international responsibilities for climate debt. *Climate Policy, 8*, 569–576.

Brainard, L. (2021). The role of financial institutions in tackling the challenges of climate change. *Speech,* IIF U.S. Climate Finance Summit: Financing a Pro Growth Pro Markets Transition to a Sustainable, Low-Carbon Economy, 18th February 2021. Available at: https://www.federalreserve.gov/newsevents/speech/brainard20210218a.htm.

Brand, U., & Wissen, M. (2013). Crisis and continuity of capitalist society-nature relationships: The imperial mode of living and the limits to environmental governance. *Review of International Political Economy, 20*, 687–711.

Buchner, B., Clark, A., & Falconer, A. (2019). *Global landscape of climate finance 2019.* Climate Policy Initiative. Available at: https://climatepolicyinitiative.org/wp-content/uploads/2019/11/2019-Global-Landscape-of-Climate-Finance.pdf.

Campiglio, E., Dafermos, Y., Monnin, P., Ryan-Collins, J., Schotten, G., & Tanaka, M. (2018). Climate change challenges for central banks and financial regulators. *Nature Climate Change, 8*, 462–468.

Carbon Tracker. (2020). *How to waste over half a trillion dollars: The economic implications of deflationary renewable energy for coal power investments* (*Report*). Available at: https://climatepolicyinitiative.org/wp-content/uploads/2019/11/2019-Global-Landscape-of-Climate-Finance.pdf.

Carney, M. (2015, September 29). Breaking the tragedy of the horizon—Climate change and financial stability. *Speech*. Available at: https://www.bankofengland.co.uk/-/media/boe/files/speech/2015/breaking-the-tragedy-of-the-horizon-climate-change-and-financial-stability.pdf.

Cavallino, P., & De Fiore, F. (2020). *Central banks' response to Covid-19 in advanced economies* (BIS Bulletin No. 21). Bank for International Settlements.

Chenet, H., Ryan-Collins, J., & van Lerven, F. (2021). Finance, climate-change and radical uncertainty: Towards a precautionary approach to financial policy. *Ecological Economics, 183*, 106–157.

Christophers, B. (2017). Climate change and financial instability: Risk disclosure and the problematics of neoliberal governance. *Annals of the American Association of Geographers, 107*, 1108–1127.

Christophers, B. (2019). Environmental beta or how institutional investors think about climate change and fossil fuel risk. *Annals of the American Association of Geographers, 109*, 754–774.

Claeys, G., & Tagliapietra, S. (2020). A trillion reasons to scrutinise the Green Deal Investment Plan. *Blog*, Bruegel. Available at: https://www.bruegel.org/2020/01/a-trillion-reasons-to-scrutinise-the-green-deal-investment-plan/.

Constâncio, V. (2020). The return of fiscal policy and the Euro Area fiscal rule. *Comparative Economic Studies, 62*, 358–372.

Crow, D. (2020, August 6). The next virus pandemic is not far away. *Financial Times*. Available at: https://www.ft.com/content/dc33f21b-740f-4be8-9947-b47439f557d2.

Dafermos, Y., Gabor, D., & Michell, J. (2021a). The Wall Street Consensus in pandemic times: What does it mean for climate-aligned development? *Canadian Journal of Development Studies/Revue canadienne d'études du développement*, 1–14.

Dafermos, Y., Gabor, D., Nikolaidi, M., Pawloff, A., & van Lerven, F. (2021b). *Greening the Eurosystem collateral framework: How to decarbonise the ECB's monetary policy* (Policy Report). New Economics Foundation. Available at: https://neweconomics.org/uploads/files/Collateral-Framework.pdf.

Dafermos, Y., Gabor, D., Nikolaidi, M., Pawloff, A., & van Lerven, F. (2020). *Decarbonising is easy: Beyond market neutrality in the ECB's corporate QE* (Policy Report). New Economics Foundation. Available at: https://neweconomics.org/uploads/files/Decarbonising-is-easy.pdf.

Dafermos, Y., Gabor, D., Nikolaidi, M., & van Lerven, F. (2021c). *Greening the UK financial system—A fit for purpose approach* (Policy Note No. 226). SUERF: The European Money and Finance Forum. Available at: https://www.suerf.org/policynotes/21233/greening-the-uk-financial-system-a-fit-for-purpose-approach.

Dasgupta, P. (2021). *The economics of biodiversity: The Dasgupta review*. HM Treasury.

De Henau, J., & Himmelweit, S. (2021). A care-led recovery from covid-19: Investing in high-quality care to stimulate and rebalance the economy. *Feminist Economics, 27*, 453–469.

Dechezlepretre, A., Martin, R., & Mohnen, M. (2017). *Knowledge spillovers from clean and dirty technologies* (Working Paper No. 135). Grantham Research Institute on Climate Change and the Environment.

Deleidi, M., & Mazzucato, M. (2021). Directed innovation policies and the supermultiplier: An empirical assessment of mission-oriented policies in the US economy. *Research Policy, 50*, 104–151.

Deleidi, M., & Mazzucato, M. (2019). Putting austerity to bed: Technical progress, aggregate demand and the supermultiplier. *Review of Political Economy, 31*, 315–335.

Deleidi, M., Mazzucato, M., & Semieniuk, G. (2020). Neither crowding in nor out: Public direct investment mobilising private investment into renewable electricity projects. *Energy Policy, 140*, 111–195.

Detter, D., Fölster, S., & Ryan-Collins, J. (2020). *Public wealth funds: Supporting economic recovery and sustainable growth* (Working Paper No. 2020–16). Institute for Innovation and Public Purpose, University College London.

DiEM25. (2019). *The Green New Deal for Europe. A blueprint for Europe's just transition.* Democracy in Europe Movement 2025. Available at: https://report.gndforeurope.com.

Dikau, S., Robins, N., & Volz, U. (2020). *A toolbox of sustainable crisis response measures for central banks and supervisors, second edition: Lessons from practice* (INSPIRE Briefing Paper). Grantham Research Institute on Climate Change and the Environment, London School of Economics and Political Science and SOAS Centre for Sustainable Finance, London.

Dikau, S., & Ryan-Collins, J. (2017). *Green central banking in emerging market and developing country economies* (Policy Report). New Economics Foundation. Available at: https://eprints.soas.ac.uk/24876/1/Green-Central-Banking.pdf.

D'Orazio, P., & Popoyan, L. (2019). Fostering green investments and tackling climate-related financial risks: Which role for macroprudential policies? *Ecological Economics, 160*, 25–37.

D'Orazio, P., Popoyan, L., & Monnin, P. (2019). *Prudential regulation can help in tackling climate change* (Blog). Council on Economic Policies. Available at: https://www.cepweb.org/prudential-regulation-can-help-in-tackling-climate-change.

Eberle, D. U., & von Helmolt, D. R. (2010). Sustainable transportation based on electric vehicle concepts: A brief overview. *Energy & Environmental Science, 3*, 689–699.

ECB. (2020). *Financial stability review, November 2020.* European Central Bank. Available at: https://www.ecb.europa.eu/pub/pdf/fsr/ecb.fsr202011~b7be9ae1f1.en.pdf.

Epstein, G. (2006). *Central banks as agents of economic development* (Working Paper No. 2006-54). World Institute for Development Economic Research (UNU-WIDER). Available at: https://www.wider.unu.edu/sites/default/files/rp2006-54.pdf.

European Commission. (2020a). *The investEU programme: Questions and answers*. Available at: https://ec.europa.eu/commission/presscorner/detail/lt/memo_19_2135.

European Commission. (2020b). *EU budget for recovery: Questions and answers on the just transition mechanism*. Available at: https://ec.europa.eu/commission/presscorner/detail/en/qanda_20_931.

European Commission. (2020c). *Questions and answers on the adoption of the EU's long-term budget for 2021–2027*. Available at: https://ec.europa.eu/commission/presscorner/detail/en/QANDA_20_2465.

European Commission. (2019a). *The European green deal* (Communication No. COM(2019) 640 final). European Commission, Brussels. Available at: https://eur-lex.europa.eu/resource.html?uri=cellar:b828d165-1c22-11ea-8c1f-01aa75ed71a1.0002.02/DOC_1&format=PDF.

European Commission. (2019b). *Guidelines on reporting climate-related information* (Communication from the Commission No. C(2019) 4490). Brussels. Available at: https://ec.europa.eu/finance/docs/policy/190618-climate-related-information-reporting-guidelines_en.pdf.

European Commission. (2018). *Action plan: Financing sustainable growth* (Communication No. COM(2018) 97). European Commission, Brussels. Available at: https://eur-lex.europa.eu/legal-content/EN/TXT/PDF/?uri=CELEX:52018DC0097&from=EN.

European Court of Auditors. (2018). *Public private partnerships in the EU: Widespread shortcomings and limited benefits* (Special Report pursuant to Article 287[4]). Available at: https://www.eca.europa.eu/Lists/ECADocuments/SR18_09/SR_PPP_EN.pdf.

Fatás, A., & Summers, L. (2015). *The permanent effects of fiscal consolidations* (C.E.P.R. Discussion Papers No. 10902). Center for Economic Policy Research.

Finance Watch. (2021).*Shaping the future or missing the past: How resilient are national fiscal plans of Germany, France, and Spain?* (Policy Report). Finance Watch. Available at: https://rethinktherecovery.org/sites/default/files/2021-04/FW_Rethink-the-Recovery_Summary-Country-Plan-Analysis.pdf.

Freeman, C., & Perez, C. (1988). Structural crises of adjustment: Business cycles and investment behaviour. In G. Dosi, C. Freeman, R. R. Nelson, G. Silverberg, & L. L. G. Soete (Eds.), *Technical change and economic theory*. Pinter Publishers.

Friedman, T. L. (2007, January 19). Opinion: A warning from the garden. *New York Times*. Available at: https://www.nytimes.com/2007/01/19/opinion/19friedman.html.

Gabor, D. (2021). The Wall Street consensus. *Development and Change*, 1–31.

Galí, J. (2020). The effects of a money-financed fiscal stimulus. *Journal of Monetary Economics, 115*, 1–19.

Galvin, R., & Healy, N. (2020). The Green New Deal in the United States: What it is and how to pay for it. *Energy Research & Social Science, 67*, 101529.
Geels, F. W., & Schot, J. (2007). Typology of sociotechnical transition pathways. *Research Policy, 36*, 399–417.
Gewirtzman, J., Natson, S., & Richards, J.-A. (2018). Financing loss and damage: Reviewing options under the Warsaw International Mechanism. *Climate Policy, 18*, 1076–1086.
Giles, C. (2020, October 14). IMF says austerity is not inevitable to ease pandemic impact on public finances. *Financial Times*. Available at: https://www.ft.com/content/722ef9c0-36f6-4119-a00b-06d33fced78f.
Giles, C. (2021, January 4). OECD warns governments to rethink constraints on public spending. *Financial Times*. Available at: https://www.ft.com/content/7c721361-37a4-4a44-9117-6043afee0f6b.
Grubb, M., Drummond, P., & Poncia, A. (2021). Induced innovation in energy technologies and systems: A review of evidence and potential implications for CO_2 mitigation. *Environmental Research Letters, 16*, 043007
Hafner, S., Jones, A., Anger-Kraavi, A., & Pohl, J. (2020). Closing the green finance gap—A systems perspective. *Environmental Innovation and Societal Transitions, 34*, 26–60.
Hall, S., Foxon, T. J., & Bolton, R. (2017). Investing in low-carbon transitions: Energy finance as an adaptive market. *Climate Policy, 17*, 280–298.
Harvey, F. (2020, June 6). Covid-19 relief for fossil fuel industries risks green recovery plans. *The Guardian*. Available at: https://www.theguardian.com/environment/2020/jun/06/covid-19-relief-for-fossil-fuel-industries-risks-green-recovery-plans.
Hepburn, C., O'Callaghan, B., Stern, N., Stiglitz, J., & Zenghelis, D. (2020). Will COVID-19 fiscal recovery packages accelerate or retard progress on climate change? *Oxford Review of Economic Policy, 36*, S359–S381.
Hickel, J. (2020). Quantifying national responsibility for climate breakdown: An equality-based attribution approach for carbon dioxide emissions in excess of the planetary boundary. *The Lancet Planetary Health, 4*, e399–e404.
HM Treasury. (2021, March 3). Remit for the Monetary Policy Committee (MPC). *Letter to the Bank of England*. Available at: https://www.bankofengland.co.uk/-/media/boe/files/letter/2021/march/2021-mpc-remit-letter.pdf.
Hodgson, C., Romei, V., & Thomas, N. (2021, March 3). Bank of England given new mandate to buy 'green' bonds. *Financial Times*. Available at: https://www.ft.com/content/f436d69b-2bf0-48cd-bb34-644856fba17f.

Hook, L., & Vincent, M. (2020, November 12). Green business reporting rules at risk of pale response. *Financial Times*. Available at: https://www.ft.com/content/ad01f2c9-9eb0-4db6-9898-220c688d16c2.

IMF. (2019). *World Economic Outlook*. International Monetary Fund. Available at: https://www.imf.org/en/Publications/WEO/Issues/2019/10/01/world-economic-outlook-october-2019.

IMF. (2021). *Fiscal monitor update January 2021*. International Monetary Fund. Available at: https://www.imf.org/en/Publications/FM/Issues/2021/01/20/fiscal-monitor-update-january-2021.

IPBES. (2019). Summary for policymakers. *The global assessment report on Biodiversity and Ecosystem Services*. Intergovernmental Science-Policy Platform on Biodiversity and Ecosystem Services, Bonn. Available at: https://ipbes.net/sites/default/files/2020-02/ipbes_global_assessment_report_summary_for_policymakers_en.pdf.

IPCC. (2018). *Summary for policymakers* (Global Warming of 1.5°C. An IPCC Special Report on the Impacts of Global Warming of 1.5°C above Pre-Industrial Levels). Intergovernmental Panel on Climate Change, Geneva. Available at: https://www.ipcc.ch/site/assets/uploads/sites/2/2019/05/SR15_SPM_version_report_L.

R.pdfIRENA. (2020). *Global landscape of renewable energy finance 2020*. International Renewable Energy Agency.

Jaffe, A. B., Newell, R. G., & Stavins, R. N. (2005). A tale of two market failures: Technology and environmental policy. *Ecological Economics, 54*, 164–174.

Jourdan, S., & Kalinowski, W. (2019). *Aligning monetary policy with the EU's climate targets* (Policy Note). Veblen Institute and Positive Money Europe. Available at: https://www.veblen-institute.org/IMG/pdf/aligning_monetary_policy_with_eu_s_climate_targets.pdf.

Kallis, G., Kerschner, C., & Martinez-Alier, J. (2012). The economics of degrowth. *Ecological Economics, 84*, 172–180.

Kattel, R., & Mazzucato, M. (2018). Mission-oriented innovation policy and dynamic capabilities in the public sector. *Industrial and Corporate Change, 27*, 787–801.

Kattel, R., Mazzucato, M., Ryan-Collins, J., & Sharpe, S. (2018). *The economics of change: Policy and appraisal for missions, market shaping and public purpose* (Working Paper Series No. 2018–06). Institute for Innovation and Public Purpose, University College London.

Kaur Paul, H. (2021). *Towards reparative climate justice: From crises to liberations* (Policy Report). Common Wealth.

Kedward, K., Ryan-Collins, J., & Buller, A. (2021). *Quantitative easing and nature loss: Exploring nature-related financial risks and impacts in the european central bank's corporate bond portfolio.* UCL Institute for Innovation and Public Purpose Policy Report 2021/02. https://doi.org/10.2139/ssrn.3922913.

Kemp-Benedict, E. (2018). Investing in a green transition. *Ecological Economics, 153*, 218–236.

Kliesen, K. L., & Bokun, K. (2020). What is yield curve control? *St. Louis Fed on the Economy Blog*. Available at: https://www.stlouisfed.org/on-the-economy/2020/august/what-yield-curve-control.

Krebel, L., Stirling, A., van Lerven, F., & Arnold, S. (2020). *Building a green stimulus for COVID-19: A recovery plan for a greener, fairer future* (Policy Report). New Economics Foundation.

Lagarde, C. (2020). The monetary policy strategy review: Some preliminary considerations. *Speech*, ECB and Its Watchers XXI conference, 30th September 2020. Available at: https://www.ecb.europa.eu/press/key/date/2020/html/ecb.sp200930~169abb1202.en.html.

Lallemand, B. (2021). *An open letter sent in February to European Union leaders asking them to review EU economic governance*. Available at: https://www.finance-watch.org/publication/reshaping-the-european-fiscal-framework-eng/.

Laplane, A., & Mazzucato, M. (2020). Socializing the risks and rewards of public investments: Economic, policy, and legal issues. *Research Policy, X 2*, 100008.

Lazonick, W., & Mazzucato, M. (2013). The risk-reward nexus in the innovation-inequality relationship: Who takes the risks? Who gets the rewards? *Industrial and Corporate Change, 22*, 1093–1128.

Lee, J.-H., & Woo, J. (2020). Green New Deal policy of South Korea: Policy innovation for a sustainability transition. *Sustainability, 12*(23), 10191.

Liddle, B. (2018). Consumption-based accounting and the trade-carbon emissions nexus. *Energy Economics, 69*, 71–78.

Lipsey, R., & Lancaster, K. (1956). The general theory of second best. *Review of Economic Studies, 24*, 11–32.

Macfarlane, L., & Mazzucato, M. (2018). *State investment banks and patient finance: An international comparison* (Policy Report No. 2018–01). Institute for Innovation and Public Purpose, University College London.

Mastini, R., Kallis, G., & Hickel, J. (2021). A Green New Deal without growth? *Ecological Economics, 179*, 106832.

Mazzucato, M. (2013). *The entrepreneurial state: Debunking public vs. private sector myths*. Anthem Press.

Mazzucato, M. (2016). From market fixing to market-creating: A new framework for innovation policy. *Industry & Innovation, 23*, 140–156.

Mazzucato, M. (2018). *Mission-oriented research & innovation in the European Union: A problem-solving approach to fuel innovation-led growth.* European Commission. Available at: https://ec.europa.eu/info/sites/info/files/mazzucato_report_2018.pdf.

Mazzucato, M., & McPherson, M. (2018). *The Green New Deal: A bold mission-oriented approach* (Policy Brief No. 4). Institute for Innovation and Public Purpose, University College London.

Mazzucato, M., & Penna, C. (2016). Beyond market failures: The market creating and shaping roles of state investment banks. *Journal of Economic Policy Reform, 19*, 305–326.

Mazzucato, M., & Perez, C. (2015). Innovation as growth policy. In J. Fagerberg, S. Laestadius, & B. Martin (Eds.), *The triple challenge for Europe: Economic development, climate change and governance*. Oxford University Press.

Mazzucato, M., & Ryan-Collins, J. (2019).*Putting value creation back into "public value": From market-fixing to market-shaping* (Working Paper Series No. 2019–05). Institute for Innovation and Public Purpose, University College London.

Mazzucato, M., & Semieniuk, G. (2018). Financing renewable energy: Who is financing what and why it matters. *Technological Forecasting and Social Change, 127*, 8–22.

McCollum, D. L., Zhou, W., & Bertram, C. (2018). Energy investment needs for fulfilling the Paris Agreement and achieving the sustainable development goals. *Nature Energy, 3*, 589–599.

Mercure, J.-F., Pollitt, H., Chewpreecha, U., Salas, P., Foley, A. M., Holden, P. B., & Edwards, N. R. (2014). The dynamics of technology diffusion and the impacts of climate policy instruments in the decarbonisation of the global electricity sector. *Energy Policy, 73*, 686–700.

Minsky, H. P. (1986). *Stabilizing an unstable economy*. Yale University Press.

NEF. (2008). *A Green New Deal: Joined-up policies to solve the triple crunch of the credit crisis, climate change and high oil prices* (Policy Report). New Economics Foundation.

Nelson, R., & Winter, S. (1974). Neoclassical vs. evolutionary theories of economic growth: Critique and prospectus. *Economic Journal, 84*, 886–905.

Nersisyan, Y., & Wray, R. (2019). *How to pay for the Green New Deal* (Working Paper No. 931). Levy Economics Institute of Bard College.

NGFS. (2020). *Guide to climate scenario analysis for central banks and supervisors* (Technical Document). Network for Greening the Financial System.

NGFS. (2021). *Adapting central bank operations to a hotter world: Reviewing some options* (Technical Document). Network for Greening the Financial System.

OECD. (2020). *Beyond growth: Towards a new economic approach, new approaches to economic challenges.* Organisation for Economic Cooperation and Development.

O'Neill, D. W., Fanning, A. L., Lamb, W. F., & Steinberger, J. K. (2018). A good life for all within planetary boundaries. *Nature Sustainability, 1*, 88–95.

Ostrom, E. (1994). Neither market nor state: Governance of common-pool resources in the twenty-first century. In *International Food Policy Research Institute*. Presented at the International Food Policy Research Institute, Washington, DC.

Ostrom, E. (2010). Polycentric systems for coping with collective action and global environmental change. *Global Environmental Change, 20*, 550–557.

Ostry, J. D., Loungani, P., & Furceri, D. (2016). Neoliberalism: Oversold? *Finance and Development, 52*(2). International Monetary Fund.

Oustry, A., Erkan, B., Svartzman, R., & Weber P-F. (2020). *Climate-related risks and central banks' collateral policy: A methodological experiment* (Working Paper No. 790). Banque de France.

Palley, T. (2019). Macroeconomics vs. modern money theory: Some unpleasant Keynesian arithmetic and monetary dynamics. *Real-World Economics Review*, 148–155.

Pekanov, A., & Schratzenstaller, M. (2020). *The role of fiscal rules in relation with the green economy* (Study requested by the ECON committee No. PE 614.524). Economic Governance Support Unit and the Policy Department A. European Parliament's Committee on Economic and Monetary Affairs.

Perry, K. (2020). *Realising climate reparations: Towards a global climate stabilization fund and resilience fund programme for loss and damage in marginalised and former colonised societies* (SSRN Paper). Available at: https://papers.ssrn.com/sol3/papers.cfm?abstract_id=3561121.

Peters, G. P., Minx, J. C., Weber, C. L., & Edenhofer, O. (2011). Growth in emission transfers via international trade from 1990 to 2008. *Proceedings of the National Academy of Sciences, 108*, 8903–8908.

Pettifor, A. (2019). *The case for the Green New Deal*. Verso.

Philipponnat, T. (2020). *Breaking the climate-finance doom loop* (Policy Report). Finance Watch.

Polanyi, K. (1957). *The great transformation: The political and economic origins of our time*. Beacon Press.

Popp, D. (2011). International technology transfer, climate change, and the clean development mechanism. *Review of Environmental Economics and Policy, 5*, 131–152.

Raworth, K. (2012). *A safe and just space for humanity: Can we live within the doughnut?* Oxfam discussion paper. Available at: https://d1tn3vj7xz9fdh.cloudfront.net/s3fs-public/file_attachments/dp-a-safe-and-just-space-for-humanity-130212-en_5.pdf.

Robins, N., Dikau, S., & Volz, U. (2021). *Net-zero central banking: A new phase in greening the financial system* (Policy Report). Grantham Research Institute on Climate Change and the Environment, London School of Economics.

Ruiz, J. R., & Stupariu, P. (2021). A Green New Deal and debt sustainability for the post COVID-19 world. *International Review of Applied Economics, 35*, 288–307.

Ryan-Collins, J. (2019). *Beyond voluntary disclosure: Why a "market-shaping" approach to financial regulation is needed to meet the challenge of climate change* (SUERF Policy Note No. Issue No. 61). SUERF: The European Money and Finance Forum.

Sager, L. (2019). *The global consumer incidence of carbon pricing: Evidence from trade* (Working Paper No. 320). Grantham Research Institute on Climate Change and the Environment.

Satow, A. (2019, March 22). Our new movement aims to propel labour into a radical Green New Deal. *The Guardian*. Available at: https://www.theguardian.com/commentisfree/2019/mar/22/movement-propel-labour-radical-green-new-deal.

Schiller, R. J. (2019). *Narrative economics: How stories go viral and drive major economic events*. Princeton University Press.

Schnabel, I. (2020, September 28). When markets fail—The need for collective action in tackling climate change. *Speech*, European Sustainable Finance Summit. Available at: https://www.ecb.europa.eu/press/key/date/2020/html/ecb.sp200928_1~268b0b672f.en.html.

Schoenmaker, D., & Van Tilburg, R. (2016). What role for financial supervisors in addressing environmental risks? *Comparative Economic Studies, 58*, 317–334.

Schumpeter, J. (1983). *The theory of economic development*. Transaction Publishers.

Simon, F. (2020, April 29). Green deal will be 'our motor for the recovery', von der Leyen says. *EURACTIV*. Available at: https://www.euractiv.com/

section/energy-environment/news/green-deal-will-be-our-motor-for-the-recovery-von-der-leyen-says/.

Spencer, R. W., & Yohe, W. P. (1970). *The 'crowding out' of private expenditures by fiscal policy actions* (Review). Federal Reserve Bank of St. Louis.

Storm, S. (2020). *The EU's green deal: Bismarck's 'what is possible' versus Thunberg's 'what is Imperative'* (INET Working Paper Series No. 117). Institute for New Economic Thinking.

Summers, L. (2021, February 4). Opinion: The Biden stimulus is admirably ambitious. But it brings some big risks, too. *The Washington Post*. Available at: https://www.washingtonpost.com/opinions/2021/02/04/larry-summers-biden-covid-stimulus/.

Svartzman, R., & Althouse, J. (2020). Greening the international monetary system? Not without addressing the political ecology of global imbalances. *Review of International Political Economy*, 1–26.

Táíwò, O., & Cibralic, B. (2020, October 10). The case for climate reparations. *Foreign Policy*. Available at: https://foreignpolicy.com/2020/10/10/case-for-climate-reparations-crisis-migration-refugees-inequality/.

Tiftik, E., & Mahmood, K. (2021). *Global debt monitor: COVID drives debt surge—Stabilization ahead?* Institute of International Finance.

Tobin, J. (1975). *Keynesian models of recession and depression.* Cowles Foundation for Research in Economics, Yale University.

Tooze, A. (2021, April 21). America's race to net zero: Does Joe Biden's climate plan go far enough? *New Statesman.*

UNCTAD. (2019). *A new multilateralism for shared prosperity: Geneva principles for a global Green New Deal.* United Nations Conference on Trade and Development.

UNCTAD. (2020). Investing in the SDGs. In *World Investment Report 2020.* United Nations Conference on Trade and Development.

UNDESA. (2020). *World Social Report 2020.* United Nations Department of Economic and Social Affairs.

UNEP. (2009). *A global Green New Deal.* United Nations Environment Programme.

Unruh, G. C. (2000). Understanding carbon lock-in. *Energy Policy, 28*, 817–830.

van 't Klooster, J., & Van Tilburg, R. (2020). *Targeting a sustainable recovery with Green TLTROs* (Policy Report). Positive Money Europe and Sustainable Finance Lab.

Varoufakis, Y., & Adler, D. (2020, February 7). The EU's green deal is a colossal exercise in greenwashing. *The Guardian.*

Vivid Economics. (2021). *Greenness of stimulus index: An assessment of COVID-19 stimulus by G20 countries and other major economies in relation to climate action and biodiversity goals* (Policy Report: February 2021 Release). Available at: https://www.vivideconomics.com/wp-content/uploads/2021/02/Greennes-of-Stimulus-Index-5th-Edition-FINAL-VERSION-09.02.21.pdf.
Volz, U., Akhtar, S., Gallagher, K. P., Griffith-Jones, S., Haas, J., & Kraemer, M. (2020). *Debt relief for a green and inclusive recovery: A proposal* (Policy Report). Center for Sustainable Finance, SOAS, University of London.
White House. (2021). FACT SHEET: The American jobs plan. *Statement*. Available at: https://www.whitehouse.gov/briefing-room/statements-releases/2021/03/31/fact-sheet-the-american-jobs-plan/.
WMO. (2018). *WMO provisional statement on the state of the climate in 2018*. World Meterological Organisation.
Wolf, M. (2020, April 9). Monetary financing demands careful and sober management. *Financial Times*. Available at: https://www.ft.com/content/dc233540-798e-11ea-9840-1b8019d9a987.
Woodford, M. (2003). *Interest and prices: Foundations of a theory of monetary policy*. Princeton University Press.
World Bank. (2020). *Poverty and shared prosperity 2020: Reversals of fortune*. World Bank.
Zenghelis, D. (2016). Decarbonisation, innovation, and the economics of climate change. In M. Mazzucato & M. Jacobs (Eds.), *Rethinking capitalism*. Wiley.

8

Rethinking Monetary Policy in the Framework of Inclusive and Sustainable Growth

Salvador Pérez-Moreno, Natalia Martín-Fuentes, and Juan-Francisco Albert

The views expressed here are those of the authors. They do not necessarily reflect those of the ECB or the Eurosystem and should not be reported as such. This work has been partially financed by the University of Malaga and the Regional Government of Andalusia (UMA18-FEDERJA-005).

S. Pérez-Moreno (✉)
Department of Applied Economics-Economic Policy, University of Malaga, Malaga, Spain
e-mail: sperezmoreno@uma.es

N. Martín-Fuentes
Economics and Business, University of Malaga, Malaga, Spain
e-mail: nmartinfuentes@uma.es

J.-F. Albert
Department of Applied Economics and IUDESCOOP, University of Valencia, Valencia, Spain
e-mail: juan.f.albert@uv.es

P. Arestis and M. Sawyer (eds.), *Economic Policies for Sustainability and Resilience*, International Papers in Political Economy,
https://doi.org/10.1007/978-3-030-84288-8_8

1 Introduction

Promoting inclusive and sustainable growth clearly constitutes an important and principal element of the 2030 Agenda and its 17 Sustainable Development Goals (SDGs) (United Nations, 2015). Goal 8 seeks to promote sustained, inclusive and sustainable growth, full and productive employment, and decent work for all. Moreover, this Goal is closely interconnected with other SDGs such as Goal 10, which aims to reduce inequalities both within and between countries, and with Goals 13–15, focused on climate change and environmental degradation.

Most governments at all levels are concerned with promoting inclusive and sustainable economic growth as a way to integrate economic, social and environmental dimensions of sustainable development and contribute to achieving the SDGs in a context characterized by two major economic crises: the Great Financial Crisis (GFC) and the crisis resulting from the Covid-19 pandemic. In this line, over the past several years there has been increasing awareness of the need for practical tools to help transform the objective of a more socially inclusive and environmentally sustainable economic growth into reality. Some plans of action have been promoted by different international organizations (see, for example, UNDP's Strategy for Inclusive and Sustainable Growth, UNDP [2017]), or the Framework for Policy Action on Inclusive Growth, proposed by OECD (2018), which also lay the foundations for more sustainable growth). These plans frequently stress the necessity of fundamental changes in the pattern of economic growth, given that so far economic growth has not had desirable environmental or social outcomes. They tend to put forward a variety of policy initiatives, mostly in terms of structural reforms in product, labour and financial markets and with regard to tax and benefit systems.

It is common that policy action frameworks for inclusive and sustainable growth neglect the potential role of monetary policy in respect to distributional and environmental issues. Traditionally, monetary policy has been understood to be neutral with respect to real variables or nearly so in the longer term. Specific mandates of central banks generally prioritize price stability, while the possibility of contributing to goals such as those related to distributional or environmental aspects is only considered within the secondary objectives. However, each monetary policy intervention is by definition not neutral, creating winners and losers of the decisions made regarding inaction or other policy alternatives. Hence, all monetary policy actions have distributional and environmental consequences, affecting intra- and inter-generational equity. Some of the major areas of the ongoing debate on future monetary policy are precisely about its potential role in pursuing and contributing to reducing income and wealth inequality and combating environmental degradation and climate change (see, for example, Colciago et al., 2019; Honoban, 2019; Matikainen et al., 2017).

Although the goals of reduced income and wealth inequality and the mitigation of climate change would always inevitably be second-order issues for monetary policy in the face of objectives such as price stability, rethinking monetary policy in the light of the distributional-environmental challenges of our times and the 2030 Agenda of Sustainable Development can be highly relevant. It would not be possible to meet the SDGs without the joint involvement of civil society and state at all levels, and deploy, develop and coordinate old and new policy instruments. Moreover, monetary policy, despite its limitations, has proved to be one of the most powerful economic policies. In consequence, it is worth exploring its capabilities for reaching objectives other than those that have traditionally constituted the core of the mandate of most central banks.

The remainder of this chapter is structured as follows. Section 2 briefly reviews the theoretical and conceptual frameworks of inclusive growth and sustainable growth. Section 3 focuses on income and wealth inequality and primary environmental problems such as climate change, key challenges within the inclusive and sustainable growth paradigm, and the present circumstances around monetary policy. Sections 4 and 5 discuss the links between monetary policy and income and wealth distribution and environmental degradation and climate change, respectively. Section 6 reflects on the extent to which monetary policy might contribute effectively to dealing with economic inequalities and environmental concerns and discusses some innovative policy proposals. Finally, Sect. 7 summarises and concludes.

2 Theoretical and Conceptual Frameworks of Inclusive and Sustainable Growth

Inclusive growth and sustainable growth are interconnected paradigms commonly used at present by academics, practitioners and international organizations in very diverse contexts. Those terms are frequently used, although sometimes it is not clear what they refer to. In this section, we briefly attempt to shed some light on the theoretical and conceptual development of inclusive growth on the one hand, and sustainable growth on the other hand.

2.1 Inclusive Growth

The debate on the economic growth-inequality nexus was strongly boosted by Kuznets (1955) in the 1950s. For much of the second half of the twentieth century, Kuznets' work was the most cited and influential framework used in explaining the potential effects of growth on inequality. His inverted U-curve hypothesis highlighted that income inequality initially increases for a time as the economy industrializes and grows, before subsequently declining. Kuznets (1955) argued that industrialization leads to a situation where households begin to migrate from the poor agricultural sector, characterized by relatively low inequality, to the richer industrial sector, where income is usually less evenly distributed, and increasing inequality. However, as an economy grows, most workers move to urban areas and only a small portion remains in agriculture, which, along with other factors such as the rise of trade unions and the development of the welfare state, tend to decrease inequality.

Based on Kuznets' hypothesis, during the 1950s and 1960s it was believed that in industrialized countries the advantages of economic growth would benefit all layers of society. The theory of trickle-down growth was developed on the premise that 'the rising tide would raise all boats', so that in the long term the growth process would have a positive effect on all segments of the economy (Aghion & Bolton, 1997; Akinci, 2018). The main idea of the trickle-down theory is based on the accumulation of wealth by the rich, which may be good for the poor since some of the increased wealth of the rich trickles down to the poor. It is assumed that growth would more likely come from those with the resources and skills to increase productive output, even though all members of society would end up benefiting from growth. Different mechanisms were presented, especially related to borrowing and lending in the capital markets, to support that as more capital is accumulated in the economy, more funds may be available to be invested in favour of the poor.

Nevertheless, as the facts demonstrated that growth was not always accompanied by a decrease in inequality, especially in the developing world, the validity of the trickle-down effect began to be questioned, highlighting the need to place more emphasis on the distributional consequences of growth. Thus, the report *Redistributionwith Growth* (Chenery et al., 1974), signed by the Vice President for Development Policy at the World Bank, was a milestone on the relevance of promoting not just growth but growth with equality. On the other hand, regarding the relationship from inequality to economic growth, the belief that inequality provides incentives for individuals to work hard, innovate, invest and undertake risks to take advantage of high rates of return (see, for example, Grusky & Szelenyi, 2018) was progressively losing its pre-eminence. In the following decades, especially in the 1990s after some years dominated by the Washington Consensus liberal approach, numerous authors put the spotlight on the negative implications of high inequality for growth. Different theoretical arguments were provided connected to the 'human capital accumulation' theory, the 'endogenous fiscal policy' theory or rent seeking behaviour and political instability and social unrest (see, for example, Alesina & Perotti, 1996; Galor & Zeira, 1993; Persson & Tabellini, 1994).

The debates regarding the links between growth and inequality highlighted the pertinence of addressing both phenomena and their various interconnections jointly and under a single strategy, even though approaches such as pro-poor growth, the immediate predecessor of the current approach of inclusive growth, which addressed growth and distribution jointly, did not emerge until the beginning of the twenty-first century.

Overall, pro-poor growth is growth that benefits the poor. We need, therefore, to define how much the poor must benefit for growth to be considered pro-poor. This way, two major approaches of pro-poor growth can be identified according to whether we consider absolute and relative approaches to pro-poorness. While under the relative approach the income of the poor is expected to grow faster than that of the non-poor, i.e. inequality declines (Kakwani & Pernia, 2000), the absolute approach only requires an improvement in the absolute income of the poor as the economy grows, irrespective of changes in inequality (Ravallion, 2004).

Focusing on inclusive growth, the first use of the term seems to belong to Kakwani and Pernia (2000), who used it as a synonym of pro-poor growth. Nevertheless, the approach of inclusive economic growth actually appeared in the mid-2000s to characterize pro-poor growth as participatory growth (see, for instance, Ianchovichina & Lundstrom, 2009; Klasen, 2010). The idea of inclusive growth is in line with the above-mentioned absolute approach of pro-poor growth, although it is more comprehensive. The World Bank defines inclusive growth as growth that allows people to contribute to and benefit from economic growth, emphasizing that while the pro-poor approach is mainly interested in the welfare of the poor, inclusive growth is concerned with productive employment opportunities for the majority of the labour force, both low- and middle-class (Ianchovichina & Lundstrom, 2009). In a similar way, OECD (2015a) defines inclusive growth as economic growth that is distributed fairly across society and creates opportunities for all. This way, while absolute pro-poor growth can be the result of direct redistributive policies, inclusive growth is characterized by pursuing the increase in productive and equitable employment opportunities. The analysis focuses on ways to increase the pace of growth by utilizing more fully parts of the labour force trapped in low-productivity activities or completely excluded from the growth process. Rather than simply redistributing resources, this approach involves enlarging the size of the economy through expanding opportunities to those previously excluded. Hence, it tends to stress that policies for inclusive growth should not only take into consideration redistributive policies as a way to reach out to those that do not participate from the direct benefits of economic growth; but particularly other interventions at the pre-market and in-market stages which allow creating opportunities for individuals across the entire welfare distribution.

2.2 Sustainable Growth

As with the term inclusive growth, the term sustainable growth lends itself to many analysis perspectives and interpretations. Thus, an analysis of sustainable growth requires an understanding of the theoretical and conceptual framework.

The origin of the concern regarding the environmental degradation connected with the pace and pattern of economic growth dates back to the 1960s and 1970s. A critical stream strongly emerged in the economic literature by questioning the limits to economic growth from an environmental standpoint. Authors such as Mishan (1967), Schumacher (1973) and Hirsch (1977) began expressing serious doubts as to the desirability of continuing to impel the ongoing economic growth of that time. They highlighted diverse shortcomings of economic growth, including various forms of externalities, from pollution to congestion of travel facilities and holiday resorts. In this line of argument, the warnings about the inevitable constraints on growth presented in 'The Limits to Growth', a report commissioned by the 'Club of Rome' (Meadows et al., 1972), had a considerable impact at the time. This report highlighted that continuous economic growth, which was characteristic of the industrial (capitalist) way of life, was not sustainable on a planet with limited resources and that a viable society should not depend on continuous growth.

In the 1980s, a particularly significant milestone was the publication of the report entitled 'Our common future', released by the World Commission on Environment and Development (1987), also known as the 'Brundtland Report', named for the Commission's Chair, the former Norwegian Prime Minister Gro Harlem Brundtland. This report explored the causes of environmental degradation and developed the guiding principles for sustainable development as it is usually conceived today. Defining and popularizing the most frequently cited definition of sustainable development to date: "development that meets the needs of the present without compromising the ability of future generations to meet their own needs" (World Commission on Environment and Development, 1987, p. 43). Note in this definition the key role of the concept of 'needs', which stressed the goal of providing for the essential requirements of society's most disadvantaged people, as well as the limitations to meet both present and future needs that technology and social organization imply for environment (see, for example, Burton, 1987; Kono, 2014). Thus, for the first time, the Brundtland Commission report attempted to understand the interconnections between economic growth, environmental problems and social equity, outlining policy recommendations that integrated all three areas and calling on the United Nations to establish a Programme of Action on Sustainable Development based on the directives proposed in the report.

In the academic sphere, the 1990s witnessed the emergence in the literature of a new strand on the nexus between economic growth and environmental quality. The Kuznets curve was applied to environmental quality by the hypothesis that the linkage between economic growth and environmental degradation follows a similar inverted U-shaped relationship (Grossman & Krueger, 1991). The environmental Kuznets curve hypothesis suggests that economic growth initially leads to a deterioration in the environment, though after a certain level of economic development, societies begin to improve their relationship with the environment and levels of environmental degradation decrease. The logic of this U-shaped relationship is that pollution grows rapidly in the first stages of industrial development because high priority is given to increasing material outputs, and people are more interested in jobs and income than in clean air and water. Nevertheless, there is a turning point at which as income rises, people value the environment more, regulatory institutions become more effective and pollution levels decline (Dinda, 2004; Grossman & Krueger, 1995). Since those pioneering works at the beginning of the 1990s, the environmental Kuznets curve hypothesis has triggered an abundant literature aimed at supporting the theoretical foundations of the specific form of the relationship and verifying or refuting its empirical evidence (see, for instance, the surveys of Dinda, 2004, and Shahbaz & Sinha, 2019).

In parallel, the idea of degrowth proposed in the 1970s[1] was taken up again at the beginning of the twenty-first century and a rich critical debate about the environmental unsustainability of the growth patterns ensued. According to the 'Degrowth Declaration' of the first international degrowth conference of Paris in 2008, this approach involves a new direction for societies that would use fewer natural resources and would organize and live differently on the basis of an equitable downscaling of production and consumption (Schneider et al., 2010). Thus, from the prevailing perspective of economic growth, two apparently incompatible aims are present in the degrowth approach: downsizing economic growth and ensuring a high quality of life. Over the last decade the degrowth debate has increasingly gained traction among academics, with a rising number of scientific publications (see, for overviews, Vandeventer et al., 2019; Weiss & Cattaneo, 2017).[2] In general, there exist two main streams in the literature from an institutional perspective. On the one hand, some authors put forward reforms of growth-based economic, political and social institutions, maintaining market and state institutions; while restructuring, for example, financial markets, tax systems and the provision of public goods and services (health care, education, pension, etc.) to be growth independent. Others, on the other hand, going beyond reforms of market and state institutions and adopting more radical proposals for change, focus on social movements and community initiatives as central agents of transformation to promote radical changes towards a new socially and environmentally sustainable economic, political and social order.

Overall, in line with the Brundtland report and the Agenda 2030 framework, sustainable growth might be seen as economic growth that meets the needs of the present without compromising the ability of future generations to meet their own needs. Obviously, there exist different views in the literature on the feasibility of sustainable growth,

[1] The term *degrowth* (*décroissance* in French) was used for the first time by the social philosopher André Gorz in 1972, even though until the 2000s it attracted little attention beyond a small circle of activists and academics (see Kallis et al., 2015).

[2] Note that other alternative approaches asserting that economic growth may be neither desirable nor indeed feasible have also gained strength in the last few years, such as the economics of 'post-growth' societies (see, for instance, Jackson, 2009).

the need to promote profound reforms in market and state institutions, or even on the idea of growth itself in terms of either GDP or economic and social well-being. What appears to be a certain consensus is on the fact that sustainable growth implicitly entails the search for a decent standard of living for all individuals, both current and future generations, incorporating a comprehensive inclusiveness approach that integrates intra- and inter-generational equity. Sustainable growth and inclusive growth could be thus interpreted as two sides of the same coin conforming the present inclusive and sustainable growth paradigm.

3 Addressing Distributional and Environmental Issues in the Current Contextual Setting of Monetary Policy

According to the theoretical and conceptual framework previously examined, it seems clear that distributional and environmental issues constitute two central elements of inclusive and sustainable growth. With regard to the former, over the last few decades there has been significant concern regarding the increasing concentration of income and wealth within industrialized countries. Since the 1980s, there exists a palpable trend towards less equal societies, although with significant differences across countries (see World Inequality Lab, 2021). This has placed the debates on economic inequality and policy alternatives to fight against it at the centre of economic debates over the last decade (Atkinson, 2015; Deaton, 2013; Galbraith, 2016; Piketty, 2014; Stiglitz, 2012). Among the causes of the increase in income and wealth inequality, a number of drivers have been proposed, such as: the deepening of globalization, skill-biased technological progress, demographic trends, changes in labour market institutions, financialization of the economy, inability of the tax-benefit systems to sufficiently reduce market income inequality, etc. (see, for instance, Aiyar & Ebeke, 2019; Grigoli et al., 2016; Heimberger, 2020; Perugini et al., 2016).

From the environmental perspective, there is growing awareness of the enormous environmental deterioration that the planet is undergoing and the consequential disturbing climate change, which put the economic prosperity and well-being of both present and future generations at risk. In this vein, climate change may be regarded as a major structural change in the world economy that has the potential to culminate in several extensively damaging environmental disasters (see, for example, Nordhaus, 2017; OECD, 2015b, 2017). The anthropogenic (man-made) contribution to cumulative carbon emissions (CO_2) that are driving temperatures upwards and, consequently, increasing the likelihood and potential scope of such dramatic events is one of the major challenges of the present. While the recipe of curbing demand for fossil fuel, either by reducing its usage or by inducing the substitution of carbon-intensive fuels by cleaner alternatives, seems clear; so far the reaction of the international community, both public and private agents, has not been sufficiently resolute. The climate change phenomenon has special features that seem to make it particularly difficult to tackle: the long-term horizon over which the risks are expected to materialize, the lack of information, and the elevated uncertainty about the potential consequences of our inactions. These issues help explain both why the response might have been insufficient so far, and why new policy alternatives should be explored.

In the following sections, we address the extent to which monetary policy might both affect and be affected by economic inequality and environmental risks. Nevertheless, it should be borne in mind the current contextual setting of central banks in advanced economies in which monetary policy would face distributional and environmental issues in the coming years. This way, it should not be forgotten that over the last decade monetary policy has been marked by low long-term interest rates. With interest rates at the effective lower bound (ELB), central banks in most advanced economies have embarked on a set of unconventional measures such as forward guidance, quantitative easing (QE), new longer-term refinancing operations (LTROs), and negative policy rates, aimed to support aggregate demand. All this has renewed the interest in the relationship between the central bank's monetary policy actions and the long-term interest rates: as central bank's actions are expected to influence the long-term interest rates primarily through the short-term interest rates, even though in certain contexts low/negative interest rates might be insufficient to overcome low growth (see, for example, Akram, 2021; Sau, 2018). Moreover, the persistence of low inflation rates despite the ultra-expansive monetary policies after the 2008 crisis has also aroused interest in the debate on the strengths and weaknesses of inflation targeting and its implications (see, for instance, Lawton & Gallagher, 2020; Tatliyer, 2017).

Under the current circumstances, two fundamental questions appear on the horizon: should monetary policy take the distributional and environmental challenges of our times into account? How could monetary policy address distributional and environmental issues in order to contribute to inclusive and sustainable economic growth?

4 Monetary Policy and Economic Inequalities

4.1 How Monetary Policy Affects Income and Wealth Inequality

Monetary policy is intended to deal with aggregate demand, seeking to stabilize prices. Therefore, its effect should be noticeable for the cyclical component of inequality, if any, while the longer-term effects on real outcomes are thought to be rather limited (Bernanke, 2015). However, the unprecedented unconventional monetary measures implemented by many central banks following the financial crisis have raised concerns about the non-neutrality of monetary policy for income and wealth inequality. In this regard, the question of whether monetary policy might have accelerated the rising trend in inequality in advanced economies has been raised (see Domanski et al., 2016). The distributional effects of such policy decisions have not only drawn the attention of academics but have also been extensively addressed by policymakers (see, for example, Bernanke, 2013, 2015; Constâncio, 2017; Draghi, 2016; Panetta, 2015; Pereira da Silva, 2021; Powell, 2020; Yellen, 2014).

Traditionally, a monetary policy able to avoid sudden and sharp deteriorations in purchasing power and to adhere to established formal targets was regarded as the main central bankers' contribution to equality. By limiting excessive inflation, the argument goes, monetary policy could help avoid pervasive consequences for those who own a larger share of their portfolios in the form of nominal assets, such as cash, which is particularly the case for the poorer (Albanesi, 2007; Galli & vor der Hoeven, 2001), hence contributing to wealth equality. However, in most OECD countries, the risk of inflation has been rather muted during the last few decades. Consequently, lately the debate about monetary policy and inequality has focused on the channels through which monetary policy decisions could affect not only wealth but also the income distribution (Amaral, 2017; Coibion et al., 2017; Colciago et al., 2019). In general terms, these concern the extent to which the different sources of income in general and, more specifically, capital and labour returns are heterogeneously affected by monetary policy. The channels identified in the income inequality literature are the following.

4.1.1 The Income Composition Channel

This income composition channel focuses on the vast heterogeneity across households in terms of the relative importance of different sources of income. Labour revenue is the primary source of earnings for most households, and more specifically, for those around the median of the income distribution, while the low end of the distribution tends to rely more on income transfers, notably pensions. Conversely, households in the rightmost part of the income distribution are much less dependent on labour earnings and instead a larger share of their income stems from financial assets and business gains. Inasmuch as income sources react differently to changes in monetary policy, distributional consequences are clearly expected. Theoretical arguments on this front are mixed. On the one hand, expansionary monetary policy might bias the income distribution in favour of the richer households in so far as capital incomes rise relative to wages (Coibion et al., 2017). On the other hand, lower interest rates might decrease interest revenue and hamper income flows especially for the poorest households, which keep in proportion more liquid accounts over their total net worth (Albert & Gómez-Fernandez, 2021). Moreover, a fall in the interest rate could reduce the present or future income of pensioners. These authors point out that the US upper middle class holds a higher proportion of pension accounts as a share of their total net worth. However, these arguments fall prey of a rather short-term partial equilibrium view. For example, while returns on savings might decrease in the short-run, savers with sufficiently diversified portfolios of financial assets will benefit from increasing prices of real assets after policy rate cuts are implemented (see Panetta, 2015). Furthermore, expansionary policies that succeed in stimulating economic activity smooth the economic cycle and contribute to greater corporate profits and real returns accrued by investors above what they could have received otherwise. The literature on the income composition channel suggests that the effect on employment earnings seems to be less ambiguous, as monetary easing is expected to increase labour demand, thereby benefiting those more reliant on labour income (see Colciago et al., 2019).

4.1.2 The Earnings Heterogeneity Channel

This channel underscores the fact that the risk of being or becoming unemployed is distributed unequally across the population and the most vulnerable households are precisely those at the lower tail of the distribution. In other words, households with lower work intensities (for instance due to fewer marketable skills) are overrepresented in the leftmost part of the income distribution (see, for example, Pereira da Silva, 2021). As a result, not all individuals are equally sensitive to downward fluctuations in the business cycle, and counter-cyclical expansionary monetary policies improving economic activity, and hence employment levels, might disproportionately and positively benefit vulnerable households, thereby reducing income inequality (see Lenza & Slačálek, 2018). Furthermore, labour earnings tend to respond differently for low and high-income households. After an expansionary monetary policy is implemented, labour income of vulnerable households tends to react more sharply to changes in the employment status. Conversely, those at the top particularly benefit from upward revisions in hourly wages (Heathcote et al., 2010; Lenza & Slačálek, 2018). According to this channel, monetary easing could reduce income inequality by fighting aggregate unemployment and the associated loss in earnings, which is one of the main drivers of income inequality. However, this effect must be analyzed on a case-by-case basis. For example, Dolado et al. (2018) focus on the capital-skill complementarity hypothesis and suggest monetary easing could increase capital demand and only generate employment for skilled workers, who tend to be more complementary to capital than unskilled workers are, thereby exacerbating income inequality.

Together with the income composition and the earning heterogeneity channels, the financial segmentation channel, is also considered in the literature. According to this mechanism, those participating actively and frequently in the financial markets occupy a better place to benefit from expansionary policy rate changes via financial earnings. This is due to the current transmission mechanism of monetary policy, which relies on the financial system. While the distributional impact of monetary policy through this channel has not been empirically addressed, theory points towards a negative contribution to equality.

The task of empirically analyzing the distributional effects of monetary policy instruments, such as open-market operations, standing facilities, minimum reserve requirements and asset purchase programmes, is fraught with difficulties. First, the coexistence and interrelationships between the different channels add complexity to the exercise, as they often exert opposing forces of different magnitudes, hence partially counteracting each other. Secondly, their dynamic patterns are also highly heterogeneous, as each one unfolds over different time horizons over which the direction of the impact might vary (for example, a negative contribution in the short run that might become positive over longer periods). Consequently, it is practically impossible to isolate the impact generated by each channel and unambiguously determine the net distributional effect of a monetary policy. Furthermore, the generalization of specific results is a risky endeavour. Effects are largely contingent and depend on a series of macroeconomic and institutional factors, and these many dimensions need to be considered jointly for each specific case.

Most studies to date do not consider all the transmission channels together, but rather capture partial effects that could be loosely attributed to specific mechanisms, providing mixed evidence (see Amaral, 2017;

Coibion et al., 2017; Colciago et al., 2019). Overall, the net distributional effect of monetary policy measures depends on the relative impact of income composition and earnings heterogeneity channels, which must be measured by the data for each specific case.

4.2 How Monetary Policy Affects Wealth Inequality

In parallel with studies examining potential effects of monetary policy on income distribution, in recent years numerous authors have also tackled some channels through which monetary policy might entail distributional effects on wealth. Auclert (2019) summarizes three main channels.

4.2.1 The Portfolio Channel

According to the empirical evidence, interest rate fluctuations lead to changes in financial asset prices (Rogers et al., 2014). Some authors point out that expansionary monetary policy could increase income and wealth inequality because asset price increases tend to benefit the top part of the net worth distribution, where stock ownership is more prevalent (Albert & Gómez-Fernández, 2021; Saiki & Frost, 2014). However, other studies point out that this effect is mitigated when housing price increases caused by the same expansionary monetary policy shock are taken into account, since the middle class and the bottom part of the net worth distribution on average own a higher proportion of their wealth in housing (Adam & Tzamourani, 2016; Lenza & Slačálek, 2018). In addition, it is important to note that high housing prices could have an impact on intergenerational inequality. Rising housing prices can negatively affect young people who want to enter the housing market (Albert et al., 2020).

4.2.2 The Fisher Channel

Unexpected inflation revaluates nominal balance sheets without households having the option to react to protect themselves from this unexpected shock, with nominal creditors losing and nominal debtors gaining. To properly analyze household exposure to the risk of unexpected movements in inflation, it is important to know their net nominal positions, which consist of nominal claims net of nominal liabilities and comprising items held both directly and indirectly via investment funds. This channel has been empirically explored by Doepke and Schneider (2006) in the U.S. and by Adam and Zhu (2016) in the euro area. They show that indebted households tend to benefit from an unexpected hike in the inflation rate, while savers are harmed. In this vein, Doepke and Schneider (2006) underline that poor households benefit, as they are the principal holders of long-maturity interest-bearing debts.

4.2.3 The Interest Rate Exposure Channel

Auclert (2019) points out that unhedged interest rate exposures (UREs), defined as the difference between all maturing assets and liabilities at a point in time, are the correct measure of household balance sheet exposures to real interest rate changes. Since monetary policy has a direct effect on the interest income flows received or paid by households, related to their interest-bearing assets and liabilities are distributed differently across households, these policies can have distributional consequences. By analyzing this channel, Tzamourani (2019) finds that households at the lower end of the net wealth distribution, younger households and mortgage holders have, on average, a higher exposure to interest rates. These households would benefit from a drop in interest rates. Similarly, Slačálek et al. (2020) show that hand-to-mouth households—with negative interest rate exposure—would benefit from a reduction in interest rates through this channel. On the contrary, a drop in interest rates would negatively affect non-hand-to-mouth households.

In addition, monetary policy could generate distributive effects through other more subtle channels. On the one hand, assuming the same rate of savings among households, the distributional effects of monetary policy on income, explained in the previous section, are reproduced in the distribution of wealth. On the other hand, monetary policy could lead to heterogeneous changes in the marginal propensity to consume and therefore in the accumulation of wealth (Auclert, 2019; Tobin, 1982).

Overall, the empirical literature on distributional effects of monetary policy on wealth shows mixed findings across channels and countries. Some studies find that expansionary monetary policy may increase wealth inequality, while others highlight the opposite (see, for instance, Albert & Gómez-Fernández, 2021; Lenza & Slačálek, 2018; Mumtaz & Theophilopoulou, 2019). In this line, given the existence of compensatory channels, empirical research tends to suggest that the effect of monetary policy on wealth inequality essentially depends on the strength and direction of asset price and interest rate responses to a monetary policy shock and the composition of different financial assets and liabilities in the household portfolio in each specific context.

4.3 Implications of Economic Inequalities for Conducting Monetary Policy

Apart from examining how monetary policy can potentially affect economic inequalities, the question of whether rising inequalities might entail consequences for the performance of monetary policy should also be considered. Macroeconomic studies focusing on the transmission of monetary policy to the real economy are largely dominated by the representative agent view, which assumes aggregate consumption is highly responsive to changes in policy rates. This paradigm abstracts from the different forms of heterogeneity, related to both income and wealth, which influence the ultimate effectiveness of macroeconomic stabilization policies (see Kharroubi et al., 2021). According to the mainstream view, monetary policy might temporarily establish policy interest rates above or below the so-called 'natural rate of interest' to achieve its objective. Consequently, and given certain time lags in the reactions of prices, monetary policy decisions affect the (real) market interest rates that prevail in the economy, which influence savings, consumption and investment decisions through intertemporal substitution. More specifically, expansionary measures reduce households' net financial income and the opportunity cost of consumption. This, in turn, disincentivizes saving, incentivizes borrowing and increases present aggregate demand. However, assuming a certain pass-through of policy rates to banks' loans and deposit rates, the magnitude of this effect depends on agents' reaction to monetary policy decisions, which in turn relies on their economic and financial situations. Therefore, not all households are as responsive as the representative agent is assumed to be; hence, heterogeneity matters.

The leftmost part of the income distribution is populated by hand-to-mouth agents that use almost the total amount of their income receipts for consumption, regardless of the prevailing interest rates. These households' discretionary spending is rather small, and hence their consumption is hardly responsive to changes in interest rates (Ampudia et al., 2018). At the opposite end of the distribution, ultra-rich households are more likely to be already satisfied with their consumption levels, hence the marginal utility they derive from additional consumption is close to zero. In this vein, households located in the extremes of the distribution tend to be particularly unresponsive to changes in policy rates. This implies a departure from the basic characterization of the 'well-behaved' representative agent, which enables a full transmission of monetary policy, given a certain level of pass-through towards financing conditions.

In this regard, the marginal propensity to consume (MPC) is distributed unequally across the population, and agents' heterogeneity is nontrivial for monetary policy (see, for instance, Ampudia et al., 2018; Kaplan et al., 2018). The literature suggests that heterogeneity in MPC is associated with the prevalence of unresponsive (that is, consumption largely unaffected by changes in interest rates) households, so that highly unequal societies might see the effectiveness of their monetary policy significantly undermined. Besides income distribution, heterogeneity in terms of wealth is also crucial, as the unequal composition of assets and liabilities across households affect their MPC. For example, after an expansionary monetary policy is implemented, the wealthiest agents might just replace liquid holdings—whose real returns have just been reduced—and rebalance their portfolios towards more lucrative, riskier and longer-term financial assets, rather than towards higher consumption expenditures. Nevertheless, empirical evidence shows that households generally do not restructure their balance sheets in response to interest rate changes (Amerkis & Zeldes, 2004). Highly indebted households, on the other hand, might prefer to pay down debt after policy-rate cuts decrease their interest payments. Therefore, the magnitude of this effect, via the intertemporal substitution, depends on how changes in nominal policy rates affect real interest rates and how strongly household consumption responds to such changes given a certain level of income. This is known as the 'direct effect' in the transmission mechanism, and refers to that which operates even in the absence of changes in household disposable labour income (Kaplan et al., 2018).

The direct impact of monetary policy shocks associated to the intertemporal substitution of consumption (i.e. how a reduction in real interest rates make agents advance their consumption plans) is only part of the story. Once responsive households set in motion an initial increase in consumption, this impulse to aggregate demand fuels employment creation, which further allows consumption to grow, hence amplifying the ultimate impact of monetary policy on aggregate demand. This indirect or general equilibrium effect works extensively through disposable income and relies on the empirical fact that not everyone is a permanent income consumer. This is at odds with the assumption made by many representative agent models, which consequently conclude that the relative importance of this indirect effect is rather small. This way, transitory earnings are transmitted to consumption (Jappelli & Pistaferri, 2010), which contributes to the effectiveness of monetary policy. The magnitude of this effect depends on how strongly disposable income changes given a certain level of real interest rates (direct effect) and the elasticity of consumption to changes in disposable income (indirect effect).

While for low-income or hand-to-mouth households the direct impact via the intertemporal substitution mechanism is rather negligible; the general equilibrium effect makes a significant difference on their demand, as consumption of these (high-MPC) agents is extremely responsive to changes in labour earnings (Ampudia et al., 2018). Consequently, in a model with heterogeneous marginal propensities to consume, income and wealth distributions have real effects. In other words, average MPC is a function of the distribution of income and wealth. In this sense, the consequences of monetary policy are intertwined with the fiscal side of the economy (Kaplan et al., 2018), and the fiscal response matters for monetary policy. More specifically, given the failure of the Ricardian equivalence theorem (i.e. debt-financed government spending might be effective as agents will not factor in the fact that taxes will have to increase in the future to re-pay such stimulus when making their consumption decisions) (Romer, 2006), expansionary monetary policies affect the intertemporal government budget constraints. This might facilitate the implementation of fiscal measures aiming to back government transfers accrued to the poorest. These, in turn, are composed of high-MPC households, which might reinforce the effectiveness of monetary policy by increasing consumption after they benefit from an increase in disposable income. Therefore, more equal societies tend to be more responsive to monetary impulses (direct effect), and monetary-fiscal coordination redistributing towards the leftmost tail, could further reinforce the transmission mechanism of monetary policy (indirect effect).

Recent literature highlights that income and wealth distributions are also central for monetary economic analysis (see, for example, Kaplan et al., 2018). Wealth and income distribution, together with portfolio and income composition, determine the distribution of marginal propensities to consume across the population and define the amplification or dampening of monetary policy relative to the baseline representative agent view. Consequently, empirically grounded heterogeneity matters for how monetary policy transmits to the real economy. Highly unequal societies unable to redistribute income towards the poorest might see the transmission mechanism of monetary policy strongly impaired.

5 Monetary Policy and Environmental Problems

5.1 Environmental Sustainability Through the Lens of Monetary Policy

Environmental degradation and climate change is an intergenerational problem with serious implications for equity between current and future generations in which action must be taken in the present to avoid the catastrophic consequences such as global warming in the future. More specifically, it should be underlined that carbon usage generates a negative externality that calls for an efficient mechanism to internalize the social costs linked to carbon emissions. However, economic agents seem to be falling prey to the paradox of the time horizon, also referred to as 'the tragedy of the horizon' (Carney, 2015), since the effects are expected to occur over a longer time horizon than the one usually considered by most economic agents, which tend to be relatively short-sighted. This problem interacts with several sources of informational market failure, such as the lack of clear, consistent and transparent disclosure and undermines the ability of markets to fully price climate-related risks and correct the externality. In general, markets face difficulties while trying to price tail events that fall outside the historical distribution (Schnabel, 2020). Consequently, markets might be systematically underpricing global warming (i.e. might be failing in demanding a higher rate of returns to carbon-intensive assets) and hence not performing their role of achieving an optimal allocation of resources.

In such a scenario, some economists advocate for well-suited climate fiscal policies, taxing carbon-intensive activities as a first-best option (Nordhaus, 2017). In this vein, higher global carbon prices would disincentivize its emission and help set in motion the carbon transition. However, the public sector is not exempt from the tragedy of the horizon: in some cases democratically elected politicians (as well as the general public) choose to optimize their current situation via postponing the much-needed reforms. In order to avoid the short-term political costs associated with the transition phase (i.e. adapting business models to the green economy might create short-term losses). This behaviour might lead to a policy failure similar to the one faced by private markets. In other words, public intervention might be sluggish when it is needed the most, as climate disasters are a function of cumulative emissions and delayed action increases consequences. Furthermore, the fight against climate change faces the additional problem of international free riding,[3] revealing the need for a coordinated reaction at the global level that might not be easily agreed.

In this context, the link between monetary policy and environmental problems, such as climate change, is not straightforward and could be addressed from different perspectives. The reaction of the different institutional sectors, together with the existence and materialization of climate-related risks, will progressively alter the macroeconomic and financial reality that guides monetary policy; for example, by influencing inflation dynamics (Lagarde, 2020). Therefore, the design of monetary policy should take into account climate-related aspects (Brunnermeier & Landau, 2020), which would be playing an ever-increasing role in the course of the decisions made by monetary authorities. This way, monetary policymakers should primarily face two major challenges. On the one hand, global warming increases the likelihood and expected magnitude of both temporary and permanent supply shocks, which complicate the conduct of monetary policy. On the other hand, climate-related risks increase the uncertainty around the economic projections that sustain monetary policymaking. In the face of the materialization of such risks, these projections are expected to suffer sudden major revisions.

Apart from reacting to climate-related trends and unexpected events, it can be asked to what extent monetary policy could directly contribute to the fight against climate change. In this sense, the incorporation of climate-related risks to published economic analyses is a significant contribution to the cause. This exercise of 'green' communication could help increase awareness about the economic implications of climate change among the general public. Unavoidably, environmental risk is and will increasingly affect the economic outlook that guides monetary policymaking, so that climate is increasingly becoming a core aspect of

[3] Climate policies implemented at a national level would be inefficient as they might end up generating carbon leakage. This is a global challenge that needs global answers.

regular analyses that back monetary decisions. While crucial, this action might be deemed subtle and even insufficient, as monetary authorities could certainly find additional ways to exert a more decisive impact.

5.2 Implications of Climate-Related Risks for Monetary Policy

In practice, implementing monetary policy consists of identifying the nature, persistence and magnitude of the shocks hitting our economies (Coeuré, 2018). The shocks associated with climate change have one attribute in common, that is their nature: climate-related phenomena are inherently supply-sided in the origin, which entail demand side effects and interplays between supply and demand effects.

From the perspective of central banks, disruptions affecting the demand-side of the economy are manageable, since they are subject to what is sometimes called the 'divine coincidence', i.e. they affect inflation and real growth in the same direction. Conversely, supply shocks imply a trade-off for monetary authorities, where preserving price stability would come at the expense of output. In order to address their potential implications for monetary policy, climate change related risks could be classified into two major groups, differing in terms of both their persistence and magnitude. However, both are of the same kind, that is, they are supply-side shocks.

5.2.1 Shocks Associated to the Transition Phase

The transition phase entails a combination of risks arising from climate-related policies, sudden preference changes and technological breakthroughs related to energy production, usage and storage. The materialization of these risks, which is already on the go, implies the re-pricing of carbon-intensive assets as awareness becomes widespread and agents react to the social costs associated with carbon emissions or to the price effect of fiscal policies taxing them. The adoption of a cleaner energy mix at a global level inevitably involves steadily growing carbon prices, which will put upward pressure on prices and change medium and long-term inflation expectations. This price incentive is precisely what would drive the much-needed technical change and resource reallocation.

On the real side of the economy, carbon-intensive assets are likely to become unused before their lifetime ends and hence mutate into stranded assets (e.g. unburnable fossil fuel reserves, inability to keep operating coal-fired industries). This destruction of productive capacity—in the short-term it might not be entirely replaced by alternative capacity—might exert a negative impact on growth and employment, at least in the short-term, due to the usually sluggish processes of reallocating resources after major structural changes. Besides the effect on the supply capacity, the adaptation of business models to a green economy might, at least in the short run, create losses and depress aggregate demand (while increasing prices). In this context, not only monetary policy but also fiscal policy could be key to avoid a sharp drop in demand. For example, the revenue from carbon taxation could be rebated via transfers or cutting other revenues (see, for example, Metcalf & Stock, 2020). A successful support of aggregate demand via fiscal policy would help alleviate this trade-off and allow monetary authorities to focus on price stability.

Monetary policy tends to overlook short-lived supply shocks, as they do not usually entail long-term consequences for aggregate prices. However, the gradual negative supply-side disruptions associated with the phase of transition towards a green economy are likely to be long-lasting and hence have second-round effects. For example, carbon taxes might entail an increase in energy prices that could end up affecting the other prices of the economy. In this sense, monetary policy makers need to closely monitor the implications of climate change and disentangle its effect from the ones corresponding to other potential sources of shorter-term inflation-output trade-offs, which are unlikely to affect the medium-term inflation outlook.

5.2.2 Shocks Related to the Materialization of Physical Risks

The concept of physical risks refers to severe events originating from global warming, such as heat waves, wildfires and landslides. These disasters exert major damage to affected economies, in as much as they are major destructors of capital (for example, homes and industries). The disruption of economic activity after such unexpected major supply shocks entails shortages of food and subsequent increases in prices that might not remain domestic, but quickly spill over internationally and generate a global impact. However, this largely depends on the dimension, recurrence and location of such catastrophes.

Physical risks could be described as 'tail risks' to economic growth that increase in a non-linear fashion following uncertain tipping points. This implies that climate-related damages are captured by skewed distributions and tipping point risks (van der Ploeg, 2020). At present, both the potential frequency and magnitude of such future disasters, as well as the time-horizon over which they might materialize are ignored. Estimating the expected present discounted value of the future marginal damages of emitting one more ton of carbon today is a truly daunting task. The only certainty is that such tail risks follow a function that increases in temperature, whose rise is influenced by cumulative carbon emissions. Unlike the transition risks, that have already started to materialize and will increasingly do so, the materialization of physical risks is expected to happen beyond the projection horizon of central banks. This implies that, unlike transition risks, these are not organically incorporated into present monetary policy decisions, which are undertaken, based on medium-term projections.

However, physical risks increase the uncertainty regarding future inflation and inflation expectations and make them more prone to suffering sharp upward revisions. Potential output and growth, and the natural equilibrium interest rate, are also expected to undergo sudden shifts in the future. In this vein, climate-related disasters are a source of volatility in the global economy, which should not be disregarded by central bankers, even in those countries theoretically less exposed to them, as globalization (for instance, global value chains) has made the global component of inflation more important than ever before.

Monetary authorities could factor these fat-tail risks in the models used to forecast macroeconomic variables and clearly communicate their impact on the uncertainty intervals regarding their projections, which would reflect the increasing probability of environmental disasters. For example, the macroeconomic models could be improved to reflect a proper assessment of climate-related financial risks (Lagarde, 2020). However, in practice the scarcity of historical evidence makes this approach very difficult.

The risks associated with climate change affect the conduct of monetary policy in different ways. On the one hand, transition measures tend to modify relative prices to curb demand towards clean energy. However, as this reallocation of resources usually takes time, high demand for carbon-intensive alternatives and high (disincentivizing) prices are likely to co-exist temporarily. This situation would lead to a gradually higher path for inflation and inflation expectations until markets alter their demand patterns to decrease (relatively more expensive) carbon emissions. Likewise, at least temporarily, economies might suffer a downward shift to reflect the loss of productive capacity. On the other hand, the materialization of physical risks will lead to sharp, abrupt revisions in these variables. As a result of both types of shocks, global warming will increase the frequency of situations whereby monetary policy has to react to supply-side shocks and hence faces the inflation-output trade-off. Both the transition phase and the occurrence of extreme events will erode the conventional policy space, which could force a rethinking of the current monetary policy framework, since non-standard or unconventional tools might become essential.

5.3 Monetary Policy in the Fight Against Climate Change

Besides leveraging on the effects arising from including climate-related risks in the normal conduct of monetary policy, central banks could also use their instruments to promote actively the fight against climate change (Brunnermeier & Landau, 2020; Honohan, 2019). In this sense, monetary authorities could reorient their monetary policy tools towards green financial assets—i.e. assets whose proceeds are earmarked for funding climate and environmental-friendly projects—and hence contribute to a reallocation of resources that deviates from the one pursued by the market. This would entail, for example, modifying the eligibility criteria of monetary policy operations to exclude bonds that finance projects in conflict with the decarbonization objectives or linking the eligibility of securities as collateral to disclosure and assessment of climate-related risks. If pursued, such decisions need to be based on clear and transparent rules that should be democratically debated.

In the conduct of monetary policy, the amount of collateralized borrowing counterparties obtained from central banks adjusts automatically to reflect underlying risk assessment in financial markets. Therefore, as investors price in climate-related risks, the haircuts applied to carbon-intensive collaterals, and used in refinancing operations would become less favourable. Likewise, these assets would increasingly become ineligible for the large-scale asset purchase operations. In other words, the correct pricing of carbon emissions automatically 'greens' monetary policy.

Along this line, according to Matikainen et al. (2017), central banks could: (i) increase transparency regarding the purchases and selection process; (ii) investigate the impact of their interventions on both high-carbon and low-carbon investment; (iii) consider options for changing their purchasing strategies, by revising eligibility criteria and using monetary policy more effectively to support long-term sustainable growth; and (iv) coordinate with fiscal policymakers and financial regulators.

This conventional approach is based on the principle of 'market neutrality', which seeks to minimize distortions in relative prices and avoid unintended effects related to disruptions affecting the information embedded in price mechanisms. However, the rationale behind maintaining market neutrality might not apply to climate change, where markets seem to be failing in fully correcting the associated externalities. If the markets failed, market neutrality might not be an appropriate benchmark, as markets themselves are not achieving an efficient reallocation of resources.

In this vein, some authors point out that the market has a bias towards carbon-intensive companies. As carbon-intensive companies, like oil and gas companies and car manufacturers, are typically also capital intensive (Doda, 2016). Market indices for corporate bonds are overweight in high-carbon companies (Schoenmaker, 2021). Matikainen et al. (2017)

estimate that 62% of the ECB's corporate bond purchases are in manufacturing and electricity production sectors. These sectors represent 59% of the Euro Area greenhouse gas emissions, but only 18% in terms of gross value added. For the Bank of England (BoE), manufacturing, and electricity production—the source for 52% of UK greenhouse gas emissions—make up 49% of the estimated purchases, but only 12% of the gross value added (Monnin, 2018).

It is important to note that in recent years, central banks in developed economies have increasingly resorted to targeted refinancing operations to fulfil their mandates. In response to the GFC, refinancing operations have become a key instrument of monetary policy to provide liquidity to financial institutions. For instance, the ECB has launched three Targeted Long-Term Refinancing Operations (TLTRO) programmes with the aim of offering banks refinancing at reduced rates for loans to non-financial corporations, as well as for non-mortgage loans to households. Similarly, in 2012 the BoE introduced the Funding for Lending Scheme (FLS) with the aim of reducing the cost of capital and increasing bank lending to households and businesses. With similar objectives, in 2016 the BoE launched the Term Funding Scheme (TFS) and in 2020 it adopted the TFS with the specific aim of supporting lending to small and medium-sized enterprises (SMEs). Similar schemes have been introduced in other developed countries, such as the Term Funding Facility (TFF) of the Reserve Bank of Australia or the Paycheck Protection Programme Liquidity Facility (PPPLF) launched by the U.S. Federal Reserve (Fed) in April 2020. With the implementation of such programmes, some central bankers argue that highly accommodative monetary policy is already helping to finance the green transition thanks to very low-interest rates and abundant liquidity provided. At the same time, however, they are aware that green finance would have to be larger than at the present, and the greening of central bank actions does not require a further loosening of monetary policy if necessary but rather a review of its monetary policy instruments (Villeroy, 2021).

Nevertheless, in practice using monetary policy to cut emissions is fraught with difficulties, as contributing to a green reallocation of resources beyond that pursued by markets is not straightforward. At present, there is not an internationally accepted taxonomy that helps to guide how every financial asset should be treated in this sense. On the one hand, a clear and consistent definition of brown assets and a quantification of their risks are essential. On the other hand, a clear understanding of the possibilities of 'olive' assets is crucial in order not to undermine the carbon transition.

In this context, many central bankers have raised concerns about adopting a more proactive monetary policy response to the climate challenge. For instance, the governor of the Bundesbank (Weidmann, 2017) expressed his opposition to the possibility of using bond purchases or the collateral policy to promote green financing. He argued that the Euro Area system's mandate is to maintain price stability, and in order to achieve this objective monetary policy should not be overburdened with other objectives. Similarly, Coeuré (2018) states that the ECB, acting in accordance with its mandate, can and should actively support the transition to a low-carbon economy mainly in two ways: first, by helping to define the rules of the game, and second, by acting accordingly, without undermining price stability. Finally, the governor of the Bank of France (Villeroy, 2019) considers that a Green QE could introduce distortions in the market, given the small size of the green bond market, and that the consideration of climate factors in collateral policy requires further study of climate risks.

6 Monetary Policy in the Face of Distributional and Environmental Challenges: Some Policy Proposals

Traditionally, central banks have not considered distributional and environmental challenges among their priorities. The primary objective of monetary policy since the 1970s in most of the developed economies has been price stability. This circumvention is motivated by the belief that monetary policy is neutral in the long run and price stability leads to higher growth and sustained welfare (Barro, 1995; Briault, 1995); in addition, there are other policies endowed with greater democratic legitimacy, such as fiscal policy, to deal with these challenges (Bernanke,

2015). In addition, a number of critics have expressed their rejection of monetary policy taking a more proactive role in distributional and environmental aspects. Some critics point out that endowing central banks with multiple objectives compromises their credibility, their independence and, consequently, the core mandate of price stability (Cochrane, 2020). Others stress that although these may be very laudable objectives, central banks do not have democratic authorization to pursue these distributional and environmental objectives. In this regard, committing to said objectives would lead to democratic, legal and ethical problems, as central banks would not be following a concise and clear mandate determined by democratic institutions (Honohan, 2019). Finally, a third frequent criticism is that monetary policies tend to alternate between expansions and contractions until price stability is reached. Therefore, in the medium term, the effect of these policies is favourable to inclusive and sustainable growth to be neutral.

However, recent studies have criticized this view and have suggested different reasons why central banks should consider distributional and environmental aspects in their actions. First, as argued in the previous sections, high inequalities could reduce the effectiveness of monetary policy due to heterogeneity in the composition of wealth and the marginal propensity to consume (Sufi, 2015), or through reductions in the long-term equilibrium interest rate (Mian et al., 2020). Likewise, climate change also implies risks for the performance of monetary policy (Brunnermeier & Landau, 2020; Lagarde, 2020). Therefore, it is possible to argue that, in defence of the primary objective of price stability, central banks should take these challenges into account (Areosa & Areosa, 2016).

Second, many central banks in developed economies have sustainable growth or equality of opportunity as a secondary objective (see Table 1). Some Central Banks, such as the Central Bank of the Republic of Argentina in March 2012, explicitly even included social equity among its objectives in its statutes. Therefore, it could be argued that central banks should pursue these secondary objectives as long as they are not detrimental to the primary objective of price stability (Honohan, 2019).

Finally, a third group of studies points out that monetary policy, especially since non-standard policies have been implemented, is far from

Table 1 Central bank mandates

Monetary area	Central Bank	Primary objectives	Other objectives
Euro Area	European Central Bank	Price stability	Sustainable development, balanced economic growth, improvement of the quality of the environment
Israel	Bank of Israel	Price stability	Promoting economic growth and employment, reducing social gaps
Japan	Bank of Japan	Price stability	Development of the national economy
Switzerland	Swiss National Bank	Price stability	Development of the national economy
United Kingdom	Bank of England	Price and financial stability	Promoting economic growth and employment (announced in 2021 that objectives will include environmental considerations)
United States	Federal Reserve	Maximum employment, stable prices, and moderate long-term interest rates	Development of the national economy
Argentina	Central Bank of the Argentine Republic	Monetary and financial stability, employment, and economic development and social equity	
Brazil	Central Bank of Brazil	Economic development	Development of the national economy
Russia	The Central Bank of the Russian Federation	Price stability	Balanced and sustainable economic development

Source Compiled with data from the IMF Central Bank Legislation Database and Dikau and Ulrich (2020) being apolitical and neutral in its actions. Gabor (2021) shows that every monetary policy decision affects the allocation of capital and creates winners and losers. Thus, according to this standpoint, anything that central banks do is unavoidably political. At the same time, as discussed above, some authors point out that the central bank's corporate bond purchases have a bias towards carbon-intensive companies (Matikainen et al., 2017). In this vein, the neutrality of monetary policy has been questioned by the German Constitutional Court, which has expressed legal doubts about the European Central Bank's (ECB) pandemic emergency purchase programme (PEPP). In this context, de Boer and Van't Klooster (2020) argue that monetary policy has a single mandate but multiple tools to achieve this objective, all legally permissible but all with political implications, including in distributional and environmental terms. Van't Klooster and Fontan (2020) assert that, from a procedural perspective, unconventional monetary policy gives central bankers broad discretion without democratic accountability. Moreover, they stress that by attempting to pursue market neutrality, central bankers fail to make their programmes sufficiently sensitive in their social and environmental consequences.

According to these arguments, and in line with the ongoing academic and practical discussions, it is worth broaching different monetary policy proposals in order to enable central banks to incorporate distributional and environmental issues among their objectives and actions. These proposals share the need to turn the challenge of the decline in long-term interest rates into an opportunity for monetary policy to help address the distributional and environmental challenges in the framework of inclusive and sustainable economic growth.

Focusing on economic inequalities, as argued in Sect. 3, the monetary policy itself has important distributional effects on both income and wealth. For example, expansionary monetary policy could reduce income inequality through more powerful job creation for workers at the bottom part of the distribution, although it could also increase wealth inequality through the appreciation of financial assets. At the same time, the significance of fiscal policy to combat inequality is well known. In this sense, the relevance of taking advantage of both policies and coordinating them in order to reduce inequality seems evident. Along this line, Arestis (2015) and Arestis and Gonzalez-Martinez (2016) propose a very close coordination between monetary and fiscal policies, as well as financial stability policies, to endow fiscal policy with greater possibilities and effectiveness. From this perspective, some authors tend to emphasize the need for closer coordination between monetary policy and fiscal policy to provide the appropriate stimulus to stagnant economies and reduce inequality through appropriate expenditure and progressive tax policies, which should be supported by monetary policy (see, for instance, Coppola, 2019; Gali, 2020).

Similarly, Bartsch et al. (2019) argue that with global interest rates near zero, both conventional and unconventional monetary policies—both of which are transmitted through the interest rate channel—are exhausted. Furthermore, they point out that fiscal policy could fail to provide enough stimulus to the economy given the high debt levels and typical implementation delays, and advocate for policy coordination in order to provide a more forceful response through explicit monetary financing and permanent fiscal expansion. They underscore that any policy innovation should take into consideration economic inequalities to tackle one of the greatest challenges of our times and to be socially acceptable. This way, they specifically point out that new digital currencies issued by central banks (CBDCs) could help bring money to citizens at the bottom of the distribution in a way that was not possible before.

From this perspective, in the face of the severe economic shock produced by the Covid-19 crisis, stimulus plans that require coordination between monetary and fiscal policy through the monetization of fiscal stimulus have been proposed. For example, Gali (2020) puts forward the financing of public deficits generated during the pandemic crisis through direct and permanent (non-repayable) transfers from the central bank to the respective governments. This measure would work in favour of the most vulnerable households that are typically more dependent on public transfers in situations of economic uncertainty and insecurity. Alternatively, for the case of the Euro Area, Jourdan (2020) suggests a transfer of €1000 to all euro area citizens in the economic recovery phase after the Covid-19 crisis. This would implicitly reduce income inequality by increasing the relative income of citizens at the bottom of the distribution by a larger percentage. Coppola (2019) and Sahm (2019) have developed similar alternatives.

Beyond the high potential of coordinating monetary policy with fiscal policy to tackle economic inequalities, some specific monetary policy instruments might be particularly relevant in reducing inequalities. For instance, some refinancing programmes such as the LTROs launched by the ECB could be made conditional on bank lending benefiting the most vulnerable households. In this sense, TLTROs might be a useful specific monetary policy instrument, as the amount banks can borrow is linked to their lending to non-financial corporations and households. This instrument ensures that monetary expansion reaches the real economy and can thus have beneficial distributional effects. Moreover, in response to the Covid-19 crisis, the Fed expanded its main street lending program to support lending to non-profit institutions. These loans improved the financing conditions of many of these institutions, including hospitals, schools and social service organizations that were in sound financial condition before the pandemic. It seems plausible that improving the financing of these institutions could help to reduce economic inequalities and should be a course of action to take into consideration in the future. Finally, directly improving the financing conditions of public treasuries could also have a beneficial distributional effect as long as this additional fiscal space is used to improve the material conditions of the most vulnerable households. Obviously, it requires fiscal programmes aimed in a progressive direction. In this regard, and contrary to what happened during the Great Recession, in 2020 the Fed created a programme of direct lending to state and municipal governments through the municipal liquidity facility. Similarly, asset purchase programmes such as the public sector purchase programme and the pandemic emergency purchase programme, launched by the ECB, have eased and improved the financing conditions of the respective governments by widening their fiscal space. These examples corroborate the importance of distinguishing between the different monetary policies instruments when assessing their distributional effects.

As far as environmental challenges are concerned, in recent years different proposals have been made on how monetary policy could address environmental challenges, such as climate challenge in a more proactive manner. With interest rates close to the effective lower bound since the GFC, several studies have concurred on the need and opportunity for central banks to incorporate climate change risks into their monetary policy strategy and adopt specific measures in this regard.

Zerbib (2017) proposes that central banks should include low-carbon bonds in central banks' collateral frameworks to contribute to the development of low-carbon bond markets. Similarly, Schoenmaker (2021) provides a method to tilt the ECB's asset and collateral framework towards low-carbon assets. According to this method, the ECB could reduce carbon emissions in the central bank's corporate and bank bond portfolio by 55%, offsetting the current carbon bias. It could also reduce the cost of capital for low carbon companies, creating an incentive for high carbon companies to reform and adopt low carbon technologies. Similarly, Monasterolo and Raberto (2016) put forward a quantitative easing programme based on large-scale purchases of new green sovereign bonds with the objective of stimulating global issuance of both bonds and green loans of sovereign green bonds. Let us recall that green sovereign bonds refer to bonds issued by governments to enable them to raise capital to implement infrastructure plans in line with national climate objectives. These authors point out that Central Bank purchases of green bonds would boost investment and reduce unemployment more than traditional quantitative easing to the extent that they would reduce the negative consequences of climate change on growth. Giuliani et al. (2017) state that when they are responsible for approving bond purchases, central banks could simplify and speed up the approval process for low-carbon bonds. They also suggest that central banks should consider providing financial support for the issuance of low-carbon assets by the market. In this sense, Hilmi et al. (2021), recommend a synergy between monetary and environmental policies in the EU and the Euro Area, specifically in the design of the non-conventional policy instruments that inject liquidity into markets. Thus, the ECB's policy of QE could potentially promote the production and use of renewable energy sources and significantly support the EU's effort to protect the environment in the pursuit of the 2030 climate and energy goals. Also for the Euro Area, Van't Klooster and Tilburg (2020) suggest the creation of green TLTROs. These programmes would be based on refinancing operations that provide cheap financing to banks if they lend according to the EU's taxonomy of green activities. Among other specific proposals, they develop a pilot programme for energy-efficient housing that could be implemented in a short period. Likewise, Monnin (2018), who recommends that central banks should mitigate the bias toward carbon-intensive sectors in their current large-scale asset purchase programmes by reflecting climate-related risk in their purchase decisions, also emphasizes these strategies.

In addition, Anderson (2015) goes one step further and proposes a 'Green QE' where the ECB and other national central banks within the Euro Area could create new money to finance lending to the private sector for green infrastructure projects and green businesses. National central banks in the Euro Area would buy bonds issued by the European Investment Bank (EIB) in exchange for central bank reserves, which would be held indefinitely on the central bank's balance sheet to finance these projects. Van Lerven (2016) for the UK has made a similar proposal.

In general, it can be stated that even though there is still some scepticism on the part of central banks to incorporate green strategies into their monetary policy tools, some central bankers are beginning to align themselves with some of these proposals. For example, the Governor of the Bank of France, Villeroy (2021), proposes to start decarbonizing the ECB's balance sheet gradually and selectively for all corporate assets, whether held on the central bank's balance sheet (purchases) or taken as collateral, excluding government securities.

7 Summary and Conclusions

In line with the inclusive and sustainable growth paradigm underlying the 2030 Agenda, nowadays it is widely recognized the importance of not only the pace but also the pattern of growth in terms of equity and environmental sustainability. At the country level, this involves identifying and implementing specific policies in order to transition to more inclusive and sustainable pathways, so that economic growth does not take place at the expense of the most disadvantaged population groups, or of environmental problems.

While inclusive and sustainable growth requires comprehensive approaches based on a wide range of public policies, it seems clear that monetary policy could play a role at the current crossroads. In this chapter, we explore the links between monetary policy and both economic inequality and environmental concerns. On the one hand, many studies argue that monetary policies are neither neutral in their distributional nor in their environmental effects. On the other hand, high inequality and environmental degradation imply challenges and difficulties for monetary policy performance. In this context, concrete proposals for innovative monetary policy are provided to address economic inequality and environmental risks under the current economic circumstances.

Beyond ethical aspects on whether monetary policy should take distributional and environmental challenges into consideration in its decision-making, our analysis supplies numerous arguments in favour of having monetary policy pay more attention to income and wealth inequality and environmental degradation and climate change than it has in the past. Rethinking monetary policy in terms of intra- and intergenerational equity, therefore, not only seems necessary, but also essential in order to contribute to meeting the SDGs, and as such should be seriously considered by academics and monetary policymakers.

References

Adam, K., & Tzamourani, P. (2016). Distributional consequences of asset price inflation in the Euro Area. *European Economic Review, 89*, 172–192.

Adam, K., & Zhu, J. (2016). Price-level changes and the redistribution of nominal wealth across the Euro Area. *Journal of European Economic Association, 14*(4), 871–906.

Aghion, P., & Bolton, P. (1997). A theory of trickle-down growth and development. *The Review of Economic Studies, 64*, 151–172.

Aiyar, S., & Ebeke, C. H. (2019). *Inequality of opportunity, inequality of income and economic growth* (IMF Working Paper, WP/19/34).

Akinci, M. (2018). Inequality and economic growth: Trickle-down effect revisited. *Development Policy Review, 36*(S1), O1–O24.

Akram, T. (2021). A simple model of the long-term interest rate. *Journal of Post Keynesian Economics* (forthcoming).

Albanesi, S. (2007). Inflation and inequality. *Journal of Monetary Economics, 54*(4), 1088–1114.

Albert, J. F., & Gómez-Fernández, N. (2021). Monetary policy and the redistribution of net wealth in the US. *Journal of Economic Policy Reform* (forthcoming).

Albert, J. F., Peñalver, A., & Pérez-Bernabeu, A. (2020). The effects of monetary policy on income and wealth inequality in the US: Exploring different channels. *Structural Change and Economic Dynamics, 55*, 88–106.

Alesina, A., & Perotti, R. (1996). Income distribution, political instability, and investment. *European Economic Review, 40*(6), 1203–1228.

Amaral, P. (2017). Monetary policy and inequality. *Economic Commentary, 1*, 1–6.

Ameriks, J., & Zeldes, S. (2004). *How do household portfolio shares vary with age?* (TIAA-CREF Working Paper). Columbia University.

Ampudia, M., Georgarakos, D., Slačálek, J., Tristani, O., Vermeulen, P., & Violante, G. L. (2018). *Monetary policy and household inequality* (European Central Bank, 2170).

Anderson, V. (2015). *Green money: Reclaiming quantitative easing*. The Green EFA Group.

Areosa, W. D., & Areosa, M. B. (2016). The inequality channel of monetary transmission. *Journal of Macroeconomics, 48*, 214–230.

Arestis, P. (2015). Coordination of fiscal with monetary and financial stability policies can better cure unemployment. *Review of Keynesian Economics, 3*(2), 233–247.

Arestis, P., & González-Martínez, A. R. (2016). Income inequality: Implications and relevant economic policies. *Panoeconomicus, 63*(1), 1–24.

Atkinson, A. B. (2015). *Inequality*. Harvard University Press.

Auclert, A. (2019). Monetary policy and the redistribution channel. *American Economic Review, 109*(6), 2333–2367.

Barro, R. (1995). *Inflation and economic growth* (National Bureau of Economic Research, 5326).

Bartsch, E., Boivin, J., Fischer, S., Hildebrand, P., & Wang, S. (2019). Dealing with the next downturn: From unconventional monetary policy to unprecedented policy coordination. *SUERF Policy Note, 105*, 1–16.
Bernanke, B. (2013, December 18). *Chairman Bernanke's Press Conference.* Paper presented at The Federal Open Market Committee, USA.
Bernanke, B. (2015). *Monetary policy and inequality*. Brookings Blog.
Briault, C. (1995, February). The costs of inflation. *Bank of England Quarterly Bulletin*, 33–45.
Brunnermeier, M. K., & Landau, J. P. (2020). *Central Banks and Climate Change*. VoxEU CEPR.
Burton, I. (1987). Our common future: The world commission on environment and development. *Environment, 29*(5), 25–29.
Carney, M. (2015, September 29). *Breaking the tragedy of the horizon–climate change and financial stability*. Speech at Lloyd's of London: London.
Chenery, H., Ahluwalia, M. S., Bell, C. L. G., Duloy, J. H., & Jolly, R. (1974). *Redistribution with growth: Policies to improve income distribution in developing countries in the context of economic growth*. Oxford University Press.
Cochrane, J. H. (2020). Strategic review and beyond: Rethinking monetary policy and independence. *Federal Reserve Bank of St. Louis Review*, Second Quarter, 99–119.
Coeuré, B. (2018, November 8). *Monetary Policy and Climate Change*. Speech, Conference on Scaling up Green Finance: The Role of Central Banks, NGFS, Deutsche Bundesbank and Council on Economic Policies, Berlin.
Coibion, O., Gorodnichenko, Y., Kueng, L., & Silvia, J. (2017). Innocent bystanders? Monetary policy and inequality. *Journal of Monetary Economics, 88*, 70–88.
Colciago, A., Samarina, A., & de Haan, J. (2019). Central bank policies and income and wealth inequality: A survey. *Journal of Economic Surveys, 33*(4), 1199–1231.
Constâncio, V. (2017). *Inequality and macroeconomic policies*. Speech at Annual Congress of the European Economic Association, Lisbon.
Coppola, F. (2019). *The case for people's quantitative easing*. Polity Press.
De Boer, N., & Van't Klooster, J. (2020). The ECB, the courts and the issue of democratic legitimacy after weiss. *Common Market Law Review, 57*(6), 1689–1724.
Deaton, A. (2013). *The great escape*. Princeton University Press.

Dikau, S., & Ulrich, V. (2020). *Central Bank mandates, sustainability objectives and the promotion of green finance* (SOAS Department of Economics, 232). SOAS, University of London.

Dinda, S. (2004). Environmental Kuznets curve hypothesis: A survey. *Ecological Economics, 49*(4), 431–455.

Doda, B. (2016). *Sector-level carbon intensity distribution* (Centre for Climate Change: Economics and Policy, 281).

Doepke, M., & Schneider, M. (2006). Inflation and the redistribution of nominal wealth. *Journal of Political Economy, 114*(6), 1069–1097.

Dolado, J., Motyovszki, G., & Pappa, E. (2018). *Monetary policy and inequality under labor market frictions and capital-skill complementarity* (IZA Discussion Paper Series, 11494).

Domanski, D., Scatigna, M., & Zabai, A. (2016, March). Wealth inequality and monetary policy. *BIS Quarterly Review*, 45–64.

Draghi, M. (2016). *Stability, equity and monetary policy*. The German Institute for Economic Research (DIW), 2nd DIW Europe Lecture, Berlin.

Gabor, D. (2021). *Revolution without revolutionaries: Interrogating the new politics of monetary financing*. Transformative Responses to the Crisis, Finanzwende, Heinrich-Böll-Foundation.

Galbraith, J. K. (2016). *Inequality. What Everyone Needs to Know*. Oxford University Press.

Gali, J. (2020). Helicopter money: The time is now. In R. Baldwin & B. Weder di Mauro (Eds.), *Mitigating the COVID economic crisis: Act fast and do whatever it takes* (pp. 57–62). VoxEU eBook.

Galli, R., & van der Hoeven, R. (2001). *Is inflation bad for income inequality: The importance of the initial rate of inflation* (ILO Employment Paper, 29).

Galor, O., & Zeira, J. (1993). Income distribution and macroeconomics. *Review of Economic Studies, 60*, 35–52.

Giuliani, D., Kidney, S., & Meng, A. (2017, November 28–29). *Recommendations for Central Banks on how to support the development of the Green Bond Market*. Paper presented at the CEP-DNB workshop on Central Banking and Green Finance, Amsterdam.

Grigoli, F., Paredes, E., & Di Bella, G. (2016). *Inequality and growth: A heterogeneous approach* (IMF Working Paper, WP/16/244).

Grossman, G. M., & Krueger, A. B. (1991). *Environmental impacts of a North American free trade agreement* (National Bureau of Economic Research, 3914).

Grossman, G. M., & Krueger, A. B. (1995). Economic growth and the environment. *Quarterly Journal of Economics, 110*(2), 353–377.

Grusky, D., & Szelenyi, S. (2018), *The inequality reader: Contemporary and foundational readings in race, class, and gender*. Routledge, Taylor & Francis Group.

Heathcote, J., Perri, F., & Violante, G. (2010). Unequal we stand: An empirical analysis of economic inequality in the United States 1967–2006. *Review of Economic Dynamics, 13*(1), 15–51.

Heimberger, P. (2020). Does economic globalisation affect income inequality? A meta-analysis. *The World Economy, 43*(11), 2960–2982.

Hilmi, N., Djoundourian, S., Shahin, W., & Safa, A. (2021). Does the ECB policy of quantitative easing impact environmental policy objectives? *Journal of Economic Policy Reform*, 1–13.

Hirsch, F. (1977). *Social limits to growth*. Routledge and Kegan Paul.

Honohan, P. (2019). Should monetary policy take inequality and climate change into account? *Peterson Institute for International Economics, 19–18*, 1–23.

Ianchovichina, E., & Lundstrom, S. (2009). *Inclusive growth analytics: Framework and application* (World Bank Policy Research, 4851).

Jackson, T. (2009). *Prosperity without growth: Economics for a Finite Planet*. Routledge.

Jappelli, T., & Pistaferri, L. (2010). The consumption response to income changes. *Annual Review of Economics, 2*(1), 479–506.

Jourdan, S. (2020). Helicopter money as a response to the Covid-19 recession. *Positive Money Europe*.

Kakwani, N., & Pernia, E. (2000). What is pro-poor growth? *Asian Development Review, 16*, 1–22.

Kallis, G., Demaria, F., & D'Alisa, G. (2015). Introduction: Degrowth. In G. D'Alisa, F. Demaria, & G. Kallis (Eds.), *Degrowth: A vocabulary for a new era* (pp. 1–17). Routledge, Taylor & Francis Group.

Kaplan, G., Moll, B., & Violante, G. L. (2018). Monetary policy according to HANK. *American Economic Review, 108*(3), 697–743.

Kharroubi, E., Kohlscheen, E., Lombardi, M., Mojon, B., & Pereira da Silva, L. (2021). Inequality and the post-covid recovery. *Bank for International Settlements*. Mimeo.

Klasen, S. (2010). Measuring and monitoring inclusive growth: Multiple definitions, open questions and some constructive proposals. *Asian Development Bank Sustainable Development*, 12.

Kono, N. (2014). Brundtland Commission (World Commission on Environment and Development). In A. C. Michalos (Ed.), *Encyclopedia of quality of life and well-being research*. Springer Reference.

Kuznets, S. (1955). Economic growth and income inequality. *The American Economic Review, 45*, 1–28.

Lagarde, C. (2020, February 27). *Climate change and the financial sector*. Speech at the launch of the COP26 Private Finance Agenda, London.

Lawton, N., & Gallagher, L. A. (2020). The negative side of inflation targeting: Revisiting inflation uncertainty in the EMU. *Applied Economics, 52*(29), 3186–3203.

Lenza, M., & Slačálek, J. (2018). *How does monetary policy affect income and wealth inequality? Evidence from quantitative easing in the Euro Area* (European Central Bank, 2190).

Matikainen, S., Campiglio, E., & Zenghelis, D. (2017). *The climate impact of quantitative easing*. Policy, Paper. Grantham Research Institute on Climate Change and the Environment.

Meadows, D. H., Meadows, D. L., Randers, J., & Behrens, W. (1972). *The limits to growth.* Universe Books.

Metcalf, G. E., & Stock, J. H. (2020). Measuring the macroeconomic impacts of carbon taxes. *American Economic Review: Papers and Proceedings, 110*, 101–106.

Mian, A. R., Straub, L., & Sufi, A. (2020). *Indebted demand* (National Bureau of Economic Research, 26940).

Mishan, E. J. (1967). *The costs of economic growth.* Staples Press.

Monasterolo, I., & Raberto, M. (2016). A Hybrid system dynamics agent based model to assess the role of green fiscal and monetary policies. *SSRN Electronic Journal, 27*, 13–37.

Monnin, P. (2018). *Central Banks and the transition to a low-carbon economy* (Council on Economic Policies, 1).

Mumtaz, H., & Theophilopoulou, A. (2019). *Monetary policy and wealth inequality over the great recession in the UK: An empirical analysis* (p. 898). Queen Mary University of London, School of Economics and Finance.

Nordhaus, W. D. (2017). *Projections and uncertainties about climate change in an era of minimal climate policies* (National Bureau of Economic Research, 22933).

OECD. (2015a). *All on board: Making inclusive growth happen.* OECD Publishing.

OECD. (2015b). *The economic consequences of climate change.* OECD Publishing.

OECD. (2017). *Investing in climate, investing in growth.* OECD Publishing.

OECD. (2018). *The framework for policy action on inclusive growth.* OECD Publishing.

Panetta, F. (2015, November 20). *The distributional consequences of monetary policy*. Remarks by Mr. Fabio Panetta, Deputy Governor of the Bank of Italy, at the Netherlands Bank, Amsterdam.

Pereira da Silva, L. A. (2021, December 11). Monetary policy, technology and inequality. *Remarks by Mr Luiz Awazu Pereira da Silva*, Deputy General Manager of the BIS, CEPR/IMF/PIIE Roundtable.

Persson, T., & Tabellini, G. (1994). Is inequality harmful for growth? *American Economic Review, 84*(3), 600–621.

Perugini, C., Hölscher, J., & Collie, S. (2016). Inequality, credit and financial crises. *Cambridge Journal of Economics, 40*(1), 227–257.

Piketty, T. (2014). *Capital in the twenty-first century*. Belknap Press of Harvard University Press.

Powell, J. H. (2020, August 27). *New economic challenges and the Fed's monetary policy review*. Speech at the Economic Policy Symposium, Sponsored by the Federal Reserve Bank of Kansas City, Jackson Hole, Wyoming.

Ravallion, M. (2004). *Pro-poor growth: A primer* (World Bank Policy Research, 3242).

Rogers, J. H., Scotti, C., & Wright, J. H. (2014). Evaluating asset-market effects of unconventional monetary policy: A multi-country review. *Economic Policy, 29*(80), 749–799.

Romer, D. H. (2006). *Advanced macroeconomics*. McGraw-Hill.

Sahm, C. (2019). Direct stimulus payments to individuals. In H. Boushey, R. Nunn, & J. Shambaugh (Eds.), *Recession ready: Fiscal policies to stabilize the American economy* (pp. 67–92). Brookings.

Saiki, A., & Frost, J. (2014). Does unconventional monetary policy affect inequality? Evidence from Japan. *Applied Economics, 46*(36), 4445–4454.

Sau, L. (2018). Coping with deflation and the liquidity trap in the Eurozone: A post Keynesian approach. *Journal of Post Keynesian Economics, 41*(2), 210–235.

Schnabel, I. (2020). *When markets fail—The need for collective action tackling climate change*. Speech at the European Sustainable Finance Summit, Frankfurt am Main.

Schneider, F., Kallis, G., & Martínez-Allier, J. (2010). Crisis or opportunity? Economic degrowth for social equity and ecological sustainability: Introduction to the special issue. *Journal of Cleaner Production, 18*(6), 511–518.

Schumacher, E. F. (1973). Small is Beautiful, London: Blond and Briggs.

Schoenmaker, D. (2021). "Greening Monetary Policy", *Climate Policy, 21*(4), 581–592.

Shahbaz, M., & Sinha, A. (2019). Environmental Kuznets curve for CO2 emissions: A literature survey. *Journal of Economic Studies, 46*(1), 106–168.
Slačálek, J., Tristani, O., & Violante, G. L. (2020). Household balance sheet channels of monetary policy: A back of the envelope calculation for the Euro Area. *Journal of Economic Dynamics and Control, 115*(C).
Stiglitz, J. E. (2012). *The price of inequality: How today's divided society endangers our future*. WW Norton & Company.
Sufi, A. (2015). *Out of many, one? Household debt, redistribution and monetary policy during the economic slump*. Andrew Crockett Memorial Lecture, BIS.
Tatliyer, M. (2017). Inflation targeting and the need for a new Central Banking framework. *Journal of Post Keynesian Economics, 40*(4), 512–539.
Tobin, J. (1982). *Asset accumulation and economic activity: Reflections on contemporary macroeconomic theory*. The University of Chicago Press.
Tzamourani, P. (2019, February). *The interest rate exposure of Euro Area households* (European Economic Review, 132).
UNDP. (2017). *UNDP's strategy for inclusive and sustainable growth*. United Nations Development Programme.
United Nations. (2015). *Transforming our World: The 2030 Agenda for Sustainable Development*.
Van der Ploeg, R. (2020, November). Macro-financial implications of climate change and the carbon transition. In *Conference in ECB Forum on Central Banking* (pp. 90–142).
Van Lervan, F. (2016). *A guide to public money creation*. Positive Money.
Van't Klooster, J., & Fontan, C. (2020). The myth of market neutrality: A comparative study of the European Central Bank's and the Swiss National Bank's Corporate Security Purchases. *New Political Economy, 25*(6), 865–879.
van 't Klooster, J., & van Tilburg, R. (2020). *Targeting a sustainable recovery with Green TLTROs*. Positive Money Europe.
Vandeventer, J. S., Cattaneo, C., & Zografos, C. (2019). A Degrowth transition: Pathways for the degrowth niche to replace the capitalist-growth regime. *Ecological Economics, 156*, 272–286.
Villeroy, F. (2019). Climate change: Central Banks are taking action. *Financial Stability Review, 23*, 7–13.
Villeroy, F. (2021). *The Role of Central Banks in the Greening of the Economy*. Speech, 5th Edition of the Rencontres on Climate Change and Sustainable Finance, Banque de France.

Weidmann, J. (2017). *Welcome and opening speech*. OMFIF Global Public Investor Symposium on Green Bond Issuance and other Forms of Low-Carbon Finance, Frankfurt: Germany.
Weiss, M., & Cattaneo, C. (2017). Degrowth—Taking stock and reviewing an emerging academic paradigm. *Ecological Economics, 137*, 220–230.
World Commission on Environment and Development. (1987). *Report of the world commission on environment and development: Our common future*. United Nations.
World Inequality Lab. (2021). *World inequality database*. Paris. https://wid.world
Yellen, J. (2014), *Perspectives on inequality and opportunity from the survey of consumer finances*. Conference on Economic Opportunity and Inequality, Federal Reserve Bank of Boston, Massachusetts, USA, October 17, 2020.
Zerbib, O. D. (2017, November 28–29). *The Green Bond Premium*. Presented at the CEP-DNB Workshop on Central Banking and Green Finance, Amsterdam.

Index

P. Arestis and M. Sawyer (eds.), *Economic Policies for Sustainability and Resilience*, International Papers in Political Economy,
https://doi.org/10.1007/978-3-030-84288-8

E

F

The manufacturer's authorised representative in the EU is Springer Nature Customer Service Centre GmbH, Europaplatz 3, 69115 Heidelberg, Germany. If you have any concerns regarding our products, please contact ProductSafety@springernature.com

Printed and bound by CPI Group (UK) Ltd, Croydon, CR0 4YY
30/09/2026
02225704-0008